D1282885

Corporatism and Change

Cornell Studies in
Political Economy

Edited by
Peter J. Katzenstein

Corporatism and Change

AUSTRIA, SWITZERLAND, AND THE POLITICS OF INDUSTRY

PETER J. KATZENSTEIN

CORNELL UNIVERSITY PRESS

Ithaca and London

THIS BOOK HAS BEEN PUBLISHED WITH THE AID OF A GRANT FROM
THE HULL MEMORIAL PUBLICATION FUND OF CORNELL UNIVERSITY.

First published 1984 by Cornell University Press.
Published in the United Kingdom by
Cornell University Press Ltd., London.

International Standard Book Number 0-8014-1716-3
Library of Congress Catalog Card Number 84-7676
Printed in the United States of America
*Librarians: Library of Congress cataloging information
appears on the last page of the book.*

*The paper in this book is acid-free and meets the guidelines
for permanence and durability of the Committee on Production
Guidelines for Book Longevity of the Council on Library Resources.*

FOR JOHNNY

Contents

Tables

Preface

The small democracies of Western Europe pose an interesting puzzle to the social sciences. Political scientists return from their travels recording the stability that these states have discovered in their corporatist arrangements. Yet economists typically view the same countries as models of economic flexibility and market competition. Across the last five years I have been attempting to develop an argument that will resolve that conundrum. The argument I advance is conditional. It applies primarily to the small corporatist states in Europe that, because of their open economies, have been vulnerable to shifts in the world economy during the twentieth century. Political stability and economic flexibility, I argue, are not contradictory but mutually contingent.

Large industrial countries are beginning to experience an increasing economic openness and vulnerability, conditions novel to them but familiar to their small neighbors throughout modern history. In the small European states this economic openness and vulnerability have made possible corporatist arrangements that are less common among larger countries. Small states thus provide something of a model by which to judge developments in large ones.

This is one of two volumes exploring the political economy of the smaller European democracies. *Small States in World Markets* develops the argument in general terms for Scandinavia, the Low Countries, and Central Europe. *Corporatism and Change* applies it to Austria and Switzerland in particular. These two volumes show how economic openness and democratic corporatism shape the politics and policy of industrial adjustment in the small European states.

Small States in World Markets argues that the interlocking crises of the

9

1930s and 1940s—Depression, fascism, and World War II—fundamentally reorganized the politics of the small European states. The democratic corporatism that emerged has been reinforced since the 1950s by the pressures of a liberal international economy. Flexible economic adjustment and a stable politics have been the result. History explains why the potential for reaching a political compromise between business and labor in the 1930s and 1940s was greater in the small than in the large industrial states. The politics of agriculture and religion before the Industrial Revolution explain why, in contrast to large countries, the small European states experienced a divided political Right and a reformist political Left in the nineteenth and twentieth centuries. In the last two centuries, furthermore, the small European states adopted a strategy of specialization for exports that has tended to narrow the gap between different sectors of their societies. And with the adoption of universal suffrage these states opted for systems of proportional representation rather than majority rule, thus showing an early willingness to share power among disparate political actors.

Although the small European states resemble each other in their corporatist arrangements and in the substance of their strategies of industrial adjustment, they show marked differences in the form of their politics and in the style of their policies. Today there exist two varieties of corporatism, one "liberal" and the other "social." The timing of industrialization, their experience in times of war, and the patterns of divisions in society help in explaining these differences among the small European states. In some of these states adjustment has global scope and is organized privately; in others, adjustment is national and public. The small European states thus choose different ways of combining economic flexibility and political stability, of making the requirements of international politics compatible with the requirements of domestic politics.

Among the small European states, I argue, the difference between these two variants of corporatism is greatest in Austria and Switzerland. I wrote *Corporatism and Change* hoping that strangers can paint good family portraits. Sketching the characteristic features of Austria and Switzerland yields a picture of two distant cousins, with predictable differences and unanticipated similarities. Austrian Social Democrats point proudly to the extension of their welfare state in the 1970s, while Swiss businessmen cherish their liberal market economy. Yet in both countries the search for consensus is a national passion. I have attempted to resist the temptation to contrast presumed characteristic traits, for example Swiss industriousness with Austrian indolence, and to build an argument around those presumptions. Rather, the systematic description I have chosen yields insights into the political incentives and structures that make the search for consensus in different settings so compelling. Such insight is central for understanding how the small European states cope in the international economy. It is also a modest step toward an interpretation of the substance and style of Central European politics.

Small States in World Markets states the argument in general terms. In comparing small and large industrial states, it emphasizes how historically shaped structures make possible a particular strategy of industrial adjustment. Since this argument risks overgeneralization, *Corporatism and Change* adds a detailed analysis of Austria and Switzerland. For a better understanding of Austrian and Swiss politics, I have followed the very recent history of four industries in trouble: watches in Switzerland, steel in Austria, and textiles in both. These industries differ along a number of dimensions, including the source of economic change, the process of internal differentiation, the typical economic actor, the political organization of the industry, and its political ties to other sectors. If viewed as four different settings for the politics of industry, this recent history varies in ways that help identify some of the enduring patterns of policy and politics.

These two books show how structure and process interact in politics. I have chosen to think through the implications of this interaction with varying degrees of abstraction. Doing this cuts against some established conventions in political science. Area specialty achieves intellectual clarity by exploring in great depth a political reality that is complex. Broad comparative studies typically seek to impose intellectual order by viewing reality from vantage points often deliberately chosen to contradict the core assumptions of a national culture. Since both methods serve their purpose, the canons of social science research have in recent years expressed the hope that, in the long run, both methods should be combined. At the end of my own marathon, I heartily agree.

I have tried to learn how to link the specific to the general. Familiarity with detail is necessary for drawing the connections between different parts of Austria's and Switzerland's political life, for discerning how these parts yield a distinctive structure, and for understanding how that structure regenerates itself in daily politics. The affinity in the subtitles of the two books thus attempts to convey my interests in linking macro- and microlevels of analysis. The industrial policies of the small European states result from distinctive structural constraints and opportunities. The politics of industry in Austria and Switzerland reconfirm on a daily basis the logic that informs particular choices. Thus both books argue that in tightly linking policy with politics, the small European states have made economic flexibility compatible with political stability.

In working on this project, I have relied on methods that are well tried in political science. Comparisons between small and large states, between Austria and Switzerland, and among different industries have been essential for developing my argument. Because I wanted to understand the constraints and opportunities provided by the corporatist structures of the small European states, I have spent a good deal of time tracing the policy process in Austria and Switzerland. I have read widely, visited Austria and Switzerland repeatedly, and interviewed more than eighty policy makers, businessmen, trade-union officials, journalists, and academics over a period of five years. I have used interviews not so much as a source for data as a way of learning from others, checking out my own ideas, and trying out new ones. But when I could not find a crucial piece of evidence in the written record, interviewing has helped me fill the gap. I have found newspaper clipping archives in Austria, Switzerland, and West Germany to be of great help in providing me with the postwar history of different industries. Using newspapers is not without risk. Schopenhauer once said that newspapers are nothing but the second hands of history—they always tell the wrong time. But newspapers provide information that is sufficiently good to hurry the researcher to the stage of probing the political significance of economic life.

This project has benefited enormously from the help of a large number of colleagues and friends. Over a period of five years they have kept talking and listening, and they have commented on what I knew were too many drafts. I have often exploited them shamelessly, used their ideas, and taxed their patience. Even when we disagreed, their reactions to my work have sharpened my ideas. Their intellectual presence has given meaning to the inevitable drudgeries of scholarship. My greatest intellectual debt is to those who actually sat down and read one or two drafts of a manuscript that originally encompassed the two volumes now published separately: William Diebold, Peter Gourevitch, Thomas Ilgen, Jeffrey Hart, Mary Katzenstein, Robert Keohane, Stephen Krasner, David Laitin, Peter Lange, Gerhard Lehmbruch, Bernd Marin, T. J. Pempel, Richard Rosecrance, Charles Sabel, Martin Shefter, Margret Sieber, Sidney Tarrow, and John Zysman. I have also received helpful comments from colleagues who read papers developing the general argument of the two books: Ronald Brickman, David Cameron, Steven Jackson, Jeanne Laux, Charles Lipson, Theodore Lowi, Henrik Madsen, Peter McClelland, Sandra Peterson, Gabriel Sheffer, and Harold Wilensky; from a group of European scholars whom I met in a series of colloquia convened by John Ruggie: Barry Buzan, Helge Hveem, Gerd Junne, and Alberto Martinelli; and from my colleagues at the Center for Advanced Study: Alfred Kahn, Natalie Ramsøy, and William Wilson. I have learned much about Switzerland from Gardner Clark, François Höpflinger, Hanspeter Kriesi, Hans Mayrzedt, Peter Rusterholz, Margret Sieber, Jürg Siegenthaler, Jürg Steiner, John Stephens, and Hans Vogel. And my insights into Austrian politics have been sharpened by Bernd Marin, Andrei Markovits, Anton Pelinka, Michael Pollak, and Kurt Steiner.

This project has been supported financially by fellowships from the German Marshall Fund of the United States (Grant no. 3-51025) and from the Rockefeller Foundation (Grant no. RF 77020-87). A first draft of both volumes was prepared while I spent a year at the Center for Advanced Study in the Behavioral Sciences, Stanford, California, in 1981–82. I am grateful for the financial support provided by a National Science Foundation Grant (no. BNS76-22943).

Over the last five years, a group of Cornell students has helped me in my research. I would like to thank in particular Mark Hansen, Gretchen Ritter, and Rhonda Wassermann. Dorothy Hong, Bruce Levine, and Diane Sousa have also assisted me.

At the Center for Advanced Study, Deanna Dejan, Barbara Homestead, and Anna Tower typed a first draft of the manuscript from which these two books eventually emerged. The staff of Cornell University's Government Department, beyond all reasonable expectations, kept on speaking terms with me while retyping several subsequent versions.

Walter Lippincott showed an early interest in this project. In its later stages he suggested a publication format that I have found congenial: two separate books, two similar subtitles, and one preface. John Ackerman read drafts of the introduction and conclusion to both volumes and gave me useful editorial advice. But my greatest debt of gratitude goes to Roger Haydon. In editing these two volumes without complaining, he learned more than he ever wanted to know about little countries. He had superb judgment on how the material of one large manuscript should be organized into two books. His tenacity pushed me to clarify my thinking; his pencil uncluttered my prose; his diplomacy left my feathers unruffled; and his humor made much of the hard work fun.

13

Some of the material in this book has previously appeared in various journals, monographs, and edited volumes. Excerpts from *Corporatism and Change* have been published in my *Capitalism in One Country? Switzerland in the International Economy*, Cornell University Western Societies Program, Occasional Paper no. 13 (Ithaca, N.Y., January 1980), which also appeared in condensed form under the same title in *International Organization* 34 (Autumn 1980): 507–40; and in "Domestic Structures and Political Strategies: Austria in an Interdependent World," in Bruce Russett and Richard Merritt, eds., *From Nation-States to Global Community: Essays in Honour of Karl W. Deutsch* (London: Allen & Unwin, 1981), pp. 252–78, which was also published, in slightly altered form, under the title "Dependence and Autonomy: Austria in an Interdependent World," *Österreichische Zeitschrift für Auswärtige Politik* 19, 4 (1979): 243–56. Material from Chapters 2–4 will appear in "Small Nations in an Open International Economy: The Converging Balance of State and Society in Austria and Switzerland," in Peter Evans, Dietrich Rueschemeyer, and Theda Skocpol, eds., *Bringing the State Back In* (New York: Cambridge University Press, 1984).

I have had all the support I could reasonably expect at home. Tai and Suzanne, I suspect, enjoyed this project. When I went to Europe, their consumption of pizza increased, and when I returned they could look forward to Austrian dirndls or Swiss chocolates. I dedicate the first of these two books to Johnny, part of a dynamic intergenerational duo that has transformed my life.

PETER J. KATZENSTEIN

Ithaca, New York

Acronyms

ASUAG	General Swiss Watch Corporation (Allgemeine Schweizerische Uhrenindustrie Aktiengesellschaft)
CNG	Swiss National Federation of Christian Trade Unions (Christlich-Nationaler Gewerkschaftsbund der Schweiz)
Comecon	Council for Mutual Economic Assistance
DAC	Development Assistance Committee of the OECD
EC	European Communities
EFTA	European Free Trade Association
FH	Swiss Watchmakers' Federation (Fédération horlogère)
GATT	General Agreement on Tariffs and Trade
GDP	gross domestic product
GNP	gross national product
GSBI	peak association of the Swiss garment industry (Gesamtverband der Schweizerischen Bekleidungsindustrie)
GWC	General Watch Corporation (subdivision of the ASUAG)
IMF	International Monetary Fund
LTA	Long Term Arrangement on Cotton Textiles
MFA	Multi-Fiber Arrangement
NATO	North Atlantic Treaty Organization
ÖAAB	Austrian Federation of Employees and Workers (division of the ÖVP)
OECD	Organization for Economic Co-operation and Development
ÖGB	Austrian Trade Union Federation (Österreichischer Gewerkschaftsbund)
ÖIAG	Austrian Corporation for Industrial Administration (Österreichische Industrieverwaltung, AG)
ÖIG	Austrian Industrial Corporation (forerunner of the ÖIAG)
OPEC	Organization of Petroleum Exporting Countries
ÖVP	Austrian Peoples Party (Österreichische Volkspartei)
SGB	Swiss Federation of Trade Unions (Schweizerischer Gewerkschaftsbund)

SHIV   Swiss Federation of Commerce and Industry (Schweizerischer
            Handels- und Industrie-Verein)
SMUV   Swiss Metalworkers and Watchmakers Union
            (Schweizerischer Metall- und
            Uhrenarbeitnehmer-Verband)
SPÖ   Austrian Socialist Party (Sozialistische Partei Österreichs)
SSIH   Swiss Watch Corporation Inc. (Société suisse pour l'industrie
            horlogère)
UN   United Nations
UNCTAD   United Nations Conference on Trade and Development
VATI   Employers Association of the Swiss Textile Industry (Verband
            der Arbeitgeber der Textilindustrie)
VEW   Austrian United Specialty Steel Works (Vereinigte
            Edelstahlwerke)
Voest   United Austrian Iron and Steel Works (Vereinigte
            Österreichische Eisen- und Stahlwerke)

Corporatism and Change

CHAPTER ONE

Introduction

Switzerland and Austria are small both geographically and in population. Like the other small European states, they have had no great impact on international politics. Indeed, it could be argued that Switzerland and Austria are distant and unimportant countries that do not warrant sustained analysis. But these two small states, under less than advantageous conditions, have been more successful than the United States and most other industrial states in mastering the economic crisis of the 1970s. It is not the insignificance of these two countries but our own ignorance that has blinded us to two success stories as notable as those of West Germany and Japan.[1]

The magnitude of Swiss and Austrian success is impressive on all counts. Austria and Switzerland restrained inflation in the 1970s and simultaneously registered two of the lowest unemployment rates in the industrial world. To be sure, because of differences in definition and reporting, unemployment statistics are not easy to compare across nations. Unemployment is affected not only by the changes in actual employment reported in Table 1, but also by demographic shifts, changes in labor-force participation, and international migration—none of which constitutes valid measures of economic success. But if we overlook these methodological difficulties for a moment, we cannot help but notice the convergence of low inflation with low unemployment in both countries. Finally, in the 1970s Austria (but not Switzerland) had one of the highest economic growth rates in the industrialized West.

Although they are both models of economic success, Austria and Switzerland perform differently along different dimensions. Low inflation in Austria and Switzerland correlates with high growth for

Austria, low growth for Switzerland. Low unemployment in both countries correlates with a growth of employment in Austria, a decline in Switzerland. As Fritz Scharpf observes, "Apparently it is possible for national economies to make separate choices regarding their relative success in the dimensions of economic growth, employment growth, and inflation control."[2] Ranking the eight countries in Table 1 by economic performance in the 1970s reconfirms the impression that, whatever their choices, Austria and Switzerland have both succeeded. This summary statistic of economic success puts Austria in the top spot, followed by Japan, Switzerland, and West Germany.

Swiss and Austrian success can be measured in political as well as economic terms. Political leaders in both countries have fashioned policies that have left largely unquestioned the legitimacy of their political institutions and practices. In both societies symbols of widespread public disenchantment are rare. Political parties and, in the case of Switzerland, the institution of direct democracy continue as the unquestioned avenues for mass political participation. Although in the election of April 1983 Austrian voters replaced a socialist government with a coalition led by the socialists, electoral changes have been small in both countries. Interest groups have not lost their hold over the social sectors they seek politically to represent. New social movements and novel forms of politics, which have grown in importance elsewhere, are insignificant in Switzerland and Austria. If legitimacy has been endangered in the 1970s, it has been by apathy rather than by large-scale public protest. In short, Switzerland and Austria are remarkable stories of political success.

Swiss success has often brought a bad press. As early as 1797 Chateaubriand observed bitterly that the Swiss were "neutral in the grand revolutions of the states which surround them; they enrich themselves by the misfortunes of others and found a bank on human calamities."[3] A contemptuous Friedrich Engels characterized the Swiss in 1847 not as opportunistic but as "poor but pure in heart, stupid but pious and well-pleasing to the Lord, brutal but broad-shouldered, with little brain but plenty of brawn. . . . They busied themselves in all piety and propriety with milking the cows, with cheese-making, chastity and yodelling."[4] Knut Hamsun, the Norwegian novelist, referred to the Swiss a few years before World War I as "the little shits in the Alps whose history does not signify anything and who have never created anything important."[5] And Hermann Keyserling wrote in 1928 that "the tourist trade broadly defined is their preordained occupation; the other things they busy themselves with are by and large unimportant."[6] In 1951 Max Beerbohm characterized them

Table 1. Economic performance of industrial states, 1961–79 (percentages)

Country	Increase in consumer price indices		Increase in real GDP		Average rate of unemployment		Increase in total employment
	1961–70	1970–79	1961–70	1970–79	1961–70	1970–79	1970–79
1. Austria	37	73	51	42	2.7	2.0	3.4
2. Switzerland	37	56	47	8	0.0	0.4	−4.9
3. Sweden	38	112	48	19	1.7	2.1	8.5
4. Germany (FRG)	28	56	51	30	1.0	3.0	−1.4
5. France	44	121	63	41	1.5	3.7	7.6
6. Japan	—	119	151	61	1.3	1.7	8.6
7. United Kingdom	38	203	28	22	2.0	4.1	4.3
8. United States	30	87	43	33	5.3	6.2	22.2

SOURCES: Organization for Economic Co-operation and Development (OECD), *Main Economic Indicators: Historical Statistics* (Paris: 1980); *National Accounts Statistics, 1950–1979*, vol. 1 (Paris: 1981); *Labour Force Statistics, 1960–1971* (Paris: 1973); *Labour Force Statistics, 1968–1979* (Paris: 1981); and International Labour Office, *Year Book of Labour Statistics 1980* (Geneva: 1981).

uncharitably as "a smug, tame, sly, dull, mercenary little race of men."[7] To the rhetorical question of what the world owed the Swiss, Graham Greene is reported to have answered disparagingly, "the cuckoo clock." And in the 1970s the French coined the term "*faire Suisse*" as a colloquial expression meaning to act selfishly.

Austria's striking performance stands in stark contrast to the fond condescension with which many foreign observers regard it. Reflecting on the Austrian tradition of antimodernism (still alive today), Napoleon observed that Austria was always one idea behind. And Clemenceau viewed modern Austria disdainfully—"*c'est ce qui reste*"— a leftover state and a state of leftovers after the breakup of the Habsburg Empire at the end of World War I. If they have any impression whatever of contemporary Austria, foreigners typically view it as the idyllic manifestation of the "five Ms": mountains, music, Maria Theresa, Mozart, and Metternich.[8] Austria, after all, is the homeland not only of sachertorte but also of "*Schlamperei*," defined in a recent article as "untidiness, unreliability, and muddleheadedness all rolled into one."[9] Austria is, in the caustic language of a popular German writer, Wolfgang Biermann, a mere "economic appendix" of the Federal Republic. And if the undeniable political and economic accomplishments of the Second Republic are recognized at all, they are often credited to nothing but extraordinary luck. A country from which the Soviet Union voluntarily withdrew after military victory succeeds in spite of itself. Austria looks nostalgically back to its imperial past as the escalator of history carries it forward to its industrial future.[10]

In a modestly self-congratulatory tone, Austria's federal press department asked the sensible question, "How does Austria do it?"[11] On the other side of their common border, Swiss self-confidence is so large that it needs no public celebration, but time and again visitors to Switzerland have pointed out that the country offers "the most striking combination of a poor country and a rich people."[12] In search of possible solutions to America's troubles, policy makers in Washington have only recently noticed that, in the 1970s, Switzerland and Austria produced economic miracles. In 1978 the American Enterprise Institute published two short monographs assessing the causes, consequences, and concomitants of Switzerland's low inflation policy.[13] In the spring of 1981, for the first time ever, the Joint Economic Committee of the U.S. Congress heard testimony from a leading foreign official, the state secretary in the Austrian Ministry of Finance, Professor Hans Seidel.[14] And later that year, the American Enterprise Institute organized a conference assessing Austria's economic miracle.[15]

Twenty-five years ago, Uwe Kitzinger argued that "a deeper study of the Swiss and Austrian system will . . . be worth attempting in due course for the caricature they offer of conditions not unknown in Anglo-Saxon countries."[16] Having lately become accustomed to America's failures, we are beginning to take an interest in the successes of others. Admittedly, Vienna and Zurich are off the well-beaten paths to Bonn and Tokyo. To those with a taste for the exotic, this book offers no recipe; but to those who would stretch their imagination, it seeks to offer illumination.

SIMILARITIES AND DIFFERENCES

Switzerland and Austria offer blurred images to the world. Their similarities and differences blend in ways that at times baffle the Swiss and the Austrians themselves. That blending is easily illustrated in the area of economic policy. In Switzerland maintaining price stability ranks ahead of defending employment levels; in Austria employment ranks ahead of price stability. The difference seems plain and simple, but it is to some extent concealed by the way these two countries have exploited the opportunities offered by the international economy. Switzerland has exported most of its unemployment by dismissing foreign workers; Austria has imported price stability by tying the value of the schilling to that of the deutsche mark. More generally, the two countries reacted in strikingly different ways to the economic crises of the 1970s. Austria chose first to counteract market developments through massive deficit spending before giving more serious consideration to its limited options for a structural policy. Switzerland, by contrast, accepted market developments in the interest of structural rationalization before undertaking a very cautious stimulation of aggregate demand. As Christian Smekal argues, "The fact that Switzerland adopted a Swiss solution and Austria an Austrian solution to their economic problems is evidence that a theory of economic stabilization must be linked to a theory of politics."[17]

But on questions of economic policy the experiences of Switzerland and Austria also converge, in ways that pose an intellectual puzzle for comparative political analysis. For example, with the tide of protectionism rising throughout Europe, the year 1981 found both Switzerland and Austria redoubling their efforts to promote free trade.[18] When French businessmen sought to shelter their capital from the newly elected socialist government of President Mitterrand, they looked to Switzerland as a European center of economic prosperity, social harmony, and political stability. A similar assessment was made by the capitalist managers of General Motors, when they decided to locate a major plant in Austria in the late 1970s. These widely admired traits flourished in the 1970s in two small states with open, vulnerable economies that constrained their political options.

It is this economic vulnerability which led to a partial convergence in economic policy, most obviously in the two states' exchange-rate policies. Because of their economic dependence on West Germany, both countries have defended monetary stability by following the hard-currency strategy of their larger neighbor. The Austrians peg the value of the schilling to that of the strong deutsche mark; thus the value of Austria's currency has rested on frequent interventions by Austria's Nationalbank (Österreichische Nationalbank) in foreign-exchange markets. The Swiss, on the other hand, let the franc appreciate autonomously against other currencies as the world's monetary system moved from fixed to flexible exchange rates. Since the late 1970s, however, even market-oriented Switzerland has at times intervened to maintain an informal link between franc and deutsche mark.

Viewed in isolation, Switzerland is a country full of contradictions. Home of the Red Cross, Switzerland is the neutral Alpine bastion that serves the international community with its "good works" and organizes its foreign policy around the principles of "neutrality and solidarity"; but Switzerland is also the bastion of international finance capitalism, whose "gnomes" daily reaffirm the old saying *"pas d'argent pas de Suisses,"* using neutrality as a base from which to elevate the principle of profitability above that of solidarity.[19] Switzerland, the tourist Mecca, is also the country that in the 1950s and 1960s imported a foreign proletariat to meet the demands of its export industry. Switzerland is the mainstay of democracy that until the 1970s disenfranchised more than half its population. Switzerland is a small, landlocked country that has virtually no raw materials and is utterly dependent on others; but Switzerland is also an economic giant compared to the giant economic dwarfs of the Third World. Switzerland is the home of economic competition—and of innumerable cartels; a model for Marx's analysis of artisanal capitalism, it is also home to some of Europe's largest corporations. Even if Victor Hugo were proved correct in his prediction that *"la Suisse, dans l'Histoire, aura le dernier mot,"* we should still ask, *"Quelle Suisse?"*[20]

Begotten by Stalin and Hitler, modern Austria also abounds in conflicting images. It features both the splendid past of a great power and the gemütliche present of a small country. Wrecked by a bloody civil war in the 1930s, Austria today is a nation at peace with itself. Because its people have only come to appreciate the difference between things German and things Austrian in the last four decades, the

Second Republic holds the distinction of being Europe's youngest nation state.[21] According to an Austrian joke, Germany's economic miracle was insignificant compared to Austria's; the Germans worked. But without appearing to try very hard, the Austrians' performance during the 1970s almost made them "Number One" in the industrial world. In this unlikely European incarnation of Japanese industrialism, "socialism and state-owned industry are superimposed on a post-imperialist society."[22] It is, however, a country with a very conservative socialism. Austria displays both a bourgeois mentality and the recurrent election of socialist governments. Judging by the salary differential between the Republic's chancellor and the director of the Vienna opera, Austrians value the sound of music at least three times as much as the political leadership. And which other country with a strong antisemitic past has elected a Jewish chancellor who champions the cause of the Palestinians? The optimistic expectations of Frederic III found their expression in a fifteenth-century acronym, AEIOU *(Austria erit in orbe ultima).*[23] But even if there were to be an Austria to the end of time, should we not ask, "Which Austria"?

For political analysis this is a confounding mixture of similarities and differences, convergences and divergences. Switzerland pursues liberal goals through insisting on economic stability. Its experience is instructive about both the possibilities and the limitations of liberal capitalism in the world economy. Of course, this Swiss exception to developments elsewhere in the world is not a recent phenomenon. To a discerning observer like James Bryce, democratic Switzerland was in the nineteenth century a political exception to the strong, European-wide current of monarchical rule, Caesarism, and bureaucratic authoritarianism. Conversely, in the late 1940s the opening pages of André Siegfried's celebrated study of modern Switzerland give the reader the impression of visiting an earlier century and a different continent.[24] Because important strains of its politics predate the emergence of the modern state, Switzerland has been viewed (by Herbert Lüthy) as an "antithesis" and "the most archaic country of the West." In another article Lüthy argues that the "few foreigners who have taken the trouble to give close study to our institutions and their workings have all been struck by their archaic, not to say anachronistic, quality."[25] Insisting on the integrity and distinctiveness of their national community, Swiss of all political persuasions deny that the country suffers from any fundamental divisions. In their cosmopolitan minds, Switzerland's position at the center of Europe symbolizes the centrist political solutions that emerge from a consensual system that pragmatically shares power while searching for a stable compromise. Jane Kramer expresses the point well: "They have based too many of their institutions—from the Swiss family to Swiss democracy—on a conviction that those institutions will reflect not the compromises of individuals living together but a kind of sublime accord."[26]

Austria pursues social goals through economic growth. Its experience is revealing about both the possibilities and the limitations of democratic socialism in the world economy. Lenin is reported to have said that "he who sups with a capitalist needs a long spoon." Austria's most important trade union leader, Anton Benya, disagrees: "What he needs above all is soup in the bowl."[27] In the opinion of Austria's Left, a war of sorts still divides the classes in a capitalist society; but, in contrast to the 1930s, the contestants have chosen different weapons. Chancellor Kreisky has characterized Austria's economic and social partnership as "a loveless marriage that works."[28] The partners in that marriage have put Austria's "small house in order," as the title of an admiring article in the *Economist* put it, thus assuring Austria of its distinctive place in the gallery of democratic socialism.[29] As Paul Lewis wrote recently, "Austrians themselves readily attribute their achievements to a remarkable social consensus—an almost-complete meeting of minds on economic matters between Socialists and conservatives, bosses and workers, rich and poor—which spares this tiny country the bruising confrontations that thwart policy-making in most other Western nations. . . . It has developed an eclectic policy of its own that combines the best of both Keynesian theories and Friedmanite monetarism, but which only works because Austrians also have a strong sense of togetherness."[30] Austria's vast nationalized sector has neither created islands of socialist production in a capitalist sea nor reinvigorated private capitalism. Instead, its presence has weakened the position of the business community without greatly enhancing the power of the state. The displacement of the business community and the state bureaucracy by the economic and social partnership and the political parties is, in the words of Andrew Shonfield, "a serious attempt to keep the conduct of undertakings which form part of the public patrimony under some kind of political surveillance."[31]

DEMOCRATIC CORPORATISM IN AUSTRIA AND SWITZERLAND

In their self-perceptions the Austrians and the Swiss emphasize their "exceptionalism" and "uniqueness." Such claims notwithstanding, this book will show that Swiss and Austrian success, both political and economic, can be comprehended in a comparative perspective. I shall, in brief, argue that democratic corporatism is central to both Austrian and Swiss success. This "democratic corporatism" has three defining characteristics: an ideology of social partnership expressed at the national level; a relatively centralized and concentrated system of interest groups; and a voluntary and informal coordination of conflicting objectives through continuous political bargaining among interest groups, state bureaucracies, and political parties. That this form of corporatism shapes the political life of both countries undercuts their claims to uniqueness. The comparative study of corporatism is a useful corrective for an intellectual insularity paradoxically at odds with these two societies' deep entanglement with the outside world.

This definition of corporatism, it should be pointed out, differs from others.[32] To some corporatism connotes the authoritarian politics of Austria, Italy, Portugal, and several Eastern European states in the 1930s. To others it refers to the organization of contemporary corporate or state capitalism, exemplified by the United States or Japan. The corporatism that this book addresses is, however, an entirely different breed. It has a democratic rather than an authoritarian politics, and it responds to political rather than to economic contradictions.

The first of the three characteristics of democratic corporatism, an ideology of social partnership (rather than class conflict), captures routine politics in societies such as Austria and Switzerland. The ideological cohesion that results does not lead to the end of political conflict. Rather, conflict is framed within vaguely held but firmly shared notions of the public good. Such notions pervade political arrangements, but they are to be found in particular in the major interest groups, which are both centralized and inclusive. The leadership of Switzerland's "peak association" of business or of Austria's trade union movement enjoys very strong powers over a compliant membership. And peak associations and unions organize a very large share of producer firms and workers. To be sure, the image of order and symmetry this interest-group system conveys is to some extent misleading; political struggles within organizations are intense. But the fact that they are decided within rather than between organizations prevents a cluttering of the public agenda with fights between different segments of business and labor. This form of corporatism, however, retains its democratic character through its close links to political parties. Electoral competition is a periodic shock to and interruption of a potentially dangerous celebration of consensus. The third defining characteristic of democratic corporatism is a particular style of political bargaining. It is voluntary, informal, and continuous; it coordinates the conflicting objectives of political actors by permitting trade-offs across different sectors of policy; and it encourages a predictability in the policy process that is conducive to flexibility on the part of actors.

Austrian and Swiss democratic corporatism has historical roots in the nineteenth century, when the differences between the two countries were more striking than they are today. In terms of sheer size the Austro-Hungarian Empire dwarfed its Swiss neighbor; but even in its most advanced provinces it lagged in industrialization far behind most Swiss cantons. Because it controlled a large and sheltered domestic market, Austria-Hungary lacked Switzerland's energy in pursuing opportunities for trade and investment abroad. Yet, as Gerhard Lehmbruch has convincingly argued, in both countries the nineteenth century saw the emergence of political practices that explain why it is common there, rather than in Germany, France, or Italy, to speak of a "typical Austrian (Swiss) compromise."[33]

The Swiss penchant for compromise stems from the country's numerous social divisions. The fear of involvement in Europe's religious warfare in the seventeenth and eighteenth centuries helped establish the principle of parity between Protestants and Catholics in several important cantons. That principle was reinforced by the constitutionally mandated strong representation of Switzerland's regions in the center. Informally, a similar proportional representation of Switzerland's different language communities is also observed. Political practices since the middle of the nineteenth century have followed a similar path away from majority rule to proportionality. A voluntary sharing of power through all-party cabinets occurred in a growing number of cantons after 1854. At the federal level, the constitution of 1848 contained provisions for a "collegial" rather than a majority-based executive branch of government. The executive thus accommodated itself easily between 1891 and 1943 to the successive inclusion of political parties representing Catholics, farmers, and workers.

Similarly, Austria's penchant for compromise can be traced back to the nineteenth century. Its roots lie in the nationality conflicts of a multi-ethnic empire rather than in its weak parliamentary tradition. The "Compromise" between Austria and Hungary reached in 1867 set a precedent for a bargained system of legislation between both parts of the empire. It also encouraged the proportional representation of different ethnic groups in the provincial governments of the Austrian half. Compromises, it was thought, could be reached only by resisting the temptations of majority rule. Austria's strong indigenous strain of corporatist theory further reinforced cooperation. It deeply affected not only the syndicalist notions of democracy of Austro-Marxism but also the political practices of the Dollfuss regime of the 1930s, and of the Second Republic.

The proximate historical origins of Austria's and Switzerland's democratic corporatism lie in the experience of the 1930s and 1940s. Confronted with the Great Depression and the spread of fascism throughout neighboring countries, Swiss business and labor concluded a "Peace Agreement" in 1937 that has lasted for almost five decades. The implications of the political experience of the 1930s were made explicit by the important constitutional amendment of 1948, which to this day stamps the procedures of Swiss-style corporatism. In the case of Austria the 1930s did not bring peace but civil war in 1934 and German occupation in 1938. The memories of this darkest period in modern Austrian history pushed the founding fathers of the Second Republic forcefully toward the adoption of an Austrian-style corporatism. They also provided powerful symbols for succeeding generations of political leaders. Thus in both Austria and Switzerland the historical foundations of democratic corporatism rest on a perception of extreme vulnerability.

Compared to the 1930s and 1940s the postwar period has been much more benign. The crisis-ridden 1930s and 1940s may explain why democratic corporatism emerged in these two societies, but, since the dark memories have faded, why do corporatist institutions and political practices persist? Two answers suggest themselves: one focuses on the international context, the other on domestic politics. Although benign, the liberalization of the international economy since the late 1950s daily reminds all political actors of the pressures of international competition that open and vulnerable economies impose on domestic political arrangements. Corporatist practices that enhance consensus are valued by all important groups as tools essential to fashioning a national strategy in the international economy. Economic openness forces on all of the central political actors the sense of being an object of international developments that they cannot control. The second reason for the persistence of Austria's and Switzerland's corporatist structures, as subsequent chapters show in great detail, lies in the way corporatist institutions are continuously relegitimized through the process of arriving at and implementing policies to compensate groups under pressure.

The analysis of corporatism, Leo Panitch argues, has become a growth industry.[34] Like most industries, its manufacturers are concentrated in a particular region, Austria and Scandinavia. Corporatist arrangements, it is assumed, are largely found where a strong social democratic or socialist party and a strong centralized trade union form an alliance to provide a backbone of closely knit political arrangements that will link political parties, interest groups, and government bureaucracies. If Austria is the paradigmatic place, economic and social problems are the paradigmatic issues for corporatist bargains. The most frequently cited bargain in the 1960s and 1970s involved a trade-off between labor markets and the political arena. Trade union leaders agreed to impose wage restraint on the demands of their rank and file in return for concessions on questions of social policy. Since the late 1950s trading wage restraint for political or social gains has been an important ingredient in the recipe that links economic changes abroad to corporatist arrangements at home, and that reinforces these arrangements through the policy process.

Swiss unions are weak compared to those of other small European states, and Switzerland's industrial relations system is decentralized. As a result, some authors have concluded that Switzerland should not be counted among the states distinguished by strong corporatism.[35] They reach this conclusion because they define democratic corporatism as part and parcel of the institutional implantation of a strong labor movement and a strong political Left. Accordingly, Switzerland is unique and Austria is paradigmatic.[36] But this book tries to establish a different interpretation. Democratic corporatism is a method of mobilizing consent in societies that occurs in the name of democratic socialism in Austria, liberal capitalism in Switzerland. The argument that attributes to Switzerland a weak corporatism on account of a decentralized system of collective bargaining and a weak union movement overlooks important features of Swiss politics.[37] To be sure, Switzerland lacks an incomes policy, a centralized system of collective bargaining, and a strong Left. But Switzerland's small size and economic openness contribute to a considerable centralization both of the system of interest groups that shapes the policy process and of Switzerland's powerful business community. An ideology of social partnership unites business and unions at the national level, and a distinctive process coordinates conflicting objectives. Thus Hanspeter Kriesi concludes, in the most comprehensive study published on the subject to date, that Switzerland features a type of corporatism unlike that in Austria and the Scandinavian countries, but which retains essential aspects of the ideological consensus, institutional centralization, and collaborative policy process that define democratic corporatism.[38]

OUTLINE OF THE ARGUMENT

All of the rich countries of the West are capitalist states and industrial democracies driven by the pursuit of both power and plenty.[39] General theories of capitalist economies, industrial societies, and political democracies postulate overarching similarities in strategy and structure—similarities that, though useful for some analytical purposes, run counter to the dominant political trends of the 1970s. The analysis of political economy aims to explain political strategies and, so far as possible, economic and political outcomes by showing how these strategies and outcomes result from the self-defined interests of actors. Thus the choice of Switzerland and Austria, paradigms of liberal capitalism and democratic socialism, is particularly promising. Although these two countries differ greatly in their political strategies and domestic structures, politics in both narrows political inequalities. This convergence, I shall argue, is the most notable consequence of their corporatist politics.

How do we analyze the Austrian and Swiss variants of corporatism? Existing work suggests three different ways.[40] Neo-Marxist interpretations focus on social forces. They insist that corporatism harnesses the European Left to the task of stabilizing an inherently unstable capitalist order. When push came to shove in the interwar years, the iron fist of capitalism used the brown leather glove of fascism for its defense; since 1945 that fist has been concealed in the red velvet glove of social democracy. Neo-Weberian scholars focus on the institutional structure of interest intermediation. Since the late nineteenth century, they argue, that structure has been the main determinant and manifestation of corporatism. In their view it was economic depressions and wars that spurred the formation of centralized economic interest groups. The third interpretation of corporatism primarily focuses on the policy process and the tradeoffs between political actors across different policy sectors.

In this book, Switzerland's and Austria's corporatism are analyzed at all three levels that inform existing interpretations of corporatism: social coalitions dominating the two societies and the effect these coalitions have on the substance of political choices; institutional structures of politics; and the policy process. Taken together the institutional structure of politics and the policy process constitute the policy network, that is, a patterned interrelationship between state and society within a domestic structure. "The actors in society and state influencing the definition of . . . policy objectives consist of the major interest groups and political action groups. The former represent the relations of production (including industry, finance, commerce, labor and agriculture); the latter derive from the structure of political authority (primarily the state bureaucracy and political parties). The governing coalitions of social forces in each of the advanced industrial states find their institutional expression in distinct policy networks that link the public and the private sector. . . ."[41] In the names of liberal capitalism and democratic socialism, Switzerland and Austria are both corporatist, though in different settings. Each has evolved a corporatism well suited to the mobilizing of political consensus that combines political stability with economic flexibility.

Normally, comparative analysis explores objects that, to the uninitiated, look similar on the surface, such as factory life in Britain and in Japan; or it points to continuities in objects that appear very dissimilar at first glance, such as France before and after the Revolution.[42] This book adopts both perspectives. Chapters 2 and 3 illustrate differences in the domestic structures and political strategies of Austria and Switzerland. Austria's democratic socialism is distinguished by a strong socialist party, a powerful and centralized union movement, extremely centralized political institutions, and policies of national adaptation and public compensation. Conversely, Switzerland's liberal capitalism is characterized by a strong, internationally oriented business community, strong conservative parties, less centralized political institutions, and policies of global adaptation and private compensation. But despite these differences, chapter 4 argues, Austria and Switzerland are both variants of democratic corporatism. In both countries we observe a narrowing of political inequalities and thus a surprising convergence of policies.

Chapters 5 and 6 illustrate how a social variant of corporatism in Austria and a liberal variant in Switzerland establish compatibility between economic flexibility and political stability in four industrial sectors: textiles and steel in Austria, and textiles and watches in Switzerland. These four industries share many of the attributes characteristic of declining industries in the 1970s: loss of market share at home and abroad, protectionist pressures abroad, domestic protectionist pressures in the face of competitive imports, and low productivity and growth even with high investment. Indeed, the growth projections for these four industries are lower than for any other in Switzerland and Austria.[43] Managing the decline of these four technologically mature industries has been a significant political problem in both countries. Yet these four industries also differ substantially one from another, and the differences between them are instructive for the argument of this book. Political commonalities observed across a range of industries so different in their economic and institutional make-up support the argument that these commonalities are not mere artifacts of the cases chosen for analysis. Finally, the concluding chapter reflects on some of the implications of this analysis.

This book argues that many roads lead to Rome. Democratic socialism in Austria and liberal capitalism in Switzerland can succeed both economically and politically. In the 1960s and 1970s they have secured legitimacy and prosperity. Their success, as I shall show, is shaped in important ways by a corporatist politics. Democratic corporatism offers a political formula by which political alliances, organized around union officials in Austria and businessmen in Switzerland, create political consensus. The essence of this democratic corporatism lies in the narrowing of political inequalities among various actors. Although Austria prefers equality to efficiency and Switzerland prefers efficiency to equality, democratic corporatism sets limits to both kinds of preferences. Corporatist arrangements thus link the requirements of political stability closely to those of economic flexibility. In doing so they make corporatism compatible with change.

CHAPTER TWO

Social Democracy in Austria

Austria exemplifies a successful social democracy whose spectacular economic performance throughout the 1970s is captured by the title of a recent study: "Prosperity amidst Crisis."[1] Against a background of oil shocks and worldwide stagflation, Austria joined the ranks of the richest countries. In 1978 Austria's per capita income had reached $7,520,* which made it the tenth-richest country in Europe and the sixteenth-richest in the world. During the 1970s Austria's unemployment rate hovered around 2 percent, one of the lowest rates in the Organization for Economic Co-operation and Development (OECD); and in the late 1970s Austria's 0.8 percent rate of youth unemployment was less than one-tenth the 11.3 percent OECD average. At the same time, Austria has managed to defend the value of the schilling. Since the mid-1970s Austria's rate of inflation has been much lower than those of all other industrialized states except Switzerland and West Germany; and in 1979 the Austrian rate dropped well below that of Germany. With the exception of the Swiss franc all currencies, including the deutsche mark, declined in value against the Austrian schilling between 1971 and 1978. In 1979 Austria ranked fifth in the world in the absolute value of its currency reserves and third on a per

*Throughout this book Austrian and Swiss currencies have been converted to dollars according to rates given in three works issued by the Organization for Economic Co-operation and Development (OECD), *National Accounts of OECD Countries*, vol. 1, *1950–1978* (Paris: OECD, 1980), p. 89; *National Accounts: Main Aggregates*, vol. 1, *1952–1978*, (Paris: OECD, 1983), p. 92; and *Main Economic Indicators* (Paris: OECD, December 1982). This book occasionally refers to the small European states. For more detail on Sweden, Norway, Denmark, the Netherlands, and Belgium as well as Austria and Switzerland, see my *Small States in World Markets*.

34

capita basis. Austria, together with Norway, achieved the highest rate of economic growth in Europe across the decade. And, unlike many other OECD countries, Austria calculates in seconds rather than in days the annual average time per worker lost in industrial disputes. Eight minor strikes involved 800 workers in 1979—an average loss of time of 8 seconds per worker per year.

These economic accomplishments of the 1970s are aspects of a longer-term economic change that has moved Austria from economic backwardness to the unaccustomed role of economic model. In the technological competitiveness of its export products, total exports, real annual investment, productivity, real economic growth, and the growth of per capita income—in all these areas Austria has, since 1960, surpassed by significant margins the average growth rates in the OECD, in the European Communities (EC), and, most important, in West Germany. In the entire OECD only Japan has exceeded the rate at which Austria has transformed its economic structure. If Austria's previous industrial history was marked by "an economic spurt that failed," this one has surely succeeded.[2] Indeed, in the late 1970s the OECD, the International Monetary Fund (IMF), and the United Nations Economic Commission for Europe registered their astonishment over Austria's uninhibited deficit spending and their approval of its success.

Austria is also a story of political success. With few exceptions Austrians view their political institutions and political practices as legitimate. Political parties and interest groups enjoy a broad base of support. And, unlike in the interwar period, political movements do not seek the government's overthrow. The 1970s have, it is true, created new problems that test Austria's established ways of conducting its political business. The issue of nuclear power, for example, created an unprecedented stalemate in Austrian politics. Regionally concentrated unemployment put a serious strain on unions, firms, and political parties. Moreover, uncertainties in international capital markets, as well as high interest rates, increasingly limited the extent to which Austria could borrow abroad to finance growth at home. But it would be a mistake to infer from such examples that the economic changes of the 1970s created stresses and contradictions that defy political solutions. Nothing could be further from the truth. Compared to the political experiences of other industrial states in the 1970s as well as to its own history in the 1920s and 1930s, Austria must be judged a great political success.

The reason for this success, I argue, lies in Austria's social corporatism. In this chapter I analyze how corporatism mobilizes the political consensus essential for coping with economic change. I address three levels of analysis: social coalitions and policy choice, institutions, and the policy process. Austria's powerful and reformist trade union movement shapes policies that stress an active employment program, a large public sector, and a generous system of public welfare, as well as policies dealing with prices, wages, and industrial adjustment. In part because of Austria's large, nationalized sector, the private business community is relatively weak and has, until recently, had a domestic orientation; it consistently sought heavy subsidies for investment and only cautiously embraced the principle of free trade. In the opening two sections I argue that the character of the dominant social coalition explains why Austria pursues a response to economic change that centers around public compensation and national adaptation. The alliance among Austria's social forces and its political choices in addressing problems of change find expression in a particular policy network. In later sections I illustrate how Austria mobilizes consensus and thus preserves the balance between flexibility and stability. Finally, I support the argument indirectly, by showing that policies adopted by Switzerland do not fit the political logic that informs Austria's social corporatism.

GROWTH-CONSCIOUS UNIONS

In Austria's social coalition, trade unions occupy the central place. Their trademark is an interest in economic growth and an indifference to questions of redistribution. The great political strength of Austria's labor movement has created a close approximation in the Second Republic to that "equilibrium of class forces" about which Otto Bauer was theorizing in the First.

Austria's strategy of public compensation and national adaptation would not be thinkable without strong unions. The organizational strength of the Austrian Trade Union Federation (Österreichischer Gewerkschaftsbund, ÖGB) is a precondition for its influence on Austria's strategy and its prominent place in Austrian politics. In 1980 the ÖGB's membership ran to about 1.7 million members, that is, about 60 percent of all blue- and white-collar employees in Austria.[3] Union membership is virtually universal in all of Austria's major firms. Furthermore, workers and employees in Austria's numerous small firms are by law obliged to be members of Austria's Chamber of Labor, which is itself an integral part of Austria's powerful labor movement. In addition, the labor movement's prominence is secured through its political penetration of key institutions in Austrian society: nationalized industries, banks, media, and, of course, the Socialist Party (Sozialistische Partei Österreichs, SPÖ), as well as Parliament.[4]

The effects of Austria's strong Left are visible even in Austrian law and Austria's Nationalbank, centers of power not easily accessible to unions in a capitalist society. For example, since it owns a portion of the stocks issued by the Nationalbank, the ÖGB sits on the bank's supervisory board.[5] Austrian judges, despite their socially more conservative views, are more liberal than Swiss judges on issues involving the rights of workers to organize.[6] Codetermination at the plant level, though relatively weak, was widespread in the nationalized industries, and it set a model for emulation in the private sector for two decades before the adoption of formal legislation in 1973.[7] More generally, throughout the postwar years Austria's labor movement has approached the economic sphere, in Kurt Shell's words, "not as a pressure group attempting to extract economic benefits for its members but as a participant shaping its decisions."[8] In a capitalist society that it helped transform, Austria's Left has moved from the theory of class struggle to the practice of social and economic partnership.

Because of its size and prominence, Austria's labor movement cannot be monolithic. But those elements of limited pluralism that do exist contribute to its extraordinary power, by increasing the organizational and financial centralization that sets off the ÖGB from labor organizations in all other industrial countries. Because of the Left's disastrous political experience in the interwar years, Austria's labor movement incorporated its political diversity after 1945 in one centralized organization.[9] Austria's centralized union shows neither the ideological differences to be found in Italy, France, Belgium, and the Netherlands nor the status differences between blue- and white-collar unions common in Scandinavia and West Germany. The ideological diversity among the socialist, Catholic, and communist factions of the labor movement finds its expression in the periodic elections to factory councils.[10] While the socialists hold decisive organizational power in the union movement, the presence of a Catholic wing both in the union organization and in the more encompassing Federal Chamber of Labor builds a link to Austria's Peoples Party (Österreichische Volkspartei, ÖVP), thus spreading the union's political base.[11] Ideological diversity has forced the dominant socialist bloc to overcome its traditional anticlericalism in dealing with the Catholic faction, on the one hand, while requiring a greater reliance on socialist rhetoric to contain the communist faction on the other.[12]

Political diversity inside the ÖGB is, paradoxically, an effective unifying force, which counteracts the numerous conflicting interests pursued by the constituent unions. Speaking for the particularistic interests of their rank and files in the different industrial unions, middle-level union officials are required by ÖGB practice to follow the policy line adopted by their political grouping inside the union. Since the socialists enjoy a predominant position in the ÖGB, this political requirement imposes unity in the face of the frequently conflicting economic interests that divide white-collar, public-sector, and industrial employees.[13]

Austria's union heavily favors the centralized exercise of influence on economic decisions at the national level over decentralized forms of codetermination within plants.[14] Furthermore, Austria's dual system of worker representation, both through the unions and through factory councils at the plant level, reinforces the centralized organizational structure and power of the union movement. The identity of interests of unions and councils is assured by the fact that elections to the factory councils determine the composition of the local union leadership. Nonunion members vote in these council elections and thus help select union officials; but this is regarded as an oddity with no particular political consequences because of the virtually universal union membership of workers in the large plants. Finally, in contrast to Switzerland, political tensions between the unions and the Socialist Party are kept to a minimum, thus further reinforcing the power of the Left. Despite the union's formal autonomy from the party system, strong links do exist, in particular between the dominant socialist faction of the ÖGB and the SPÖ. Important political questions such as the employment problems of Austria's coal mining industry were, for example, settled in informal and secret bargaining sessions between Chancellor Bruno Kreisky and the head of the trade union, Anton Benya. Party and union links are sustained by a broad array of twenty-eight satellite organizations that provide the followers of Austria's Left with an integrated system of social and cultural services from cradle to grave.[15] Moreover, almost one-half of the SPÖ members of Parliament are union officials on either a full-time or a part-time basis, and, since 1971, the president of the ÖGB has also been the president of Parliament.[16] This fusion of union and party leadership makes open conflict between the two organizations very rare. It greatly strengthens the labor movement when its interests are affected in the wide range of policy choices that follow from Austria's strategy of domestic compensation.[17]

In these choices the ÖGB reveals the prominent position that it occupies in politics. The SPÖ's social policy initiatives come not from

Vienna, as in the First Republic, but from collective bargaining in the nationalized industries. For example, several key provisions incorporated in Austria's social security reform of 1956 had been won through collective bargaining in Austria's nationalized industries a few years earlier.[18] From the perspective of the Left, Austria's strategy of public compensation requires political control over the economy, which is achieved neither through a free market nor through political plans but through economic policy that emphasizes jobs, growth, productivity, and the ability to adjust to change. The Left views its own importance as at least equal to that of Austria's business community.[19] Thus, its policy choices reflect a broad and system-wide rather than a narrow and class-specific definition of workers' interest. In the 1950s and the late 1970s, a union policy of deliberate wage restraint was designed to strengthen Austrian exports in world markets. In the 1960s and 1970s, productivity bargaining and a countercyclical wage policy complemented and reinforced the strategy of national adaptation that informed government policy. And the gradual development of Austria's system of income policy goes, in each and every instance, back to the political initiatives that the union leadership took in the late 1940s, mid-1950s, and early 1960s.[20]

The union's orientation toward the common weal has had its costs. In hoping to further the objectives of social democracy through a strategy of growth rather than through distributional struggles, the Austrian union movement was prepared in the late 1960s and early 1970s to accept substantial losses in the relative share of gross domestic product (GDP) accruing to labor.[21] The OECD's *Economic Surveys* noted this several times as "an atypical development" in the prolonged upswing of the business cycle then being experienced by the industrial world.[22] The gains of 1974–75, stemming from very large real wage increases in the face of a world recession that Austrian economists had not accurately projected, were offset by the sharp drop in the wage share in 1978–80. A decade of socialist rule has not altered the size of the wage share in national income,[23] and Austria's growth policy has, at best, left unaltered the inegalitarian distribution of income and wealth. Indeed, it is more likely that the policy has reinforced an inequality which the union movement is committed, at least in principle, to erase.[24] Instead of emphasizing the goal of social equality in programmatic demands and ideological debates, the Austrian union leadership has chosen to involve itself politically in those arenas of economic and social policy most critical to Austria's strategy of domestic compensation.[25] As Sarah Hogg reports, "The unions and their members know that their power lies in their ability to bargain without ever letting negotiations come to the point of outright confrontation. Hence they have become an indispensable part of the machinery of economic management."[26] In short, the Austrian trade union has steered away from radical socialism toward conservative social democracy.

The dominant position that this reformist labor movement occupies in political life explains in large measure Austria's pursuit of national adaptation to and public compensation for economic change. Policies dealing with employment, public expenditure, social welfare, prices and wages, and industrial adjustment clearly reflect the union's political preference, which is to link international competitiveness to national well-being. As the deputy chancellor said in 1977, "For Social Democrats the first objective of economic policy . . . is to secure and create jobs."[27] For example, that Austria's public enterprises should enhance the economic stability of the Second Republic has been declared government policy since the minister of Transport and Nationalized Industries, Karl Waldbrunner, issued a circular in the early 1950s requesting public enterprises not to reduce employment in times of recession.[28] In the 1950s and 1960s public firms laid off fewer workers in times of recession and hired fewer workers in times of rapid growth.[29] In the 1970s Austria's large nationalized companies similarly acted as buffers, to protect Austria's domestic labor markets from higher rates of unemployment.[30] Through a variety of policies—including suspending the practice of temporarily "borrowing" employees from other firms, accelerating the shift of employees out of declining into more promising product lines, taking advantage of the social security system's provision for early retirement, and increasing the role of vocational training programs—Austria's nationalized industries operating in declining sectors gradually absorbed the sharp reduction in business activity in 1975 and distributed the necessary reduction in employment over several years. In Austria's overall nationalized sector, however, employment increased while productivity declined between 1973 and 1977. In the private sector the relation was reversed.[31] Austria's nationalized banks have also cooperated with the government's "socially responsible" employment policy, by propping up ailing firms among their subsidiaries as well as by bailing out some private firms at the brink of bankruptcy.[32] Generally speaking, the government's policy is not to defend every job but to ensure that the total number of jobs remains the same. Thus, economic change is accepted as a way of life, but it calls for a deliberate policy of compensation.

The defense of full employment is not simply left to Austria's vast nationalized sector. Between 1970 and 1975 employment in the public sector increased by 20 percent, and between 1974 and 1979 the number of employees in the public sector narrowly defined (excluding nationalized firms, education, and health) increased by 47,000.[33] Felix Butschek argues that "the overall expansion in tertiary sector employment was less due to a favorable situation in the market for qualified personnel, but more to the political decision to expand specific public sectors which in Austria still lagged behind those of other countries."[34] In 1976, in relation to total government spending, expenditures for public sector employment were almost twice as large in Austria as in Switzerland.[35] Furthermore, because of a 10 percent unemployment rate in some parts of the Austrian periphery, regional policy (in the Eastern part of the country in particular) was explicitly designed to defend existing jobs and to create new ones. A shorter work week was introduced in 1975, partially intended to spread fewer jobs among more employees. About 33,000 workers accepted early retirement with advantageous financial conditions. Minimum annual vacation was extended from three to four weeks. Without these and a host of other specific measures in the areas of education and vocational training, Austria's unemployment rate in the late 1970s would probably have been three times as large as the reported 2 percent figure.[36] The costs are measured in larger budget deficits, diminished productivity, and growing balance-of-trade deficits—key political challenges for the SPÖ government after 1979.

Because nationalized industries and the public sector support the government's goal of full employment, Austria has a labor-market policy less far-reaching and less expensive than Sweden's. In the late 1970s, for example, the Austrian government spent about 2 percent of its budget on labor-market policies; the Swedish figure was about four times higher. But the employment effect of Austria's policy was twice as great as that of Sweden's.[37] With its emphasis on vocational training, Austria has deployed its resources selectively. In the late 1970s Austria was one of the few industrial states that could provide, through an extensive apprenticeship system, gainful employment to virtually all of its young. In 1980 a comprehensive system of vocational counseling extended to 127,000 young people deciding on careers. In addition, the federal government made available about 15,000 apprenticeship grants at a total cost of $6.18 million. Since 1976, furthermore, the government has subsidized the apprenticeship programs of firms that employ more youngsters than they actually need.[38]

This commitment to full employment is stronger than in Switzerland, even in the face of less favorable labor-market conditions. In Austria the annual average growth of population of working age is expected to increase from 0.2 percent in 1960–75 to 6.9 percent in 1975–90. In Switzerland the corresponding figures are 14.9 and 3.1 percent for the two periods.[39] In order to maintain full employment, Austria will have to create about 30,000 jobs annually throughout the mid-1980s. Austria's labor-market policies will thus remain indispensable. Between 1970 and 1979 expenditures for an active labor-market policy increased by a factor of ten, from $6.2 million to $60 million.[40] In contrast to most industrial states the average duration of unemployment decreased between 1974 and 1979, and hidden unemployment is not a problem in Austria.[41] In introducing the SPÖ's Economic Program of 1981 the secretary of the party, Karl Blecha, reaffirmed that unemployment does not "naturally follow" from general economic conditions and that the realization of the right to work is the central task of the government's economic policy.[42]

The government's effort to protect Austrians from wide fluctuations in economic activity is clearly reflected in the area of public expenditure. Fiscal policy has been facilitated by the traditionally wide discretion that the Austrian government has enjoyed on questions of public finance, especially before 1963.[43] For example, in 1953 a long-term investment program was set up to modernize and extend Austria's highway system, railroads, and postal services; it provided the government with expenditures "which could be varied up or down at the discretion of the Minister of Finance."[44] In an attempt to curb inflation during the high economic growth of the early 1970s, Austria adopted a restrictive fiscal policy. And the premature repayment of government debt, freezing of surplus revenues, postponement of expenditures, and creation of reserves during the inflationary years of the early 1970s led to only modest increases in public debt. This gave the Austrian government some financial leverage, which permitted deficit spending in the mid-1970s in the wake of the first oil shock and subsequent worldwide recession.[45]

Austria's government has relied on a wide range of fiscal policies to strengthen domestic demand and thus to maintain high levels of employment. After 1973 the government increased public investment expenditures, created new tax incentives for private consumption, and generously promoted private investment.[46] As a result, the debt of the federal government increased sharply.[47] In the first quarter of 1976, 80 percent of all borrowing on Austria's capital market was by the public sector, compared to 50 percent a year earlier.[48] Although Austria's income taxes paid as a percentage of gross earnings increased more markedly than in any other OECD member state in the late 1970s, the deficits in the government's budget have remained very large.[49] Between 1974 and 1977 Austria's public spending substantially exceeded the statistical norm among the OECD countries.[50]

Budget deficits were financed largely through short- and medium-term borrowing, both at home and abroad.[51] Between 1970 and 1974 the debt of the federal government almost doubled (from $1.82 billion to $3.26 billion); in the next five years, between 1974 and 1978, the debt more than quadrupled (from $3.26 billion to $13.8 billion); and it doubled again between 1978 and 1982. Austria's foreign indebtedness increased by a factor of seven between 1973 and 1979, compared to a mere threefold increase in its domestic debt. By 1981 slightly less than half of the government's debt was foreign. In support of this policy Austria's new banking law of 1979 was especially designed to attract foreign capital. Responding to attractive interest rates in 1980, foreigners shifting funds to Austria could enjoy more secrecy, higher interest rates, and more far-reaching tax exemptions than in Switzerland. The additional inflow of foreign capital has largely gone into Austrian government bonds, thus helping to finance simultaneously the deficits in Austria's balance of payments and government budget.[52]

Because the government has been compelled to adopt a policy of prolonged rather than temporary deficit spending, the danger of a long-term deterioration in the balance of payments has increased, and government officials are now more fearful that the weight of interest charges will strain government finances. In 1980, only 10 percent of the federal budget contained budget items over which the government had some discretion.[53] Should Austria's borrowing abroad to finance prosperity at home be impaired in the future, the long-term political debates may well circle around the feasibility and desirability of having Austria's Nationalbank directly finance budget deficits. In the medium term, though, Austria's fiscal policy is confronting another problem and is steering a less controversial course. A growing divergence between an increasing propensity to import and a declining effectiveness of deficit spending in a small, open economy confronts the Austrian government in the 1980s with new problems.[54] Because of this constraint, as well as rising levels of public debt and external indebtedness, Austria's fiscal policy was much more restrained after the second oil shock of 1979–80 than it had been after the first shock of 1974–75. The head of Austria's Nationalbank concluded that "quite a number of tax increases during the course of recent years as well as cuts in expenditure have alleviated the problem to some extent, but have not been able to bring about adequate elbow room for an active budget policy during the next phase of a more serious recession."[55]

Austria's sizable expenditures for social welfare provide built-in economic stabilizers that assist the government in its effort to shield the Austrian economy from international turbulence. Compared to those of the other advanced industrial states, both large and small, and especially compared to Switzerland, Austria's public expenditures for social welfare are very large. Throughout the postwar years the Austrian government has outspent Switzerland by sizable though declining margins.[56] But unlike Switzerland Austria has only expanded its mature welfare state incrementally in the postwar years. An index of the extensiveness of different social welfare programs shows Austria to be close to the European norm since 1945, ahead of Switzerland by a very substantial margin but lagging somewhat behind Norway, Sweden, and the Netherlands by 1970.[57] In the late 1960s and early 1970s public spending on social welfare was about twice as large in Austria as in Switzerland, and, in the case of old age pensions, the most expensive of all social welfare programs everywhere, Austria spent significantly more than any other OECD member state.[58] In sharp contrast to Switzerland, virtually all of Austria's working population and dependents are covered by legislation; provisions such as the fourteen-month payments for pensions and the payment of child allowances until the age of twenty-one are more generous than in Switzerland; and pension levels are pegged to a wage index, permitting recipients to partake in the economy's productivity gains.[59] This high level of public welfare spending explains why the difference between the earnings received by employees and the labor costs paid by employers is much larger in Austria than anywhere else in Europe. The average hourly earnings of Austria's manufacturing workers are the lowest in Europe, while the proportionate importance of social charges in the wage bill (about 90 percent) is among the largest.[60] Until the late 1970s average taxes paid as a percentage of gross earnings were lower in Austria than in any other OECD country, but the social security contributions paid by Austria's average employee were exceeded only by those paid in the Netherlands.[61]

The philosophy underlying Austria's earnings-related social insurance system differs greatly from Switzerland's provision of minimum benefits (which, it is expected, will be supplemented by voluntary, private insurance benefits). The "replacement rate" of Austrian pensions is more than twice as high as in Switzerland. In Austria, pensions amount to more than one-half of the earnings in the last year of work; in Switzerland, they amount to less than one-fifth.[62] Since Austrian pensions are considered adequate, very strict regulations govern poverty assistance, while, as Max Horlick shows, "Switzerland represents the opposite; since the old-age pension was not meant to be sufficient and since the system is young and payments are small, the controls for means-tested benefits are, so to speak, relaxed."[63] Only 7 percent of Austria's expenditures for old age pensions are financed through means-tested benefits; in Switzerland the proportion is twice as high.[64] Austria's restrictive approach is the sign of a welfare state that, in contrast to Switzerland's, is both mature and extensive. But a comparison with Switzerland does not uniformly favor Austria. For example, compared to Switzerland Austria suffers from substandard housing; and only in the 1970s did Austria catch up with Switzerland in the proportion of its working population covered by sickness insurance.[65] These occasional exceptions notwithstanding, the quality and the range of Austria's publicly funded social welfare policies are attested to by the fact that only two years after the Council of Europe adopted the European Social Charter in 1961, the Austrian government signed it. Switzerland, on the other hand, is still not able to follow suit.

At the same time, however, Austria has not proved vulnerable to the public disenchantment with the massive growth of taxation required to finance public services that surfaced in the 1970s, especially in Scandinavia. Austrian welfare expenditures have increased less sharply in the last two decades than those in Scandinavia or the Netherlands, countries that had surpassed Austrian spending levels by the mid-1970s. Correspondingly, between 1965 and 1977 increases in social security payments and taxes were much lower in Austria than in the OECD as a whole. Indeed, in comparison to West Germany and Switzerland Austria's tax load, heavily weighted toward social security, no longer looks as heavy as it once did. In both 1965 and 1978 Austria's average tax burden was greatest among these three countries, but its lead had shrunk from 9 to 3 percent in comparison to West Germany and from 67 to 22 percent in comparison to Switzerland.[66] Because Austria's growth of social welfare expenditures was comparatively slow in the 1960s and 1970s, the adjustment of the Austrian welfare state to lower rates of economic growth in the years ahead, though difficult, will probably be achieved more easily than elsewhere.[67]

Austria's national adaptation to developments in the international economy is also illustrated by its widely noted incomes policy (politically negotiated price and wage increases), which has helped to achieve relative cost-competitiveness in international markets and thus contribute to full employment and economic growth. Although estimates of the extent of Austria's price regulations vary widely, most observers agree that prices are determined by demand in only limited market segments. In the late 1960s about one-fifth of all goods and services, one-quarter of total output, and one-half of all consumer prices were subject to administrative or political control.[68] This extensive intervention in markets is facilitated by the high degree of concentration in Austrian industry; about one-half of industrial turnover occurs in sectors in which the top four firms control at least 50 percent of sales.[69] The importance attached to the regulation of prices is unambiguously expressed in the legislation of the 1970s. The "liberal" Cartel Law of 1972, for example, notes that "because it is important to the securing of stable prices, public regulation of prices for the most important agricultural products, raw materials and industrial goods will continue."[70] Austria's system of price administration is based not only on a list of goods and services enumerated in its long-standing Price Regulation Law but also, since December 1974, on a general emergency provision that permits a temporary restraint of any price increase found to be excessive.[71]

That this provision had not been invoked by the late 1970s illustrates the self-restraint with which the SPÖ government approached its anti-inflation policy. Distinctive of Austria's incomes policy is "the virtual absence of government . . . and the absence of compulsion."[72] The most important instrument of price regulation in Austria is not administrative but political. Through its voluntary but effective rulings on price increases, the Subcommittee on Prices of the Joint Commission (Paritätische Kommission) in fact establishes a uniform price level at the specified maximum level. The effect has been an officially encouraged, informal cartelization of a substantial part of the competitive segments of the Austrian economy.[73] This system of price regulation is reinforced by Austria's Cartel Commission, in which the major interest groups sitting on the Joint Commission have in effect assumed the powers of the judiciary. In 1975–76 63 cartels covered about 250 producers, 700 goods, and 17 services.[74] Since 1973, furthermore, the number of nonbinding price recommendations issued by business or trade associations has also increased greatly.[75] One-half of Austria's total industrial production experiences no more than "limited" competition; that proportion declines to 40 percent if foreign goods are included in the calculation. International prices thus do not determine domestic price levels in Austria.[76]

At the same time, it would be a mistake to overestimate the political control that Austria's system of price regulation imposes on markets. Corresponding to the widely noted phenomenon of "wage drift," which offsets some of the effects of centralized collective bargaining, Austria experiences a "price drift" in response to its far-reaching attempts to fix prices politically. Two-thirds of all Austrian firms grant rebates; four-fifths differentiate in their pricing between domestic and foreign markets.[77] The effect of firm behavior is to negate in part the oligopolistic price leadership of the Joint Commission. Nonetheless, in the 1950s and 1960s price fluctuations in Austria were less cyclical than in the other small European states, which in turn exhibited fewer price fluctuations than the large industrial states.[78] Although the opening of the Austrian economy to world markets in the 1960s and 1970s reduced the efficacy of its incomes policy, a recent study concludes that between 1965 and 1979 only one-third of Austria's inflation rate can be explained by its international component.[79] By comparative standards, therefore, Austria retains an impressively far-reaching grasp on prices.

Equally important to Austria's incomes policy is a system of wage restraint implemented in the most centralized system of collective bargaining in the advanced industrial world. The inclusion of wages under the jurisdiction of Austria's incomes policy in 1962 was due largely to the pressure of an ÖGB leadership intent on securing its position against the leadership of its constituent members. The Subcommittee on Wages of the Joint Commission does not interfere with the process or outcome of collective bargaining but simply approves the initiation of negotiations for a new agreement and, at times, influences the duration of contracts. Thus Austria's union leadership has an impressive level of control over union organization: the power to engage with business in collective bargaining rests with the leaders of the ÖGB, not with the Chamber of Labor or the individual unions. Although in practice the ÖGB delegates the negotiation of agreements to industrial unions or their subdivisions, no agreement stands without the ÖGB's consent.[80] Furthermore, the central leadership, not the constituent unions, exercises full control over all union finances in general, and over strike funds in particular.[81]

As a result, collective bargaining agreements in Austria are highly centralized. In 1968 only 3 percent of the 602 agreements were concluded at the level of the firm, compared to 32 percent at the federal and 65 percent at the provincial level.[82] Data for the 1950s and the 1970s show that the move from the level of the firm to the national level is one of the distinctive features of Austria's system of labor relations.[83] Moreover, this centralization is reinforced by the rules governing Austria's incomes policy. Cost increases that firms incur because of supplementary wage agreements they have negotiated with their works councils at the plant level do not constitute valid grounds for demanding price increases before the Subcommittee on Prices. Austrian firms thus have a great incentive to bargain only with the ÖGB.[84]

Austria's unions subscribe to the linking of productivity and wage increases over the course of a full business cycle and do not seek to reach their broader social and economic objectives through collective bargaining. Acutely aware of the consequences of wage levels for Austria's position in the international economy, the unions satisfy their broader political demands through political rather than through economic bargains.[85] As I have noted before, the success of this strategy is illustrated by the fact that the "social wage"—benefits paid by employers—in Austria is among the highest in Europe. Austrian employers pay 90 percent of the effective wage in the form of supplementary charges.[86] In the words of ÖGB leader Benya, "You can't separate an incomes policy from a social policy."[87]

The union's wage demands tend to be countercyclical. The union imposes wage restraints in times of economic expansion and requires wage increases in excess of productivity gains in times of recession.[88] Austria's reaction to the second oil shock of 1979–80 illustrates the political capacities that the union's centralized policy of wage moderation provides as an essential ingredient in Austria's incomes policy. In sharp contrast to the strongly countercyclical, upward move of wages in 1974–75, the union reinforced its commitment to Austria's international competitiveness and a favorable investment climate through remarkable wage restraint. Basic wage increases in 1979 were the lowest in the 1970s. And in 1980 basic wage increases did not compensate for the rise in inflation, thus leading to a fall in net real earnings for the first time in three decades.[89] In the words of the long-time head of the ÖGB, "The trade unions . . . do not simply raise demands, . . . they also contribute actively to all measures necessary for reconsolidation of our economy."[90]

The overall economic effects of Austria's incomes policy are not easily assessed. By most accounts it has succeeded psychologically: it dampens excessive inflationary expectations in decisions on wages and prices. A recent empirical investigation gives credit where it is due, yet concludes on a cautionary note: Austria's incomes policy does not have a strong effect on wage levels.[91] The unambiguous determination of the economic effects of policy is not an easy task. Yet in the

1970s, the Austrians argue, incomes policy was an essential pillar of support for Austria's cost competitiveness in international markets. The linking of the Austrian schilling to the strong deutsche mark required some form of domestic arrangement to counteract the appreciation of the schilling against other currencies. Using overly optimistic forecasts for 1975, business and labor concurred on wage increases that in hindsight were far too high; but both adopted remarkable restraint from 1976 onward. In Austria's system of incomes policy the mistakes are made and corrected jointly. In the words of a leading representative of the business community, Austria's political management of markets walks a very narrow path between political and economic necessity. "Monetary stability without high levels of employment is politically unthinkable. Full employment without monetary stability is economically infeasible."[92]

NATIONALIZED BUSINESS

Austria lacks an internationally oriented and powerful business community to advocate the Swiss solution to change—global adaptation and private compensation. In the early Second Republic Austria's business community was largely nationalized; it distinguished itself by a preference for organized domestic markets compatible with national adaptation and public compensation. Austria's average share of capital income between 1950 and 1969 was by far the lowest among the OECD states, less than half the figure reported for Switzerland.[93] And, according to one recent survey, "Austria has a higher degree of public ownership than any other western economy—higher, even, than the most western of its communist neighbors, Jugoslavia."[94]

The roots of Austria's vast public sector must be sought not only in the legacy of a strong monarchical past and a strong labor movement but also in the vagaries of history. A strong middle class never emerged in Austria. At the end of World War II, the newly established Austrian Parliament unanimously decided to nationalize virtually all of the assets seized by the Germans after Austria's *Anschluss* in 1938. And when the Soviet Union withdrew from Austria in 1955 it relinquished its grip on hundreds of Austrian enterprises, which further enlarged Austria's public economy. Thus, the nationalization of a large portion of the means of production was not so much an expression of the class struggle in a capitalist society as an assertion of Austria's national independence in the conflict among nations. In the Austrian context, nationalization can be taken literally, as "making national."[95] This Austrification of capitalism has prevented a recurrence of the experiences of the 1930s, when Austria's big steel firms, under tight control by German trusts, sharply reduced their employment (while actively supporting Austrian fascism and Nazism) or of the postwar years when Austria's oil industry, controlled by the Soviet Union, only produced for foreign demand (while lending support to Austria's Communist Party).[96]

The Austrian state owns virtually all of the country's transportation, communication, and power industries, a number of state monopolies including tobacco and salt, the two largest commercial banks, and seven of the eight largest joint stock companies. Of all joint stock companies "in 1969, federal authorities accounted for 45 percent of total shares, regional authorities for 12 percent, and nationalized banks for 10 percent. Multinational corporations and Austrian private enterprise accounted for 13 percent each."[97] Concentrated in basic materials and semifinished products, Austria's state-owned enterprises constitute about one-fifth of total gross industrial output and one-third of total exports.[98] The state-owned enterprises employ 28 percent of Austria's industrial workforce, the same proportion as for foreign firms; Austrian private firms account for the balance of 44 percent.[99] About one-sixth of the Austrian workforce is employed in enterprises directly or indirectly owned by the federal government. When one adds employees in the public sector narrowly defined—such as civil servants, police, and teachers—the public sector accounts for close to one-third of Austria's national output.[100]

Furthermore, the importance of public ownership in the economy is greatest among Austria's largest firms. Firms such as the Voest-Alpine steel combine play a critically important part in an economy otherwise characterized by relatively small private firms. It does not really matter whether one measures firm size by turnover, exports, or number of employees:[101] among Austria's fifty largest corporations, nationalized firms account for more than two-thirds, private firms for little more than 10 percent, and foreign firms for about 15 percent of the total.[102] Austria's fifty largest firms account for more than half of Austria's total industrial production,[103] yet Austria's state-owned giant firms are small by international standards. Only two Austrian firms, the Voest-Alpine and the national petroleum company, can be found among the world's largest four-hundred.[104]

By all yardsticks, then, the economic basis of liberal capitalism is extremely weak in Austria. Often protectionist inclinations in Austrian industry, especially among Austria's medium-sized and small firms, and the large size of Austria's public economy give ample support and ample room for maneuver among the business segments for Austrian strategy. Besides vast holdings in industry, the government owns the two largest commercial banks, the two largest insurance companies, and a host of other financial institutions. Because of the banks' substantial direct ownership or indirect control of a large number of subsidiaries, the Austrian government could indirectly control an even larger part of Austrian industry. Calculating the extent of the banks' ownership and control of industry is as much a pastime in Austria as are guesses about the hidden assets of the three largest banks in Switzerland. By most accounts Austria's nationalized banks own about 10 percent of the nominal capital of all joint stock companies, and their subsidiaries have about 60,000 employees.[105] In addition the nationalized banks have at their disposal a variety of instruments falling short of ownership, which, while defying all attempts at precise calculation, enhance their dominant position in Austria's economic life.[106]

Extensive nationalization heavily influences the character of Austria's business community; for example, it has always been cautious about international markets. This is illustrated by the hesitation with which it has followed the developments abroad toward the internationalization of production structures. As late as the mid-1960s, Austria's traditional capital shortage prompted severe criticism of policy measures designed to facilitate the export of goods and capital as ill-advised attempts to drain the country of resources badly needed in the modernization of the economy.[107] But increases in Austria's currency reserves in the late 1960s and early 1970s made capital export preferable, in the government's eyes, to either imported inflation or the revaluation of the schilling.[108] In the 1970s the declining international competitiveness of some parts of Austrian industry reinforced this tendency. Austria's nationalized industries, especially petrochemicals, oil, and metals, gradually moved to develop sales and, at times, production facilities in foreign countries. South Africa and Greece under the colonels were among the countries where the establishment of production sites were either seriously considered or took place; the political preferences of social democracy apparently play no part in such decisons.[109] In the 1970s the Austrian Corporation for Industrial Administration (Österreichische Industrieverwaltung, AG, ÖIAG), a holding company for the government's nationalized firms with 116,000 workers and sales of $3.9 billion in 1976, founded slightly more subsidiaries abroad than at home. Its top management explicitly hopes to follow the Swiss model, reserving core areas of production, management, financing, and research and development to the home country while developing an international organization of sales outlets and production sites.[110]

Since Austria's nationalized firms are the flagship of Austria's political Left and the prime target for achieving its social objectives, this recent change in orientation reflects the forceful effect that international markets have had on deep-seated political habits. None of this, however, justifies premature conclusions concerning the convergence of two forms of "Alpine capitalism." The value of Austrian investments abroad in 1980 was only one-quarter of the value of foreign investment in Austria.[111] And, despite growing internationalization, a recent survey of Austrian banking reveals both the predominantly domestic orientation of Austria's financial institutions and the inapplicability of the Swiss model in the Austrian context.[112] Furthermore, in its recent moves Austrian business has been emphasizing foreign sales organizations while Switzerland has for a long time emphasized foreign production. Finally, Austria's investments abroad are miniscule. In 1945 Austria had lost virtually all of its foreign assets. By 1971 Austria's domestic industrial production exceeded production abroad by a factor of more than 100; for Switzerland, the factor was 1.5.[113]

Private business plays a subordinate role compared to both Austria's vast nationalized sector and its trade union. Hence there has been no serious conflict to date over Austria's pursuit of national adaptation and political compensation, as Austria's foreign trade and investment policies illustrate. But the growing importance of direct foreign investment by foreign firms may impart an international dimension to that national strategy of adaptation, as well as to Austria's business community, in the 1980s and 1990s.

Compared to a tradition of protectionism dating back to the beginning of the nineteenth century, Austria's gradual liberalizing of its import trade during the past two decades constitutes an important break with the past. Besides reducing its tariff barriers Austria has, like most of the industrial states, taken limited steps to grant preferential market access to the developing countries. Furthermore, during the last decades the speed of multilateral tariff reductions has increased greatly within the framework of various international institutions such as the General Agreement on Tariffs and Trade (GATT), the European Free Trade Association (EFTA), and the EC.[114] Austria has reduced protection to levels common among the major industrial states.

Compared to Switzerland's liberalization, however, Austria's is distinguished by hesitation and delay. At the beginning of the 1980s Austria's tariffs not only remained much higher than those of Switzerland but also exceeded those of the Benelux countries and of Scandinavia.[115] Early efforts at import liberalization in 1953 were carefully designed to leave domestic producers unaffected; indeed, the calculation of Austrian tariffs based on the value rather than the weight of imported goods resulted in an increase in the average level of protection in 1955.[116] In the late 1950s only one-half of Austria's trade with the OECD countries in domestically produced manufactured goods was liberalized;[117] and Austria had liberalized less than half of its trade with the United States and Canada—the lowest figures among all small European states.[118] By 1965 Austria was the only small European state still reserving the right to claim exceptions to the full application of GATT rules, under Article 35 of the GATT, in relations with new members acceding to the organization.[119] In 1963–64 it took direct U.S. pressure in the form of bilateral conciliation procedures under Article 22 to change Austrian protectionism in several agricultural and industrial products.[120]

Even though liberalization accelerated in the 1960s and 1970s with the impetus of first joining EFTA and later signing a free trade agreement with the EC, Austria has retained relatively high tariffs against third countries. The average Austrian tariff on industrial products exceeded the Swiss average in 1976 by a factor of four and was the highest among the small European states. Yet despite this high level of protection, the average percentage cut in tariffs to which Austrian negotiators agreed in the Tokyo Round of tariff reductions in the 1970s was the second lowest among all of the small European states. Furthermore, the difference between the linear cut to which all governments agreed in principle and the actual cuts Austria offered was far greater than that for any other small European state, pointing to the strength of protectionist political forces inside the country.[121] Later than the rest of Western Europe and much later than Switzerland, Austria liberalized trade with Japan in 1976.[122] Finally, Austria was less immune than Switzerland to rising protectionism in the late 1970s. For example, Chancellor Kreisky followed the demands of small businessmen in 1977 in publicly supporting nontariff barriers in industrial sectors, such as garments, threatened by low-cost imports from Asia. Since 1978 the Austrian government has sharply increased a special excise tax on imported, luxury consumer goods, especially automobiles; and it has followed the EC in adopting restrictions on free trade, especially in steel.

To the extent that it is enmeshed in economic relations beyond the OECD, the Austrian government has primarily concentrated its energies on developing economic relations with the socialist economies of

Eastern Europe while Swiss firms have followed market incentives toward deeper involvement in the Third World. Switzerland's international orientation is global; Austria's is regional. The geographic and economic position of Austria's large nationalized industries, the political commitment toward strengthening detente in Europe, and the desire to find new export markets led the government in the 1970s to maintain the strong, historical ties that bind Austria to its former empire in the East. In the 1960s and 1970s, the 15 percent of Austrian exports shipped to East Europe was about four times larger than Switzerland's and about three times as much as the West European average.[123] Joint ventures with Eastern European countries numbered more than 140 by the end of 1976. Austria also leads in joint ventures, twenty-seven in all, that socialist governments had by 1977 located in small European states; in contrast, they had located only eight joint ventures in Switzerland.[124] When the Eastern European states expressed growing interest in trade, industrial cooperation, and joint ventures with the West in the late 1960s, Switzerland's business community, remembering the expropriations of the late 1940s, reacted with massive indifference.[125]

Austria used its strong political ties with the East to organize its own export drive in Eastern Europe in the 1970s.[126] In consultation with Austria's business community the federal government has assisted Austrian companies and trade associations to conclude numerous contracts with Eastern European state trading organizations.[127] Most importantly, the government greatly extended credit facilities for trading partners in the East. Between 1974 and 1980 net claims by Austrian banks on Eastern-bloc countries increased from $433 million to $4.02 billion. In addition, commercial credits by Austrian exporters stood at $1.27 billion in 1980.[128] While Austria's nationalized export credit and insurance bank guarantees about 40 percent of Austria's total exports, it covers virtually all Eastern exports. Of the bank's cumulative guarantees of $12.29 billion, about $4.95 billion (41 percent) cover Austria's Eastern trade. The bank's system of export finance also supports Austria's commercial offensive in the East, for the success of export promotion in Eastern European markets hinges on financial guarantees. In 1979 the bank had loans outstanding to East Europe totaling more than $1.9 billion, 42 percent of its total credits; and it had provided credit assurances for $3.2 billion, 44 percent of all assurances.[129] Since Poland accounts for about one-half of the total, Austria ranks among that country's major creditors. In an effort to support exports, Austria granted total credits amounting to more than $861 million to Poland during the worldwide recession of

1975–76. The government-owned export bank broke with the normal international practice of reserving long-term credit for trade in investment goods and extended such credits for the purchase of Austrian consumer goods.[130] Apart from strengthening Austrian exports, this tactic was based on the hope that in the latter half of the 1980s imported coal from Poland would make up for some of Austria's growing energy consumption.

Optimistic expectations about the growth of Austria's trade with Eastern Europe have been disappointed. In comparison to the growth of total trade, Austria's Eastern trade did not increase substantially during the 1970s. Moreover, economic prospects in Eastern Europe look increasingly troublesome in the 1980s; it has been argued that Austria's deep involvement in Eastern Europe is an Achilles heel of its trade policy.[131] Austrians, however, tend to discount these economic risks. The government in its Eastern trade is exploiting a growing trend in international commerce toward large, state-to-state contracts that permit sales below market prices through government-negotiated subsidies in interest rates. Nationalized firms, which account for one-quarter of Austria's total export trade, give the Austrian government a capacity to engage in trade negotiations with its Eastern European partners that it has been eager to exploit.

Austria has refused to relinquish political control over imports once and for all. For example, although Austria became the first OECD country to extend GATT regulations to its trade with Eastern Europe, in 1975, the government insisted for its own protection on what amounts to an escape clause should bilateral negotiations fail in resolving disputes over particularly sensitive import items. Despite the elimination of virtually all quotas in the 1960s, the legal foundations for government intervention in foreign trade continue to exist in the 1974 Amendment to the Trade Act of 1968.[132] The Austrian government has at its disposal legislation that protects domestic producers against foreign dumping and assures orderly conditions in Austrian markets. The importance of these legal provisions lies not in their existence, which is hardly unique to Austria; rather, they signal to the world a commitment to retain political control over the potential impact of international markets.

That insistence on exercising control is reinforced by the preponderant position that Austria's government occupies in financial markets. The government relies on a variety of policies that spur business investment at home, to a degree utterly alien to Switzerland. Although an overwhelming share of a firm's investment could be written off in the first year in the late 1970s, the dependence of private firms on external sources of investment capital has continued to increase.[133] This provides the government with an opening that it has pursued with a variety of policies. "Austria currently boasts one of the most extensive . . . investment promotion systems in the industrialized world."[134] Between 1970 and 1980 direct subsidies and other forms of financial aid increased from $96 million to $548 million; and the tax savings of business due to indirect measures more than sextupled from $200 million to $1.31 billion.[135] Direct subsidies for agriculture remained constant between 1967 and 1974, but they quadrupled for industry to nearly $100 million by 1974.[136] With a combined total of publicly guaranteed investments of $1.16 billion in 1967 and almost ten times as much, $11.4 billion, in 1976, public liability companies have also sharply increased their levels of operation.[137]

Since the mid-1970s the government has tried to supplement its financial resources with the capital and technological know-how of foreign firms. Austria's courtship of foreign multinationals is a new element, which, in the interest of modernizing the country's industrial structure may, over time, give its business community and its strategy of adaptation a more international orientation. Austria's suspicions about the political risks of foreign ownership ran strong in the 1950s and 1960s. A stable political climate, comparatively low wages, and a strategic location close to Eastern European markets brought Austria a steady stream of direct foreign investment, especially from West Germany and also from Switzerland, estimated at $4.39 billion at the end of 1980.[138] Between 1955 and the late 1960s the wage differential with southern Germany as well as Austria's membership in EFTA encouraged West German firms to open subsidiaries across the Austrian border. The Austrian government supported this development only feebly. But a sharp break in policy occurred in the late 1960s, when for the first time the ÖVP government permitted foreign firms such as Siemens to cooperate with state-owned firms, and when the SPÖ lost its confidence that a state-planned economy could work effectively without the injection of foreign capital. Although the Austrian government had provided potential foreign investors with information about labor-market conditions since 1956, it was only in 1969 that the Ministry of Commerce, Industry and Trade started offering comprehensive information services tailored to the specific needs of foreign firms that consider locating a subsidiary in Austria. In a statement before Parliament in April 1970, the newly elected SPÖ government affirmed the importance it attached to foreign capital for the success of its regional and sectoral policies.[139] The 1970s saw government policy change to the point where it eventually embraced the maxim, "If you can't home-brew technological advance, bribe it in."[140] The deliberate and active bidding for investments by the largest multinational corporations was explained by an aide to Chancellor Kreisky: "Our economy is largely dominated by medium-size and small companies, and we frankly need the know-how and the new technologies which only the very big companies with their extensive research and development activities can give us."[141]

Apart from its social peace and political stability Austria offers, often in direct competition with Switzerland, large financial incentives to foreign companies.[142] These incentives are structured so as to make them particularly attractive to large foreign firms once a new plant has come on stream; they include, in particular, high depreciation allowances and generously low corporate tax rates, and credits at subsidized rates. Like other countries Austria also subsidizes start-up costs, which weigh more heavily with smaller firms. Between 1969 and 1977 the proportion of industrial employees working in foreign-owned firms increased from 18 to 28 percent.[143] Political unease about the growth of direct foreign investment, which still lingers, has been offset both by the perceived economic advantages and by the political protection that the Second Republic derives, unlike the First, from the government's vast holdings—especially among the largest corporations in Austria's basic industries. Among the top twenty industrial firms in Austria, only four were foreign-owned in 1979.[144]

The electrical engineering and automobile industries provide two instructive examples of Austria's policy on questions of direct foreign investment. At the end of World War II, all the major firms in the electrical engineering industry were nationalized; today, this particular industry is more penetrated by foreign firms than any other.[145] The two major foreign firms, Siemens and Philips, jointly employ about 70 percent of the industry's workforce.[146] The history of this development is complex but deserves to be told because it precisely charts Austria's changing relation to the world economy during the last three decades.[147] In this fully nationalized industry the Soviet Union's return of production facilities in the mid-1950s created both overcapacity and severe competition. At the prompting of the conservative ÖVP, two of the four firms then dominating the industry merged in 1959, and the new company accounted for one-half of industry sales. But excessive competition among the remaining firms, both in domestic and in foreign markets, continued to reduce prices and profits. After years of arduous negotiations and in cooperation with a new holding company for Austria's nationalized industries, the Elin Union merged in 1967 with one of the two Siemens subsidiaries.

57

By 1972 the process of industrial concentration with multinational participation was completed. As a result the publicly owned holding company, the ÖIAG, acquired a 44 percent minority participation in Siemens's consolidated Austrian subsidiaries. The relation between Austria's national champion and the multinationals now dominating the industry is thus highly symbiotic, reflecting a conscious policy to work with rather than against leading foreign firms.

The recent history of the automobile industry similarly illustrates the government's favorable attitude to foreign firms. Due to American influence, postwar Austria refrained from building an indigenous passenger car industry, instead signing a licensing agreement with Italy's largest manufacturer, Fiat.[148] Less than 6 percent of the 1.1 million cars registered in Austria in 1969 were domestically produced. This economic dependence proved costly: West German, French, and Italian cars sold in Austrian markets at mark-ups reported to vary between 2 and 27 percent.[149] In the late 1970s nearly one-third of Austria's total balance-of-trade deficit was due to the import of automobiles.[150] The Austrian government thus induced a number of foreign car manufacturers, among them Daimler, BMW, and Renault, to contract with Austria's Steyr-Daimler-Puch for a larger share of components to be produced in Austria.[151] Furthermore, Chancellor Kreisky himself and his government pulled out all the stops in an attempt to attract a foreign firm to build a large-scale assembly plant in Austria.[152] After numerous disappointments involving Porsche, Volkswagen, Chrysler, Fiat, Mitsubishi, and Ford, the Austrian government finally reached an agreement with General Motors. General Motors committed itself to invest $720 million in an engine and transmission plant, leaving open the possibility of moving to full assembly sometime in the 1980s. The Austrian government agreed not only to pay one-third of all start-up costs but also to provide many additional financial benefits. Each one of the 2,800 new jobs will cost the government about $95,000, about nine times as much, some critics charge, as the average newly created job in Austria. But the government was willing to pay a very high price to reduce Austria's balance-of-payments deficit through the production of engines and transmissions solely for export, and to create a large number of new jobs.

Like the sustained export drive in Eastern markets, foreign capital alleviates the government's concern over the deficits in current accounts. Without Austria's large, profitable tourist industry, the country's trade balance would have been a very serious obstacle to the domestic growth that the government pursued throughout the 1970s.

In the early 1970s Austria's tourist economy was about twice the size of Switzerland's, and the receipts from this industry accounted for 30 percent of the value of Austria's exports of goods and services. In the OECD only Spain exceeded this proportion.[153] Foreign-exchange earnings due to tourism are ten times higher in Austria than the average in all OECD countries. Yet during the 1970s Austria's total trade deficit grew much faster than the surplus in its tourist trade. Receipts from tourism covered about 90 percent of the trade deficit in the early 1970s but only 50 percent in the late 1970s.[154] For this reason the government also decided to tax Austria's rapidly growing transit trade to supplement the slower growth of its tourist trade.[155] Since Switzerland occupies a more profitable niche in the international division of labor, its government does not have to tax foreign trucks. Swiss banks, insurance companies, and multinational corporations more than compensate for a relatively small tourist industry. In 1976 Switzerland's rapidly growing net balance of foreign services was almost four times as large as Austria's.[156]

POLITICAL INSTITUTIONS

The strong position of Austria's reformist and growth-conscious trade union and the subordinate role of a private business community with a national orientation shape a broad spectrum of policies, encompassing employment, public spending, social welfare, prices and wages, industrial adjustment, and foreign trade. Though union and business are necessary, however, they are not sufficient; policy networks as well as social forces shape these policies and politics. One of the defining elements of democratic corporatism, after all, is that relatively centralized and broadly based interest groups form part of an institutional structure that shields the process of political bargaining from external disturbances. Austria supports the point.

The political weakness from which the Austrian government suffered between 1945 and 1955, in the face of Allied occupation, reinforced the historical prominence of Austria's interest groups.[157] Indeed, those interest groups have been characterized as constituting both a "non-ideological corporative state" and a "democratically disguised chamber state."[158] Distinctive of this state is its centralized, publicly licensed economic chambers, in which membership is compulsory. (On the average, each working Austrian belongs directly to three economic interest groups and, through his or her place of work, indirectly to two additional groups.)[159] Although Austria's economic

59

chambers have public functions and up to a point act with public authority, they are not, strictly speaking, governmental institutions and lack powers of enforcement. On the other hand, the chambers only partially resemble voluntary associations. Public law defines their membership and organizational mission, and, even though the government cannot influence the internal process of decision making in the chambers, it enjoys the right of legal supervision.[160] The Federal Economic Chamber (Bundeskammer der Gewerblichen Wirtschaft) represents the crafts, commerce, and industry, and business interests more generally; the Federal Chamber of Labor (Kammer für Arbeiter und Angestellte) speaks for wage and salary earners, as well as for consumer interests. There are also chambers of agriculture (Landwirtschaftskammern) at the provincial level. Austria's most important private interest groups, the Federation of Austrian Industrialists (Vereinigung Österreichischer Industrieller) and the Austrian Trade Union Federation (the ÖGB), cooperate closely with "their" respective chamber.[161]

There exists, of course, ample room for conflict between "natural" partners and for "perverse" temporary alliances. For example, the Federal Chamber of Labor, as representative of consumer interests, has had an interest in trade liberalization that dovetails neatly with the demands of the Federation of Austrian Industrialists for a more internationally oriented, outward-looking export policy. Since the Federal Economic Chamber represents the myriad small firms most likely to be adversely affected by import competition, it has been a less enthusiastic proponent of liberalization. Law, tradition, and expertise assure these groups a central role in the development of major legislation and in the implementation of policy. The continuity in their leadership and their osmotic relations with political parties make them powerful spokesmen in Austrian society. Andrew Shonfield scarcely exaggerated when he wrote that "the corporate form of organization seems to be almost second nature to the Austrians."[162]

At the behest of the trade unions, the Federal Chamber of Labor was established by public law in 1920.[163] Since membership in the chamber is compulsory for all employees, it strengthens the position of the Austrian Trade Union Federation among those parts of the labor force otherwise difficult to organize.[164] The chamber maintains close contact with the union and provides information, advice, and policy analysis on general economic and social problems that have a bearing on the union's stance in collective bargaining. Furthermore, the candidates standing for office in the chamber's internal elections are drawn from the main political organizations, primarily the socialist faction, active inside the ÖGB. This assures the SPÖ of a dominant position in the Chamber of Labor.[165] Since 1945 the chamber has guaranteed Austria's labor movement formal and influential representation in all stages of the policy process. Its voice typically carries weight on all issues involving social welfare. For example, 73 of its 138 amendments to or changes of the original draft of Austria's social security legislation of 1956 were taken into account in the final version of the bill; and 238 of the 254 improvements of the act that it, together with the ÖGB, requested between 1955 and 1961 were adopted as government policy.[166]

Unlike in other small European states, the Trade Union Federation encompasses blue-collar workers, and private- and public-sector employees. The ÖGB strictly controls the fifteen constituent unions from the top in collective bargaining, strategy, use of finances, and policy debate. For example, in 1978 the central union organization controlled more than four-fifths of the membership dues of about $83 million; the constituent unions received less than one-fifth.[167] While estimates vary as to the size of the centrally administered strike fund, it may run as high as $100 million.[168] The task of reaching agreements within Austria's inclusive trade union organization is of critical importance to the formulation and implementation of Austrian strategy. As I argued above, the political diversity within the ÖGB works to reinforce the dominant position of the socialist union leaders over the interests of other factions and constituent unions, and contains the particularistic interests of different segments of the labor movement. And in Austria's dual system of labor representation through both unions and factory councils, conflicting interests are harmonized within the labor movement. Union leaders are in charge of resolving the numerous grievances of the rank and file. A recent, careful, comparative analysis of the organizational structure of national union federations echoes and confirms the findings of other studies in concluding that, among all of the advanced industrial countries, Austria has the most centralized trade unions.[169]

Austria's business community is organized in a broadly based organization that is a body of public rather than private law, with compulsory rather than voluntary membership. The 1946 legislation that established this system of business representation was directly linked to the nationalization of a large fraction of Austrian industry and finance. Virtually all Austrians work in plants associated with the Federal Economic Chamber.[170]

It was only in 1946–47 that Austria's two distinct historical traditions of business representation in politics were welded together. Dating back to 1848, Austria's economic chambers had traditionally enjoyed considerable influence in national policy making but lacked the organizational presence at the grass roots necessary to wield power effectively. On the other hand, Austria's professional organizations, which had their origins in ancient guilds, were always strongly represented at the local level but lacked political access to decision makers in Vienna. By combining the territorially organized, centralized economic chambers with the functionally organized, decentralized professional associations, Austria gave its postwar business community great political cohesion.[171] The Federal Economic Chamber has six sections incorporating about 130 professional organizations under the headings of commerce, industry, trade, banking and insurance, transportation, and tourism. It covers virtually all Austrian enterprises, both private and public, and it speaks for about 250,000 members who overwhelmingly support the ÖVP.[172]

The sheer size and heterogeneity of the chamber's clientele make the forging of a consensus that permits Austria's business community to speak with a single voice an important political task.[173] Furthermore, the political task of establishing a durable consensus within the chamber is, as Max Mitic and Alfred Klose argue, of decisive political significance for the state.[174] Establishing such a consensus is frequently very difficult because, they continue, "conflicts of interests between different segments of business are often much greater than between employers and workers."[175] Against strong opposition, the formation of consensus in the Federal Economic Chamber among many competing sectors of business is helped by involving the grass-roots level, by relying in most instances on the principle of unanimity rather than majority, by offering wide-ranging and substantial services, especially to the small and medium-sized firms that constitute the bulk of the chamber's membership, by the inability of financially strong firms to withdraw from the organization, and, finally, by the presence of centralized chambers and peak associations of workers and farmers that require the business community to unite in the political struggles over policy.[176] Once the chamber chooses its position, however tenuous, it becomes authoritative for all members; this tends to avoid particularistic demands by narrow segments of business.

The Federation of Austrian Industrialists, by way of contrast, has a much smaller, voluntary, and homogeneous membership of about 4,000; it balances the underrepresentation of industrial interests in the Federal Economic Chamber.[177] Since it faces fewer internal restraints, the federation is more flexible, maneuverable, and outspoken on controversial issues than the chamber is in normal practice.

Even so, the federation maintains intimate contacts with the chamber and, in particular, with its industry section. Because the federation represents big private firms and can raise large sums of money for political campaigns, its views are heeded by politicians and chamber members. Conflicts of interest between the two organizations, while rare, do seem to occur on some critical economic issues. For example, the federation approved of the government's effort in the late 1960s to create national champions by encouraging the concentration of firms within industrial sectors as well as its courting of multinational corporations in the late 1970s; the chamber viewed both policies critically or indifferently. More importantly, the last two decades' gradual movement toward economic liberalization severely tested consensus in Austria's business community. A system of business organization that traditionally inhibited competition at home favored protectionism or autarchy in its relations with the international economy.[178]

More generally speaking, conflicts between the two organizations are likely to exist on issues that pit big corporations against small firms and that separate internationally oriented growth sectors of industry from domestically oriented mature or stagnant sectors. The official division of Austria into "red" (socialist) and "black" (conservative) thus conceals "the many combinations of interests that are not only possible but actually do exist presently in Austrian politics."[179] These conflicts among different segments of business can mute its power or make it acquiesce in or compromise with the political strategies proposed by the union or the government. Although impressive in comparison with business associations in larger countries such as West Germany, Austria's business associations, compared to the unrivaled centralization of Austrian unions, have a less uniform purpose and experience intermittent public controversies.

At first glance the organizational structure of the government and the prominence of the state bureaucracy appear to duplicate the centralization of political power in Austria's system of interest groups. The Second Republic can draw on a strong administrative tradition dating back to the mercantilist unification of the German core of the Habsburg Empire under Maria Theresa and her son, Joseph II, in the eighteenth century.[180] Furthermore, Austria's federal system is weak, and Vienna remains the undisputed center of the country's political life. Indeed, over the last three decades Austria's state bureaucracy has steadily expanded. Measured by the number of officials per capita, Austria's welfare bureaucracy is larger than that of any other Western European country, and civil service pensions as a share of earnings are the largest in Europe.[181] Austria's bureaucracy is intimately involved in the political relations between unions and business as well as in the formulation and implementation of national strategy. In the eyes of the public, at least, the state bureaucracy is a very powerful institution.[182]

But the realities of Austrian political life are more complex. Cohesiveness and *esprit de corps,* and with them bureaucratic power, are undercut by political parties. The "waning of the opposition" in Austria's consensual domestic structures has been accompanied by a "waning of the governmment."[183] Instead of a powerful state bureaucracy dominating politics and orchestrating policy, Austria has a broadly based policy network in which the state bureaucracy is only one—and by no means the most important—actor. Inside that network the authority of the state bureaucracy, though important, is not overwhelming; outside, political initiatives by particular agencies or ministries would lack often the legal basis and always the legitimacy necessary to translate political blueprints into practice. In the words of a high-ranking official, Professor Hans Seidel, "It is very important that the government not impose or not introduce measures which have not been approved by these groups."[184]

In its relations with Austria's major economic interest groups, the bureaucracy acts from a position of relative weakness.[185] Staffed according to the proportionate strength of Austria's two main parties in Parliament, government ministries are surrounded by a comprehensive system of advisory councils that help to formulate and implement much of Austria's social and economic legislation. In the area of foreign economic policy, for example, such advisory councils were of critical importance in the liberalization of Austria's commercial policy and retain their importance on questions of antidumping, domestic market disturbance, and export credit.[186] Despite Austria's sizable public sector, the OECD finds "the desire to limit state intervention in the economy to what is strictly necessary. . . . There exists an inclination to let the business world assume all the tasks which it is considered better able to handle than is the state."[187] As a result, as in Switzerland but in contrast to West Germany, informal consultations and arrangements rather than formal legislation provide the instruments for many of Austria's policies.[188] Throughout the postwar period the Austrian state bureaucracy has acted the part of "honest broker." The senior civil service perceives itself as an "impartial political force," an attitude that can be traced back to the very origins of Austrian bureaucracy. Today, permanent political neutrality abroad finds its mirror in the exercise of "neutral" statecraft at home. Virtually all political strategies affecting Austria's position in the international economy must be discussed with, ratified, and sometimes implemented by the powerful interest groups. United in their dislike both of vigorous state intervention and of market competition, these groups typically prefer Austria's secretive, centralized, and often informal bargaining.

The weakness of the state bureaucracy is evident even in those areas where it plays a very prominent role, as, for example, in Austria's nationalized industry. Government intervention is remarkably restrained. Austria's nationalized firms make their contribution to the stabilization of employment and investment, but they vigorously resist direct forms of political intervention and conduct a large part of their business along the lines of commercial profitability. The formal instruments of control at the government's disposal are quite limited. Since the nationalization acts of 26 July 1946 and 26 March 1947 transferred the shares of the affected firms to the Second Republic, "The only way the state is able to exert an influence on the enterprises is by exercising its rights as a shareholder."[189]

As early as 1949 the Austrian government gave up all serious attempts at economic planning.[190] From that year dates the beginning of the organizational fragmentation of the public sector. Nationalized industries and nationalized banks were put under the jurisdiction of different ministries, and the First Nationalization Act's mandate for coordinated economic policy was repealed.[191] Subsequent developments have reinforced the neutralization of state power. For example, Austria's petroleum industry lacked vertical integration for periods in the 1950s and 1960s because of its organizational ties to different government agencies.[192] Since Austria's nationalized firms have the same legal standing as private firms, they have neither special management associations nor different collective bargaining mechanisms.[193] The management of nationalized firms, not the government, decides the amount of profits to be reinvested and the amount to be paid out to the government in the form of dividends.[194] As a final example, countercyclical stabilization policies that rely on the employment and investment decisions of nationalized firms cannot simply be imposed, as the programs of 1962 and the 1970s illustrate. Instead, these policies need the full prestige of the cabinet and the support of the political parties in the delicate negotiations that the government conducts with public-sector firms.[195]

The organizational fragmentation of the public enterprises and the relative lack of government control were clearly recognized by both the ÖVP and the SPÖ, and were mirrored in the reorganization drives that the two parties initiated when they seized full control of the government in 1966 and 1970, respectively.[196] The ÖVP simplified organization by establishing a central, nationalized holding company in the late 1960s that left the Austrian Industrial Corporation (ÖIG) with very little control over individual firms and enterprises.[197] In the early 1970s the SPÖ converted the ÖIG from a trust company to a joint stock company, the ÖIAG, and slightly increased the power of its central headquarters; but the SPÖ also refused to enlarge the government's limited formal control.[198] What Dennison Rusinow noted in 1966 is still true today: Austria's nationalized industries display "the characteristics of nationalization and of state capitalism, but few of the characteristics of socialization. . . . For better or for worse, the role of the state as owner is largely passive."[199]

POLICY PROCESS

Social corporatism is typified by a policy process that coordinates the conflicting objectives of political actors through uninterrupted bargaining in the policy network. These bargains primarily center around questions of employment and investment, and the government is involved in many of them, at least indirectly. The reconciliation of competing group interests often involves explicit trade-offs across different issues.

In Austria, the formulation and implementation of policy on questions affecting the management of the economy reveal a remarkable concentration of power. In full assurance of the support of the major interest groups and political parties, which they control, a handful of political leaders shape all strategic decisions.[200] "It is a democracy with a strong flavor of oligarchy, where almost all the decisions are taken by hard-headed men talking together in smoke-filled rooms behind closed doors."[201] This concentration of power occurs in a political setting that does not recognize a distinction between public and private. Lines of formal authority are typically blurred. As bodies of public law, some of Austria's major interest groups exercise, in addition to their normal, autonomous operations, administrative powers delegated by the state. This subjects them to the supervision of the government, which cannot function adequately without the expertise that only the interest groups command. Equally ambiguous is the relation among party elites, Parliament, and cabinet ministers who are normally members of particular interest groups, often their spokesmen, but rarely their tools. The informality of Austria's policy process engendered by these interlocking corridors of power is revealed in what might be called government by commission and is best illustrated by the Joint Commission as the lynchpin of Austria's celebrated incomes policy.[202] "Incomes policy in Austria has to be regarded as an essential part of the broader concept of what we call 'Social Partnership,'" noted the state secretary for Finance. He defined it as "a durable cooperation between the representatives of labor, business and agriculture."[203]

The Joint Commission is a curious institution. It is both an instrument for the regulation of wages and prices, and a center for steering Austrian society. Some see in it an executive organ of the government's economic policy; others view it as an extraordinary preserve of powerful groups against the state. According to the commission's own definition of its mission, which matches the OECD's assessment, it lacks some of the characteristics essential for conducting an incomes policy. On the other hand, its practice of institutionalizing wage and price controls predated the recommendations of the OECD by several years and exceeded other countries' experiments in this policy sector both in its intentions and in its results. The divergence between the sharp increase in the average number of annual requests for price increases (up from 176 in 1957–64 to 425 in 1973–78) and the decrease in the estimated proportion of prices covered in the economy (down from 60 percent of producer prices in 1960 to 50 percent in 1980) illustrates a characteristic of the commission: it is both more and less than an institution for the conduct of an incomes policy.[204]

In the late 1940s the challenge of inflation had been countered by a series of five wage-price agreements, concluded by the major producer groups without government participation. When inflation threatened again in the late 1950s, the ÖGB and the Federal Chamber of Labor succeeded in convincing both business and government that the time had come for a formal institution. The result was the Joint Commission.[205] Composed of representatives of business, labor, and government, the commission was provisional (permanently, as it turned out) and lacked legal standing. Its decisions are not backed by formal sanctions, and it acts only on the basis of unanimous decisions.[206] Its growing power is reflected in the fact that it broadened its activity from a consideration of prices (1957) to wages (1962), and to economic issues more generally (1963). This increasing policy competence was accompanied by a centralization of power within the commission and the delegation of specific questions to its subcommittees on prices and wages, as well as to the Advisory Council for Social and Economic Affairs (Beirat für Wirtschafts- und Sozialfragen).

The meetings of the Joint Commission serve as a forum for informal and far-ranging consultations over issues of strategic importance for Austria rather than hard bargaining over specific issues, which typically takes place in the subcommittees. Since the late 1960s the presidents of the labor, agriculture, and economic chambers and the ÖGB have met prior to the convening of the Joint Commission to settle all outstanding issues in secret *(Präsidentenvorbesprechung)*. Furthermore, every three months the leaders of the major interest groups meet under the auspices of the Joint Commission to discuss Austria's economic situation in light of the most recent data presented by the director of Austria's Economic Research Institute *(Wirtschaftliche Aussprache)*.[207] With government officials, including the chancellor, present but not voting in the hundreds of meetings that the commission has held since its inception, it illustrates the traditionally subordinate role that the government and state bureaucracy have played in Austria's system of "multilateral corporatism."[208] Rather than initiating political strategies, the Austrian government is expected to ratify decisions reached in negotiations between Austrian interest groups;[209] it insists on consultation but not codetermination in the shaping of critically important economic and social choices.

The commission's Subcommittee on Prices meets at least once a week.[210] Individual firms and entire industrial branches must submit their requests for price increases through the Federal Economic Chamber with data sufficient to show, in general terms, that the proposed price increase can be justified in terms of increased costs. At times the quality of the data has become a source of contention between members of the subcommittee; union spokesmen have thus far been unsuccessful in persuading business representatives of the need to base the subcommittee's rulings on detailed data that reflect the profitability of firms. Typically, requests for increases are granted by the subcommittee, although often by a smaller margin and sometimes with some delay.[211] Requests directly affecting the whole economy are referred to the Joint Commission, which regulates about one-third of Austria's prices. An additional 20 percent of the prices of all goods and services in the consumer price index are fixed administratively, in areas such as food, energy, and public services. The remaining half, many of them prices of imported goods, are determined in the market without direct political intervention.[212] The political attempt to regulate prices in an open economy has often proved impracticable, and has curtailed further growth in the commission's power. It was for such reasons that, when Austria's Left pleaded in 1965 for much stricter supervision (including controls on imported goods), the business community refused to go along.[213]

In contrast to the Subcommittee on Prices, government officials do not sit on the Subcommittee on Wages.[214] Austria's system of collective bargaining is thus entirely free from administrative interference. Furthermore, the sanctity of free collective bargaining is reflected in the fact that the Subcommittee on Wages has no right to approve or to determine particular wage agreements. Instead, it approves the initiation of new rounds of collective bargaining and can influence the duration of contracts in the interest of a balanced wage policy. Constituent unions of the ÖGB must submit their requests to the ÖGB leadership, which relies on its influence over the Subcommittee on Wages, particularly the queuing of requests for wage increases, as a way to shape the union's general wage policy. Its countercyclical wage policy kept the increases in unit labor costs comparatively modest between 1955 and 1970. At the same time, the system allowed room for sizable supplementary agreements at the plant level and thus for sizable wage drift—which, however, did not impair the international competitiveness of Austria's economy.[215] That competitiveness was temporarily threatened only by the brief wage explosion of 1974–75.

Finally, the third leg of the Joint Commission is the Advisory Council for Social and Economic Affairs.[216] Intended by the Austrian Left as an adaptation of France's system of indicative planning, widely admired in Europe in the early 1960s, the council has remained a fundamentally political institution. Its mission has been to prepare reports thoroughly grounded in research and often subcontracted out to experts not identified with major political parties. De facto, the council's numerous reports on a wide range of social and economic issues have adhered to the principle of public unanimity and to constraining internal controversy. While few doubt it has contributed to greater expertise on questions of economic policy, its work reflects the primacy of interest groups.

Austria has witnessed the emergence of a "political technocracy" in sharp contrast to the French "planning technocracy."[217] While agreeing with the older generation of political leaders on a growth strategy, the younger political technocrats pushed for the adoption of modern and "rational" policy instruments. The new breed of experts, which was associated with the council in the 1960s, lost little time in advancing their careers within the major interest groups and the two main parties. Today the technocratic impulse remains inextricably linked with Austrian politics. While the lack of technical expertise that Austria's civil service commands on questions of economic policy is still sometimes astonishing, a new generation has moved into positions of power and influence, especially at middle levels. That generation knows that important economic choices require a deliberate neutralization and standardization of several sources of economic information. When assessments of economic developments differ, this technocratic solution no longer works. Political leaders then rely on their political intuition and a mix of tactical and strategic thinking.[218] Questions of economic and social policy are judged to be simply too important to be left to specialists.

How can this political management of the economy and the institutionalization of political conflict work so smoothly without sanctions?[219] The answer to this question is relatively straightforward in the case of Austria's major interest groups. The groups' veto power acts as a protective shield, which makes possible the establishment of far-reaching compromises that need no sanction other than a skillfully deployed threat. The union's support of the Joint Commission is not surprising, since the commission merely reinforces the central position of the ÖGB vis-à-vis the industrial unions engaged in wage negotiations, without in any way interfering with Austria's cherished system of free collective bargaining. The reasons for individual firms' compliance with the restraints on price increases are more complex.[220] In the late 1950s the implicit threat of selective tariff reductions may have been important; in some instances, such as in 1962, tariffs were in fact reduced ahead of schedule to stem inflation.[221] Today compliance may be helped by the accepted practice of submitting demands for inflated price increases, which are passed by the Subcommittee on Prices once suitably reduced; by the mere existence of extensive information on most major firms in the files of the Joint Commission; and most importantly by the firms' continuous reliance on and need for the help and support of the peak associations of business. The expectations of their customers, including the vast public sector, make price increases not ratified by the Joint Commission appear highly suspect. The possibility of a firm's submitting requests for price increases covering whole sectors of industry appeals to the traditionally strong cartelistic instincts of the Austrian business community. Finally, the political context in which Austrian firms operate frequently imbues them, and especially the large firms, with a definition of their own interest that is sufficiently broad to incorporate a calculation of the effects of particular pricing strategies on workers, consumers, and the whole economy. Such calculations are not the same as altruism. They lead to firm behavior that takes its cues not only from the market but also from the system of economic and social partnership in which that market is embedded.

The commitment of Austria's political elite to the Joint Commission

as the core of Austria's entire system of collaborative policy making
was perhaps most apparent in the early years of one-party government after the ÖVP's electoral victory in 1966. Under the leadership
of Chancellor Josef Klaus, the ÖVP decided that the end of the Great
Coalition between the two major parties called for redoubled efforts
to strengthen the economic and social partnership uniting Austria's
major interest groups. For example, in the interest of preserving the
Proporz between "black and red," the government in 1966 relinquished its right to vote in the sessions of the Joint Commission.[222]
When the SPÖ assumed governmental power in 1970 it followed the
ÖVP's precedent.

Even though a decade of socialist rule has not altered the institutional underpinnings of Austria's system of economic and social partnership in any of their fundamentals, that partnership is open to
subtle evolution. Reinforced in part by the ÖVP in the late 1960s,
centralization in decision-making style is beginning to foster a notable
increase in personalism. The "Bonapartist" tendencies that could be
observed in the late 1970s contrast sharply with the "faceless" leadership of Switzerland's participatory institutions. Tolerated, encouraged, and exemplified in the 1970s by the dominant role of
Chancellor Kreisky, that personalism was also displayed at times in the
relations between Finance Minister Androsch and union leader
Benya.

For a brief period in the early 1970s Chancellor Kreisky had even
attempted to govern without the social and economic partnership. He
apparently hoped to construct the kind of alliance between farmers
and workers that had propelled Scandinavian social democracy to
political victory in the 1930s. But the policy failed and the chancellor
quickly returned to a reliance on the partnership. A few years later,
and with some justification, the business community complained that
the social and economic partnership was being robbed of its political
substance. In those years Finance Minister Androsch was preparing
the instruments of a more active state role, for possible use in times of
greater economic crisis or greater socialist hegemony. At the same
time the SPÖ leadership warned the younger generation of SPÖ ac-
tivists against putting the maximization of group interest ahead of a
cooperative relationship with business in the Joint Commission. One
Austrian official, reflecting on the erosion of the political basis supporting the social and economic partnership went so far as to suggest,
prematurely as it turned out, that "the cat has vanished and only the
grin remains."[223] Even if it wanted to, the Federal Economic Chamber,
for example, simply cannot afford to walk out of the Joint Commis-

sion and thus damage the whole system of institutions of which it is a part. For reasons of size, only the 8,000 largest of its 170,000 member firms fall under the jurisdiction of the Joint Commission.[224] The remainder share with the general public a very strong commitment to the partnership. In some ways the Joint Commission is a political prison from which the Austrian business community cannot escape— because it is both inmate and warden.

Foreign observers, in particular, have attempted to gauge the effects of Austria's collaborative policy process on the performance of the Austrian economy measured in terms of growth, unemployment, and inflation. Although the results have been less than clear-cut, the verdict has been cautiously approving.[225] Of greater importance for this book's argument are the consequences of Austria's policy process for the organization of power in the country and the future capacity to make effective policy choices. One such consequence has been to reinforce the pervasive politicization of Austrian society and economy. Because they would erode the power of key institutions such as the Joint Commission, mechanical approaches to the problem of inflation, such as monetarist indexation, have little chance of being adopted.[226] A second consequence has been to spread, quickly and efficiently, an awareness of how different types of economic adversity are affecting different parts of society.[227] In Austria, as in Switzerland, "The rule is that everybody can talk to everybody about everything."[228]

Because joint decision making is inextricably bound up with the exercise of mutual control, the political incentives to participate in Austria's never-ending process of forming consensus are very strong for all actors.[229] The government trades its partial political emasculation for a predictable formulation of policy and its easy implementation. The business community accepts political controls over the market in the interest of ensuring social stability and averting costly strikes. For the ÖGB, a "responsible" and "restrained" participation in economic policy making tends to equalize power by extending union influence beyond the area of traditional collective bargaining. Finally, this policy process is continuously strengthened by the compatibility of the actors' political objectives: the commitment of the business community to the goal of full employment as well as its tolerance of nationalization, on the one hand, and the union's pursuit of productivity-based wage bargaining untempered by efforts to achieve greater equality in the distribution of income and wealth, on the other.[230]

Following Bagehot one could argue that Austria's economic and social partnership has converted the Austrian Parliament from the "efficient" to the "dignified" part of the Austrian constitution. A further centralization of power through personalist rule in a system of one-party government may eventually have a similar effect on the institutional underpinnings of the economic and social partnership.[231] For the time being, though, it remains true that, as financial journalists have observed, "Austria's consensus is really something that is reached at the top. The general public concurs while reserving the right to grumble."[232] The weakness in Austria of the large-scale radical or neopopulist opposition movements that have sprung up throughout Western Europe shows that the institutional support of the economic and social partnership remains intact.[233] Heeding an eighteenth-century Austrian maxim—"All for the people, nothing through the people"—the Joint Commission has succeeded in transcending the two ideological opposites of the First Republic, Ignaz Seipel's capitalist corporatism and Otto Bauer's nationalized socialism.

SOCIAL CORPORATISM AND POLITICAL PARTIES

Political parties stand at the center of Austria's social corporatism. Between 1945 and 1966 the partisan manifestation of Austria's distinctive political structure was the Great Coalition between the SPÖ and the ÖVP. The legacy of political conflict and economic adversity—the economic hardship and political turmoil of the interwar years, the civil war of 1934, World War II, and German and Allied occupations—had created a durable consensus among competing party elites. All recognized the virtues of political demobilization and of strict limitations on unilateral political initiatives, imposed through carefully worked out political compromises.[234] These compromises channeled political leaders' energies into the intricate details of political bargaining through which they sought to protect, or marginally to enlarge, their own power base and the benefits accruing to their respective constituencies. Tough political bargains struck between tightly linked party and interest-group elites have succeeded in reaching political compromises on virtually all significant political issues since 1945.[235]

Since the end of the Great Coalition in 1966 Austria has moved to a system of one-party government dominated first by the ÖVP and, since 1970, by the SPÖ. In the late 1960s, the establishment of numerous powerful advisory councils to various ministries, including the important Ministry of Finance, greatly enhanced both the access and the power of the SPÖ opposition, and it left Austria with the odd combination of a one-party government heading bipartisan ministries. Staffed according to the power of the two parties in Parliament *(Proporz),* these councils typically relied on the principle of unanimity and were powerful in the formulation and implementation of policy.[236] In important policy arenas where the ÖGB would have been excluded because, unlike the chambers, it lacked legal standing, these advisory councils informally included the union. The ÖGB reciprocated these concessions of the ÖVP. The extension and reinforcement of Austria's collaborative arrangements after 1966 were honored by a sharp decline in Austria's strike rate. The five-year average of strikes and hours of work lost in industrial disputes was about twelve times smaller in the years 1967–71 than it had been in 1962–66.[237] In the 1970s this institutionalized willingness to cooperate successfully managed politically explosive questions of business-cycle policy, codetermination, and the reduction of the work week. In so doing, it proved its durability and adaptability in times of heightened political controversy and increased economic crisis.[238] The share of legislation passed with the votes of the two main parties increased from 80 percent in 1966–70 to 90 percent in 1971–75.[239] It mattered little that in 1970 the SPÖ took control of government away from the ÖVP.

Critical to Austria's social corporatism is a proper balance between the autonomy of interest groups and their dependence on political parties. Too much autonomy from political parties would not only risk the democratic character of Austria's corporatism but make for explosive conflict among interest-group and party elites. Too much dependence on political parties would tie interest groups directly to the competitive relations among parties and thus risk the consensual bargaining that now occurs.[240] Social corporatism in Austria recognizes the potential veto power of both business and labor. This recognition has encouraged the harmonization of diverging interests in a political context that continues to distinguish between "red" and "black."[241] In strict observance of *Proporz,* equal representation is given to the peak associations representing the interests of business and agriculture, which are linked to the ÖVP, and to the ÖGB and the Chamber of Labor, closely connected with the SPÖ. Political leaders of both major parties are thus assured of continuous, easy access to all important decision arenas and to full, mutual consultation. The government's intermediary role in group bargaining tries to assure, on the whole successfully, that the potential veto power of each side does not lead to

74

stalemate. Indeed, the very concept of "partnership" among groups that are politically divided reflects the symbiotic relation that results from the groups' potential veto power over substantial policy change. While the business community and the ÖVP prefer a broad interpretation of Austria's "social partnership" that protects private property from political interference by sublimating class conflict in society, the labor movement and the SPÖ push for a narrow interpretation of the "economic partnership" that has as its defining element the political management of a small, exposed economy.

Austria's Great Coalition, continued after 1966 by other means, has sociological and electoral underpinnings in a society still marked by very notable class and status divisions, regional disparities, and intermittent, carefully controlled ideological conflict.[242] The class conflict that ended in civil war in the 1930s pitted the "red" East of the country against the "black" West. Since 1945, gradual changes in partisan identification of voters and the electoral strength of the two main parties have somewhat diluted this coalescence of regional and class divisions. But compared to the horizontal segmentation of Swiss society, Austria's social structure still remains vertically segmented into different "political camps" *(Lager)*. Both major camps have vast networks of ancillary organizations penetrating Austrian society, and both still recruit a very high proportion of the electorate as party members. Even if one takes the lowest membership estimates for the ÖVP, the one-quarter of the electorate that holds party cards is undoubtedly the highest figure for any center-right party in the industrial world; in fact, it exceeds the average party membership of the total Swiss electorate. Other estimates of the ÖVP's membership exceed by up to 10 percent the 30 percent of the electorate who are card-carrying SPÖ members.[243] One major purpose of elections for the duration of the Great Coalition is still retained in part today; elections, in Uwe Kitzinger's words, "furnish a revised index of strength according to which the organized groups can bargain to settle their differences."[244]

The central position of the political parties in Austria's social corporatism is reflected in the restraints that they impose on the power of the state. The role of the federal bureaucracy is to facilitate agreements between Austria's powerful interest groups, and through them Austria's parties, rather than to impose its own solutions.[245] Before 1966 political power was centralized in institutions that bypassed the state bureaucracy. The coalition government between the ÖVP and the SPÖ was essentially managed by the coalition committee rather than by the state bureaucracy. This committee provided the parties' leaders with a forum for settling virtually all important political issues in secrecy, outside the cabinet and the Parliament and unimpeded by the state bureaucracy.[246]

Political parties not only bypassed but penetrated the Austrian bureaucracy. Austria's higher civil service is staffed largely by university graduates who are members of the ancillary academic organizations of the two major parties. This increases the thorough politicization of the Austrian state.[247] Party membership among Austria's senior civil servants is larger than in the private sector, while the number of party officials is smaller.[248] *Proporz* has thus reinforced the decentralization inherent in all large-scale bureaucracies. An acute observer of Austrian politics concluded in the 1960s that "the result is a quantitative and qualitative politicization of almost all aspects of public life."[249] The breakup of the Great Coalition in 1966 shifted the forum for high-level decision making not to the cabinet and the senior civil service but to the top echelons of political parties and their ancillary interest groups. Politicization at the top thus voided independent political initiatives of the state bureaucracy in its relations with industrial sectors or individual firms. But politicization has also restrained the bureaucracy from becoming an instrument fully controlled by the SPÖ government. After a decade of socialist rule, Austria's bureaucracy has retained its predominantly conservative coloration.[250] All important initiatives of the state bureaucracy are carefully screened by an elaborate network of institutions in which Austria's main contestants for power, who perceive themselves as both "partners" who cooperate and adherents of opposing "camps," are represented.

Besides bypassing and penetrating the state, political parties also encircle it through numerous institutions that they control through their many ancillary organizations, including the major producer groups. These institutions normally take the form of powerful advisory committees, staffed jointly and in equal proportions by representatives of business, labor, and at times other interest groups. They encircle the entire executive branch of government when it deals with social and economic issues broadly defined. An incomplete listing in the late 1970s counted, at the federal level alone, fifty-six of these committees covering issues such as investment, taxation, industry, prices, social insurance, foreign workers, labor markets, cartels, transportation, research and development, agriculture, exports, imports, tariffs, foreign trade, and foreign aid.[251] Some informed observers talk of as many as two hundred commissions and advisory bodies of the federal government.[252] Although Austria's federalism is weak, these institutional mechanisms for consultation, deliberation, and policy implementation have also been established in all of the provinces. Seven of the nine provinces, for example, mandate by law a system of proportional representation of the parties in the executive branch of government. These provinces are governed to this day by black-red coalition governments of conservatives and socialists. At all levels of government these advisory bodies essentially assemble, day after day, the same people in different rooms. In situations where the political consensus cannot be created for a particular decision or for the development of a policy, these advisory commissions often provide the arenas for deliberately avoiding decisions.

The dominance of interest groups and the penetration of the state bureaucracy by political parties have created an osmotic relation between groups and bureaucracy that has in many instances enlarged the size of the groups' staff and reinforced the groups' central power over their subordinate units. For example, the groups exercise highly effective control, although in practice it is greater in the case of wages than in that of prices, over access to the two subcommittees of the Joint Commission. Since they play the role of gatekeeper, they in effect reinforce the centralized exercise of power in both the Federal Economic Chamber and the ÖGB.[253] In a system with a Parliament as impotent as Austria's, the executive branch of government risks delegitimation on questions of economic and social policy. But the extensive participation of interest groups in policy making contains that threat.[254]

Austria's consensual system of governance has broadened beyond the formulation and implementation of an incomes policy that, according to many observers, lies at its core.[255] Gerhard Lehmbruch, for example, sees Austria's distinctiveness compared to other European states in the "spillover" of its "neo-corporatist" policy making beyond business-cycle policy toward the inclusion of investment, employment, and broader issues affecting the management of the economy such as cartel legislation and codetermination.[256] The interest groups have been growing in prominence in matters of policy since their power to regulate the behavior of prices and wages was first institutionalized, informally, in the late 1950s.[257] In the 1960s the groups' role in policy implementation was successively broadened to incorporate, among other issues, economic forecasting and advice, and labor-market policy (including the allocation of quotas for foreign workers), as well as agricultural, social, industrial, regional, and commercial policy. The role of the economic partners is less central but still important in areas such as research and development, the media, taxes, and transportation.

Arguing that the scope of Austria's social corporatism is broad is, however, not the same as arguing that it is unlimited. Political conflict between the partners is sufficiently intense to prevent, for example, overarching economic planning, tax, or social policies. Vienna's new city hospital testifies to Austrian limits. Although planning started in 1955, the hospital will probably not be completed before the end of the 1980s. The original cost estimate has increased by a factor of seventy, and, at a 1980 cost of about $3.2 billion, it will be the most expensive hospital ever built anywhere in the world.[258] Other issues such as family, abortion, education, and cultural affairs more generally, have not lent themselves to an accommodative style of policy making. The question of nuclear energy highlights these limitations with particular clarity. On an issue that had originally cut right through Austria's entrenched partisan alignments, and after prolonged political struggles, the Austrian government was forced to resort, for the first time in the history of the Second Republic, to Switzerland's most favored political device, the referendum. The policy debate did redefine the issue to some extent along partisan lines. But the completed yet inoperative reactor at Zwentendorf remains an expensive testimonial to the limits of Austria's corporatist system of governing by group consensus; the idle plant costs about $75 million a year in loan repayments and maintenance charges.[259]

ALTERNATIVES FOREGONE

Social corporatism in Austria mobilizes and maintains a strong political consensus around a strategy of national adaptation to and public compensation for economic change. The strategy reflects the central position that a reformist trade union organization occupies in Austrian politics. Significantly, policies that have been essential to liberal corporatism across the Swiss border in coping with economic change have not been great successes in Austria. The differences between the two countries are evident in political alternatives that Austria has foregone in the way it frames and implements policies in the areas of research and development, foreign labor, and export promotion. These areas illustrate political possibilities that Austria's social corporatism does not pursue.

Research and development policy points to the limits on private policies of compensation in Austria. Austrian firms lag far behind their Swiss competitors in the selective specialization and product innovation that bring a highly competitive position in world markets.

Instead, Austria enjoys a relatively strong position where its market position is easily threatened, in the development of innovations either in traditional industrial sectors like metals and paper or in the traditional segments of advanced industries.[260] Despite their strength in fundamental research, Austrian firms lag in the commercial application of innovations to the development of new products and new production processes.[261] Rather than being developed indigenously, through substantial research and development in Austrian firms, technological progress is typically imported in the form of machinery and investment goods.[262] In 1967, for example, Austria paid more than sixteen times as much for the import of investment goods embodying largely foreign technology (10 percent of its gross national product [GNP]) as for its own research and development programs (0.6 percent of GNP).[263] Although Austria quadrupled its research and development expenditures as a share of GNP from about 0.3 percent in 1963 to about 0.9 percent in 1970 and 1.4 percent in 1980, and tripled the federal government's expenditures in the 1970s, such increases are in fact far smaller than what had been planned in the late 1960s.[264] Today Austria has one of the lowest research and development budgets among the advanced industrial states and lags far behind Switzerland's research-intensive industry.[265] Reflecting on Austria's traditional policy of covering its research and development needs through the import of investment goods, Vice Chancellor Androsch observed in 1977 that "this easy and cheap way to acquire knowledge and new technologies will become more and more difficult in the future."[266]

But in the past this policy was very successful in improving Austria's position in technologically advanced export markets. The balance between research-intensive industrial goods and overall industrial exports improved greatly and so did Austria's balance of trade in high-technology goods in sectors such as chemicals, machinery, and electronics. According to one study, the share of high-technology and research-intensive products increased from 27 percent in 1960 to 43 percent in 1971 and 53 percent in 1978.[267] Like Japan, Austria has successfully used its technological backwardness to achieve a rapid transformation of its industrial capacities. But unlike Japan, Austria has not succeeded in developing leading technologies in relatively secure market niches. All the statistical indicators point to a relative decline in Austria's own contribution to technological advance. Thus Austria's share in the total number of industrial licenses in domestic markets dropped from 27 percent in 1960 to 19 percent in 1970, and, compared to the other industrial states, Austria issues very few patents abroad.[268] The imbalance between the import and export of licenses, patents, and trademarks is reflected in the growing deficit between receipts and payments. That deficit increased from $5.88 million in 1960 to $89.8 million in 1979, and doubled between 1969 and 1974 alone.[269] In 1967 Austria's ratio between payments and receipts of 3.6 was the largest in the small European states; and Austria spent 29 percent of its total research and development expenditures for foreign patents and licenses as compared to about 10 percent in most other Western European countries.[270] In the late 1970s Austrian expenditures still exceeded receipts by a factor of four.

These figures point to Austria's persistent and probably growing technological dependence. The negative consequences are perhaps best illustrated by Austria's experience in the research-intensive electrical engineering industry, which in 1972 received only 15 percent of the government's total research and development budget ($908,000). Although the proportion of funds spent in the industry on research and development was twice as high as the Austrian average of 0.7 percent of industrial gross production, it was only one-half of what, on the average, was spent by the other advanced industrial states.[271] In the leading producer countries in this particular sector (the United States, Britain, West Germany, and Sweden) between 20 and 30 percent of the total national research budgets is generated by the electrical engineering industry; in Austria the corresponding figure was in 1969 only 11 percent.[272] Furthermore, among the small European states Austria was the only country to spend more than half of the industry's research and development budget on electrical-mechanical engineering products, a traditional area of strength, rather than on future growth segments like electronics.[273] Even though Austria's industry has the technological capacity to produce electronic equipment, its machine tool industry, for example, imports all of its electronic steering components.[274] A research and development budget that is by international standards limited and relative technological backwardness occur in an industry dominated by foreign firms, which largely finance their product developments in their home markets and mainly use their Austrian subsidiaries for the assembly of components.[275] In this particular industry, Austria, it could be argued, shares to some extent in the branch-plant economy characteristics of some developing countries.

In contrast to Switzerland, Austria relies to a lesser extent on an imported workforce.[276] Like most other states in Western Europe, Austria admitted foreign workers in increasing numbers during the 1960s. At the peak, in 1974, its 220,000 foreign workers constituted only about one-fifth of Switzerland's foreign workforce in absolute numbers; and the 9 percent of Austria's working population that was foreign was less than a third of the Swiss figure of about 30 percent. Like Switzerland, Austria reduced the number of foreign workers rapidly after 1974. By 1976 the total number had dropped by 50,000, compared to Switzerland's 250,000, and the relative share in Austria's workforce stood at 6 percent, compared to Switzerland's 20 percent.[277] Furthermore, the rate at which it reduced its foreign workforce was slower (22 percent) than in Switzerland (28 percent). These data support the argument that a strategy of international adaptation is less central to Austria than to Switzerland.

Finally, as is true of Switzerland, Austria's growing involvement in world markets since 1945 is reflected in policies designed to strengthen the country's export performance.[278] However, these policies reinforce the impression that Austria's government is more fully involved than the government of Switzerland in foreign economic policy. After 1945 Austria quickly reestablished commercial relations with a large number of its traditional trading partners in Western Europe, but the underlying orientation and overall economic consequence of Austria's integration into the postwar international economy was to secure rather than to enlarge traditional export markets.[279] This orientation was also evident in the prolonged Austrian debate over European integration.[280] Deep-seated reservations concerning Austria's full integration into world markets persisted until the early 1970s. When, for example, Austria experienced high economic growth, full employment, and a balance-of-payments equilibrium before 1974, the government turned a deaf ear to the demands of the export sector for stronger support. As late as 1973 a sales rebate on exports was eliminated without compensation because exports were then viewed as an undesirable stimulant of inflation. Since 1973, the mounting pressures of a prolonged economic downturn and increasing international competition have compelled the Austrian government to reconsider the importance it attaches to a further promotion of its export trade.

The recent expansion of state support for Austrian exports is an attempt to compensate for the downturn in the international economy, and the balance-of-payments and employment problems that downturn has created for Austria. Unlike Switzerland, Austria has publicly organized and administratively unified its export insurance and financing programs. They have grown by leaps and bounds. Although their establishment dates back to 1950, and although they have been continuously enlarged and modified, particularly between

1964 and 1967, recent changes in both complexity and scale have been impressive.[281] With annual growth rates of about 30 percent in the 1970s, the proportion of Austrian exports guaranteed by the publicly owned Control Bank increased from 13 percent in 1968 to 40 percent in 1980.[282] Furthermore, spurred by the rapid deterioration of Austria's balance of trade since the mid-1970s, the proportion of export trade covered by Austria's export financing schemes increased from 6 percent in 1975 to 27 percent in 1981.[283] This system of export financing has been dependent on international capital markets. Between 1975 and 1980 foreign net borrowing by the Control Bank increased from $253 million to $2.24 billion, respectively 48 and 95 percent of its total borrowing.[284]

The government's increasing role in the support of Austria's export trade is also reflected in the financing of Austria's extensive system of foreign trade delegations. As the *Economist* reported, "No government, except that of Japan, tries so hard to promote trade through commercial delegations as the Austrian one."[285] In the 1950s and 1960s the organization of Austria's foreign trade missions relied critically on the financial and organizational support of the peak association of business, the Federal Economic Chamber.[286] By the mid-1970s the chamber had developed a computerized system that stored information on 4,800 firms and more than 17,000 products, thus covering more than 90 percent of all exporters. Seventy of Austria's eighty trade missions have direct access to this data bank, which is consulted about sixty times a day. The traditional weakness of Austria's numerous medium-sized and small firms in marketing is at least partly offset by this concerted effort in which, in recent years, the government's financial involvement has markedly increased. These developments reflect a partial move toward an active policy of export promotion. Today there exists a strong tendency in Austria to argue that only an export policy that follows the Swiss model will assure economic prosperity in the next two decades. Thus, a recent government study projects a one-third increase in Austria's export intensity by 1990.[287]

But viewed in a comparative perspective that includes Switzerland, this projection appears improbable. A good illustration of the different attitudes of the two states on questions of export policy is provided by the controversies that surround the shipment of arms in Austria but not in Switzerland. The creation of a national armaments industry was considered vital to securing Austria's neutrality after 1955. Since Austria's Defense Ministry purchased domestically produced equipment at premium prices, Austria's army can now cover 60 percent of its total weapons purchases from domestic suppliers.

About two dozen companies employ some 3,000 workers on defense contracts. The largest, Steyr-Daimler-Puch, generates about one-quarter of its annual turnover of $800 million in military hardware. From its Greek subsidiary this nationalized firm circumvents Austria's export restrictions and sells directly to the warring factions in the Middle East. More than 50 percent of Austria's armament production of $600 million is exported to customers in forty countries. Quite apart from the international pressures to which Austrian policy is occasionally exposed, this export orientation generates domestic controversies simply unheard of in Swiss politics. In 1977 Austria's minister of Defense, Karl Luetgendorf, was forced to resign after it became public that he had backed the sale of arms to Syria; in 1980 the opposition of the trade unions and the left wing of the SPÖ stopped a government contract with Chile.[288] Unlike Switzerland, Austria at times ranks other objectives higher than export sales. Austria's more active export promotion since the mid-1970s was necessary to maintain the relative export intensity of the Austrian economy. In contrast, Switzerland's less far-reaching support policy permitted a substantial further increase in the export intensity of the Swiss economy. The typical Swiss firm is better positioned in international markets than its Austrian counterpart.

Austria's political strategies and structures run counter to many of the generalizations of Left and Right. Blessed with full employment, low inflation, and high growth, Austria in the 1970s exemplified a successful strategy of deficit spending, at a time when policy makers throughout Europe turned to other ways of conducting their economic policies. The political endurance of Austria's party system contrasts with the political decay of established party systems in many European countries. And Austria's interest groups do not show the signs of advanced decomposition so marked in many other industrial countries, particularly the larger ones. Social stability and political normality in Austria contrast with instability and crisis elsewhere. Europe's misery is illuminated fully only by Austria's miracle. To those who argue that the fin-de-siècle of democratic socialism has arrived, Vienna offers food for thought.

CHAPTER THREE

Liberal Capitalism in Switzerland

Recent experience confirms an old truth: Switzerland offers a view of the past that works. In 1978 Switzerland was the richest country in the industrialized world, with a GNP of $13,853 per capita. On a per capita basis the Swiss also led the world in individual savings ($5,200) and currency reserves ($3,370). Between 1975 and 1978 Switzerland raised the proportion of exports of goods and services in its GDP by an astonishing eight percentage points, from 36 to 44 percent. Despite its almost total dependence on foreign energy, its current account surplus in 1978 was more than 40 percent of the total OECD surplus. Two years later, after the second oil shock, its deficit was less than 1 percent of the OECD total. In 1979 Switzerland's $21 billion currency reserves surpassed those of the United States. Between 1971 and 1978 the Swiss franc appreciated by 100 percent. The country's inflation rate, moreover, dropped from more than 10 percent in 1974 to 1 percent in 1978.[1]

Yet Switzerland is the only advanced industrial country that has never regained its pre-1973 level of output. Because it rationalized production and continued its redeployment of industry abroad, Switzerland laid off foreign workers and women, reducing its labor force by about 12 percent between 1973 and 1976. Despite the loss of about 340,000 jobs, however, its official rate of unemployment was only 0.3 percent in 1980, lower than that in any other advanced industrial state. Government expenditures have since 1970 increased faster than in any other OECD country, yet Switzerland cut its budget deficit by one-third in the midst of a general recession, in 1976–77. Real GDP dropped by more than 7 percent in 1975, one of the largest declines in the OECD and, indeed, a much greater drop than had been recorded in any one year in the 1930s; yet in 1977 Switzerland's real GNP increased by 4.3 percent, which exceeded the growth rate of all other OECD states.

Switzerland is also a political success story. In the eyes of an overwhelming proportion of its citizens, Swiss institutions and policies are legitimate; and Switzerland's plebiscitary democracy helps recreate this legitimacy through frequent votes on major issues. This is not to deny that strains in Swiss politics have increased, as the rapid economic changes of the 1970s posed new problems that seriously tested Switzerland's established political arrangements and choices. Programs proposed by the federal government are now being voted down more frequently than they were in the 1950s and 1960s. Rule by emergency decree is on the increase, especially on issues touching on Switzerland's position in the international economy. Europe's restless youth can even be seen and heard in Zurich. But it would be wrong to infer from these illustrations of growing strain that the economic changes of the 1970s have created a debilitating crisis in the very structure of Swiss politics. Nothing could be further from the truth. Compared to the political experience of other industrial states, and compared to Swiss history during the 1920s and 1930s, Switzerland has weathered well the storms of the 1970s. As one journalist observed, only half mockingly, "Switzerland is a paradise for tourists and conservatives. A conservative tourist can have a particularly good time there. . . . Switzerland is a great place to visit. It is not a bad place to live either."[2]

Switzerland's success derives from its willingness to let market forces create efficient combinations of factors of production while at the same time appreciating the importance of compensatory political gestures in maintaining a broad consensus on this market-driven process of adjustment. In democratic corporatism, economic flexibility is contingent on political stability. This chapter illustrates how Switzerland mobilizes consensus to master economic change. The analysis is carried out at the three levels identified in chapter 1: social coalitions and policy choice, political institutions, and the policy process. An internationally oriented business community shapes policies dealing with economic change that stress international trade and investment, and intensive research and development efforts, by Switzerland's large corporations. Swiss unions are relatively weak, have conservative leanings, and must accept, or support on their own accord, the employment of a large foreign workforce, a tight-fisted approach to public spending, and a far-reaching privatization of social welfare. Sections 1 and 2 argue that the social coalition shaping the choice of policies explains why Switzerland's response to economic change can be summarized as global adaptation and private compensation. This alignment of social forces, and the substantive political choices with which that alignment addresses economic change, finds distinctive expression in the institutions and the process of political bargaining that constitute Switzerland's policy network. Sections 3 to 5 show how Switzerland mobilizes a corporatist consensus that makes possible a delicate balance between economic flexibility and political stability. Finally, Section 6 traces some policies that have been vigorously pursued across the Austrian border but that do not appear to suit Switzerland's liberal corporatism.

INTERNATIONAL BUSINESS

The most distinctive feature of Switzerland's powerful business community is its international orientation. Measured both by the ratio of foreign over domestic production and on a per capita basis, Switzerland's direct foreign investments are much larger than those of the United States or Britain.[3] Switzerland's corporations can be said to be, in every sense of the term, "at home abroad."[4] One knowledgeable observer of Swiss business, Jürg Niehans, concludes that "multinationalism helps to equalize the economic opportunities between firms of small and large countries. It is not, as it is sometimes argued, a new offensive weapon of large, developed countries to gain economic dominance. It is the traditional defense of small, developed countries to preserve economic equality."[5]

It is not easy to estimate the magnitude of funds that Swiss corporations own or shift abroad. Indeed, because of the traditional secrecy shrouding the operations of most of Switzerland's corporations, some of the data are so unreliable that the government stopped collecting them in 1970.[6] But by all accounts Switzerland's capital exports have increased dramatically since the end of World War II. The outflow of capital increased from $733 million per year in 1967–69 to $3.243 billion in 1973–75. By the mid-1970s Switzerland had joined Britain as the number two foreign investor, well behind the United States but well ahead of West Germany, Japan, and France. Among the small European states Switzerland's rate of capital export in the mid-1970s exceeded that of the Netherlands by a factor of 2.6, Sweden by 8.4, Belgium by 13.8, Norway by 25.0, Denmark by 32.3, and finally, Austria by 111.5.[7] Switzerland's gross assets abroad increased from $11.81 billion in 1960 to $108 billion in 1975, and its net assets increased from $6.95 billion to $62.8 billion. These latter figures correspond to 81 and 113 percent, respectively, of Swiss GNP.[8] Net returns on capital have increased at an even faster rate: from $162 million in 1960 to $2.01 billion in 1975.[9] Returns on capital are critically important in adding strength to the current-account balance and in covering Switzerland's traditional trade deficit.[10]

Corporations held one-third of Switzerland's net foreign assets, some $21 billion, in the form of direct foreign investment in 1975.[11] The shift of funds has accelerated greatly since 1945, especially to Latin America, which receives about two-thirds of Switzerland's direct foreign investment. Between 1966 and 1971, for example, the rate of Switzerland's foreign investment doubled, and Switzerland recorded the fourth-largest increase in the rate of growth of its direct foreign investment (behind Japan, West Germany, and Sweden).[12] Swiss corporations are more involved in the internationalization of production than firms in any other country. In 1970, for example, the fraction of foreign over domestic production of the fifty largest firms was 0.66 in Switzerland as compared with 0.28 in Britain, 0.17 in the United States, 0.06 in West Germany, 0.02 in Japan, and less than 0.01 in Austria.[13]

Switzerland resembles other small European states in the relatively large role that its giant corporations play in the economy. Switzerland's fifty largest corporations account for a little over half of Switzerland's total domestic and foreign production. While this is comparable to the Austrian case, it is substantially above levels for the large advanced industrial states.[14] Furthermore, Switzerland's giant multinationals, and especially the six largest—Nestlé, Ciba-Geigy, Hoffmann-LaRoche, Alusuisse, Brown Boveri, and Sandoz—have between 95 and 71 percent of their employees and between 95 and 63 percent of their sales abroad. Most global in its orientation is the Nestlé Corporation, with only 4.7 percent of total sales in domestic markets.[15] But Nestlé is only the most extreme example; its international orientation is characteristic of all Switzerland's large corporations. Thus, more than two-thirds of the employees of Switzerland's thirty-five largest manufacturing firms work abroad. Between 1967 and 1977 domestic employment in industry shrank by almost one-quarter. Employment by Swiss corporations in low-wage countries increased by two-thirds, and the rate of employment growth abroad was twice as high in 1972–77 as it had been in 1967–72. In the late 1970s, nine of the top ten industrial groups were investing funds faster abroad than at home, and eight of these groupings produced more in their foreign plants than they did in Switzerland.[16] The degree of international involvement, however, varies with firm size. Among the thirty-five largest corporations, the top five companies employ five-sixths of their labor force abroad, but the figure for firms ranked thirtieth through thirty-fifth drops to one-tenth.[17]

The indirect consequences of these statistics for the structure of Switzerland's economy are very important. Even though the growth of Switzerland's large multinational corporations has not exceeded the growth of Swiss GNP, the fact that these firms are shifting an increasing share of their manufacturing operations abroad has helped accelerate the growth of Switzerland's service sector, both in production and in exports. In summary, as Niehans writes, "the Swiss multinationals, while not the most aggressive or dynamic sector of the economy, are its solid, durable, and resilient backbone."[18] Their heavy international involvement justifies, especially for some of the very largest firms, the characterization of Switzerland's business community as "big business without a home market."[19]

The international orientation of Switzerland's corporations strengthened in the 1970s. The appreciation of the Swiss franc sharply increased their inclination to redeploy an even greater share of manufacturing operations abroad. But a second reason also deserves mention. Like large multinationals in other countries, Swiss corporations, because of their very size, have direct access to international markets on which to raise the capital for their foreign investments. Unlike most multinationals, however, Swiss firms have built up hidden assets *(Stille Reserven)* across the last hundred years. Such financial strength buttresses their independence from the federal government and the banks. These assets are, by all accounts, very large; one of the reasons why Swiss companies are so secretive about their finances may well lie in the fear that the very size of their assets, once publicly known, would invite public debate about Switzerland's system of business taxation.[20] Because of their vast assets, Swiss firms have greeted with diffidence the Investment Risk Insurance scheme created in 1970 to encourage investments in less developed countries. In both scale and growth, Investment Risk Insurance has been insignificant compared with Export Risk Insurance. Between 1970 and 1976 only thirty-three investment projects, totaling under $56 million, were insured; at the end of 1977 outstanding guarantees amounted to only $32.9 million, that is, only 16 percent of the sum that the government had made available.[21]

Switzerland's banking community has in recent years grown by leaps and bounds. Today there is one bank for every 1400 Swiss— 4,700 branch offices in all.[22] More importantly, Swiss banks, and especially the three largest, are truly financial empires, inextricably linked with developments in international markets. The same is true of Switzerland's important insurance and reinsurance companies, which generated about 60 percent of their business abroad in the 1970s.[23] In terms of sheer size, Switzerland's financial community is imposing: in 1980 the balance sheet of just the five largest banks amounted to $74.38 billion, while in 1975 the balance sheet of all Swiss banks totaled $125 billion.[24] The proportion of the banks' capital and reserves in their total balance sheet is the highest in the industrial world: Switzerland's 8.3 percent exceeds by far the figures for the United States (6.4 percent), West Germany (3.4 percent), and Japan (1.2 percent).[25] Furthermore, it is common knowledge that the banks typically underreport their total assets; one rule of thumb common among Swiss bankers is to double the figures the three largest banks report, thereby arriving at a rough guess of their total assets. Thus the Swiss Credit Bank could absorb a loss of more than $420 million in 1977 by liquidating some of its hidden assets and still show the same profit as in the preceding year.[26] As in other economic spheres, the Swiss banking industry is becoming increasingly centralized; the relative share of the five largest banks in total assets increased from 26 percent in 1945 to 45 percent in 1974.[27] This financial muscle has increasingly translated into employment. With employment shrinking in manufacturing, the financial sector recorded high growth rates in employment in the 1970s; even in the crisis year of 1975 employment increased, by about 4 percent.[28]

The banks are deeply enmeshed in international operations. Transactions with foreign customers increased from about 8 percent of the total balance sheet in 1938 to 15 percent in 1958, and about 33 percent in 1972. For the five largest banks the figure stood at just under 50 percent in 1972.[29] The five big banks conduct about two-thirds of their business abroad, where most of their growth now occurs.[30] Between 1963 and 1972, for example, foreign lending increased by a factor of six as compared to a mere doubling of domestic loans.[31] The foreign assets of Swiss banks grew from $4.3 billion in 1965 to $48.8 billion in 1976, almost one-half the size of U.S. assets abroad at current exchange rates; and the number of foreign branches increased from eleven in 1965 to forty-five in 1976. The Union Bank of Switzerland and the Swiss Bank Corporation are members of the select club of international banks acting as "primary" lenders in the Eurodollar market.[32] The international operation of Swiss banks and their receipts for services rendered have greatly strengthened Switzerland's balance of payments. In 1979 short-term credits were swapped among central banks; it is no accident that the $4 billion that Switzerland's Nationalbank (Schweizerische Nationalbank) contributed exceeded the Austrian quota by a factor of sixteen (as well as exceeding the quota of all the other small European states combined).[33]

Although Swiss industry and Swiss banks generally share an international orientation, they have occasionally disagreed over policy. Under the system of fixed exchange rates of the 1960s, for example, the undervaluation of the Swiss franc reinforced the position of Swiss exporters on world markets. It also increased the influx of foreign funds, thus enlarging the money supply and fueling inflationary pressures throughout the domestic economy. In the debate about the dangers of "imported inflation" industry and finance took different sides. Generally speaking, Swiss bankers opposed, unsuccessfully, the inflationary consequences of Switzerland's export strategy. The export-induced boom of 1958–64 finally subsided only when the government and the public became convinced that it would result in an unacceptably high, permanent rate of inflation.[34] The restraints then imposed attempted to apportion the economic costs equally between industry and finance without doing substantial damage to either. In 1970 Switzerland's strong export lobby was even more successful; it stopped the government outright from curbing inflationary pressures by imposing a temporary export levy.[35] But because the magnitude of international capital movements was still relatively small in the 1960s, the inflationary consequences were less pronounced and the political defeat of the banks less visible. Under the system of flexible exchange rates prevailing throughout most of the 1970s, industry and finance were also affected differently. Numerous and far-reaching regulations, which the Nationalbank adopted in the attempt to stem the growing tide of speculative, short-term capital moving into the country, severely curtailed some of the banks' most profitable operations. But large industrial corporations were well positioned to adjust, due to their global operations. The result was a multitude of quarrels but no general war between these two prominent segments of the Swiss business community.

Because of the similarity of their conciliatory pursuits of profits, relations among the different segments of the Swiss business community are, by and large, excellent. For example, the appreciation of the franc in the 1970s sharply increased the inclination of the business community to redeploy its manufacturing operations abroad. There is widespread agreement among the Swiss that this policy brings only benefits. The traditionally close relation between foreign trade and capital export is reflected today in the very high correlation between the net exports of investment goods and direct foreign investment.[36] At least in the short- and medium-term, export trade and direct foreign investment are thought to be compatible and mutually supportive. Moreover, the investment strategy and lending practices of Swiss banks at times help industry: they do not neglect long-term goals for the sake of short-term profits, and they consider the impact of particular events or developments on the whole economy rather than only on the banks' particular interests.[37] This has been evident since the mid-1970s in export financing and in temporary support for industries in need of structural readjustment. The agreement between industry and finance is furthered by a far-reaching system of interlocking directorates, a private equivalent to the politically constructed links in Austria's social corporatism. Switzerland's "universal" banking system leads to much direct participation by bankers on company boards. In 1971, for example, a total of forty-seven members of the supervisory boards or boards of managers of the three largest banks also served on the supervisory boards of the seven largest industrial corporations.[38] Furthermore, Switzerland has internationally oriented financial holding companies, which also reinforce and reflect the intimate relations between industry and finance. In 1976 there existed 17,000 holding companies, including many foreign ones, which had many of their production facilities located abroad.

Even though an internationally oriented industrial and financial community is the dominant force in Switzerland, there also exists a much smaller and less powerful national business sector. The commanding heights of industry and finance express in their daily operations a firm conviction in the principles of economic liberalism. In the national sector, on the other hand, protection and cartels are the magic words. While this segment of the business community has mustered sufficient political strength to stave off many of the threats of a liberal market economy, it is much too weak to impose its own vision of society on other sectors. Still, its existence helps explain why, for example, Switzerland has been called "the most highly cartelized country in the world," why a giant multinational like Brown Boveri can belong to an international export cartel covering heavy electrical engineering products virtually without domestic opposition, or why the Catholic Peoples Party (Christlich Demokratische Volkspartei), unlike its West German counterpart, values the principle of freedom of contract more than the principle of competition.[39] These facts illustrate how far Switzerland "is removed from the Smithian image," and that Switzerland is marked, as the OECD notes, "by a pluralist concentration of economic responsibilities in an associative rather than a collective sense."[40] Switzerland relies on private coordination.

These restrictive practices have left their mark on Switzerland's business community. The Cartel Commission stands as a symbol of the gradual move toward liberalization that has characterized economic policy since the end of World War II. However, the commission is, by most accounts, very lenient in its approach to decartelization. In applying the law it consciously values the protection of the "economic personality" of a firm or group of firms more than the principle of competition.[41] The greatest conflict of interest exists between cartels of small firms in weak industrial sectors such as parts of the textile industry, on the one hand, and large firms in strong industrial sectors such as chemicals, on the other. This tension pits cartels and economic nationalism against multinationalism and economic internationalism. When the conflict is articulated and resolved in the Vorort, the major peak association of business, the liberal policy preferences of international business typically prevail. When, on the other hand, the Vorort opposes the interests of the Swiss Association of Small Business (Schweizerischer Gewerbeverband) or the Swiss Farmers' Union (Schweizerischer Bauernverband), the outcome may at times be in doubt.[42] But as long as the farming community is guaranteed its protected status, the nationally oriented business community lacks the political support necessary to challenge the internationally oriented business sector.

The appreciation of the franc in the 1970s led to increased foreign competition in Swiss markets, which has given the move toward liberalization a stronger push than have two decades of cautious decartelization. Because of these competitive pressures, the national business community is in retreat. Between 1966 and 1972, the total number of firms in Switzerland shrank by more than 15 percent;[43] an even larger proportion of firms closed between 1973 and 1979, especially in the cartelized and protected sectors of the economy. A national business community that had sufficient political strength to withstand the international business community in, for example, the prolonged debate over Switzerland's cartel law is now quite powerless as liberal foreign trade policy seriously restricts its traditional preserves in domestic markets.

The strong position that international business enjoys in Switzerland is reflected in a strategy of global adaptation to and private compensation for economic change. Political choices on questions of foreign trade as well as on research and development unmistakably reflect the view of the Swiss business community. With few exceptions

Switzerland has adhered in the international economy to a deeply engrained liberalism that predates the Industrial Revolution. In a comparative perspective the extensive and often unilateral tariff reductions of the 1950s left Switzerland with negligible tariffs on imports.[44] By 1956, for example, 98 percent of Switzerland's trade with Western European countries was free of restrictions, as compared to 8 percent for Austria.[45] In the early 1960s, prior to the Kennedy Round, Switzerland's average tariff rate on industrial products was 8 percent, as compared with Austria's rate of 19 percent.[46] Switzerland's accession to EFTA in the late 1950s, multilateral tariff negotiations in the Kennedy and Tokyo rounds, the granting of preferential tariffs to less developed countries in the late 1960s, the unilateral extension of most-favored-nation status to the Eastern European states, and the agreement with the EC in 1972—all imposed further downward pressure on tariffs that, by any standards, were already low. In the 1960s, for example, about 15 percent of imports entered Switzerland at tariff rates ranging from 10 to 13 percent, while 50 to 60 percent of imports entered at 4.5 percent or lower.[47] A 1979 economic study issued by the U.S. Congress concluded that at the end of the Kennedy Round negotiations on tariff reductions Switzerland's average tariff rate was 3.9 percent, the lowest rate among small European states (Austria's rate was 15.4 percent). In the late 1960s Switzerland's rate was by far the lowest among advanced industrial states.[48] In the round of multilateral tariff negotiations concluded in 1979, Switzerland's compromise formula for calculating tariff cuts bridged the gap between the EC proposal for harmonization and the U.S. preference for linear reduction. Ironically, Switzerland is probably alone among the eighteen major industrialized countries in experiencing a small welfare loss as a result of the latest round of tariff reductions.[49]

For Switzerland, foreign policy and foreign economic policy are inextricably linked. About three-fifths of the 424 bilateral treaties concluded since 1945, twice the OECD average, deal exclusively with economic matters.[50] According to the frank assessment of one Swiss official, "Switzerland's consistent policy of neutrality creates the most advantageous conditions for unrestricted commercial expansion in all markets."[51] Switzerland thus has oriented its involvement in foreign trade beyond the industrial world, unlike Austria, toward developing countries rather than Eastern Europe. While Switzerland imports about 5 percent from the less developed countries and the state trading countries of Eastern Europe, it sends 15 percent of its total exports to the developing world, almost four times as much as it exports to socialist countries.[52] Switzerland's policy, especially in Latin

America and the Middle East, reflects the mixture of laissez-faire liberalism and export promotion that more generally characterizes its strategy in world markets.[53] In approaching problems of development Swiss diplomats have, on the basis of their country's experience, always extolled the virtues of private initiative and market solutions. Since the first United Nations Conference on Trade and Development in 1964, Switzerland has been a staunch defender of a liberal approach to problems of international trade and aid. In this respect little has changed in the last twenty years. In the Nairobi meetings of UNCTAD (1976) Switzerland again articulated the liberal position, and in the talks between North and South in the mid-1970s Switzerland emphasized technical matters rather than politics, worked in the Finance Commission where its voice carried weight, and did not align itself with the (at times far-reaching) compromises that the Netherlands and Sweden proposed.[54] While prudence prevented any overt support of the initially strong opposition of the United States and West Germany to the demands of the South, the Swiss, there can be little doubt, agreed with the American and West German position.

Switzerland's uninspiring record in international aid also expresses this liberal inclination. By all accounts the Swiss have been stingy in living up to what they call the principle of "solidarity" in their foreign policy. Switzerland falls far short of meeting the target, 0.7 percent of GNP, of the OECD's Development Assistance Committee (DAC). Private capital movements, taking the form of export credits and direct foreign investment, in 1975 matched public aid. In 1977 public aid amounted to 0.19 percent of GNP, as compared to 0.30 for Austria. This was so far below the OECD average of 0.31 percent that the DAC, uncharacteristically, voiced public criticism.[55] On the other hand, Switzerland's credit provisions for the less developed countries have been generous. In the mid-1970s its $291 million share in the "Third Window" that the World Bank opened for the less developed countries hit hardest by the increases in the price of oil, and its $720 million contribution to the Witteveen Facility of the IMF, illustrate how in North-South relations Switzerland has acted on questions involving its "vital" interests, such as the debt issue and expropriation. Political calculations and a commitment to helping the poor explain why in 1979 Switzerland agreed to cancel $69 million or 90 percent of the developing countries' debt (as compared to Austria's $4 million and 15 percent).[56] And, together with the Netherlands, West Germany, Great Britain, and the United States, the Swiss government has been in the forefront in negotiating agreements that are mostly inspired by the OECD Draft Convention on the Protection of Foreign Property.[57]

The official purpose of Switzerland's aid policy is to increase the capacity of the less developed countries to absorb a growing share of Switzerland's exports and direct foreign investment.[58] Switzerland is more willing than most other advanced industrial states, however, to accept the consequences of the export offensive of low-cost producing countries. This liberal stance is grounded in Switzerland's own economic interests. Switzerland exports five times as many industrial products to the developing countries as it imports.[59] Even though Swiss trade with non-oil-producing less developed countries amounts to only 2 percent of the trade of all advanced industrial states, Switzerland's share in the export surplus registered in that trade is 10 percent.[60] Furthermore, while Switzerland is slower than most other European states to impose temporary or permanent import restrictions on products from less developed countries, it is, in keeping with liberal premises, equally opposed to granting them preferential treatment. Self-critical in tone, a report of the federal government issued in the 1970s concluded with refreshing candor that "compared to the efforts of other advanced industrial states our previous efforts to increase imports from less-developed countries have been minor."[61]

Despite this far-reaching liberalization of imports, Switzerland has not renounced all of the instruments of protection. Protectionist forces in Switzerland could, for example, support a 1958 tariff reform because the simultaneous shift to an ad valorem base of tariff calculations meant that rates were lowered for only one-tenth of the items on the tariff schedule, while they were increased slightly for a full two-thirds.[62] Prior to its full membership in the GATT in 1966, Switzerland reserved the right to renounce unilaterally the most-favored-nation status of any trade partner. In the 1970s Switzerland resorted on several occasions to the option of issuing import certificates. These are, however, exceptions. In the 1950s, 1960s, and 1970s the core of Swiss policy has been to apply to itself the principles of economic liberalism that it has recommended to others.

On questions of foreign investment Switzerland's image is that of the quintessential small state with open borders. Switzerland's political stability, military neutrality, and financial discretion are the foundation for the German maxim that "money alone does not bring happiness; you must also have it in Switzerland."[63] Old maxims express today's economic realities: by law the Swiss franc has the highest gold coverage of bank notes in circulation among all major currencies. If Switzerland's gold reserves were valued at market prices in 1982, each franc note was backed 300 percent. This is no more than a token of the multiple sources of investors' confidence in Swiss currency.[64] Historically, the secrecy of Swiss bank accounts was adopted to protect political refugees and their relatives from Nazi espionage in the 1930s. But since 1945 Switzerland has benefited from the influx of foreign capital from foreign firms and governments as well as tax dodgers and military dictators.

Exports account for an overwhelming amount of production in the main branches of Swiss industry: 60 percent in machinery, 85 percent in chemicals, and more than 95 percent in watches.[65] Switzerland's export policies are thus the closest the government has come to an activist economic policy in the 1970s.[66] There was agreement in Switzerland that the crisis of the 1970s had to be met through stepped-up efforts in export promotion rather than through selective import restrictions. Export promotion is, in fact, next to fiscal policy, the government's main countercyclical policy measure. Indeed, a programmatic survey of Switzerland's position in the international economy published in 1945 recognized its importance.[67] Similarly, in 1978 a comprehensive analysis of the changing position of Switzerland in the international economy concluded that "the modern version of Swiss laissez-faire economic policy is export promotion."[68] In contrast with measures adopted in Austria and elsewhere, though, Switzerland's export policies reveal the limited instruments that the government has at its disposal, and they illustrate the pervasive power of the private sector, in particular the banks. The overwhelming export effort still rests in the private sector with individual firms and a number of newly founded, privately organized export promotion groups designed to make medium-sized and small firms more competitive in international markets.[69]

Several institutional changes reflect Switzerland's intensified export drive in the 1970s.[70] The machinery of government was streamlined, and some attempts were made to train diplomats and political personnel in economic analysis. An Information Office for Export Finance was created in the mid-1970s. Switzerland's commercial diplomacy has been strengthened through the addition of so-called "trade delegates" affiliated with the embassies in some important growth markets in the Third World. In supplementing Switzerland's foreign chambers of commerce this system of trade delegates is a modest step that imitates the export promotion strategy developed by the Austrian government during the last three decades.[71] The trade delegates come under the jurisdiction and supervision of the semipublic Swiss Trade

Development Office, which was given an additional government allocation in 1976 and was extensively reorganized in 1977. In the late 1970s it handled about 10,000 requests annually from among the 7,000 firms that export.[72] At the same time, however, institutional reorganization and financial support favoring Swiss exports cannot be viewed as the central ingredient of Swiss success. The $2 million of financial aid granted to Switzerland's export drive in 1972 was minor in comparison with the $7.1 million average of five other small European states, and the $8.8 million spent by Austria.[73]

Far more important to Switzerland's export drive on world markets than outright aid is the federal Export Risk Insurance. Created during the Great Depression in 1934, it is currently governed by legislation dating back to 1958.[74] It is constantly honed and strengthened; in December 1975, for example, the Nationalbank decided to add to the scheme's reserves some $60 million that the bank had accumulated from negative interest rates charged on foreign deposits held in Switzerland.[75] Although Switzerland's export insurance maintains its traditional purpose of covering various forms of political risk, it has been the main source of assistance to Swiss exporters trying to cope with the decline in their prices and profits brought about by the Swiss franc's appreciation in the 1970s. Because of that appreciation Swiss exporters, unlike their competitors in all other industrial states, are entitled to retain their foreign-exchange profits. The extension of insurance coverage to exchange risks occurred in late 1973. In 1975, 9 percent of total payments for damages concerned losses due to currency changes; only two years later, in 1977, that figure had jumped to 70 percent.[76] In line with the practice of other countries, maximum coverage was raised from 85 to 95 percent in 1975.[77] But more important than this change in regulations was a change in the spirit of administering them. The Export Risk Insurance became very supportive of small firms in consumer goods industries, which have confronted the greatest difficulties in recent years.

The increase in the volume of insured export business has been very rapid. New commitments rose from $146 million in 1960 to $1.55 billion in 1975, and $3.33 billion in 1977. The total commitment of the federal government as lender of last resort to Swiss exporters increased from $204 million in 1960 to $1.17 billion in 1973, $3.1 billion in 1975, and $15 billion in 1980 (including $6 billion for foreign-exchange risk guarantees).[78] Furthermore, while in 1968 70 percent of export insurance covered trade with less developed countries, by 1976 that proportion had declined to 48 percent.[79] The Export Risk Insurance has thus been an important ingredient in

Switzerland's successful defense of established positions in its traditional export markets in the OECD; in the late 1970s it covered between 15 and 20 percent of Switzerland's total export trade.[80]

Of comparable importance to Switzerland's export drive has been its generous system of export finance, which relies almost exclusively on the private banking sector and in particular on the three largest private banks: the Union Bank of Switzerland, the Swiss Bank Corporation, and the Swiss Credit Bank. Throughout the nineteenth and twentieth centuries Switzerland has had interest rates well below those of most other countries. This provided a basis of strength that the Swiss exploited to maximum advantage in the 1970s.[81] In the mid-1970s preferential short-term credits were granted to Switzerland's hard-hit consumer goods industries (as will be discussed in chapters five and six). Medium-term credits (two to five years) are also very cheap. Swiss interest rates of about 5 percent were by far the lowest in any advanced industrial state. Corresponding rates averaged 9.4 percent in five small European states and slightly over 7 percent in the large advanced industrial states.[82] In short, Switzerland's export financing system provides credits at a rate so far below the 7.0 to 8.5 percent range stipulated in the OECD's first international agreement on export financing of 1976 that Switzerland simply refused to sign.[83] The combined effect of these policies led to a dramatic 23-fold increase in private export credits to developing countries, from $40 million in 1975 to $916 million in 1977.[84]

These different ways of promoting exports are much more important than attempts to stimulate Switzerland's domestic demand. The multiplier for exports exceeds that for both government expenditures and domestic investment by, respectively, 30 and 60 percent.[85] Despite this efficacy, some of the government's initiatives were greatly constrained. For example, in 1979 Swiss voters defeated, for the third time in the 1970s, a proposal to adopt a value-added tax and the export rebates that normally accompany it; Austria and the other small European states had already shifted to that form of taxation and indirect export promotion by the late 1960s. Switzerland's export insurance covers only political risk and excludes, unlike Austria's, commercial and investment risks. Furthermore, in contrast to Austria, export credits are normally limited to a maximum repayment term of five years. Moreover, most of the special measures adopted to strengthen Swiss exporters had been terminated by the end of 1980. Yet these restraints on government policy have not mattered much. A number of private-sector arrangements and initiatives, especially in the financing of exports, proved adequate in the 1970s. With the exception of the period of the Swiss franc's dramatic appreciation in 1978, Switzerland's credit terms were sufficiently attractive to support its export strategy.

Switzerland's tendency to compensate privately for economic change is illustrated by a type of research and development policy that has found no favor in Austria. In blending modern scientific discoveries with indigenous artisan skills, "Switzerland was saved from the temptations of mass production and condemned to superiority."[86] Switzerland's specialized export goods rely on a high value added. The franc value of each ton of exports is about seven to eleven times greater than the value of each imported ton.[87] But while the Swiss government is fully aware that an increasing specialization of Switzerland's industry is, within the context of its present strategy, both necessary and inevitable, it is the large corporations that define and implement the country's research and development policy. Perhaps for that reason, Switzerland has always heeded the counsel of prudence in following a limited rather than a general research and development policy. Like many other European countries Switzerland set up its own National Science Council in 1965; but because "*le défi des cantons*" outweighed "*le défi américain*" the council was given only advisory rather than policy-making powers.[88]

While the government funds some research, especially at university institutes, Switzerland's research and development policy is distinguished by the business community's active opposition to government sponsorship. Both in 1943 and 1959 Swiss industry spurned offers extended by the federal executive to involve the government more prominently in research and development issues.[89] Indeed, at the request of the National Science Council, the major association of business, the Swiss Federation of Commerce and Industry (Schweizerischer Handels- und Industrie-Verein, SHIV), has since 1966 taken responsibility for the collection, interpretation, and dissemination of data on questions of research and development. These data illustrate the overwhelming influence exercised by Switzerland's large multinational corporations. While small- and medium-sized firms concentrate their research and development resources on improving engineering processes, the large corporations, which account for about three-fifths of total research expenditures, are mapping long-term strategies for product innovation. In contrast with most other European states, where the relative share of privately funded research has dropped, the private sector has provided a constant 80

99

percent of Switzerland's research and development budget since the early 1960s. Most of the research is therefore conducted in the area of applied rather than basic research.[90] In fact atomic energy is the only research area that has remained the special prerogative of the government. In sum, as Felix Streichenberg writes, "in the organization and support of industrial R and D Switzerland is a special case and perhaps the only country where privately-based industrial research has emerged on a case-by-case basis which is applied and unusually economical."[91]

Because they are largely financed by its huge corporations, Switzerland's research expenditures rank well above those of Austria. In 1958, for example, Switzerland's research and development expenditures were, on a per capita basis, seven times as large as those in Austria.[92] Total public- and private-sector expenditures roughly doubled between 1962 and 1967, passing one billion francs ($231 million) by 1965. Between 1969 and 1975 the rate of increase slowed somewhat, with research expenditures reaching $1.4 billion in 1975. As a proportion of GNP research and development expenditures increased steadily from 1.6 percent in 1964 to 1.9 percent in 1967, and to 2.2 percent in 1975, compared to less than 1.4 percent in Austria.[93] Moreover, considering the far-flung international operations of Swiss firms, it is remarkable that two-thirds of their research and development is still conducted at home.[94]

The success of Switzerland's research and development efforts is particularly striking in a historical perspective. In following a strategy of industrial imitation Switzerland had lax patent laws until the turn of the century.[95] In some areas of textile processing Switzerland lacked patent legislation until 1959, and it joined the International Patent Institute as late as 1960. Today industrial imitation by others leaves the Swiss unperturbed.[96] On a per capita basis the number of patents registered inside Switzerland is much greater than in any other country in the world. In 1965, for example, Switzerland's figure was one-third higher than corresponding figures for Japan, Sweden, and West Germany, ranked numbers two through four.[97] If measured in terms of the relative number of scientific authors, Switzerland ranks first among the small European states and second in the world.[98] After the United States, Switzerland is the second-largest exporter of technology, and roughly one-quarter of worldwide technology exports originates in Switzerland.[99] This Swiss ingenuity pays. Receipts from licenses and patents increased from about $69.5 million in 1957 to $139 million in 1967, and to more than $316 million in 1973.[100] In short, Switzerland's research and development policy plays a central role in maintaining international competitiveness.

REFORMIST UNIONS

Unions occupy a subordinate position in Switzerland's social coalition and exhibit a conservatism that derives from their relative political weakness.[101] Although that weakness has been reinforced by the prosperity and full employment of the past generation, the deeper political reasons lie in the structure of the Swiss economy and the policy choices of the trade unions. Switzerland's decentralized manufacturing industry, small plant size, and, in the 1970s, an accelerating shift of labor from industry to services have adversely affected its trade union movement. Between 1950 and 1965 Switzerland's export strategy made the secondary sector of the economy the largest in any advanced industrial state. Therefore the most important constituent union of the Swiss labor movement, the metalworkers and watchmakers, could proudly report a 30 percent increase in membership. For the labor movement as a whole, however, the picture differed. After very rapid increases in membership in the aftermath of World War II, the total has stagnated around 450,000 since the mid-1960s.[102] One survey reports that the proportion of the industrial work force organized by the Swiss Federation of Trade Unions (Schweizerischer Gewerkschaftsbund, SGB) declined between 1955 and 1971 in every region of the country but one canton.[103] By 1970 the share of the industrial workforce organized in the SGB and the other blue-collar unions had plummeted from its all-time high of 49 percent in 1955 to 33 percent. But after 1973 a sharp contraction in Switzerland's secondary labor market, primarily affecting foreign workers and women, led to an increase in the proportion of blue-collar workers who are union members, from 33 percent in 1970 to 45 percent in 1978. During the same period the unionization of Switzerland's total work force also increased from 30 to 38 percent, a little more than half of the corresponding figure for Austria.[104]

The weakness of Switzerland's union movement also stems from its internal political divisions. Within the union movement there exists a substantial difference between the moderate metalworkers and watchmakers union, and the more militant public employees union, as well as more radical industrial unions such as the printers, construction and wood workers, and the chemical, textile, and paper workers.[105] In 1968, for example, an initiative was launched to reduce the work week to forty-four hours. The SGB Central Commission followed the metalworkers in opposing the move, while the more radical unions backed the initiative, thus provoking a "crisis of unity."[106]

Of greater importance, though, are the differences between Switzerland's Social Democratic Party (Sozialdemokratische Partei) and the trade union movement. In the only elite survey probing this problem, fewer than half of the party and union leaders polled expressed satisfaction with party-union relations.[107] The basic source of tension is a clash between the unions' private-sector strategy and the party's preference for public-sector activity. Symptomatic of this difference in political orientation was the bitter conflict between party and unions in the late 1960s. When the Social Democratic Party introduced its demand for a national pension plan, roughly following the Swedish model, it was adamantly opposed by the unions: they insisted, instead, on extending existing union pension funds.[108] The fundamental difference in orientation explains why, at the request of the unions, all direct references to collaboration between party and unions were removed when the party statutes were revised in 1966.[109] Disagreements persisted in the 1970s, when, for example, the Social Democratic Party chose not to offer parliamentary support to union-inspired attempts to reform Switzerland's vocational training system.

The export of capital has further reinforced the Swiss unions' long-standing weakness. Direct foreign investment by Switzerland's multinational corporations and the more general export offensive of Swiss industry impose limitations on the unions. The implicit threat to withdraw operations from Switzerland is, of course, not to be discounted as a strong influence on union behavior simply because it is rarely stated explicitly. But of far greater importance is the moderation that the need for competitive prices for Switzerland's industrial exports imposes on wage demands at the level of the firm. The unions are wholehearted supporters of the present export strategy, which has brought their members great prosperity while severely limiting their leaders' margin of choice.[110] In the interest of maintaining Swiss adaptability in the face of rapid changes in the international economy, unions have not been averse to letting marginal firms go under because, until now, there has been no scarcity of jobs for laid-off Swiss workers. Dependence on world markets has forged ties between employers and workers—ties that, especially in times of economic crisis, blunt the edge of disputes in collective bargaining.

The weak position of the unions and the Social Democratic Party in

Switzerland's social coalition is illustrated by the fact that of the 82 extraparliamentary committees established between 1974 and 1976, union officials were appointed to only one-quarter the number of seats alloted to business; furthermore, not a single committee was chaired by labor officials.[111] The intricacies of Switzerland's electoral laws also tend to weaken the Left's political position. One electoral analysis concludes that in the seven federal elections held between 1931 and 1959, the Social Democratic Party was underrepresented in Parliament by about 7 percent while the Liberal Party (Liberal-demokratische Partei) was overrepresented by about 4 percent.[112] What sketchy evidence exists about senior civil servants suggests that socialists are dramatically few in number.[113]

In the rare cases where the Left attempts to challenge Switzerland's business community on key questions of economic policy, it normally encounters defeat. On the issue of codetermination, for example, the unions were decisively defeated in the 1970s. On the question of stricter bank regulations, which arose with a number of spectacular bank failures in the late 1970s, the Social Democratic Party succeeded only after considerable difficulties in collecting the hundred thousand signatures necessary to hold a referendum.[114] This weakness of Switzerland's labor movement can be illustrated with economic statistics. The relative share of Swiss labor in GDP is well below corresponding figures in any other OECD country and is the reason why, in sharp contrast with other industrial states, a strong secular trend favors capital's rather than labor's share.[115] Switzerland has seen a "de facto integration of Social Democracy and of the unions into a national consensus."[116] The threat of fascism and the Great Depression converted Switzerland's revolutionary socialist party to a social democratic party in 1935, when it dropped its demand for a dictatorship of the proletariat. Equally important, after 1945, when the communist unions had split from the SGB, the union leadership was free to pursue a "humanitarian social order" without nationalization of the means of production.[117] The unions today regard as secondary the question of whether this new social order will achieve its humanitarianism under the auspices of liberal capitalism or those of democratic socialism.

The weak position and conservative orientation of the unions are reflected in Switzerland's policies for employment, public expenditures, and social welfare. In sharp contrast to Austria, Switzerland pursues a strategy of adaptation on questions of employment that relies largely on its foreign workers. Although the total number of Swiss jobs had declined by 15 percent from the peak level of 1973, in

1980 Switzerland suffered a serious manpower shortage and enjoyed a 99.7 employment rate.[118] Traditionally, labor mobility to and from Switzerland has been very high, but, without the dramatic increase in the numbers of foreign workers, Switzerland's postwar economic fortunes would have been very different, especially in the 1960s and 1970s. Switzerland's industrial expansion, fueled by the insatiable demands of its export industries, led to an influx of more than a million foreign workers. These workers formed more than 17 percent of the total population and more than 30 percent of the active workforce at the peak of the boom, in the early 1970s.[119] Despite the political backlash from Switzerland's traditional Right, headed by James Schwarzenbach, the effects of worldwide stagflation, and a 28 percent reduction in the number of foreign workers between 1973 and 1977, Switzerland still has a much larger proportion of foreign workers than any other European country.[120]

Switzerland's first postwar recession, in the late 1940s, foreshadowed how it would deal with the prolonged recessions of the 1970s. Although plans for an extensive public works program were shelved, Switzerland avoided any serious unemployment problem by almost halving its foreign workforce, from 140,000 in 1947 to 75,000 in 1950.[121] Throughout the postwar period, unions and business agreed with the government's explicit policy to lay off foreign workers first. In the 1970s the system worked exactly as in the late 1940s. Through return migration, a ban on further hiring, and the expiration of contracts, that is, through what one observer has called "the play of market forces rather than coercion," about 250,000 foreign workers were eliminated from the Swiss workforce between 1973 and 1976, as compared to the 90,000 Swiss citizens who belonged to the secondary labor market.[122] Without relying on the harsh method of deportation and with only a few cancellations of work permits held by people already in Switzerland, this policy gave what a Swiss Federal Commission calls "decisive relief" from the pressures on labor markets.[123] Emil Küng calculates that "the level of unemployment would be well over ten percent if the departed foreign workers were counted as unemployed."[124] As one critical observer noted, given America's growing labor force and citizen workers who cannot be deported, Swiss-style employment policies would have produced a 1978 U.S. unemployment rate approaching 30 percent.[125] Paraphrasing William James, such critics might well conclude that the Swiss appear to have found their (im)moral equivalent of the welfare state.

On the question of foreign workers, union leaders have supported a policy that sharply constrains the unions' political choice.[126] Since only 10 percent of the SGB membership is composed of foreign workers (as compared to 50 percent in 1912, when "foreign" meant "German"), a large foreign workforce cuts the unions' presence in Switzerland's industrial workforce, as the 1970s illustrated, by 10 to 15 percent.[127] It is thus understandable that the SGB, in particular, has viewed the enormous growth of the foreign workforce since the mid-1950s with mixed feelings. In 1959 the SGB was the first major group in Switzerland to speak out in favor of an upper limit of 400,000 (at a time when the number of foreign workers had reached 450,000 in the summer season); and throughout the 1960s the unions always supported proposals that sought to diminish significantly the increasing number of foreign workers. While the focus of union concern shifted, especially among the rank and file, from job protection and the securing of welfare gains in the 1950s to the preservation of a distinct Swiss identity in the 1960s, it became increasingly clear to union leaders that the Swiss economy could no longer function without a very large, permanent foreign workforce. Confronted in the late 1960s by the popular Schwarzenbach proposal for a drastic across-the-board cut in the foreign workforce, the union leadership, like all other important interest groups and political elites, chose to support the government in opposing such demands. The result was a very serious conflict within the labor movement, which frequently became public. As a result membership resignations in the metalworkers union, for example, increased by as much as 50 percent. More recently, in 1981, the Social Democratic Party and the unions split, though in muted form, in a referendum campaign concerning the improvement of the status of seasonal workers. The party supported the referendum while the trade union federation did not take a stand. As François Höpflinger explains, "Many Swiss trade unionists feared for their own job security if control over foreign labor was removed to the extent proposed under the amendment."[128]

Only one-third of Switzerland's unskilled workforce is Swiss.[129] But it should also be noted that Switzerland depends heavily on attracting highly trained scientists, engineers, and technicians, who are indispensable to its export strategy. By any international standard Swiss university enrollment and expenditures on education are paltry. In 1959, for example, despite its enormous lead in research and technology, Switzerland lagged behind Austria in university enrollments; by the mid-1970s there had been little change.[130] Yet plans for university expansion, opposed vigorously by the business community, were voted down in 1978. Switzerland has thus chosen to rely heavily on foreign researchers. In the 1960s the number of foreign researchers moving to Switzerland sharply increased. In the late 1960s one-third of professional researchers had received their university degrees abroad, and more than 40 percent of Switzerland's engineers had been trained abroad and were in fact immigrants.[131] Switzerland is thus one of the few countries in Europe to have experienced a massive "brain gain."

Employment policy has created international pressures to which Switzerland has, to varying degrees, been forced to accommodate itself. Between 1946 and 1964 Switzerland's official policy was to rotate its foreign workforce. Because they affected so many Italian citizens, the severe discriminatory practices that were part and parcel of that rotation, especially in social and economic welfare rights, created tension in the relations between Switzerland and Italy. Now largely forgotten, for example, is the policy of requiring foreign workers to contribute to Switzerland's pension plan and accident insurance for at least five years before establishing their own eligibility, as compared with only one year for Swiss citizens. The 1964 bilateral agreement between Italy and Switzerland was the first of a series of agreements that assures foreign workers today of a legal status equal in most respects to that of Swiss citizens.[132] Not all discrimination, though, has been abolished. For example, income taxes for foreign workers, in contrast to Swiss citizens, are withheld at source. Several cantons do not subscribe to international conventions and still refuse to pay social assistance to needy foreign workers.[133] Moreover, Switzerland's treatment of its Italian seasonal workers, a "strategic pillar" of Swiss labor markets, continued to place a significant strain on the political relations between the two countries throughout the 1960s and 1970s.[134] In 1977 the Italian under-secretary for Foreign Affairs threatened to charge Switzerland with human rights violations at the Belgrade Conference.[135]

Foreign pressure is the lesser of two reasons that may reduce Switzerland's foreign workforce as an economic buffer in the 1980s. The greater reason is the growing proportion of foreign workers who have established permanent residence and are thus well protected against the possibility of deportation. The proportion of foreign workers who have lived in Switzerland for at least ten years increased from 10 percent in 1959, to 25 percent in 1965, 40 percent in 1970, and 70 percent in 1977.[136] It is therefore not surprising that in the spring of 1981 Swiss voters rejected by a margin of five to one a constitutional amendment that would have ended some of the harshest forms of legal discrimination against seasonal workers, the one segment of the foreign workforce that Switzerland can still use to adjust to changes in the world economy. Discrimination includes the requirement to leave Switzerland if unemployed, incomplete social security coverage, a prolonged prohibition on workers' being joined by other family members, and restrictions on changing jobs and places of residence while in Switzerland.[137]

Switzerland's inclination to compensate privately for adverse economic change reflects the relatively weak position of the unions and the political Left, and it is illustrated by a distinctive type of fiscal and welfare policy. In sharp contrast to Austria Switzerland did not attempt to offset the deflationary consequences of the two oil shocks and worldwide recession of the 1970s with an expansionary fiscal policy. Symptomatic of the Swiss attitude was the government's reaction to an unanticipated budget deficit in 1975. At the height of economic crisis, an emergency session of Parliament cut the public contribution to Switzerland's expanding public pension fund far more than any other government program. A proposed annual subsidy of $508 million was slashed by $209 million; the contributions of employers and employees were raised to make up the difference.[138] In addition the government reduced by 10 percent its support of private health insurance.

This exercise of fiscal restraint matches Switzerland's traditional preference that the government should play a minor role in the economy. But the economic and political pressures of the 1960s and 1970s have resulted, in Switzerland as elsewhere, in a bigger role for the public sector. Increasing demands for social infrastructure investment, which fell especially on cantonal and local governments, largely explain why the proportion of GNP spent by all levels of government in Switzerland increased from about 18 percent in 1960 to 22 percent in 1970, and 29 percent in 1976. During the same period total public-sector spending, including parapublic insurance schemes and nationalized firms, increased from 28 percent in 1960 to 34 percent in 1967, to 44 percent in 1976.[139] Because of the deep recession federal government subsidies increased from $1.01 billion and 28 percent of the federal budget in 1973 to $2.24 billion and 35 percent of the budget in 1976. Between 1947 and 1970 the federal government did not have to go to capital markets to finance its expenditures. But since 1971, it has regularly run budget deficits, and they have spurred intense political debate. By 1979 the total debt of the federal government was $10.22 billion, about 15 percent of GDP.[140]

Switzerland is thus not immune to pressures on the public purse. Yet in 1967–69 and in 1972–76 public spending was still lower than in any other small European state and ranked barely above the spending levels of the Japanese government.[141] Furthermore, compared to the high growth of central government expenditure between 1972 and 1974, the annual percentage change between 1975 and 1979 declined more drastically for social security and education than for any other budget item.[142] Servicing the public debt has not "crowded out" private investments in Switzerland's capital markets. And, since three-quarters of Switzerland's taxes are raised directly and are thus visible to a conservative electorate that enjoys the rights of a plebiscitarian democracy, budget deficits averaged only 0.7 percent of GNP, or $440 million, between 1973 and 1978.[143] Nevertheless, concern about the continued deficit in the federal budget had not abated in the late 1970s, and the federal government reduced its budget deficit substantially during the economic recession of the early 1980s.

During the last forty years, Switzerland's public sector has not increased uninterruptedly in relative size. In 1974 it was slightly larger than in 1939, smaller than in 1945, and larger than in the early 1960s.[144] The very limited role of the federal government's fiscal policy is illustrated by the three economic recovery programs that it adopted in 1975–76.[145] The collapse of Switzerland's oversized construction industry, and the sharp decline that the Swiss economy experienced more generally, prompted the government to spend about $800 million, which created a total of some 25,000 jobs in 1976 and 1977.[146] Compared to the 21,000 and 12,000, respectively, registered as unemployed in these two years, the size of the program might be considered generous; but the comparison is misleading. In its most serious and sustained economic crisis of the twentieth century Swiss industry lost close to 350,000 jobs in the mid-1970s: about one-fifth of its employment in industry and about one-tenth of all jobs in the economy. Almost two-thirds of lost jobs were held by foreign workers. The employment created through this program was of very modest size and was designed as such. The government hoped to increase real GDP by 2 percent in 1976 as compared to an actual decline of more than 7 percent.

Switzerland restricts government activities considered normal in Austria and elsewhere. The operation of Switzerland's employment stabilization fund reinforces this impression of government restraint. Established in 1951, the fund was used for the first time in 1975–76, to compensate for weak demand in industries particularly hard hit by the recession of the 1970s. Firms that had in good times invested a portion of their profits in government bonds were entitled to redeem them and to receive additional federal, cantonal, and local tax rebates amounting to $30 million. A report assessing the efficacy of the program judged the $160 million of investments thus created to be grossly insufficient to effect a stabilization of macroeconomic significance.[147] In sum, all the political signals in Switzerland point to continued fiscal frugality and government restraint, at least at the federal level. Far from prompting fundamental changes in orientation, the crisis of the world economy in the 1970s left untouched the Swiss commitment to policies indebted to the principle of private compensation.

Nowhere is this clearer than in the character of Switzerland's welfare state. Although they have expanded in the 1970s, Switzerland's publicly funded social welfare programs remain remarkably modest by Austrian standards. Instead, Switzerland has built a private social welfare state. Its private insurance system consists of a plurality of organizations in both the private and the public sector.[148] In the mid-1970s Switzerland had about 17,000 private insurance schemes with about 1.5 million members—about one-half of Switzerland's workforce.[149] Employers and employees jointly contribute 10 percent of the total wage bill to private insurance schemes, a figure that exceeds the mandatory 8.4 percent for the public pension plan. When, as part of the 1972 reform, this private insurance system was made an obligatory supplement to the public pension plan, the additional cost to employers and employees was a relatively low 2 percent. This indicated that the unregulated growth of the 1950s and 1960s had extended coverage (of variable quality) to about four-fifths of the Swiss workforce.[150]

Exempted from all federal taxes and enjoying substantial cantonal tax preferences, private insurance funds are important instruments of private capital formation. Private pension plans rely on a method of financing that differs from that of the public fund, and throughout the postwar years they have generated revenues roughly twice as large as expenditures.[151] In 1970 their assets were about thirty times as large as the pensions paid out.[152] In effect, these private insurance schemes are a form of forced savings. In 1976 alone expenditures amounted to $920 million, compared to $3.52 billion of revenues.[153] In the 1960s and 1970s the reserves of private insurance funds have had a major effect on Swiss capital markets.[154] Indeed, one study estimates their total savings over the next two decades to be $120 billion.[155] Individual firms also benefit from this system. Between the 1950s and the 1970s about one-third of private pension savings were granted as credits to companies, especially for long-term investment. In 1976 this amounted to $6.8 billion.[156] In the 1960s and 1970s it was common practice that employees changing jobs could not transfer the contributions that employers had made to the employee's private pension plan; employees' contributions were transferable, at times without interest payments.[157]

The private character of Switzerland's social welfare system is further reinforced by the great importance attached to individual savings. Several statistics illustrate the point. Between 1948 and 1969 personal savings increased four times as fast as per capita income. In 1973 the average balance in Swiss savings and deposit accounts was roughly twice as large as in the United States or West Germany. Fourteen percent of Swiss citizens own stocks and 28 percent own either stocks or bonds. Just under 30 percent of total insurance premiums are generated by individual insurance.[158] Indeed, the average Swiss buys more insurance than the citizen of any other country in the world, and in the late 1970s the Swiss spent a larger share of their income on insurance than on either food or education.[159]

In its high level of individual savings Switzerland ranks just behind Japan. This results from a long-standing and deliberate policy of trying to keep taxes low. In the mid- and late 1960s Swiss taxes were by far the lowest in small European states and hovered just above Japanese rates, and Switzerland's rate of taxation remains comparatively low today.[160] Low levels of taxation benefit business both directly and indirectly. Sizable individual savings permit, for example, the employer's share of total social security contributions to be lower (just under 50 percent) than that in any other advanced industrial state. Furthermore, one study shows a decline in the relative share that employers contributed to public welfare plans in the 1950s and 1960s. This, in turn, increases the profitability and competitiveness of Swiss firms, and indirectly facilitates increases in real wages. The share of taxes and social security contributions in the total wage bill is lower in Switzerland than in any advanced industrial country other than the United States and Canada.[161] In keeping with its emphasis on private-sector activity, Switzerland lost revenue from foregone corporation taxes to the level of 2.9 percent of GDP in 1975, a figure far higher than in any of the other six countries for which data are available.[162]

Compared to all other advanced industrial states Switzerland was a notable latecomer to publicly organized, compulsory social welfare policies. Compulsory social security legislation was introduced as late as 1947; disability insurance and unemployment insurance were only introduced in 1959 and 1977, respectively; proposals for a national health plan were voted down several times in the 1970s.[163] An index of social insurance coverage in the advanced industrial states shows Switzerland at the very bottom of the list in 1970; and the gap between it and other countries had widened between 1950 and 1970.[164] Comparisons of public social welfare expenditures in the advanced industrial states confirm the impression that Switzerland is a welfare "laggard" among its peers. According to one study, Switzerland's social security spending increased from 9.5 to 11.4 percent between 1966 and 1971; these figures were only about one-half of those for Austria, and they were substantially lower than for the larger European countries, ranking barely ahead of the United States and Japan.[165] Unlike Austria's public social welfare system, Switzerland's was originally designed only to provide a minimum level of existence. Since employee pensions and individual savings are the core of this "privatized welfare state," Switzerland, in sharp contrast to Austria, has an extremely small benefit program as a percentage of the final wage bill.[166] But the Swiss proudly point to the fact that in contrast with most other advanced industrial states the underlying philosophy of their public insurance is universal coverage, including the self-employed and, especially, those in agriculture, rather than a more selective coverage of blue-collar workers. Furthermore, the ratio between the maximum and the minimum pensions paid is a relatively low two-to-one, and there exist no upper limits for salary contributions to the public pension fund.[167] These indications of solidarity notwithstanding, Switzerland's system of public compulsory insurance in the early 1970s was modest in size and lagged behind similar systems in most other countries.

Compared to the size of private insurance schemes and the magnitude of individual savings, the importance of the public pension fund sharply increased in the 1970s.[168] But despite this increase, Switzerland's strategy of domestic compensation still relies on a social welfare policy that gives a particularly prominent place to the private sector. In general terms, Switzerland differs from other countries not so much in the magnitude of its total expenditure on social welfare as in its mode of financing. In the late 1970s between 18 and 25 percent (depending on the statistical definition) of Switzerland's net national product paid for social policy measures financed by public and private insurance systems.[169] A comparison with Sweden, the welfare state par excellence, leads to three interesting conclusions.[170] First, Switzerland lags somewhat, but not much, behind Sweden in the total expenditures of its public and private insurance systems. Second, the statistical difference reflected in the data would probably disappear if private savings were included in the comparison. Finally, compared with Sweden, Switzerland provides relatively more generous support for high-income categories than for average income levels. Switzerland may thus be said to be both a rich welfare state and, considering the importance of private savings, a welfare state for the rich. In sum, Switzerland's privately based social welfare state reflects a strong craving for security distinctive of Swiss society in general: "From cradle to grave the Swiss is insured against everything."[171]

POLITICAL INSTITUTIONS

Swiss policies and politics are shaped not only by particular social conditions—an internationally oriented business community and a conservative union movement—but by the form these coalitions take in the policy network. In Switzerland's system, relatively centralized and broadly based interest groups linked to institutions are effective in shielding the policy process from exogenous shocks. Although their numbers reach into the thousands, Swiss interest groups yield an orderly picture.[172] National organizations thoroughly penetrate economic life and converge in a small number of peak associations. In contrast to Austria, these groups, rather than political parties, are the decisive actors in policy making. Among the major reasons often cited are the groups' superior personnel and resources; their national (rather than cantonal or local) organization and outlook; and their prominence in the preparliamentary bargaining that shapes policy decisions. Group membership is broad; according to one public opinion survey, 68 percent of the respondents in the early 1960s belonged to an occupational association. That figure substantially exceeds the 15 to 20 percent of the electorate with party memberships.[173] In short, as Christopher Hughes says, "Swiss democracy is geared to pressure groups; it is a form of government calculated to call such groups into existence and give them power. The system could conceivably continue for a time without parties, but without pressure groups it would not work at all."[174]

On questions of the international economy, the Vorort is the most important peak association of Switzerland's business community. One knowledgeable observer of Swiss politics calls it "the strongest unofficial political force in Switzerland, and one which calls into question the whole working of Swiss democracy."[175] It is more than a normal pressure group trying to protect narrowly defined business interests. Instead, because of Switzerland's small size and exposed position in the international economy, the Vorort's stance on critical issues is distinguished by the fact that it considers the effects that particular policies would have on Switzerland's political and economic system as a whole. It focuses on policies that affect Switzerland's position in the international economy or relate to the general principles governing Switzerland's market economy. A staunch defender of economic liberalism, the Vorort opposes the protectionist tendencies of Switzerland's domestically oriented business community; it seeks to block most developments that would enhance the power of the state in economic policy; and it advocates a liberal and internationalist stance on questions of domestic and foreign economic policy.

In sharp contrast to the major business associations of most other European states, the Vorort is very centralized in representing the interests of both the secondary and the tertiary sectors of the economy. Even though its 108 sections reflect more than twenty diverse branches of the Swiss economy, the central staff that coordinates the Vorort's affairs is minimal, by any standard, and has remained the same size for the last forty years.[176] The great diversity of economic interests represented in the organization makes the formation of internal consensus, especially between business groups involved in the domestic and those in the international sectors of the economy, essential to the accomplishment of the Vorort's liberal objectives. Central political questions of the last two decades such as imported inflation, foreign workers, or European integration have often divided the business community deeply. Although we know very little about how consensus is reached within the organization, it is clear that, on virtually all questions, the Vorort has arrived at a workable compromise that it represents effectively in national politics. There are no contemporary analogues to the open dissension that immobilized the Vorort during the great tariff debates at the turn of the century. The reason for the Vorort's successful representation of business interests in Swiss politics probably lies in Switzerland's version of "democratic centralism": geographically diverse groups and different economic interests come to adhere to a common political position through frequent consultations within a centralized peak association. The importance of this type of representation is evident throughout Swiss politics. In contrast to the Vorort, for example, the Swiss Association of Small Business is not dominated by large firms; yet it, too, is very effective in organizing on a territorial basis the exports of Switzerland's numerous small and medium-sized firms.

The fact that the Vorort speaks for diverse segments of the business community gives its voice special weight in its relationship with other organized groups and with the federal bureaucracy. The Vorort's relations with the Federation of Swiss Employers' Organizations (Zentralverband Schweizerischer Arbeitgeberorganisationen) are excellent. By mutual agreement the federation focuses on questions of collective bargaining and social policy, but the Vorort retains a large informal influence. In contrast, disputes with organizations representing the domestically oriented segments of business, the Swiss Association of Small Business, and the Swiss Farmers' Union are at times heated.[177] Yet this is the only exception to a remarkably uniform and coherent pattern of institutionalized representation of business interests.

By way of contrast, the political structure of Swiss unions is marked by a much greater decentralization and much lower levels of concentration. In the early 1970s, besides the Swiss Federation of Trade Unions, one could count five other major unions with a total membership of about 270,000.[178] Not surprisingly, then, "Switzerland's employees lack a formally organized unity."[179] That lack of unity is clear within the SGB as well. The SGB is composed of sixteen industrial unions, but relations with its largest and most important constituent union, the metalworkers, are not free from conflict and less close than, for example, the relations between the West German Union Federation (Deutscher Gewerkschaftsbund) and its metalworkers union (IG Metall).[180] Three particular sources of organizational fragmentation can be noted. One is the split between the seven craft and eight industrial unions organized under the umbrella of the SGB. Although more than 90 percent of the SGB membership is organized in the eight industrial unions, the special character of Swiss industry (for example, its strength in highly specialized products and its vocational training system) makes the split between industrial and craft orientations more important in the decentralization of the SGB than the percentages might lead one to expect.[181] A second source is the split between blue- and white-collar unions in the private sector. Finally, the existence of denominational unions, particularly the large Swiss National Federation of Christian Trade Unions (Christlich-Nationaler Gewerkschaftsbund der Schweiz, CNG), has encouraged organizational fragmentation. For reasons of demography, the proportion of the unionized industrial workforce represented by the SGB declined from 85 percent in 1930 to 82 percent in 1950, and 77 percent in 1973, while corresponding figures for the CNG increased from 10 to 11 to 17 percent. An attempted merger of the two unions, initiated by the SGB, failed in 1963.[182]

But relations between the SGB and the CNG also illustrate that one should not overstate the organizational fragmentation of Swiss unions. Cooperation between these two major associations of labor, based on a mixture of solidarity and opportunism, has been close on many occasions. Furthermore, claiming partisan and religious neutrality, the SGB has become unquestionably the most important labor organization speaking out on national issues that affect Switzerland's entire labor force.[183] Moreover, the reduction in the number of unions organized under the umbrella of the SGB, from more than fifty in 1900 to sixteen in the 1970s, illustrates a long-term trend toward less fragmentation within the SGB.[184] Despite these countervailing tendencies, which are notable in comparison to the trade unions in several of the large industrial states, the organization of the Swiss labor movement must be judged fragmented in comparison to Switzerland's institutionally more unified business community, as well as in comparison to Austria's centralized trade union.

The Swiss state is distinguished by a decentralization characteristic of neither business nor unions. The strict separation of powers stipulated in Switzerland's constitution is observed in practice; in a system distinguished by its political elite's accumulation of roles there is virtually no overlap in personnel between Parliament and the executive branch of government. In contrast with Austria, members of the Federal Council (Bundesrat) are forbidden to hold offices simultaneously in major interest groups.[185] In the formulation and implementation of policy the government must take full account of the cantons and of interest groups. If it does not secure at least tacit support for its policies in these diverse quarters, its policy is always open to challenge at the polls. Generally, the government's resources and institutional capacities are very limited. Even if a controversial bill were to be passed in the Federal Assembly, it could often not be implemented without the assistance of the centers of power outside government. The decentralization of Switzerland's state institutions, especially in comparison with those in Austria, is extreme. With some justification, therefore, Switzerland has been characterized as a "prescription for central non-government."[186]

This prescription is reinforced by an executive, the Federal Council, which embodies the principles of administrative efficiency rather than of partisan politics. Two institutional practices illustrate this depoliticization of the executive. First, the seven members of the government serve in a dual capacity as elected political heads of their departments and simultaneously as senior civil servants.[187] Second, the federal counselors do not indicate in public the position they have individually taken on political issues; and they refrain from open criticism of decisions reached jointly.[188] Swiss practice stands the British doctrine of the collective responsibility of the cabinet on its head: secrecy has become the trademark not of a partisan but of an administrative type of executive politics.

The encroachment of bureaucratic habits and norms into the arena of executive politics illustrates the neutralization of state power rather than the existence of a powerful civil service. The federal bureaucracy lacks officially sanctioned career patterns and the guarantee of lifetime employment, and it observes the dictates of a linguistic *Proporz*. Compared with that in Japan or in Britain, the professional civil service is not strongly united by common social background, training, or outlook.[189] Indeed, because of the closely knit character of Switzerland's political elite in general, the absence of a cohesive state elite is particularly striking. In a country totally averse to doctrines of statism, the civil service has very limited resources and information. Instead it relies heavily on the cooperation of organized groups. With good reason the Swiss insist that the "Vorort in Zurich sets the switches for the government in Bern" *(Im Züricher Vorort werden die Weichen für Bern gestellt).*

Switzerland's federal bureaucracy is relatively small (32,000) and the rate of increase since 1945 has been comparatively slow.[190] It compensates for its small size through a "militia" system of dispersed administration, which primarily relies for expertise and administrative capacity on the major interest groups and individuals. Because it leaves so many tasks, especially on questions of economic and social policy, to the major economic interest groups, it risks turning "into a series of guild-like fiefs."[191] In 1977, for example, there existed a total of 834 government committees; 334 of these were extraparliamentary commissions, staffed, in the majority, by outsiders. For every one of the 4,000 higher or middle-level civil servants with academic training on one of the 334 advisory committees, there existed a seat for an outside "expert."[192]

Switzerland's direct democracy restricts the exercise of power by the federal government. In 1977 and again in 1979, for example, the government's effort to adopt a value-added tax was defeated by referendum. If compared to provincial or local authorities, Switzerland's federal government receives the lowest share of tax revenues among all the OECD countries, be they unitary or federal—29 percent, as compared to an OECD average of 58 percent. As a result, the implementation of policy typically involves complex bargaining between different levels of government.[193]

The weakness of the Swiss state is reflected in its relations with the Nationalbank and the private banking system. The Nationalbank is virtually free from government interference in its monetary policy, and this autonomy puts it in the delicate position of mediating relations between the government and the financial community. Yet in this position the Nationalbank can rely on few of the instruments of monetary policy that are standard equipment for other central banks. Changes in the discount rate are largely ineffective because drafts are rarely used in Switzerland; normally the discount rate is a "passive" policy instrument, which may, at best, have some "psychological" effect. In its open market policy the Nationalbank is severely restricted because Switzerland's government debt excludes short-term notes. Furthermore, because the Nationalbank lacks the legal basis for imposing a minimum reserve requirement to expand or contract the money supply, it regulates the money supply through interventions in foreign-exchange markets.[194] In the absence of most of the formal instruments of policy, the Nationalbank has relied on informal "gentlemen's agreements," fifteen in all between 1927 and 1970.[195] Most of these agreements have dealt with the question of how to control the influx of foreign funds fueling the flames of inflation. Although there havebeen occasional sources of conflict and tension—including debates over the monitoring of capital exports—the Nationalbank has, through its "subtle and restrained" exercise of power, by and large succeeded in arriving at informal compromises.[196] And the power of the Nationalbank has been greatly enhanced by the system of floating exchange rates, to a point in the late 1970s where its management of the Swiss franc in international capital markets became vastly more important than any business-cycle policy that the government might devise.

Formal political supervision of Swiss banks is weak. The Banking Commission (Eidgenössische Bankenkommission) is independent of the government. Although the commission's position has been strengthened somewhat in the 1970s, its ineffective supervision of Switzerland's six hundred banks has been attested to, for example, by the scandal surrounding the Crédit Suisse in 1977 and the closing of the Banque Leclerc in 1978.[197] But even these spectacular episodes left the banks' operations largely untouched by political intervention. Musing about the political implications of these incidents, one Zurich official expressed a widespread consensus: "Well, it doesn't mean that banks are going to lose any of their freedom. It just puts a limit on how far they can go."[198] In early 1982 the Banking Commission ruled that in the future Swiss banks had to disclose in their balance sheets the extent to which they have drawn on hidden assets to absorb losses; another banking official viewed this as a typical Swiss compromise.

"You still can have hidden reserves, but you no longer can have hidden losses."[199] In any case, whatever formal supervision may exist is much less important than the informal relations tying the private banks to the Nationalbank. Private ownership of the Nationalbank makes it unique among the central banks of the advanced industrial states. The bank operates under some political controls and returns a part of its earnings in the form of dividend payments to the cantons and to private shareholders.[200] Its board of directors is under the supervision of a system of commissions controlled by both the banks and the government. This inner circle of power has been viewed by one observer "as a financial *Gemeinde* [commune] where citizenship devolves on the managers of companies whose balance sheets are larger than SFr. 500 million."[201] The self-regulation of the Swiss banking community illustrates the weakness of the Swiss state.

POLICY PROCESS

Switzerland relies on a policy process that prizes the coordination of conflicting objectives through uninterrupted political bargaining in the policy network. This feature of Swiss everyday politics is so noteworthy that the country has been characterized as moving since 1945 from a "voting democracy" *(Abstimmungsdemokratie)* to a "bargaining democracy" *(Verhandlungsdemokratie)*.[202] Although the scope of the policy process is broad, it excludes questions of investment and employment which are left to the discretion of business, and of free collective bargaining between business and unions. Furthermore, the restraint with which the state intervenes in economic and social issues facilitates a policy process that primarily centers around the reconciliation of different group interests; trade-offs across issues are normally left implicit.

Switzerland's move to a "bargaining democracy" among groups was decisively strengthened by the power that the "Economic Articles" of the Federal Constitution conferred in 1947 upon Swiss interest groups. This constitutional innovation extended legal recognition to the great power that economic groups had accumulated during the Depression and World War II, when they were entrusted with a growing number of public tasks. All groups likely to be affected must be consulted prior to a change in legislation, and the government can rely on them in the process of implementation. For the unions, in particular, the Economic Articles represented a vitally important recognition of their public role *(Ordnungsfunktion)*. The effect of the

Economic Articles has been to move the decisive arena in which policy choices are fashioned away from deliberations in parliamentary committees and the government's emergency powers. Instead, center stage is given to a pre- and extraparliamentary formation of consensus between interest groups, including the unions, and the state bureaucracy.[203]

Consensus forms at the levels both of policy formulation and of policy implementation. Although procedures vary from case to case, the initial drafting of a bill is typically done under the auspices of the Federal Council by the appropriate department or by a working committee that draws on several departments of the federal government. The federal bureaucracy often receives assistance in its work from specially convened expert committees, which reflect the interests of the groups most affected by the bill, or through informal consultation with these same groups. In other words the initial proposal of the bureaucracy normally reflects or anticipates the political position of the main protagonists; typically, it does not reflect an independent position of the state.

Cantonal governments and the relevant interest groups are then invited to a second round of consensus formation, in which the original legislative proposal is revised and elaborated. So-called "expert commissions" are typically created on an ad hoc basis to consider the initial legislative proposal. The years between 1970 and 1977, for example, saw the establishment of two hundred advisory commissions. In sheer numbers the federal and the cantonal governments dominate the composition of these commissions, but members of the affected interest groups and outside experts are also well represented.[204] All those represented share in the inclination to conceal these commissions' political nature. Interest groups often put intense political pressure on the government in order to get the "neutral" expert of their choice appointed. These "miniature Parliaments of interest groups" have the essential political purpose of providing a commonly accepted data base and framework for analysis.[205] The fact that they manage to do so in a technocratic language that depoliticizes issues is the distinctive trait of a state grounding its policies in a broad consensus about basic political choices.

The third step in the formulation of policy is the "consultation" *(Vernehmlassung)* mandated by the Economic Articles of 1947, which submits the consensus reached in the expert commission to a more public test. Consultation takes the form of direct testimony and the submission of written statements, in which the large economic associations are heavily represented. Between October 1969 and June 1971, for example, the government initiated thirty-five consultations. The biggest interest groups were involved in between 20 and 27 of these consultations, while more than 300 other groups were only consulted between one and four times.[206] The government's overt purpose is to obtain further information and to elicit the views of the private sector; but its covert and more important political purpose typifies the "bargaining" form of democracy that has emerged in postwar Switzerland. The large interest groups rely on the implicit threat of challenging proposed federal legislation through a popular referendum should their wishes not be adequately reflected in the final version of the bill submitted to Parliament. The political power that all of the major interest groups exercise as well as the prominence accorded to consultation have prompted one observer to dub these groups issue-specific "economic shadow cabinets" of the private sector.[207]

The final draft of the legislation is revised once more by the relevant department or by a working committee of several ministries to reflect the new consensus that has emerged during consultations. The Federal Council then submits the final bill to Parliament, where it is considered and debated by the appropriate committee within each House or a specially created ad hoc committee. Even at this stage the important interest groups are present. Their spokesmen in parliamentary hearings act either as "delegated representatives" (if employed on a full-time basis by their organization) or, more typically, as "interested intermediaries" (if serving the organization in a part-time or honorific capacity). Upon reaffirmation of the policy consensus in parliamentary committee, the full House votes on the bill clause by clause. Generally speaking, the early stages in the formation of consensus are of decisive importance, especially the initial drafting of the proposal and its first discussion in expert commission. Relying on different sources of data, two studies reach the conclusion that Parliament makes no changes, or only minor changes, in 80 percent of the bills that it considers.[208]

The implementation of policy offers a second expression of the Swiss penchant for consensus building through policy. Characteristic of Switzerland's "militia system of administration" (*Milizverwaltung*) is the large number of administrative commissions associated with particular departments; these commissions are very active in implementing and supervising policy. The Department of Economic Affairs alone is reported to have had more than sixty such advisory committees in 1961.[209] In 1977 more than four-fifths of the 834 advisory commissions established at the federal level were permanent; many of them were involved in implementing policy. Of equal importance are the standing commissions of the federal government. Very few detailed analyses of this complex system exist; one such study admits that the number of committees cannot be clearly ascertained. Estimates in the early 1970s ranged from "more than 200" to "more than 400."[210] The standing commissions provide the government with information and advice on a continuous basis, and offer a convenient forum for discussion. Representation on these commissions is heavily skewed in favor of the big interest groups—agriculture, small business, labor, and industry—and rules regarding representation are carefully spelled out. They include what groups will be represented and how many delegates each group is permitted to send. In many instances standing commissions are composed on a "parity" basis with equal numbers of representatives of labor and employers (agriculture, small business, and industry). Only ten interest groups held seats on more than six of the one hundred sixty commissions that one analyst counted in the late 1960s.[211] Although the deliberations of the standing commissions cover a wide range of technical and broad political issues, the experts serving on them, often key officials in interest groups and professional associations, stress the technical, nonpolitical nature of the commissions' work.[212]

The elaborate way in which a lasting consensus on questions of public policy is established remains open to challenge by the institutions of direct democracy. Those institutions, however, have at the same time been fundamentally affected by the process of consensus formation. There exist two different types of popular referenda, compulsory (*obligatorisch*) and optional (*fakultativ*).[213] All changes in the constitution, extraconstitutional emergency decrees, popular initiatives, and certain types of international treaties are subject to the compulsory referendum; they *must* be submitted to a popular vote. All legislative proposals, general federal decrees, or constitutional emergency decrees are subject to the optional referendum; they *may* be submitted to a popular vote, if a certain number of citizens or cantons so requests within a given period of time.

Since the end of World War II, the importance of Switzerland's direct democracy in the formation of consensus has varied. At no time have popular referenda been supplanted by interest-group bargaining. For example, on questions such as foreign workers or the size of the government's budget, the original intent of direct democracy, popular control over government, has been preserved. Typically, though, the threat to challenge proposed legislation through the referendum, rather than the referendum itself, has become the critical bargaining chip for every group representative.[214] Between 1971 and

1978, for example, all issues that had been resolved through a genuine compromise among the leaders of the main interest groups were accepted at the polls; all other proposals made subject to popular approval were voted down.[215]

Dubbed by Max Imboden the "*malaise helvétique*," an increasing political apathy of the voting public has mirrored the growth of complex political bargaining and compromise that gradually replaced the traditional mixture of rule by emergency decree, popular referendum, and inertia. For example, nine referenda were held in 1952; only one was held fifteen years later. Between 1945 and 1959 a total of 59 referenda was held, as compared with 26 between 1960 and 1969; over the same two periods the annual average declined from 4.1 to 2.6.[216] Furthermore, despite this drop in the number of referenda, voter turnout declined from 54 percent between 1945 and 1959 to 43 percent in 1960–67. At the same time, the electorate's acceptance rate increased from 42 to 62 percent.[217] Previously, the referendum had been a potential stumbling block for the government's policy initiatives. In the 1960s that picture changed: only two government proposals subject to a compulsory referendum were rejected by the voters, and in revised form both were eventually passed.[218]

In the 1970s, however, when economic and social problems became more pressing, the groups' bargaining strategy of relying on the threat of referendum has produced some conspicuous failures. For example, on critically important questions involving regional planning, fiscal policy, codetermination, federal security forces, taxation, and health insurance, no compromise capable of withstanding the challenge of a popular vote was reached; voters rejected all of these major legislative proposals. Furthermore, compared with the annual average of 2.6 proposals (compulsory and optional referenda) on which the electorate had voted in the 1960s, the 8.3 average between 1970 and 1978 reversed the decline. This dramatic threefold increase in absolute numbers, from 26 to 75, reveals the limits of consensus through interest-group bargaining. While voter turnout declined slightly, from 43 percent in 1960–69 to 42 percent in 1970–78, the electorate's acceptance rate of government proposals dropped from 62 to 49 percent. The federal government has been encroaching in one issue after another upon the traditional, constitutionally mandated prerogatives of the cantons; hence, the number of issues subject to compulsory referendum has increased more sharply—from 5 (19 percent of the total) in 1960–69 to 21 (28 percent) in 1970–78—than government legislation subject to optional referendum—up from 8 (31 percent) in 1960–69 to 12 (16 percent) in 1970–78. In sum, in the

1970s Switzerland's political elites were straining harder to achieve a workable consensus on major policy questions. With increasing frequency they found the consensus they had reached challenged and overturned at the polls.[219]

Direct democracy has been used both defensively, as an obstacle to change, and offensively, as an instrument of change. Defensively, it has permitted shifting coalitions of conservative forces to prevent the delegation of political instruments to the political leadership in Bern. For example, in the 1950s and 1960s parliamentarians in Bern favored more government intervention in the economy by overwhelming majorities, while fewer than 50 percent of Swiss voters tended to support such measures.[220] In the 1970s, direct democracy has been used offensively by political outsiders and ad hoc groups to register their disapproval of unsolved problems stemming from Switzerland's political and economic successes in the 1950s and 1960s.[221] Significantly, political opposition has not come from the unions; they have been fully integrated into the pre- and extraparliamentary process by which consensus is built. Still, a growing number of political actors has, in the 1970s, seized on direct democracy as a potent weapon to combat Switzerland's consensual political elites. These actors have forced a growing reliance on rule by emergency decree.

The institution of direct democracy has thus both facilitated and impaired consensual policy making. Switzerland's slow but effective method of establishing a policy consensus is purchased at the cost of political immobility and a lack of policy innovation by the federal government.[222] The growing strains of the 1970s suggest that in the 1980s it will take considerable political skill to maintain the delicate balance between the "technical success and political backwardness" that characterize public policy making in Switzerland.[223] At the same time Switzerland's referendum democracy has forced innovative policies on some crucial issues, such as the nuclear law. And it has helped to defuse the political explosiveness the issue acquired in more centralized domestic structures such as Austria's.[224]

Although serious, these challenges have so far not succeeded in displacing Switzerland's established way of making policy. The search for consensus is elaborate and occurs in many arenas. In fact on any important question, a minimum of consensus between the head of the relevant federal department and the groups most affected is necessary to start the decision sequence.[225] Although the sequence of policy debate is not formally fixed, the various group consultations shape the version of the bill that the federal department in charge will eventually send to Parliament. The central feature of this complex process of political bargaining is the fact that all the interested groups are directly represented at every site of the policy debate and at every stage of the process; group representatives and bureaucrats argue with one another again and again until a workable and acceptable compromise has been reached.

LIBERAL CORPORATISM AND POLITICAL PARTIES

Distinctive of Switzerland's domestic structure is the "cooperative regulation of conflict" between business and labor, between internationally and nationally oriented segments of business, between industry and finance, and between industry and agriculture.[226] Because of the opportunities extended by the liberalization of the international economy since the late 1950s, Switzerland has shifted away from the state-centered corporatist arrangements of the 1930s and 1940s toward a liberal corporatism. This liberal corporatism integrates all important political actors and sources of potential opposition, diffuses conflict, and compensates for the lack of policy instruments in the hands of government. As Paul Hofmann claims, "The people who really count in this country are a few hundred men who know one another, having gone to the same schools and served in the same army units. They may belong to different political parties or competing firms or interest groups, but there is a basic consensus among them to defend the status quo."[227] Very few national associations, perhaps as few as five, constitute the inner core of Switzerland's corporatism. In Hanspeter Kriesi's words, "For Switzerland it is indeed true that (almost) everybody cooperates with (almost) everybody."[228] Since consensus is fashioned in numerous arenas with multiple access points, groups typically lack an overall institutional strategy and let ad hoc decisions or short-term tactical considerations determine their behavior.[229] Uncertainty about who is, and who is not, wielding power on a particular issue is one of Switzerland's trademarks. Because of this uncertainty, Jürg Steiner notes, "Swiss decision situations are not a kind of summit conference of representatives from specific segments of society."[230] Switzerland is thus an infertile ground for the more centralized political consultation that distinguishes Austria's social corporatism. Yet despite the differences in form in the two countries, both corporatist arrangements are compatible with an extraordinary degree of political collaboration.

The leaders of the Swiss business community are intimately linked to the political elites and are actively involved in the conduct of Switzerland's economic policies. Even a company as global in outlook as Nestlé takes great interest in Swiss affairs. In 1974 that company's chief executive officer took a seat on the Banking Council, which, at least nominally, supervises the Nationalbank; and in 1975 he was appointed by the Federal Council as a member of the Swiss Commission for Foreign Trade Policy.[231] It was therefore not entirely unexpected that a group of shareholders would publicly object in 1981 to Nestlé's plan to appoint a West German national to run the company. They wrote that "Nestlé enjoys an extraordinary and privileged position in Switzerland. It is thus inconceivable—in the long term—that Swiss nationals shouldn't assume the chairmanship or the post of managing director."[232] Although their demand attracted little support, the company's new chairman, chosen in 1982, was Swiss.

The links between public and private spheres are numerous. About one-half of the politically most important actors in the 1970s had worked in both the public and the private sector.[233] As Hughes argues, "The officer corps of Switzerland's army constantly refreshes the contacts of Swiss elites from all walks of life. Many leading civil servants keep open the possibility of joining Swiss corporations at least some time in their career, a system made possible by the renewable four-year contracts rather than appointment for life of Switzerland's civil service. . . . Federal Councillors retire willingly to a governing board of big industry."[234] Students of Swiss politics have many names for this system of collaborative policy making, interpreted here as a particular form of corporatism: concordance system, bargaining democracy, *Proporz* rule, amicable agreement, consociationalism. The doctrine of limited government finds its embodiment in a centralization of power within participatory institutions that cultivate compromise.[235]

A clear institutional manifestation of Switzerland's corporatist structure is the Federal Council, an all-party government that included one member of the Social Democratic Party between 1943 and 1953, and two since 1959. "On election night, the TV-networks cannot declare *the* winner of the election because the election is not structured in such a way that there would be a clear winner or loser at the national level."[236] There exist no procedures such as no-confidence votes in Parliament or national referenda to bring down a government. The widespread institutional practice of proportional representation *(Proporz)* of religious, linguistic, and regional groups also extends, albeit in modified form, to economic interest groups. On economic and social issues Switzerland is distinguished by a distaste for adversarial politics and competitive decision making. Instead, the typical mode is consensual. That consensus does not take the form either of an "amicable agreement" among a few leaders or of majority rule.[237] Instead, "decision by interpretation" is based on a mixture of the counting of heads and the weighing of status characteristic of what one knowledgeable observer has called a "hierarchical decision pattern with a strong manipulative element."[238]

The coalition that Switzerland's four main political parties have formed in the federal executive for the last twenty-five years has distinctive sociological and electoral underpinnings. Switzerland's cultural diversity divides organized group life along religious, ethnolinguistic, and regional lines. It has prevented a Left-Right continuum from emerging as the central axis for political conflict.[239] By any objective measure, Switzerland exceeds all small European states in its religious diversity, and it is a close second to Belgium in its ethnolinguistic diversity.[240] Cultural diversity encourages a regional fragmentation in Swiss politics, which has resulted in a strong tradition of localism. But because the demographic characteristics of a people do not determine their perceptions, cultural diversity is, as Jürg Steiner and his associates have noted, not the same as subcultural segmentation.[241] On this a large number of studies all point to the same conclusion: the political effects of Switzerland's cultural diversity are mitigated by a complex pattern of cross-cutting cleavages.[242] Subcultural identification, including the identification of workers, is weakened by the fact that linguistic divisions cut across religious, class, and regional lines. Thus Switzerland's social structure, in contrast with that of Austria, is characterized by horizontal rather than vertical segmentation; and Switzerland's subcultural groups, compared with those of the Netherlands and Belgium, also seem less divided.[243]

Several other factors inhibit ideological conflict through a weakening of the power of political parties. Swiss federalism weakens the development of overarching loyalties such as a national or a class consciousness, and instead, reinforces a strong particularism. Political actors coalesce in inconsistent majorities on issues that are often either unique to particular parts of the country or perceived differently within them.[244] It does not matter for the purpose of this argument whether the boundaries between different subcultures are vague or sharp;[245] Swiss localism and federalism are not conducive to the emergence of a class-based politics at the national level.

Furthermore, it is a general axiom of Swiss politics that power does not reside in Parliament. Underpaid and understaffed, Swiss members of Parliament meet only during four three-week sessions each year.[246] The principal concerns of members of Parliament often lie in cantonal and local affairs rather than in the issues of national politics. Moreover, parliamentarians typically sit and act as representatives of pressure groups. In the late 1960s almost two-thirds of the two hundred members of Parliament, as compared to only one-half in Austria, were working either full-time or part-time for various interest groups.[247] Their presence may explain why Parliament has more than twenty economic and professional interest-group caucuses, which cut across party lines.[248]

But quite apart from the impotence of Parliament and its permeation by interest groups, Switzerland's political parties are weakened by their lack of ideological coherence and by the tradition of direct democracy. Political parties lack ideological coloration because they only get involved in the deliberation of policy at a relatively late stage, when all that remains is to ratify a consensus that has already formed.[249] Since parties have to appeal to the extraordinarily diverse constituencies that make up the Swiss electorate, they typically mute any emphasis on ideology.[250] Finally, Switzerland's system of direct democracy expresses the political issues of the day.[251] The permanent state of electoral mobilization at all levels of government has mitigated against a centralized party organization. And, to the extent that some of the referenda and initiatives of the last two decades have taken on the character of single-issue movements separate from organized partisan politics, they have reinforced an atrophy of political parties that in other countries has only recently become a source of widespread concern. As Jonathan Steinberg observes, "The plebiscitarian component of Swiss democracy thus results in a total politicization of Swiss politics which leads to its opposite, a lifelessness in daily politics and indifference to it."[252]

Yet underneath the consensual surface and prosperity of Switzerland's politics lurks the split between Left and Right. On religious and linguistic issues subcultural segmentation is weakening. But this is not true among the young for issues relating to social class.[253] Switzerland's class cleavage now generates virtually all of the central issues in Swiss politics, with the one exception of the political status of the Jura. To the extent that parties merge with their ancillary interest groups in Swiss politics, the notable alliance is that which ties ethnically or religiously based unions to their respective parties. Finally, in the perceptions of Swiss voters the parties of the Left still have a distinct anti-establishment image.

The scope of Switzerland's liberal corporatism is broad. It probably covers a wider array of issues than do comparable collaborative arrangements in Austria. At the same time, though, the character of

Switzerland's dominant social coalition has largely removed from the agenda of collaborative consultation and decision making those issues thought to be the unrestricted prerogative of business in a capitalist economy: investment and employment. On this point the difference with Austria could not be greater. The Swiss are often full of pride about the consensual style of their system of governance and the political stability of their institutions, which rest on a far-reaching depoliticization of economic issues. At the same time the Swiss are not particularly eager to recognize that underneath their corporatist arrangements there continue to exist economic and political tensions rooted in the capitalist nature of Swiss society. Indeed, to the Swiss the very term capitalism connotes intense conflict, a conflict that liberal corporatism, they argue, has succeeded in diffusing.

Alternatives Foregone

Policies that across the Austrian border have been central to how a system of social corporatism copes with change have not taken hold in Switzerland. This difference between two forms of democratic corporatism can be traced clearly in the areas of employment and incomes policy, which illustrate political possibilities not pursued in Switzerland's system of liberal corporatism.

Switzerland's domestic employment policy is rudimentary. The recent history of the Swiss unemployment insurance system illustrates the point. Two decades of prosperity and overemployment in the 1950s and 1960s explain why the construction of a partial social welfare state excluded compulsory unemployment insurance at the federal level. By the early 1970s only one-sixth of Switzerland's employees was covered by unemployment insurance. Moreover, in the mid-1970s the federal government was refused the right to conduct a more active manpower policy focused on retraining. Effective protection against structural readjustment, a government spokesman concluded, simply could not be fashioned politically "unless an economic crisis accelerates matters."[254]

In 1975–76 labor markets contracted with a rapidity that exceeded even the disastrous downturn of 1931–32.[255] The economic effects of that contraction could not be restricted to the stock of migrant workers and Switzerland's secondary labor market; some of the impact was also felt by the indigenous, unionized Swiss workforce. For example, in 1974 Switzerland's largest industrial union, the metalworkers, paid 202 recipients $42,967 in union unemployment compensation; in

1975 the union had to support 30,000 recipients at a cost of $14.7 million. These figures roughly parallel the reported increase in Switzerland's unemployment, from 111 persons in 1974 to over 33,000 in 1976. The government quickly increased the per diem rate of support and extended the period of eligibility for receiving payment.[256] Such provisional government measures afforded the necessary breathing space for rapidly developing and accepting an obligatory unemployment insurance scheme at the federal level. It came into effect in 1977 and, for the first time, required financial contributions from individual firms. Although Switzerland's tight labor markets have concealed the fact from many, the Swiss government values security, especially job security, and thus social stability. Mass unemployment both after World War I and in the 1930s left an indelible mark on the country's collective memory. Thus the threat of widespread unemployment remains the one trigger that could quickly enlarge the federal government's limited role in the area of social welfare. For the time being, though, Switzerland's strategy of international adaptation makes this improbable. Because Switzerland's full employment was largely maintained through its strategy of global adaptation, the fund accumulated $1.5 billion in reserves over the next four years; in 1980–81 contributions were reduced from 0.8 to 0.3 percent of the wage bill.[257]

Because the Swiss union movement will not trade a stronger position in labor markets for a weaker position in politics, it has adamantly opposed any curtailing of free collective bargaining. As a result, Switzerland has no incomes policy. After the devaluation of the franc in 1936, the government threatened to pursue a strict incomes policy by arbitrating wage disputes; in 1937 employers and unions in the metals and watchmaking industries signed a widely celebrated Peace Agreement, Switzerland's version of the "historic compromise."[258] For the government this was a calculated move toward strengthening corporatist arrangements; for business it was a tactically motivated compromise to ward off what it perceived as government pressure for legally binding contracts; for the unions it brought de facto recognition of their role in collective bargaining equal to that of business; finally, for the country as a whole it introduced a system for settling wage disputes that would eventually spread to virtually all industrial sectors. Although it lacked legal force, the frequently implied stipulation of a "peace obligation" *(Friedenspflicht)* to all intents and purposes eliminated strikes and lockouts. Instead, a multitiered system of arbitration between employers and unions excludes the government and handles virtually all disputes at the level of the plant or the industrial sector. A generation of prosperity and full employment has since diminished the importance of Switzerland's system of collective bargaining. Swiss industrialists and workers are satisfied with their peaceful labor relations; Swiss strike statistics are among the lowest in the world.[259] Switzerland's workers became an army that never marched.

For a variety of reasons industry-wide collective bargaining agreements (Gesamtarbeitsverträge), covering about two-thirds of the industrial workforce in the 1960s and 1970s, offer a misleading picture of centralization.[260] Collective bargaining is decentralized, and any trend toward national-level bargaining has remained stalled because agreements during the last three decades have only provided a "floor"; plant-level agreements add substantial benefits. A generation of labor scarcity has led to a dramatic narrowing of wage differentials in labor markets, thus making unnecessary a centrally coordinated campaign in favor of wage solidarity.[261] The national unions are only weakly represented at the plant level, and their position is not helped by the de facto indexation of wages to the cost of living as a notable feature of Swiss collective bargaining. Decentralization is due not only to the regional and linguistic diversity of the country but also to the fact that the employers' organization has preferred, with the consent of the unions, a large number of collective bargaining arenas in order to maintain the economic flexibility and adaptability of the economy.[262] Compared with statistics from West Germany, for example, the number of contracts in the Swiss metals industry is disproportionately large; a sizable number of agreements are concluded at the level of the plant. In striking contrast with the peak association of the business community, the Vorort, the employers' association is decentralized to such an extent that it leaves complete autonomy to its different branch organizations.[263] The union federation thus features a corresponding decentralization in its collective bargaining jurisdiction. Such decentralization prevents the unions from broadening their influence to other areas of policy. Yet despite these numerous impediments, the unions remain firmly committed to autonomous negotiations with employers. These negotiations guarantee and reaffirm union power; they assure greater adaptability to economic change; and they have succeeded in substituting "industrial peace" for "industrial armistice."[264]

Only once in Switzerland's postwar history, in 1948–49, was there a faint chance that an incomes policy might have superseded free collective bargaining in the interest of Switzerland's competitiveness in world markets.[265] But the experiment collapsed when the unions, because of their political weakness, refused to accept the extension of a temporary wage freeze. Since then, in times of inflationary pressures, Switzerland has largely relied on an ineffective system of price supervision. Such a system was, for example, retained after 1949 because price supervision was then facilitated by the prevalence of cartels. In the early 1950s, "a free price [was] the exception in the Swiss economy."[266] After another failure to establish an incomes policy in 1957, the accelerating inflation of the early 1960s was met first by the recommendation of self-restraint by the peak business association and, when that effort failed, in part because of the exclusion of the unions, by government measures affecting, in particular, the construction and banking industries. In 1972 the government once again sought to curb inflation; it proposed five emergency measures, including a supervision of prices later amended by Parliament, for symbolic reasons, to supervise wages and profits as well. Reluctant to give up their strong position in Switzerland's tight labor markets, the unions again strongly objected. A constitutional amendment debated at length and finally ratified, in modified form, by popular referendum deleted all references to wage and price supervision or control. With the lapsing of price supervision in 1978, three decades of intermittent inflationary pressures had witnessed the failure of four attempts to create an institutional machinery for an incomes policy.

Switzerland's economic and political success lies in the capacity to combine economic flexibility with political stability. The international economy contributes significantly to Switzerland's success. Without the option of sending home a quarter of a million foreign workers, Switzerland in the 1970s would have experienced an unemployment rate in excess of 10 percent and a political crisis of very large proportions. At the same time Switzerland's success rests on a policy network that mobilizes consent for coping with change. Interest groups that rely on Switzerland's direct democracy, rather than parties, the state bureaucracy, or the government, are central to the perpetual reaffirmation of this political consensus.

The efficiency with which they have organized their Alpine fortress assures the Swiss of their distinctive contribution to the theory and practice of liberal capitalism. With some justification Switzerland has been called the "ultimate triumph of permissive government."[267] By maintaining its competitive position in the international economy, Switzerland's capitalism produced embourgeoisement rather than immiseration. This is evident in the incorporation of the unions in Switzerland's political economy. Switzerland's liberal corporatism thus creates the political conditions critical for dealing with economic change.

Switzerland's political strategies and structures make it an exception to virtually all the easy generalizations that proponents of the Left and the Right see in "the structural crisis" of capitalism and the "crisis of ungovernability" of liberal democracy. And Switzerland defies all economic orthodoxies with its enviable economic record of maintaining full employment while sharply reducing the total number of jobs, of achieving relative price stability while unsought foreign currencies pushed its money supply upward, and of becoming the most prosperous industrial country while drastically reducing the size of its economy in the mid-1970s. While multiparty systems throughout Europe show growing signs of instability, Switzerland's system endures with only imperceptible changes. Moreover, its main interest groups manage to live side by side with single-issue movements that have proved antithetical to the political bargains of interest groups in many other European countries. A haven of stability and consensus, Switzerland provides a marked contrast to instability and conflict elsewhere. To those who argue that "business civilization is in decline,"[268] Switzerland should be living proof that capitalism is alive and well in at least one country.

CHAPTER FOUR

Democratic Corporatism in Austria and Switzerland

Austria and Switzerland have different domestic structures. In Austria a centralized union and a large public sector dominate the political scene. The pursuit of a strategy of national adaptation and public compensation reflects the very weak position of the internationally oriented segment of the business community. Conversely, international business and finance are the central actors in contemporary Switzerland. The strategy of global adaptation and private compensation that Switzerland pursues in the international economy mirrors the victory that international business has won over the domestically oriented business community, as well as over Switzerland's unions and the political Left. Although in both countries labor and business accommodate their diverging interests in a policy network whose form they partly shape, Austria's institutions are more centralized and politicized than Switzerland's.

The policy process of these two countries differs in the scope and the mode of bargaining. In Austria bargaining focuses on economic issues and, in particular, on crucial questions of investment and employment. In Switzerland the scope of bargaining is broader and more readily includes noneconomic issues, but it excludes investment and employment. The Austrian mode of bargaining tends toward trilateral relations among unions, business, and the state, while Switzerland's characteristic mode is bilateral, and involves business and unions or industry and finance. Trade-offs across different sectors of policy tend, therefore, to be more explicit in Austria than in Switzerland. Finally, both Austria and Switzerland forego policies that, across their common border, appear as natural choices. Table 2 summarizes, in quantitative terms, some of the basic differences in the character of

Table 2. Business and labor in Switzerland and Austria

	Switzerland		Austria	
	Rank[a]	Value	Rank[a]	Valu
A. *Business community by degree of national or international* *orientation* (1971)				
1. International production in foreign subsidiaries as percentage of exports	1	236%	7	
2. Direct foreign investment per employee in $	1	$3,077	7	$ 1
3. Export per employee in $	4	$1,906	7	$1,04
4. Total balance sheet of the three largest banks/GNP	1	1.070	6	0.21
5. Average of (1) to (4)	1		7	
B. *Structural attributes of labor movements* (1965–80)				
6. Average of labor force unionized (%)	7	24%[b]	5	5
7. Organizational unity of unions[c]	5.5	0.7	1	1.
8. Confederation power in collective bargaining[c]	7	0.4	1	0.
9. Scope of collective bargaining[c]	7	0.8	2	1.
10. Works councils and codetermination[c]	7	0.3	3	1.
11. Average of (6) to (10)	7		2	
C. *Relative power of Social Democratic parties*				
12. Social Democratic average electoral base of government (1956–73)[d]	6	31	4	4
13. Percentage of total vote going to Social Democratic parties in election closest to 1970	7	23%	1	5
14. Percentage of years during which Social Democratic parties participated in government (1956–73)	1.5	100%	4	7
15. Percentage of cabinet portfolios held by Social Democratic parties (1965–81)	6	29%	1	7
16. Average of (12) to (15)	5		2	
D. *Institutional measures of the centralization of business and labor*				
17. Associational monopoly of business peak associations[e]	1.5	10	4	5
18. Associational monopoly of unions[f]	7	7	3	3
19. Average of (17) and (18)	2.5		5.5	

SOURCES:

Row 1: Peer Hull Kristensen and Jørn Levinsen, *The Small Country Squeeze* (Roskilde, Denma Institute of Economics, Politics and Administration, 1978), p. 121.

Rows 2–4: Herbert Ammann, Werner Fassbind, and Peter C. Meyer, "Multinationale Konzerne Schweiz und Auswirkungen auf die Arbeiterklasse in der Schweiz," mimeo (Institute of Sociolo University of Zurich, 1975), pp. 106–7.

Rows 6–10, 15: David R. Cameron, "Social Democracy, Corporatism, and Labor Quiescence: Representation of Economic Interest in Advanced Capitalist Society" (paper presented at Conference on Representation and the State: Problems of Governability and Legitimacy in W ern European Democracies, Stanford University, October 1982), tables 6 and 4.

Rows 12–14, 18: Philippe C. Schmitter, "Interest Intermediation and Regime Governability in C temporary Western Europe" (paper prepared for the 1977 annual meeting of the Ameri Political Science Association, Washington, D.C., 1–4 September 1977), Appendix.

Row 17: Vorort des Schweizerischen Handels- und Industrievereins, "Der Aufbau der europäisc Industrie-Spitzenverbände: Ergebnisse einer Umfrage (Stand: Ende 1975)," mimeo (Zur 1977), p. 16.

  a. Ranking measured among the seven rich small European states (Switzerland, Austria, Net lands, Belgium, Sweden, Norway, and Denmark).

(Additional footnotes on opposite pa

business and labor in these two countries. Compared to each other and viewed in the broader context of other small European states, Austria and Switzerland are polar types of democratic socialism and liberal capitalism.

But these differences are only one part of the story. There are also substantial similarities in the politics and policies of the two countries, similarities that justify calling them variants of democratic corporatism. For example, the sketchy data on institutional centralization (Table 2, rows 17 and 18) illustrate with numbers what the analysis of the previous chapters established with words: in both countries the dominant actor, unions in Austria and business in Switzerland, is highly centralized. Analyzing the relationship between business and unions thus brings to light a degree of similarity that an analysis focusing exclusively on the structure of either business or unions does not reveal.

These variants of democratic corporatism lead to similar political consequences. Both countries integrate state and society very closely. They have stable institutions that shield the process of political bargaining from external shocks. Relying on broadly based, centralized peak associations to limit the public agenda by creating a durable internal consensus, they leave the state bureaucracy relatively passive and lacking in autonomy. The policy process in both countries is predictable. Continually modifying and reaffirming the consensus on political strategies and structures, it relies on intricate political bargaining between peak associations and the state to compensate for the relative passivity of the state bureaucracy. Finally, it incorporates virtually all important sources of potential opposition.

It is, of course, true that despite similarities the content of policy and the form of politics differ in Austria and Switzerland. For example, in labor-market policies the tendency to marginalize specific social strata—guestworkers, women, and old people—is greater in Switzerland's liberal than in Austria's social corporatism. But nothing points to a serious conflict over the distribution of power in either

---

b. This figure is close to the minimum for the postwar period. The departure of foreign workers used a sharp increase in the figure to 38 percent by the late 1970s. If this higher figure is taken, vitzerland's rank in row 6 changes from 7th to 6th while its rank in row 11 remains unchanged.

c. The methodology for assigning scores to different countries is explained in Cameron, "Social emocracy, Corporatism, and Labor Quiescence," notes 59–63.

d. This indicator measures the percentage of the vote in the preceding election of the party or rties in government which was obtained by social democratic parties.

e. This indicator varies from 0 to 12. It measures the number of business organizations in differ- t economic sectors that are included in the peak association of business.

f. The methodology for assigning scores is explained in Schmitter, "Interest Intermediation."

state. Geared to the achievement of different objectives, both variants of democratic corporatism have a distinctive capacity to mobilize political consensus for change.

THE NARROWING OF POLITICAL INEQUALITIES

Corporatist arrangements in Austria and Switzerland entangle in a densely woven fabric those political opponents who in the large industrial states would normally choose to walk their different ways. The full institutional penetration of society and the relegitimizing of these institutions through an uninterrupted formulation and implementation of policy continuously retrace and mend the fabric's seams and borders. The mobilization of consensus is facilitated by the narrowing of inequalities between actors in both Austria's democratic socialism and Switzerland's liberal capitalism. In capitalist societies business enjoys an inherent advantage over labor. But in Austrian capitalism the power of the strong, business, and the state is circumscribed; in Swiss capitalism the power of the weak, the unions, and the state is inflated. This narrowing of power differences is not a "natural" covergence between two actors—business and unions, and their respective allies—that have equal standing and command similar resources in a capitalist economy. It is, rather, a deadlock forced by the need actors perceive for political cooperation within the constraints and opportunities of corporatist structures. The consequence of this narrowing of power differences in both societies is to strengthen their corporatist arrangements.

Austria. Often misunderstood as merely a mode of reconciliation, Austria's social corporatism is both a safety valve and a fire engine. It is a safety valve in that it provides for a politically safe release of political tension, a fire engine in that it offers a means for containing escalating conflicts. Its major political consequence is to constrain the power of actors favored by the very structure of Austria's capitalist state: the business community, which owns the means of production, and the state, with its far-reaching grasp over most domains of Austria's society and economy.

The nationalization of most of the large industrial and financial corporations has shifted power away from Austria's business community toward a trade union eager to share in the exercise of power. This shift provides the economic foundation for a balance of power between the two major parties, the SPÖ and the ÖVP, as well as their ancillary organizations representing the interests of labor and business. The distinctiveness of that balance lies in a political accommodation of diverging policy objectives. It works through bargains that bypass the state bureaucracy and implicitly or explicitly acknowledge the veto power each of the main contestants enjoys over substantial deviations from Austria's strategy of national adaptation and public compensation.

Though Austria is essentially capitalist, its political system constrains the power of the business community. The organizational structure of the conservative ÖVP is perhaps the most obvious example.[1] The ÖVP is not a unified party but a coalition of three federations. The numerically weak Business League traditionally exercised a very strong ideological and political influence over the party, an influence that only waned in the 1970s. The Federation of Employees and Workers (ÖAAB) is the largest of the three federations and enjoys the broadest electoral appeal. The third is the well-organized and well-represented Peasant League, whose political influence in Austria has diminished only slowly because of its inclusion in many of the country's central institutions.

The splits within and between the different factions of the ÖVP weakens the business community. Internal splits within the Business League, for example, are as numerous as in the Federal Economic Chamber and include political issues such as the pursuit of a hard or a soft exchange-rate policy, of a more or less liberal tariff policy, and of a liberal or a regulated distribution system in domestic markets. Furthermore, business interests in the ÖVP also include the Federation of Austrian Industrialists, which represents the interests of large, private firms, as well as the Federal Economic Chamber, spokesman for small industry, artisans, the service sector, and the professions. Constructing a compromise among these different business interests normally means moving away from the pursuit of an unambiguous and clear-cut position favoring free enterprise toward a negotiated stance that approximates a consensus favoring some control of markets. This tendency is reinforced by the fact that the influence of the Business League inside the party gradually declined in the last decade, while the influence of the employees' federation increased.

But the ÖAAB's ideological orientation derives more from the authoritarian corporatism of the 1930s than from the policies advocated by the Business League or the ÖVP in the 1950s. Furthermore, as the ÖVP element with the greatest electoral appeal, the ÖAAB provides an important bridge to Austria's union movement. In fact it represents the Christian Democratic unions, which, in terms of sheer size, dominate the public-sector unions, the fourth largest constituent union of the trade union federation. The political ascendance of the ÖAAB thus created in the ÖVP of the 1970s a mirror image of the SPÖ's views of the 1950s. Austria's social corporatism promises the ÖVP access to economic and social policy making in what is sometimes viewed (erroneously, as this book argues) as a "union state." And corporatist structures permit adjudication at the top of the manifold problems that Austria's system of codetermination has created since 1974 at the plant level. In many ways the powerful ÖAAB consists of "closet social democrats" who would never permit the ÖVP to formulate an aggressive business policy. This explains, for example, why in 1980 the ÖAAB demanded massive subsidies for Austria's beleaguered steel industry. The effect is to impede the political articulation of a "natural" business point of view. As in Switzerland, institutional cross-penetration incorporates most sources of opposition in such a way as to ensure a consensual politics.

As a result, business denies itself the exercise of full entrepreneurial autonomy. Business is part of a network of political forces that condition firm behavior in ways so fundamental that it is impossible to characterize that integration as either "voluntary" or "constrained." In important ways the Austrian business community takes its cues from the very system of social and economic partnership. A large nationalized sector and a government that (through its procurement policy and investment subsidies) tangibly affects business prosperity are obvious constraints on the unilateral exercise of market power. So is the participation of the business community, jointly with the unions, in a wide variety of arrangements of economic and social self-administration.

One good example of business's abrogation of market power is to be found in the area of pricing.[2] Price increases granted by the Joint Commission acquire a moral sanction in the eyes of the public; more important, other segments of the business community insist on Joint Commission approval as a certificate of proper—that is, not excessive—profit rates. Furthermore, Austria's business community relies, probably more than the business community of any other advanced industrial state, on the services and political contacts provided by its peak association. In a country that has experienced different forms of price controls throughout the last fifty years, even large, foreign-based multinational corporations accept from their subsidiaries a pricing and employment policy that is peculiarly Austrian in taking its cues not only from the market but from a collectively tolerated system of market supervision. Uncertainty about multiple potential sanctions in Austria's complex policy network and anticipation of strong, hostile union reaction, exercised either directly or indirectly via the government, result in private businesses limiting their own power to set price levels for their products.

At the same time, though, Austria's corporatist structures gave the business community considerable protection against an increasingly dominant Left in the 1970s. Austria's nationalized firms are members of the Federal Economic Chamber. Thus, the main organization representing the economic interests of small business receives financial support from the large public firms that it opposes in politics. Throughout most of the 1970s, for example, the SPÖ minister of Industry and Trade insisted on unanimity in the ministry's advisory bodies on virtually all important issues affecting the structure of Austrian industry. This procedural rule gave Austrian business a stronger voice on policy than would otherwise have been the case. The 1981–82 financial reorganization of Austria's second largest, nationalized bank with public funds also illustrates the point. Negotiations were conducted between the finance minister and the bank's management. Only in the final stages was the parliamentary opposition, the ÖVP, consulted and asked to support the plan. Chancellor Kreisky's conciliatory stance overcame initial ÖVP opposition. The eventual compromise between the SPÖ and the ÖVP required biannual reports from the board of managers to the committee the two parties had appointed in 1981 to supervise subsidies to Austria's steel industry.

A precarious balance between conflict and cooperation has been maintained throughout the postwar years. It has survived because it has always been the weaker political actor that has more strongly cherished Austria's corporatist system. Thus in the 1970s Austria's business community was even more strongly attached to the social and economic partnership than were the trade unions.[3] Furthermore, because economic crisis makes cooperation more valuable, the growing power of corporatist structures increases the power of the business community. In the regions where the crisis of the steel industry has been particularly acute, Styria and Upper Austria, Austria's social and economic partnership now operates at a regional level. Typically, right before provincial and federal elections consultations and compromise become infrequent. But immediately after the ballots are counted, business and unions, ÖVP and SPÖ, jointly decide on a course of action. The struggle over the distribution of power in Austria, conditioned as it is by developments in the international economy, is not zero-sum but positive-sum. In short, the very system of social and economic partnership that constrains the power of the business community also impedes the sanctions in the hand of the unions and the government.

The assertiveness of political parties is the main reason for the passivity of the bureaucracy; Austria has experienced a partisan neutralization of state power. As Uwe Kitzinger notes, "Positions which involve major actors of economic decision-making are thought to entail ideological opportunities and power—therefore to be a vital matter for the parties and the people."[4] Yet the ÖVP and the SPÖ have persistently disagreed on the role of the public sector in the economy. As a result, the potential for political control over the economy that the sheer size of Austria's public sector offers to the bureaucracy has remained partly unfulfilled. The ÖVP has traditionally been interested in limiting the scope of the public sector and in having management conform to "economic" considerations. SPÖ leaders, on the other hand, have always argued that a planned and a market economy are mutually complementary; the nationalized sector in particular should therefore consider the effects of its strategy on the whole economy (and in particular on labor markets) rather than on company profits alone. These conflicting conceptions of the purpose of economic power have blunted both the potential for state intervention in the economy and the potential for invigorating competition in Austrian markets. In the partisan penetration of Austria's nationalized industries and nationalized banks, as well as the institutional requirements of its industrial policy, the political parties have neutralized state power.

It is, however, worth stressing that this neutralization of state power was the result of intense partisan conflict within Austria's supposedly consensual political milieu. For the last generation political control over Austria's public economy has been determined at the polls. Control was reflected before 1966 in the reorganization of ministerial responsibilities negotiated by the two main parties in their coalition agreements; after 1966, in the administrative reorganization of public enterprises imposed after the ÖVP's and the SPÖ's electoral victories, respectively of 1966 and 1970.[5] And throughout the postwar period *Proporz* power was most immediately exercised in nationalized firms through the political staffing of top-level and middle-level management positions.[6] In fact, for the nationalized sector the *Proporz* system was legally sanctioned in 1956. This explains why as early as 1959 the impartial UN Economic Commission for Europe concluded that "although the public-enterprise sector in Austria is large (and comprises more monopolies than elsewhere) it has greater independence from governmental control [than in the U.K.]."[7] But political power is shared, and thus neutralized, not only between but within firms. In the mid-1960s the United Austrian Iron and Steel Works (Vereinigte Österreichische Eisen- und Stahlwerke, Voest) was often viewed as a citadel of "red" power; yet three of the six top management positions—the chairman of the board, the assistant general director, and one of the two assistant directors—were in fact staffed by the conservative ÖVP.[8]

The move to one-party government since 1966, the internal reorganization of the public enterprises in the late 1960s and early 1970s, as well as the SPÖ's gradual and successful implantation in power in the 1970s, have tended to diminish this explicit politicization of economic life.[9] It is, however, by no means clear that apparent depoliticization "really means kicking the other side out," as a leading bureaucrat predicted in 1966.[10] The holding company for Austria's nationalized firms, the ÖIAG, set up by the Socialist Party in the early 1970s, retains key elements of the *Proporz* legislated in 1956 even though these elements are not codified in the company law that governs other parts of the ÖIAG's behavior. Its supervisory board, for example, is not elected at the annual shareholders' meeting. Instead, fifteen members are nominated by the political parties according to their strength in Parliament, and three members are nominated by the government.[11] This arrangement grants the ÖVP a very substantial representation of its interests while assuring the SPÖ of a working majority. In the 1970s the ÖVP controlled appointments to 61 of 136 positions available on the supervisory boards of the nationalized firms under the control of the ÖIAG. Five of ten chairmanships, and 18 of 37 directorships, were also held by managers with close ties to the ÖVP. The SPÖ controls virtually all of the other positions. "The allegiance of these politically appointed managers to their respective parties varies from case to case," writes Erich Andrlik, "even though practically all are members of party suborganizations that unite them within an informal club-like atmosphere."[12] Chancellor Kreisky repeatedly reaffirmed the continued validity of this institutionalization of Austria's corporatism.[13] Besides constraining state power his reaffirmation accords to the ÖVP, as the voice of Austria's business community, a political presence and power in Austria's political economy that both limits and enhances its position.

The partisan neutralization of the power of the state bureaucracy is also evident in the bureaucracy's relations with Austria's nationalized banks.[14] Throughout most of the postwar years the banks succeeded in keeping government at arms' length while running their industrial empires largely according to market criteria.[15] The political autonomy of the banks benefited from their partial reprivatization between 1956 and 1959, the federal government's growing need for credit in the 1960s and 1970s, and the banks' comparatively strong capital base.[16] Despite the formidable powers that legislation governing credit institutions gives to the Finance Ministry, the government has in practice delegated most of that power to the several associations of banking institutions.[17] Furthermore, between 1949 and 1970 the Finance Ministry rested, without interruption, in the hands of the conservative ÖVP, which was not interested in a further development of the government's instruments of financial intervention. Since 1970 the SPÖ government has continued to acknowledge the ÖVP's strong representation in top financial positions and has resisted the temptation to reduce sharply the ÖVP presence and influence in Austria's nationalized banks. Reflecting on the first two decades of the Second Republic, one of the foremost students of Austria's nationalized industries concluded in 1964 that "in Austria the large nationalized investment banks have so far been singularly negligent in lending their services to the public sector."[18] By the end of the 1970s one could argue in a similar vein that "Austria's Socialists say comfortably that they need the conservative Peoples' Party to run the state-owned banks."[19]

Despite their economic importance, the nationalized banks have never become as much of a political football as the nationalized industries. Nonetheless, the Austrian *Proporz* has ruled here as well. Throughout the postwar years the largest nationalized bank, the Creditanstalt, has been "black" and the second largest, the Länderbank, "red."[20] Because of the mounting burden of bad debts, the Länderbank's board of managers was summarily dismissed in the spring of 1981; but the principle of parity representation of business and unions, black and red, was strictly adhered to in its replacement. The appointment of the ÖVP's main parliamentary spokesman on economic questions, Professor Stefan Koren, as president of the Nationalbank in 1978 also illustrates that political power continues to be shared in the 1970s. One detailed study of the role of the Nationalbank concluded in the early 1960s that "in practice the National Bank in Austria does not depend as much on the government as on the two main political parties and the major interest groups."[21] At the end of the 1970s another analysis captured the spirit of the economic and social partnership, which domesticates political conflict without abolishing it, by characterizing the situation in the following terms: "In principle the National Bank is independent. In practice it always acts in agreement with the Ministry of Finance. Some might even say that the Ministry of Finance always acts in agreement with the bank, but no one does, because the two appear to act as perfect partners, even though they disagree in public."[22]

The SPÖ's attempt to establish the institutional machinery for an active industrial policy will serve as a final illustration of the partisan neutralization of state power. In the late 1960s Austria's bureaucracy suffered from organizational weaknesses that impaired its ability to conduct coherent policy.[23] The Ministry of Industry and Trade was reorganized so as to include sections dealing with particular branches of industry, and some of its civil servants received additional training. Between 1968 and 1970 six different policy measures were initiated, through which the Austrian government hoped to encourage innovation and reform in Austria's traditional industrial structure. But only two of these—the establishment of the Industrial Research Promotion Fund and the Working Group for the Promotion of Patents—were specific policy measures.[24] New sectoral data were regularly collected and published from 1973 on.[25] The nationalized banks, however, were very reluctant to go beyond mostly limited financial rescue missions in defense of full employment. Thus the SPÖ government pressed ahead with the development of new institutions in preparation for an active industrial policy. But the limitations on that policy were soon apparent. The new Commission for Industry, set up in 1976 and chaired by the chancellor, evolved, not as the ÖVP had feared, into a centralized planning agency. Instead, it became still another body of consultation in charge of preparing detailed position papers on important industrial sectors. Nor did the commission push for a policy of concentration, as the busines community had feared. It instead encouraged, in its early sessions, an enlargement of cooperative relations between Austria's medium-sized and small firms.[26] Since the SPÖ's natural alliance partners are found in large-scale industry, this policy amounted to a strengthening of the political base of the ÖVP opposition, which typically favors small and medium-sized firms. In short, from the very outset the commission began to operate not as a lever in the hands of government bureaucrats eager to alter Austria's industrial structure, but as another institutional pillar reinforcing Austria's corporatist structures.

Social corporatism in Austria constrains the power of the strong, narrows power differences, and constantly recreates itself while making room for political bargains that permit economic flexibility. But the amelioration of class conflict depends in part on a convergence of political objectives that is essential to the country's political consensus and stability. As the U.S. Congress was told, "Social partnership . . .

not only means we all sit in the same boat; it also means that we are willing to steer the boat in a direction upon which most of us agree."[27] Political accommodation always remains complex and uncertain precisely because the institutional constraints of the domestic structure shape the political objectives of the actors without fully determining them. As Chancellor Kreisky explained, "The left-wing people are opposed to the social partnership and the right-wing people are opposed to it, both for different reasons. . . . What we have done in Austria is a process of sublimation of class values. We found a much more sublime way for our divergences. And it works. . . . without institutionalizing it. If we institutionalize it, we would kill the system. Do you know why? Not because I am against institutions, but because this system has only one real sanction—to say that we shall leave the table. We are not obligated. We are not compelled. This threat, to leave the table, is the strongest reason for remaining at it."[28]

Switzerland. Switzerland's liberal corporatism creates its own institutional pressures for cooperative bargaining and a consensual politics. Among these pressures are the political presence of two legislative chambers, the influence of the cantons, a two-tiered legislative process in which constitutional revisions often precede important legislative changes, an extraparliamentary process of policy formation, and, most importantly, the popular referendum and initiative. These institutional constraints point to the very strong, institutionally anchored veto positions for all important groups. The result, often discussed in Switzerland, is a decidedly status-quo-oriented policy process, which prizes small steps. Large-scale policy changes are not easily accomplished. The main political consequence of Swiss corporatism is to enhance the strength of the structurally weak Left in the country's governing social coalition and to make possible, under certain conditions, the mobilization and application of state powers otherwise left dormant.

Its weakness notwithstanding, Switzerland's labor movement reveals surprising strength. Part of the power of labor unions derives from the extremely favorable conditions in Swiss labor markets during the past thirty years. Because of labor scarcity the unions successfully resisted repeated attempts to contain inflation through curtailing free collective bargaining. Furthermore, collective bargaining covers a wide range of issues: it includes social welfare measures (such as supplementary child allowances) settled in other countries by national legislation. Unions conceive of their role not merely as collective bargaining agents *(Tarifpartner)* but also as social partners *(Sozial-*

partner). They thus include in their negotiations with employers issues other than the regulation of conditions of work. In comparison with West Germany the Swiss government's social welfare measures are inferior; but the metalworkers union's social insurance schemes are considerably more extensive and generous than corresponding plans of West Germany's Metalworkers Union. The difference is most striking in the areas of unemployment, pensions, accident, and sickness.[29] Through this system unions have gained a political stature in Swiss politics that they deeply cherish, especially in light of the Left's otherwise unenviable political position. "We defend ourselves," wrote a former president of the metalworkers union and the union federation, "against the attempts of social policy makers of all political colorations to plunder our agreements with employers."[30] The metalworkers union thus regarded as a success the fact that in Switzerland's metal industry of the 1960s, gross wages took a much larger share of the total wage bill than in either Italy or France.[31]

The antistatist instincts reflected in the strength and durability of private insurance thus agree with the preferences of the labor movement. In the late 1960s Switzerland's Federation of Trade Unions (SGB) defended tenaciously, and in the end victoriously, the principle and practice of private insurance against the efforts of the left wing of the Social Democratic Party to establish a unified, national pension plan.[32] As this conflict demonstrated, Swiss unions value the principle of organized self-help more highly than the principle of collectivism. Self-help carries its own costs, however. For example, Switzerland's largest industrial union, the Swiss Metalworkers and Watchmakers Union (Schweizerischer Metall- und Uhrenarbeitnehmer-Verband, SMUV) had in the mid-1960s a strike fund of $3 million. Over $25 million, on the other hand, were invested in social insurance schemes for its members and thus withdrawn from direct union control.[33] Even if one takes account of the "absolute peace obligation" *(absolute Friedenspflicht)* in Swiss collective bargaining, this investment pattern amounts to nothing less than unilateral disarmament.

Since 1947 public law has sanctioned the elevation of the unions above the role of mere collective bargaining agents. In explicit recognition of the unions' law-and-order role in industrial relations *(Ordnungsfunktion)* collective agreements often stipulate that unions are entitled to collect dues *(Solidaritätsbeiträge)* from nonmembers.[34] The law also provides for an "extension of a collective agreement" *(Allgemeinverbindlichkeitserklärung)*, which stipulates that under certain conditions an agreement reached between the employers' association and the union must be adhered to both by members and by nonmembers within an industrial sector or occupational group. In other words, private contractual agreements can acquire the force of public law.

The well-institutionalized relations between the unions and the government bureaucracy and business make the SGB today the most important interest group by any formal measure of representation in policy making.[35] In the late 1970s the Social Democratic Party occupied the Ministry of Finance and the Foreign Ministry, key positions for organizing Switzerland's relations with world markets. The top official in charge of questions of domestic economic development is a former union official.[36] The Swiss Left enjoys institutional representation on all important advisory committees and expert commissions, which mark the decision nodes in Switzerland's policy network. And on all issues, all groups, including the unions, potentially affected by government policy have a constitutional right, honored in daily practice, to participate in the process of "consultation" *(Vernehmlassung)*. A group's implicit threat to challenge policies it cannot support by organizing a referendum vote strengthens the position of the Left and Switzerland's compulsion to compromise.

But because they hold a central position in the formulation of policy, especially on issues of social policy, the unions do not rely on the referendum, which is the policy instrument of the political outsider.[37] During the last thirty years the unions have not launched a single major referendum campaign. Moreover, despite their greater financial resources, the unions have been much more hesitant than the Social Democratic Party in launching popular initiatives.[38] The unions do not need such unilateral initiatives: the policies framed in, for example, the area of social welfare have included all of the major demands of the labor movement, simply because the unions have been present at all stages of preparliamentary consultation.[39] It comes, therefore, as no surprise that the unions are among the most avid defenders of the principle of group autonomy. They join Switzerland's business community in actively opposing any form of incomes policy that would disrupt free collective bargaining; and unions participate actively in shaping Switzerland's privatized welfare state.[40]

In contrast to the unions, the Social Democratic Party has a much stronger inclination to rely on direct democracy.[41] This inclination has remained strong despite an abatement in political conflict over issues of economic policy, which ran high when the social democrats first joined the government between 1944 and 1952, and despite the serious financial constraints under which the party operates. As none of the numerous political initiatives sponsored by the Social Democratic

Party since 1945 has been approved at the polls, the resolution of intraparty tensions rather than the expectation of electoral success has been the prime reason for the party's continued preference for direct popular participation in policymaking. Direct democracy makes tolerable the political cross-pressures between a party leadership that has been part of the government since 1959 and a rank and file that frequently prefers playing an opposition role.[42]

The special role of the Swiss unions on questions of collective bargaining and social welfare thus ameliorates some of the basic inequalities of power among Switzerland's main political actors. But as a recent, comprehensive study demonstrates in convincing detail, there is still a yawning gap between amelioration and elimination.[43] Contrary to Swiss ideology, notions of proportional representation in policy making are restricted to regional and linguistic differences; they do not encompass socioeconomic differences.[44] On questions of economic policy, in sharp contrast to Austria, the Swiss unions and the political Left play an insignificant role. And even in their area of greatest strength, social policy, Swiss unions cannot impose solutions; they can only veto those which they oppose.[45] Although the unions are integrated into Switzerland's liberal corporatism, their representation is numerically inferior to business, lacks the combined weight of business interests, and locates them closer to the marginal groups in Swiss society than is true of any segment of the business community.[46] The cumulation of political roles, which in Austria is a sign of the power of the Left, is in Switzerland a sign of weakness.[47] That weakness is reflected in the widespread criticism of the decision-making process by elite members of the unions and the political Left.[48]

The irony is that, this criticism notwithstanding, the unions and the Left have become prisoners of Switzerland's corporatism. They embrace it as the only conceivable political mechanism by which decisions favoring union interests can be reached under the watchful eye of a fragmented and overwhelmingly conservative electorate.[49] The unions find it very difficult to challenge any of the fundamental political premises of the entire system. The result has been that the class cleavage lurking underneath the consensus has found no expression in existing institutions; that the political demobilization of young workers is very far advanced; and that the unions and the Left lack a strategy for change informed by their own theoretical debates or specific objectives.[50] Indeed, the unions' primary objective now is to broaden membership. They aim to reinvigorate their organizational structure in an effort to counteract the deleterious consequences of the last twenty years as well as the apparently inevitable shrinking of the industrial workforce in the coming decades. The change in the name of the largest industrial union, the metalworkers, from a "worker" to an "employee" union in 1972 illustrates these concerns.[51] Ironically, the cooptation of the labor movement is partly voluntary because, unlike in Austria, the unions and the political Left subscribe to the notion of a rough equivalence of economic policy, dominated by the business community, and social policy, heavily influenced by the unions.[52]

Switzerland's liberal corporatism artificially enhances the power of the Left. It is, for example, easily forgotten that the Social Democratic Party was accorded two seats on the Federal Council in 1959 not so much due to its own strength as to the intense conflict between the two dominant bourgeois parties, Liberals and Catholics. In 1968 twenty of Switzerland's twenty-five cantons featured coalition governments in which the social democrats were included; but nowhere did the Left control a majority of the cantonal executive.[53] Furthermore, the power of the unions and the Left in Switzerland's policy network rests heavily on the special delegation of public power, especially in the areas of collective bargaining and social welfare. That delegation strengthens a weak sector of society, the labor movement, in the same way that tariffs protect agriculture and a lenient enforcement of cartel legislation protects domestic business. The strength that all these social sectors derive from the delegation of public power is considerable; but it is a brittle kind of strength, which does not compensate fully for the fundamental asymmetry in power relations in Swiss society.

Nor is this only true of the unions and the Left: under certain conditions the power of the Swiss state is also inflated. It would be a mistake to view either the government or the state bureaucracy as impotent. The government provides information and direction to the work of the Federal Assembly, which is by all accounts its inferior in both power and status. Furthermore, (and somewhat paradoxically), the government's weakness vis-à-vis well-organized interest groups can also act as a source of strength. With so much power resting in the private sector, the inevitable divisions and conflicts between groups frequently elevate the government to the role of an arbiter, enjoying wide discretionary powers.[54] Through adroit choice of institutional arenas for discussion and careful timing of the policy process the government can achieve an important impact on policy.[55] And, at least in terms of numbers, the federal bureaucracy and the cantons dominate the early stages of the critically important preparliamentary consultation.[56]

State strength also manifests itself in other dimensions of Swiss life. Economic and security affairs are for the Swiss, as for the Japanese, intimately linked. In the area of agricultural policy, for example, this linkage has encouraged policies that show the Swiss state in a position of unaccustomed strength and decisiveness.[57] The need to increase self-sufficiency in agriculture was one of the important lessons that the Swiss learned from World War II. In 1939 Swiss agriculture covered only 30 percent of domestic consumption of bread cereals and produced virtually no fruit or vegetables. By 1975 more than 70 percent of bread cereals and fruit, and 40 percent of vegetables were domestically produced. In addition, the Swiss are self-sufficient in meat and potatoes.[58] These dramatic changes in self-sufficiency resulted from a self-conscious and consistent policy. Every five years the Swiss formulate a plan in which they decide what Swiss agriculture should produce and in what quantity. Such plans have also affected Switzerland's foreign trade policy in the area of agriculture. Switzerland decided in favor of joining the GATT in 1966 only after it had been exempted from the principle of free trade in agriculture—a unique occurrence in the annals of the organization.

But the move to self-sufficiency brought with it a chronic oversupply of dairy products and the threat of long-term environmental deterioration (due to the intense application of fertilizers and the growing volume of untreated sewage). In the late 1970s, therefore, Swiss policy began to limit the number of cows permitted per acre. The move to self-sufficiency thus required further action from an ever more active Swiss state attempting to cope with the unintended consequences of its policy. Irirangi Bloomfield describes the change thus: "As liberal economic values with their emphasis on short-term factor costs erode the traditional ethic of stewardship of natural resources, an increasingly intrusive type of governmental intervention has been undertaken to protect the future. . . . There were policy options open which enabled Switzerland to act and at a level of intrusion and coercion that the Swiss themselves profess to abhor."[59] Carried by a broad political consensus and embedded in an ideology that cherishes individual liberty as a component of rather than an antidote to communal collectivism, the Swiss state, under conditions of crisis, can call upon residues of strength easily overlooked.[60]

Experience in other arenas of policy confirms this suggestion. On questions like defense or money that touch the very core of Switzerland's vital interest, the laborious process of collaborative consultation, characteristic of almost all other economic and social issues, is less prominent.[61] For example, in contrast to Austria, a portion of

Switzerland's low tariffs on imports is a levy imposed to help finance a vast program of economic preparedness in case of war. This is part of a larger program of civil defense, which aims to protect 90 percent of the Swiss population against nuclear attack.[62] The country's constant state of military preparedness is reflected in the fact that, forty years after the end of World War II, about one-half of the total federal bureaucracy is employed by the Defense Department.[63] And, as a scandal in Switzerland's intelligence community revealed, in the latter part of the 1970s Switzerland had not one but two top-secret government intelligence services. Both were directed by the same official, who, in addition, also headed a parallel private organization.[64] When the Queen of England visited Switzerland in May 1981, British journalists were astonished by the extent of security precautions, which some likened to those of well-established dictatorships.[65]

The issue of foreign workers also enhances the role of state authority and reflects an underlying, forceful state presence often overlooked. Switzerland's fascist movement never won a wide following in the 1930s, but the country's xenophobic streak did intensify fears of foreign influence. Restrictive immigration laws, which are still in force today, date back to that period.[66] Moreover, the federal Aliens' Police is singularly efficient and omnipresent in identifying illegal immigrants. Working in close cooperation with the cantonal labor-market authorities, it is a highly visible symbol of state power.[67] Furthermore, the dramatic expansion in the number of foreign workers in the postwar years has had little effect on the country's restrictive naturalization policy. In the late 1970s more than one-half of Switzerland's aliens possessed the formal qualifications of twelve years' residence for naturalization; but fewer than 10 percent of those eligible have been granted citizenship since 1951. In 1975 the number of naturalized foreign workers was 10,000, or about 1 percent of the foreign workforce.[68] The strong role of the state was also reinforced by the adoption of a highly restrictive immigration policy in the 1970s; it relies on a quota system and is administered by the federal government rather than the cantons.[69]

In the area of foreign economic policy close relations among business, the unions, and the government have helped to enhance state power.[70] Compared with the other small European states (as well as with the large, advanced industrial countries) the intimate connections between business and government are unique.[71] These connections consist of informal, personal consultation as well as institutionalized contacts. Parapublic institutions such as the Trade Development Office and the recent growth of "mixed" trade commissions organizing Switzerland's commercial relations with the Soviet Union, Iran, and Saudi Arabia provide arenas in which government officials and business representatives cooperate in the implementation of commercial policy. It is standard practice for Swiss business to be directly represented in international trade negotiations.[72] Furthermore, there exists a Consultative Commission for Foreign Trade Policy, which the Federal Council is obliged to consult on all important trade questions. Its thirty to forty members, drawn from the major interest groups, do not agree on the main policy question through majority vote but through prolonged discussions that lead to compromise solutions accepted by all.[73]

Due to the need to increase Swiss export competitiveness, this consultative commission was supplemented in 1975 by the Advisory Committee for Foreign Economic Policy. It draws on a more restricted circle of groups and now serves as the major speaker for Switzerland's export industries.[74] It, rather than the consultative commission, hammered out the series of policy decisions designed to strengthen the export sector in 1975 and 1976. The true center of power, the Permanent Delegation for Economic Negotiations, is still more exclusive than either the consultative commission or the advisory committee. It lacks any legal foundation for its power.[75] Its membership is not fixed but is normally restricted to top government officials, the leaders of the main interest groups, and a small and variable number of guests who are invited depending on the subject matter under discussion. Invitations to attend particular sessions are extended to individuals rather than to their institutions, and the permanent delegation keeps no written records. Here all the threads run together as, under the auspices of the state, one small group settles the fundamental decisions that Switzerland confronts in the international economy.

It is not unheard of for the solutions fashioned in these exclusive circles to be challenged at the polls. In 1976, for example, a coalition between voters of the traditional Right who distrusted Switzerland's increasing involvement in international organizations and voters of the new Left opposed to international financial institutions joined forces in a referendum. They managed to veto a bill, already passed by both houses of the Federal Assembly, that would have extended a loan to the International Development Agency.[76] But in a broader perspective such public incursions into the interlocking corridors of power are very rare in the area of foreign economic policy. Between 1920 and 1974 seven of the eight foreign-policy measures that the government had to subject to popular referendum passed; only one of the fourteen popular initiatives brought against government policy was accepted.[77] Normally, then, the public does not challenge the close cooperation between peak associations and the government in the area of foreign economic policy. André Jäggi and Margret Sieber summarize the situation: "In general, the decision-making in foreign economic policy is different from the decision-making on domestic issues. The efficiency, flexibility, and quickness of centralized oligarchic foreign economic policy is functional with regard to the rapid changes of the international economic regime. The rather conservative, pragmatic, and time-consuming consociational decision-making . . . is functional with regard to democracy and legitimacy."[78]

The strict limitations imposed on the power of the decentralized Swiss state are themselves, as in the United States, a source of fundamental strength, especially in times of economic crisis. The Swiss constitution is, in Jane Kramer's words, a "kind of working brief, always redescribing and redefining its authority."[79] Popular vote has amended this brief ninety times since the last constitutional revision of 1874. Reliance on bypassing democratic practices in times of crisis has historical precedents. For example, between 1919 and 1939 one-half of all federal laws and decrees were issued under the constitution's emergency clause, and were thus removed from all popular control. Sixty percent of these measures were passed between 1930 and 1938.[80] In the 1950s and 1960s, by way of contrast, the political process was typically marked by long, complex bargaining and informal agreements. The anti-inflation program of 1964, drawn up, debated, and adopted within a week in an atmosphere of crisis, was a notable exception.[81]

But since the early 1970s that exception has almost become the norm. For example, with the advent of flexible exchange rates the emergency decree for the protection of the currency of 1971 accords the Federal Council and the Nationalbank broad discretionary powers that they have constantly used throughout the 1970s.[82] A more stringent anti-inflation program (1972), regional planning policy (1972), fiscal policy (1975), and the unemployment insurance scheme (1975–76) are prominent examples of a growing reliance on rule by emergency decree. Between 1971 and 1976 the government issued nine extraconstitutional emergency decrees, all of which were approved by the obligatory referendum (between 1949 and 1970 only three such decrees had been issued). Similarly, between 1971 and 1976 the government issued fifteen constitutional emergency decrees, about 10 percent of the total number of bills passed and about 15 percent of the significant political issues, none of which was appealed by the optional referendum stipulated by the constitution (between

1949 and 1970 only seven such decrees had been issued).[83] Rule by emergency decree reduces the number of points of intervention in the policy process, as well as the number of participants.[84]

Thus, direct democracy in the 1970s challenged a growing share of political decisions. But because of its corporatist process of policy making, Switzerland has stopped far short of reverting to the crisis pattern of the 1930s. Generally speaking, its extraparliamentary politics exhibits predictable compromises among all of the major actors. Swiss corporatism strengthens the weak, narrows political inequalities, and creates the political context necessary for economic flexibility. The political accommodation of different social forces occurs in the consensual framework of a liberal corporatism that enhances the power of the unions and the state, and restricts potential sources of opposition. An elaborate process of building durable compromises brings together the same well-organized major interest groups around different tables.

Corporatist politics relies on a combination of collective representation and collective self-discipline. In the temptations it holds and in the transformations it effects, corporatism has a comparable though not equivalent impact on both labor and business. Neo-Marxist interpretations tend to stress, as John Stephens does, that "corporatism represents a deadlock in the class struggle in which working-class economic and political power is sufficient to force substantial concession from capital but insufficient actually to take control of the accumulation process."[85] But this line of reasoning often fails to examine the different roles business plays in capitalist societies as different as Switzerland and Austria, and thus offers a one-sided interpretation of corporatist politics. In Switzerland and Austria corporatism is not a guise for stabilizing capitalism by extracting concessions from labor. Democratic corporatism is a mechanism that integrates conflicting class interests in a broader conception of national welfare informed by the vulnerabilities that beset open economies. The secret to its political success, in both its Swiss and its Austrian incarnations, rests on the ability to strike a balance between the social pressures for political competition, on the one hand, and the market-generated pressures for political compromise, on the other.

In a book published sixty years ago, the Austrian socialist Otto Bauer coined the phrase the "equilibrium of class forces" as a precarious precondition justifying, in times of great national crisis—the loss of an empire, hyperinflation, starvation, and internationally imposed stabilization policies—the formation of temporary cross-class alliances.[86] During the last generation, different corporatist arrangements have routinized that precarious precondition. One result has been a relative narrowing of political inequalities among business, labor, and the state. Of course, the political compromises reached in both Switzerland and Austria are always imperfect. Indeed, Count Taafe's aphorism on the balancing of interests between the Austrian and Hungarian halves of the nineteenth-century empire aptly characterizes bargaining in Austria and Switzerland today: a state of "good-tempered dissatisfaction." But the narrowing of political inequalities to be found in both variants of democratic corporatism induces political actors, more than in other domestic structures, to compromise rather than to maximize their interests. As a result, corporatist structures have a large capacity to absorb politically the consequences of economic change.

CONVERGENCE IN POLICY

Democratic corporatism explains some otherwise anomalous convergences in how Switzerland and Austria respond to economic change. On questions of industrial policy and investment by foreign corporations, for example, the activities of cantonal governments and the provisions of Swiss corporate law fill the void left by the seemingly passive federal government. Conversely, in a number of different areas Austria's political instruments for intervention in the economy are surprisingly limited.

In Switzerland's federal system, the economic crisis of the 1970s prompted a number of cantonal governments to develop their own regionally specific industrial adjustment policies. Generally speaking, the most active cantons were those saddled with declining industries suffering from problems of structural adjustment. The structural problems of Swiss industry were thus met politically and, in sharp contrast to Austria, in a regionally decentralized manner. Political responses relying on tax and land-use policy, as well as limited subsidies and loan guarantees, were designed to attract new firms to declining regions or to strengthen and diversify the production structure of ailing corporations. Of Switzerland's twenty-five cantons, eight had enacted what might be called a "program for industrial policy" in the late 1970s, and another four were in the process of doing so. Most of the remaining cantons had at their disposal a variety of legislative instruments to pursue similar objectives. Whatever their legislative base, the cantonal programs stressed a variety of incentives but, significantly, avoided large expenditures. Furthermore, because of differing economic circumstances, policy implementation varies widely, from an administrative mode where the policy is carried by a broad consensus, as in Neuchâtel, to a collaborative mode where the policy is contested, as in Solothurn. Careful analysis suggests that policies of industrial adjustment have been carried out in an ad hoc manner informed by short time horizons; the cantons are thus unlikely sources for effective, long-term policies of structural transformation.[87]

But an embryonic industrial policy can also be found in the Swiss private sector. Firms unable to finance their investment programs through retained earnings turn to the large private banks for credit or access to capital markets. It is no longer altogether uncommon to hear calls for the banks to provide limited venture capital for the promising investment projects of relatively small firms, projects with strong potential growth effects for other business segments. Furthermore, Swiss banks are occasionally pressed into preserving firms central to the health of sizable segments of Swiss industry. If industrial policy is debated anywhere in Switzerland, it is in the financial community—but the debate is still conducted in whispers.[88]

Thus, in times of crisis bank lending policies appear to be geared at least in part to easing the pain of transition and change in selected sectors of industry. Switzerland's banking sector, moreover, includes 29 cantonal banks, with assets of more than $54 billion in 1980; many of these banks derive their capital from cantonal governments. Some of them rival the large five private banks in size, and, since even the Nationalbank is privately owned, these cantonal banks are the closest thing the country has to state banking institutions. Unlike private banks they have to date operated almost exclusively in domestic markets. Acknowledging special interest in and obligation to the cantonal economies does not, however, interfere with their insistence on strictly commercial considerations in their credit policies. Exceptions do, of course, occur. For reasons of social policy, between 1967 and 1978 cantonal banks charged consistently lower interest rates for home mortgages than did the private banks. And even in the area of industrial policy, cantonal banks are at times tempted to ignore the market principle. In the late 1970s, the tiny Nidwaldner Kantonalbank ignored this precept in a wave of cantonal chauvinism and, as a result, ran up substantial losses from its overly benevolent support of debt-ridden local companies.[89]

Switzerland has also taken precautions against foreign capital buying out Swiss firms against their wishes. In general, the government is very liberal in its treatment of the foreign ownership of Swiss firms. The annual inflow of direct foreign investment increased from \$197 million in 1967–69 to \$517 million in 1973–75. (These figures are substantially above the \$39 million and \$126 million reported for Austria in the same periods.)[90] Priding itself on a full reliance on markets, the OECD reports, Switzerland does "not subject the establishment of international enterprises to any special rules."[91] Only the intermittent control of currency speculation and short-term capital movements has provoked brief exceptions to this liberal stance. The Swiss government has no agency monitoring or screening foreign investment; unlike in Austria, cantonal governments or communes rather than the federal government extend incentives favoring either local or foreign companies; and reporting requirements are identical for foreign and domestic firms.[92] Furthermore, Swiss law contains no restrictions on the nationality of shareholders.

But this cosmopolitan image is as deceptive as the notion that market forces in areas affecting Switzerland's vital interests have unrestricted play. Permissive government regulations on questions of foreign investment must be viewed together with legal rules governing corporate behavior that in fact impede foreign takeovers. The majority of the board of directors of Switzerland's joint stock corporations must be Swiss citizens who live in Switzerland. And when it comes to questions of ownership, Switzerland's banks and its multinational corporations, for all their international orientation, remain very much Swiss. Specific provisions of Swiss company law assure that ownership will remain in Swiss hands.[93] Different types of stocks have different voting rights at annual stockholder meetings. Registered shares (*Namensaktien*) carry the same voting right per share as regular stock certificates even though they have, typically, been issued at a fraction of the price of regular stock certificates. Registered shares are reserved for specified groups of individuals, for example, family members or Swiss citizens. They cannot be traded on the open market. And normally Swiss corporations have issued registered shares in sufficient numbers, and to the right people, to control any contest over ownership. Furthermore, the company's board of directors must agree to any change in the ownership of these shares, and agreement can be denied without disclosure of the reason. Shareholders typically give the banks a power of attorney to vote their shares at the annual meeting of stockholders, and the banks' normal policy is to support the corporation's board of directors. Finally, because Swiss companies are permitted to conceal their "hidden assets," foreign firms find it almost impossible to assess the value of a Swiss company targeted for takeover. This whole system of regulations and practices assures a small number of Swiss owners control over Swiss firms. When Sandoz attempted to take over McCormick in the spring of 1980, it could do so from an uncontested domestic base: an overwhelming majority of Sandoz shares are owned by Swiss. As Robert Metz reported, "It appears to be virtually impossible for a non-Swiss to take over one of Switzerland's resident corporations."[94]

Equally noteworthy are the limitations imposed on political intervention in Austria. For all its self-proclaimed activism, the Austrian industrial policy is distinguished by a restraint of government power and an inclination toward improvisation. In the 1960s, for example, political debates and policies concerning industrial adjustment followed rather than preceded the gradual restructuring process of 1961–68 and was voided by the phase of export-led growth that began in 1968. In the 1970s Austrian policies focused primarily on cushioning the impact of external change in the defense of jobs rather than on generating new jobs through the acceleration of large-scale industrial modernization. Political speeches at times made Austria's industrial policy appear like the grander political designs for structural transformation so prominent in the Japanese and French efforts of the 1960s and 1970s. But in reality Austria's policy consisted of a series of small-step adjustments. A recent sympathetic assessment of a decade of socialist industrial policy concluded in 1981 that the programmatic demands of the SPÖ have not been met; put simply, "the Socialist government has not succeeded in implementing its industrial policy objectives."[95] The financial instruments at the disposal of the government have become increasingly fragmented and have impaired central political direction. And the state's generous investment incentives have not been sufficiently selective.

Austrian policy makers, like their counterparts in Switzerland, are aware of the importance of market pressures that cannot be overridden. Considering the enormous size of the state's ownership of or control over industry, it is striking how cautiously it has conducted industrial policy.[96] Throughout the postwar period the government has attached a much greater importance to an indirect and global, as contrasted to a direct and sectoral, approach to industry. As in Switzerland, a hard-currency policy throughout most of the 1970s forced Austria's export industries to defend their competitive position strenuously in world markets, through adjusting to accelerating changes in production structures and product mixes. The effect has been a reinvigoration of Austria's industrial structure through indirect rather than direct government action. Meanwhile, the state's massive investment subsidies are allocated largely in indirect ways, and not selectively. Even if one were only to consider the 15 percent of total investment subsidies granted on a selective basis, the state bureaucracy typically responds to the approaches of individual firms and their banks. It is very rare for the state bureaucracy itself to propose specific investment projects.[97]

On this point political debate started in the late 1970s. Some segments of the SPÖ were then beginning to argue that investment support through accelerated depreciation allowances should become less important than the creation of selective incentives for innovative firms and new product lines.[98] For example, under one of Austria's interest subsidy schemes, a total of $310 million is being made available between 1978 and 1984 for projects deemed desirable from a structural and employment point of view. But this does not change the general character of the Austrian policy.[99] In the mid-1970s indirect investment subsidies exceeded direct subsidies by a factor of nine.[100] Judging by the intense political opposition the SPÖ's new approach has created in Austria's business community, it is likely to supplement rather than replace existing indirect approaches. Furthermore, in the 1980s the government will lack the massive amounts of capital necessary to correct the heavy bias of existing policies toward general, indirect investment support.

Political restraint can be observed in other economic policies that have a direct bearing on industrial adjustment. Austria's countercyclical fiscal policy does not approach what in the large industrial states would be called medium-term planning of public finance. In fact, medium-term forecasts of public expenditures were not introduced until the mid-1960s and since then have only been applied with considerable hesitation.[101] Finance Minister Wolfgang Schmitz's observation in 1967 that these forecasts "do not predict what will happen nor do they prescribe what should happen" held true throughout the 1970s.[102] In general, public expenditures are not the favored tool by which the government sets clear political priorities over the medium or long term. This limitation on the government's power is illustrated by the obstacles to its policy of deficit spending. For example, the federal government has never exercised great control over the spending decisions of provincial and municipal governments—a source of political weakness. Compared to that of the provinces, the federal government's role as a tax collector actually diminished in the 1970s. And throughout the 1960s and 1970s these lower levels of government did not follow, and at times acted against, the anticyclical expenditure policy of the federal government. For example, in the 1970s the SPÖ controlled both the city government of Vienna and the federal government in Vienna; but the expenditure policies of these two governments diverged widely across the decade.[103]

Other episodes also point to the pervasive political restraints on the Austrian government, inhibiting its active pursuit of economic intervention. By and large the government lacks the ability to influence strongly the investment (as contrasted to the employment) decisions of the nationalized sector. When one of the most profitable and successful nationalized firms, Austrian Airlines, chose new telephone equipment in 1976, Siemens, as the representative of Austria's "domestic" industry, was underbid by a Swedish company and lost a very large and lucrative contract.[104] Austrian Airlines wanted the best product for the lowest price and had no interest in furthering the government's procurement and research and development policies.

On questions of export finance, market considerations continue to shape the policies of Austria's Control Bank. In its two-tier system of interest rates the variable portion fluctuates widely in response to changes in international capital markets. Furthermore, in striking contrast to the case in Switzerland, Austria's export support programs could not be targeted on particular industries or products but were generally applied. As financial contributor to as well as benefactor of these programs, the business community was unable to agree on a list of priorities for funding.[105] Moreover, the veto that the Nationalbank imposed on the extension of export credits for the financing of production periods of less than a year (typical of consumer goods industries) also illustrates the limitations imposed on the government's efforts to spur exports. Under the guise of export promotion, such credits, the bank argued, amounted to a politically motivated improvement of the capital base of particular firms or industrial sectors. And this, it thought, was antithetical to the tenets of Austria's market economy.[106] In this instance as well, Austria's restrained approach is in striking contrast to Switzerland's selective and energetic support of its export-oriented consumer goods industries.

The federal government has even lost control over the expenditure decisions of a number of independent funds set up in the 1960s and 1970s with the aim of improving the infrastructure of the economy.[107] Its numerous investment programs are very complex—and to many, utterly confusing. One recent study, commissioned in the late 1970s by the federal government, concludes, "What Austria's selective structural policy lacks more than anything else is clarity. As long as all these activities and programs are devoid of a comprehensive development and structural budget spanning at least one legislative period, the danger persists that only insiders will know and be able to make use of the programs that exist."[108] This description hardly fits an activist socialist state eager to restructure its economy. It does, however, capture the logic of Austria's social corporatism and the unending sequence of compromises by which different groups and sectors are compensated for changes in international and domestic markets.

Restraints on the government are evident in its recent moves toward more selective methods of industrial intervention. The establishment of two small Capital Participation Corporations in 1977 was designed to strengthen the capital base of dynamic firms in industrial sectors with high growth potential.[109] Although the establishment of such corporations had been debated since the late 1960s, implementation was stalled for the better part of a decade because of the clash between the government's insistence on a centralized and publicly funded corporation and the business community's preference for multiple, privately based institutions. The structure of the two small corporations set up in 1977 largely follows the 1969 recommendations of the business community.[110] Not only do these corporations not offer the government an instrument useful for an activist policy; it is in fact quite reasonable to interpret their establishment as a government attempt to allay fears in the Austrian business community, widespread in the mid-1970s, that pushing ahead with large industrial projects would undermine further private initiative in Austria's market economy. The compromise that the SPÖ and the ÖVP reached in December 1981, concerning sharp increases in subsidies for the steel industry, obliged the government to increase both the number of these sources of venture capital for private firms and the scale of their operations, without state intervention. ÖVP support for subsidies to the nationalized steel industry was traded against SPÖ support for additional aid for Austria's medium-sized and small firms in the name of an investment-oriented growth strategy. Austria's *Proporz* required subsidy packages of roughly $125 million each for the "red" and the "black" portions of the program.[111] Such political bargains aimed at satisfying conflicting demands are facilitated by Austria's corporatist structure. As a former state secretary reflects, "So much admired abroad, the Austrian model is based on . . . a parallelism of plan and market. . . . The ideology of our 'framework planning' is thin and pragmatic. It expresses skepticism more than conviction. Austria is small and therefore easily comprehended. Everybody understands very well the imperfections of both market competition and state planning."[112]

In summary, both Switzerland and Austria express political conflicts over economic choices in the language of social partnership rather than in that of class conflict. The terms of political discourse result from both external and domestic determinants of politics and policy. They do not signify that political conflicts have been replaced by the cooperative pursuit of the national interest. In both countries political actors pursue different interests and adhere to different visions of the good society. But through their policy networks these differences are harnessed together in an unending process of small-scale political adjustments. Although institutional form and the character of the policy process differ in the liberal and the social variants of corporatism, the political consequence of these two variants of democratic corporatism are, as I have argued in this chapter, essentially the same: they succeed in restraining the unilateral exercise of power, in narrowing political inequalities between actors, and, as the next two chapters will show, in organizing these actors to support political strategies that cope flexibly with economic change.

CHAPTER FIVE

The Politics of Change in the Textile Industry

Chapters 2 and 3 analyzed Austrian and Swiss politics by focusing on the social coalitions, political institutions, and policy process that have permitted both countries to achieve extraordinarily high levels of economic success and political legitimacy in the postwar world. Rather than emphasizing the differences between Austria's democratic socialism and Switzerland's liberal capitalism, chapter 4 stressed their similarities under the more general heading of democratic corporatism. This and the following chapter will combine differences and similarities by showing in greater detail, both at the sectoral and at the firm level, how the social and liberal variants of corporatism have dealt politically with economic crisis.

The corporatist compact is open to different kinds of choices. Layoffs, for example, are more readily accepted in Switzerland than in Austria. But the Swiss textile industry illustrates also how corporatism encourages the adoption of countermeasures that reinforce consensus. Conversely, Austria's interventionist instincts notwithstanding, in textiles as in the rest of industry political leaders are fully aware of the fact that they must meet market competition. Striking in both cases is the capacity of political actors to conceive of their self-interest in broad rather than in narrow terms, and to resist the temptation of sacrificing long-term interests to short-term considerations. This capacity to behave strategically, as I argued earlier, is both an outcome of democratic corporatism and at the same time one of its essential political reinforcements.

The political predominance of either business or labor instills a broad conception of self-interest. Aware of the importance of social harmony to its overall success, the business community in Switzerland does not strictly oppose concessions to hard-pressed industrial sectors or segments of sectors. Conversely, the labor movement in Austria is interested only in slowing down, not in opposing, economic change. In each case, a broad conception of self-interest reinforces the country's political stability and economic flexibility. In sharp contrast, weak business communities or weak labor movements have a narrow conception of self-interest. They tend rigidly to oppose their domestic opponents and, confronted with economic threats to their existence, advocate policies inimical to adaptation, such as tariffs or job protection. This is not the characteristic response in Switzerland and Austria. Their corporatist arrangements mobilize political consensus, though under dramatically different political conditions. The corporatist ideology of social partnership is sustained in Switzerland by the need to pacify labor in the interest of international competitiveness; in Austria, by the weakness of the business community in the face of competition from world markets. Differences between the economic interests and political ideologies of union officials and businessmen, as well as in the centralization and politicization of Austria's and Switzerland's corporatist arrangements, have important consequences for different parts of society. But the inclusionary characteristics of corporatism in both its variants explain why consensus is mobilized successfully.

In times of economic crisis, the distinctive feature of democratic corporatism—the narrowing of political inequalities—becomes crucial to the political system's ability to reconfirm its own legitimacy. Industries are internally split in complex ways that make it relatively easy for the peak associations of business to ally with a particular industry segment, a segment that broadly favors existing political arrangements and policies. At the same time the cooperative stance of the government and the unions serves to keep dissident industry segments attached to corporatist structures. As a result, and despite massive economic dislocations, political alliances challenging these structures did not appear in Austria in the 1970s and were never more than embryonic in Switzerland. Thus, corporatism acts like a shock absorber of economic dislocations. It succeeds in recreating its political legitimacy by the manner in which it shapes the responses of political leaders to economic adversity.

In macroeconomic terms Switzerland and Austria have done well; all the available statistics attest to the proposition. Yet those statistics conceal wide variations in particular industrial sectors and particular firms. Some industries have seen permanent decline over the last two decades; textiles and watches in Switzerland and textiles and steel in

Austria have all experienced adverse economic change of a very great magnitude. These four industries approximate the conditions under which large industrial states have typically opted either for protection or for policies of structural transformation. Until the mid-1970s the Swiss watch industry and the Austrian steel industry enjoyed international positions of strength atypical for the industries of small states. Swiss watches dominated world markets in terms of sales, Austrian steel in terms of technological innovation. The two industries were also central in their national politics. Conversely, in both countries the textile industry occupies a weak position in international markets. Stiff foreign competition and the loss of domestic market share and jobs have undermined the industry's position in domestic politics. Despite these differences, political and economic leaders in both countries have succeeded in deflecting potential challenges to the overarching design of their political life by assisting those in adversely affected industries to adjust to change. As Gerhard Lehmbruch writes, "Generally speaking, industrial policy and, in particular, restructuration of industries in distress appears to be a field where corporatist arrangements on the 'meso' or 'micro' (firm) level are of increasing importance."[1] Through their adjustment policies the Austrians and the Swiss have maintained their corporatist political arrangements; and they have managed through a flexible response to external pressures to live with change rather than attempting to thwart it.

Four cases illustrate how corporatism succeeds in mobilizing consensus. They do so by showing how Switzerland and Austria accept outcomes dictated by market forces. Switzerland acknowledges the power of the market freely, in both textiles and watches. In the 1970s hundreds of firms and tens of thousands of jobs were eliminated in both industries without much public debate and without political protest. But in the case of large firms, again without debate and without protest, the Swiss found a way to organize an enormously complex, far-reaching, and expensive assistance program on the basis of private initiative. The acceptance of market outcomes thus has its limits, even in Switzerland. Conversely, Austria's aversion to accepting market outcomes provoked large-scale government intervention in textiles between 1975 and 1978. But the government's willingness to absorb the costs of change had its limits—limits imposed by the constraints of Austrian politics, by the mounting costs of subsidies in an era of shrinking resources, and by the government's evident failure to assure an adequate and stable level of employment. In the end the collapse of the textile industry in Eastern Austria was accepted without great public repercussions. The crisis of Austria's steel industry, which has intensified in the early 1980s, also reveals a similar mixture of unwillingness simply to accept the dictates of the market and capacity for enhancing competitiveness through rationalization and diversification. Beyond certain limits market outcomes are accepted even in Austria. Thus, despite their different starting points and political inclinations, Switzerland and Austria converge in their response to market outcomes. In times of crisis, Switzerland is forced toward market intervention, Austria toward market acceptance.

This convergence is also to be seen in the political responses *not* chosen by these countries. Since the Swiss government lacks most of the instruments normally considered indispensable for an industrial policy, it is hardly surprising that no policy of sectoral transformation has been developed. But one might have expected an expedient government policy, trying to export at least some of the costs of change suffered by domestic producers to other countries, particularly those in the Far East pressing hard on Swiss firms. But despite insistent political demands from firms in the watch and textile industries, no such policies have been seriously debated, let alone tried. Conversely, with a less internationalized economy, and a more limited tradition in and lesser commitment to the principle of free trade, Austria has at times taken recourse to modified forms of protection, shifting some of the costs of change to foreign producers of textiles and steel. Yet one might have expected the government, which controls all the instruments for an industrial policy and enormous resources in the area of economic policy, to exploit the crisis that attend economic failure in order to develop long-term policies of sectoral transformation. But to date no such comprehensive policies have been asked for or developed. The Swiss state refrains from protectionism because it lacks power over its trade partners abroad. The Austrian state does not restructure its industry wholesale because it lacks power over its society a home. Instead, both countries pursue flexible industrial policies that emanate from their corporatist domestic structures.

The textile industry illustrates the predicaments of consumer goods industries of the First Industrial Revolution, experiencing low rates of economic growth and severe import competition.[2] Its numerous medium-sized and small firms are, typically, still family-owned and operated. Successful Swiss and Austrian producers occupy profitable market niches with specialized products. They do not enjoy positions of market power as measured by a firm's relative invulnerability to both its sources of supply and its market outlets.[3] Because the workforce tends to be foreign and female, the position of labor unions is

Table 3. The textile industry in Switzerland and Austria

	Switzerland		Austria*	
	Textiles	Garments	Textiles	Garments
Employment	*(thousands)*			
1970	60[a]	48[b]	66[c]	36[d]
1980	36[e]	28[b]	45[f]	33[d]
Firms	*(number)*			
1970	727[a]	1019[b]	714[g]	550[d]
1980	501[e]	631[b]	565[f]	510[d]
Average firm size (1980)	*(% of industry's employees)*[h]			
under 19	5	9	4	4
20–99	31	49	20	38
100–499	33	35	49	51
over 500	11	7	27	7
Research and development expenditures	*(% of total R and D)*			
1969	2.3[i]		1.0[j]	
1975	1.7[i]		2.0[j]	
Export intensity	*(% of total production)*†			
1970	47[i]	24[b]	41[j]	21[j]
1980	64[i]	32[l]	70[f]	43[d]
Import penetration	*(% of total production)*†			
1970	54[i]	78[b]	44[j]	17[j]
1980	70[i]	120[l]	80[f]	45[k]

SOURCES:

a. *Textilindustrie 1975* (Zurich: Schweizerische Textilkammer, 1976), p. 48.

b. Gesamtverband der Schweizerischen Bekleidungsindustrie, "Die Bekleidungsindustrie im Überblick: Eine permanente Dokumentation" (Zurich, May 1982), p. 13. Data are for 1971.

c. Hans Wehsely, "Industriepolitik in den siebziger Jahren: Rückblick und Ausblick," *Österreichische Zeitschrift für Politikwissenschaft* 1981/1, p. 30. Data are for 1969.

d. *Die österreichische Bekleidungsindustrie: Weissbuch 1980* (Vienna: Fachverband der Bekleidungsindustrie Österreichs, 1980), pp. 12, 17, 27. Export data are for 1979.

e. *Textilindustrie 1980* (Zurich: Schweizerische Textilkammer, 1981), p. 45.

f. *Die österreichische Textilindustrie im Jahre 1980* (Vienna: Fachverband der Textilindustrie Österreichs, June 1981), pp. 2, 31, Appendix Table 8.

g. *Chemiefasern Textilindustrie* no. 5 (May 1981), p. 364. Data are for 1971.

h. Swiss figures are from *Statistisches Jahrbuch der Schweiz 1981* (Bern: 1981), pp. 160–61; Austrian figures are from *Statistisches Handbuch für die Republik Österreich 1981* (Vienna: 1981), p. 314.

i. Silvio Borner et al., "Structural Analysis of Swiss Industry 1968–1978: Redeployment of Industry and the International Division of Labour" (Basle: Industrial Consulting and Management Engineering Co., 1978), pp. 52–53, 71. Figures are based on gross values and are for the years 1970 and 1977.

j. Beirat für Wirtschafts- und Sozialfragen, *Vorschläge zur Industriepolitik II* (Vienna: Ueberreuter, 1978), pp. 95, 103.

k. *Jahrbuch der österreichischen Wirtschaft 1979/2* (Vienna: Bundeskammer der gewerblichen Wirtschaft, 1980), p. 106.

l. Gesamtverband der Schweizerischen Bekleidungsindustrie, letters to the author, June 1982.

(Additional footnotes on opposite page)

typically weak. And, although they are often in great need of credit, medium-sized and small firms have only very limited access to external sources of funds. With such a profile, the industry is not easily organized in centralized business or trade associations; and it is not easily managed by government bureaucrats.

The decentralization of the textile industry and the vulnerability of many of its firms encourage it to seek industrial adjustments that would export the costs of change through direct intervention between domestic and international markets. The industry typically looks for protection against foreign competition in a variety of forms including ad hoc measures, such as voluntary export restraints and invisible tariff barriers, and more systematic measures, such as the Multi-fiber Arrangement, which, at the international level, coordinates policies of the OECD countries and low-cost producers in the Third World.[4]

Table 3 presents some of the statistical data that characterized the Swiss and Austrian textile industry across the 1970s. In terms of employment, Austria's textile industry was slightly larger and shrank less drastically, especially in the hard-pressed garment segment. The reduction in the total number of firms gives evidence of both the greater stability in Austrian markets and the greater decentralization of the Swiss textile industry (reflected in the data on average firm size). The rapid opening up of Austria's textile industry during the 1970s left it more exposed to world markets than the Swiss textile industry. Finally, the relative share of the total research and development budget devoted to textiles, though small in both countries, increased sharply in Austria and declined in Switzerland. These statistical data provide useful reference points for the case histories of the two textile industries.

Considering the economic dislocations that these two industries have suffered in the last two decades, one might expect them to respond to growing international competition by attempting to change the very nature of their respective social compacts—to change, that is, the way political life is conducted. This, I shall argue, is not what has happened. The national mobilization of consensus in both Switzerland and Austria around the task of meeting economic change managed to include the textile industries. Textiles thus pro-

---

*The existence of a large number of very small firms *(Gewerbe)* not covered by a separate industrial census impairs the strict comparability of the data, but it does not invalidate the broader trends reflected here.

†Because the Swiss data are based on gross values, the data may not be strictly comparable.

vide an excellent case for examining how the shift in economic factors of production is helped or hindered by the nature of politics. In sum, that is, they illustrate how corporatism copes with change.

SWISS TEXTILES

Despite a long-term decline in relative importance in both employment and exports, textiles and garments together ranked fourth among Switzerland's major industries in the late 1970s.[5] In the postwar years the garment industry expanded at a much greater rate than textiles, and employment in these two industries grew slightly from 104,000 in 1950 to 115,000 in 1971.[6] As in the rest of the Swiss economy, the postwar availability of cheap foreign labor was essential to economic expansion. Foreign workers held 12 percent of jobs in the textile industry in 1950, 36 percent in 1960, and 50 percent throughout the 1970s.[7]

Investment by foreign producers was also notable in the industry's economic expansion in the 1960s. By 1968 direct foreign investment amounted to $162 million, about one-fifth of total foreign direct investment in Switzerland. By the late 1960s foreign firms employed between 10 and 20 percent of the textile industry's total workforce.[8] Only the capital-intensive petroleum industry was more heavily penetrated by foreign capital. In the 1950s, 1960s, and 1970s the international orientation of the industry was also reflected in the growing share of products sold in world markets. Textile exports, less than 40 percent of production in 1959, grew to about 60 percent in 1979; garments, from 10 percent to about 30 percent.[9]

But Switzerland, as elsewhere, saw accelerating problems in the 1970s. Employment in textiles declined sharply: the 45 percent reduction between 1971 and 1981 was well above the average rate of decline in other Swiss industries.[10] In 1974–76 alone, between 15 and 20 percent of the workers lost their jobs; about 15 percent of the remaining workforce went on short hours.[11] The number of firms also decreased sharply, one reason being the decrease in foreign demand for Swiss products as the Swiss franc sharply appreciated in value.[12] Another reason was the growing penetration of Swiss markets by imports, especially of low-cost garments. Between 1967 and 1977 the negative trade balance in the garment industry quadrupled, and in 1980 it was $1.02 billion. Between 1971 and 1981 imports from Asia more than trebled their share in total textile imports, from 6 to 19 percent.[13]

These adverse developments in market conditions were reinforced by politics. The industry has suffered greatly from its failure to change Switzerland's manpower and exchange-rate policies. Since about half of its total workforce and virtually all of its unskilled labor is of foreign origin, the industry greatly benefited from the unrestricted inflow of foreign labor in the 1950s and 1960s.[14] The sharp restrictions that the federal government imposed in the 1970s on any further influx of foreign labor created an acute labor shortage in the industry, especially in times of strong market demand (as in 1977, for example, when employment increased by 8 percent). Throughout the 1970s the industry's call for a more "flexible" government approach to the question of foreign labor permits elicited no response. This political impotence reinforced the industry's rationalization, which will accelerate the declines both in employment and thus, indirectly, also in electoral strength.

Equally important, Switzerland's textile industry protested vociferously, but to no avail, against the relentless upward movement of the Swiss currency throughout the 1970s.[15] For an industry that depends on exports for survival, the franc's dramatic appreciation in 1978 created a crisis that surpassed the sharp downturn of 1975 and rivaled the experience of the 1930s. The textile industry fought hard for far-reaching deviations from Switzerland's liberal stance in the international economy, but its call for strict currency regulations or restrictions on capital movements fell on deaf ears. Those temporary measures which the Swiss Nationalbank did adopt in response to the demands of export industries—such as the imposition of negative interest rates and temporary restrictions on foreign investments in Switzerland—were ineffective. Other industrial sectors could counter the severe costs of a hard-currency policy more easily because of their sizable production facilities located abroad. But since 1945 Switzerland's textile and garment industry had veered little from its traditional strategy, producing high-quality products at home with advanced technologies. The industry thus confronted a very serious challenge.

The political defeats and economic hardships of the 1970s, as well as the anticipation of harder times to come, spurred concerted efforts to overcome the industry's institutional fragmentation and, it was hoped, its political impotence. The Bührle conglomerate was calling for the formation of a peak association as early as 1967.[16] The number of trade associations diminished from 54 in the late 1950s to 48 in the late 1960s, and 35 in the mid-1970s.[17] Growing pressures due to Switzerland's free-trade arrangement with the European Communities in the 1970s were anticipated in a flurry of organizational mergers in the late 1960s; by 1972 they had resulted in the formation of the industry's first peak association, the Swiss Textile Chamber (Schweizerische Textilkammer), which organizes firms involved in all stages of production. It is, however, a relatively weak organization, designed only to reinforce the informal consultation and cooperation that typified the industry in the 1950s and 1960s.[18] In fact, the Textile Chamber concerns itself with questions of economic policy largely by delegating different tasks to different member organizations; for example, it leaves issues of collective bargaining to two different employers' associations.[19] Its major purpose is to coordinate the industry's diverging interests and to represent them in politics as best it can. Yet it lacks a centralized structure and a clear mandate; thus, its reliance on the unanimity principle in reaching decisions is a symptom of the serious limits that impaired its operations in the 1970s.[20]

Given this pattern of fragmentation in intrasectoral interest representation, one might expect to see the industry attempt to capitalize on the political strength of Switzerland's peak business association, the Vorort. But the Vorort represents financial and industrial interests that strongly oppose any sustained interference with market principles and any prolonged attempt to slow the pace of economic change. Thus, in its demand to slow down the appreciation of the franc through administrative intervention in foreign-exchange markets, the textile industry faced the overwhelming opposition of Switzerland's major banks and giant multinational corporations. While the banks saw their economic interests threatened more directly than the multinationals did, both opposed a change in policy because they were committed to the economic, political, and philosophical precepts of economic liberalism. Moreover, on the issue of increasing the number of foreign workers in some of the "good" years after the deep recessions of 1974–75 and 1978–79, the textile industry confronted the unrelenting opposition of the federal government backed by a strong grass-roots movement, which by about 1970 had succeeded in defining the goal of Switzerland's manpower policy as a long-term reduction in the number of foreign residents.

The industry's political weakness is reinforced by Swiss regionalism. In only six of the twenty-six cantons did the industry account for more than one-fifth of the labor force in the 1970s. Furthermore, internal conflicts in the industry remain very serious. Particularly prominent are conflicts between firms located in the eastern canton of St. Gallen, which specialize in high value-added products for world markets, and firms located in the canton of Zurich, oriented more toward domestic markets. In the late 1970s it was not uncommon for the different segments of the industry to continue their disagreements within the Vorort on important questions of foreign trade and government support, despite intensive, informal bargaining and the concerted efforts of the Textile Chamber to forge a united stand. Since the Textile Chamber enjoys neither a seat nor a vote in the Vorort, it is seriously constrained in any effort to represent the interests of the industry more effectively within the business community at large.

The fact that the textile industry rarely spoke with one voice in the deliberations of the Vorort diminished even further the industry's already slim chances of building a coalition with other industries, such as watches, that might have advocated different policies. In fact on some important policy choices the textile industry was defeated not by the banks and the multinationals but by the interests of related industries. For example, textile producers suggested at times that they would derive more benefits from Switzerland's textile and machinery industry if the pace of international technological diffusion were to be slowed. Since Switzerland accounts for more than one-fifth of total OECD trade in textile machinery, and since the Swiss industry is increasingly selling its licenses worldwide, the textile sector's interest in monopolizing technological know-how is understandable. But all such attempts were bitterly opposed by the textile machinery producers, who are highly competitive in world markets and have no interest in indirectly subsidizing the declining fortunes of Swiss textile producers by sacrificing opportunities for sales and profits overseas. In its objections the textile machinery manufacturers could count on the support of virtually all other competitive branches of Swiss industry.[21] Thus, lacking the power to change policies central to Switzerland's strategy in the international economy, the textile industry had little choice but to rely on its own initiative to remain competitive in global markets.

Confronted with the adverse changes and political defeats of the 1970s, Switzerland's textile industry redoubled its export offensive in world markets, at the cost of declining profits, and maintained high rates of investment. In the hope of securing their long-term viability, firms chose a combination of quantitative decline and qualitative growth, supplementing the industry's traditional export strategy with a new emphasis on the foreign production so common in other branches of Swiss industry.[22] This export orientation requires high investments. Even in the midst of the deep recession of 1974–75, the industry's investments at home were reported to be about six times as high as the annual average that one group of European experts recommended for maintaining a modern and competitive textile indus-try into the 1980s.[23] Furthermore, the industry's efforts to remain competitive could, despite political differences, draw on its traditional links to the textile machinery industry—a source of considerable strength. At the expense of its own research and development the textile industry continued to acquire patents and licenses from the textile machinery industry as well as the chemical industry.

The industry's concerted efforts to modernize and rationalize its production structures, and thus maintain its competitiveness in inter-national markets, are evident even in the gloomy statistics of the 1970s. In 1974–75, for example, exports of textile and garment prod-ucts decreased by only 5 percent, as compared to an average of 8 percent for Switzerland's manufactured products as a whole and more than 20 percent for watches.[24] Although unable to offset the widening trade gap in garments, Switzerland's surplus in textile trade still doubled in the 1970s.[25] Moreover, the average value of Switzer-land's textile exports exceeded the average value of textile imports by one-half.[26] In the expanding foreign markets for high-quality textiles, Switzerland's industry remains highly competitive.

For this reason Switzerland's trade policy in textiles remained lib-eral throughout the 1970s. Although Swiss tariffs on textile products are among the lowest in the world, the issue of cheap imports from less developed countries, in sharp contrast to the case in Austria and other advanced industrial states, was not a prominent concern for the industry. Under the provisions of the Multi-Fiber Arrangement Switz-erland negotiated no voluntary export restraints, nor did it impose quantitative restrictions of any kind. In contrast to the European Communities, Switzerland was willing to extend the Multi-Fiber Ar-rangement in 1977 without imposing further restrictions on the tex-tile exports of the less developed countries. Unlike Austria, Switzerland never joined the Long-Term Arrangement on Cotton Textiles (LTA), designed to restrict the growth of textile exports from less developed countries. The far-reaching penetration of Swiss mar-kets by foreign products reflects this consistently liberal import policy. Indeed, the degree to which textiles produced in the less developed countries have penetrated Swiss markets is far greater than in Austria or in the European Communities.

The industry's defeats in the 1970s on national manpower and foreign-exchange policies simply replayed on a wider stage its lack of success in affecting national policy during the previous decade. In-deed, the industry's political strength has been profoundly debilitated by its export orientation, which consistently constrains its own demands for protection. It does so for the simple reason that a much greater proportion of textile imports is reexported than is consumed in Switzerland. Aware of the sharp limits that protectionist demands face, those segments of the garment industry hurt in particular by foreign imports, such as the stocking industry, are increasingly advocating "Buy Swiss" campaigns as a partial remedy to market pressures exerted by foreign producers. The primary reason that segments of the industry demand selective import protection is to use it as a lever in political negotiations to open additional foreign markets for Swiss exports. Limited as it is, protectionism is thus presented by the industry as an additional tool of export promotion.[27] Compared to those of Austria's textile industry, these are modest protectionist aspirations and achievements. They reflect the political climate of a country where liberalism is so deeply entrenched that government contracts designed to support the Swiss garment industry were in 1979 extended, in at least one instance, to an Austrian producer complaining of unfair discrimination.[28]

In an effort to compensate the industry for its political defeats on the central issues of manpower and foreign-exchange rates, and to cement ties between government and industry in areas where an ambivalent agreement existed—a liberal trade policy—the government extended limited and temporary forms of economic aid in times of great crisis during the 1970s. As part of a special "Program for the Alleviation of Economic Difficulties" (Botschaft über Massnahmen zur Milderung wirtschaftlicher Schwierigkeiten), the Swiss army placed a sizable order of $18 million in 1979, which benefited many of the garment industry's weaker firms. In a burst of patriotic fervor and concerned about the health of Swiss soldiers on cold winter nights, the garment producers delivered undershirts that were, some claimed, large enough to warm the soldiers' kneecaps. In the late 1950s the army's procurement policy for textile and garment products had been decidedly procyclical; this order, timed to counteract the business cycle, thus represented some help for hardpressed firms.[29] An anticyclical procurement policy would hardly seem a political victory of significant proportions in neighboring Austria, but in Switzerland's political economy it represented a modest gain for the textile industry.[30]

On the whole, however, government efforts to subsidize the industry, either directly or indirectly, have been very limited. Even in the worst of times the industry has always extolled the principle of self-help. Acknowledging the usefulness of temporary export supports, one of the industry's leading trade journals argued that such measures could not be justified over longer periods of time.[31] And while the president of the peak association of the garment industry welcomed a government subsidy for the industry's privately organized export promotion, he insisted at the same time that the "state should not have the capacity to influence economic life or to change industrial structures and thus to replace the decisions of the entrepreneur."[32]

It should be noted that the industry did receive substantial assistance in its export drive of the 1970s; but it is typical of Switzerland's political economy that the assistance did not come from the government.[33] In the mid- and late 1970s the textile producers received a variety of credit facilities from the Swiss Nationalbank as well as from the large private banks. Such preferential credits were designed to enhance their competitive position in world markets.[34] In the spring of 1975, the Association of Swiss Banks and the Swiss Nationalbank concluded an agreement that made short-term export credits available at preferential rates to consumer goods industries such as textiles and watches. In 1976 the big commercial banks further agreed to extend ten-year export credits at fixed, rather than variable, rates to those same consumer goods industries. By the end of 1977, the Swiss Bank Corporation alone had opened credit lines of $54 million, including $12.5 million for textile producers; its subsidization of interest rates, the bank claimed, cost $2.08 million in 1977 and $5 million between 1975 and 1977.[35] Another estimate talks of an annual subsidy of $10.4 million, three-fifths being financed by the private banks.[36] The industry's reliance on these preferential export credits increased more than eight-fold across the middle of the decade, from $38.75 million in 1975 to about $333 million in 1977.[37]

Export Risk Insurance was extended to include coverage for the risks stemming from currency realignments. Firms in the textile industry apply to their trade association rather than to a federal commission for their export risk insurance. The Textile Chamber, in turn, receives an allocation of fixed country quotas at prevailing rates from a federal commission. Furthermore, between 1976 and 1978 the Swiss Nationalbank agreed to enter forward exchange markets on behalf of the textile industry, at lower than commercial rates. Although they helped an industry short of cash, these measures, some critics charged, amounted to nothing less than concealed export subsidies. Adopted on a six- or twelve-month basis, they were extended several times before lapsing in 1980, when the Swiss franc's appreciation abated. All these concessions were intended to help industrial sectors, such as textiles, believed to be in the midst of far-reaching structural adaptation.

This assistance of the industry's export drive by the banks was reinforced by less costly government policies. In 1975 Swiss embassies in Spain and Iran were instructed to prepare market studies for Swiss textile exports.[38] The textile industry followed up with a lengthy and detailed proposal concerning the establishment of foreign trade representatives, who could be attached to Switzerland's 87 embassies, 39 consulates general, and 61 consulates.[39] The government accepted the proposal, modeled after Austria's elaborate system for promoting exports, in amended form and implemented it in six embassies covering Switzerland's exports in the Persian Gulf, the Far East, Africa, and Latin America. Finally, as most other forms of financial assistance wound down in 1979 and 1980, the federal government decided to contribute a subsidy of $1.98 million to the industry's collective export promotion.[40] In sum, although it had suffered stinging defeats on the central policy choices affecting its economic well-being, the industry did not break away from Switzerland's corporatist arrangements. Organizing a broad political challenge by a coalition of industries disadvantaged by Switzerland's strategy promised few rewards; but acquiescence brought its own compensations.

The corporatist web enmeshing the textile industry was particularly tight in the industry's relations with labor. Crisis strengthened cooperation rather than confrontation. One sign was that in textiles, as in other industries, there emerged new forms of institutional cooperation between employers and unions in a "Mixed Commission" (Gemischte Kommission).[41] The commission is staffed on a parity basis by representatives of the Employers Association of the Textile Industry (Verband der Arbeitgeber der Textilindustrie, VATI) and the leadership of the four unions engaged in textile collective bargaining. Created under conditions of economic crisis in 1975, the commission provides a forum for consultation and exchange of information, discussion of issues affecting the industry, and a further institutionalization of cooperative relations. Designed to aid the creation of consensus through a free exchange of information, particularly before collective bargaining commences, the Mixed Commission is a sector-specific institutional response to strengthen the social partnership between employers and employees at a time when the industry was laying off large numbers of workers, introducing short hours, and confronting the painful issue of rapid adaptation to changing market conditions. By 1977 the Mixed Commission had become a model for a system of "Personnel Commissions" (Personalkommission) at the level of the plant, which, it was hoped, would "inform," "discuss," and "codetermine" issues of workplace relations.[42] A response to the unions' codetermination demand of the mid-1970s, these personnel commissions are designed to institutionalize at the plant level the cooperative relations between business and unions already evident at the level of the sector.

Business and unions could cooperate more easily because the loss of jobs was concentrated among foreign workers and women, who made up 75 percent of the industry's workforce, rather than among the core of the union movement, Swiss male workers. The sharp reduction in the textile and garment industry's labor force in the 1970s did not alter the ratio between Swiss and foreign workers. Absolute numbers, however, show the importance of the industry's stock of foreign workers. Of 44,000 jobs lost across the decade, only 46 percent were held by Swiss citizens. Although a discriminatory policy did not affect foreign workers, women were dismissed in disproportionately large numbers. Federal officials have studiously avoided tracing what has happened to this part of the workforce. We can speculate that women returned to their homes in a culture permeated by the traditional values of women as homemakers and economic dependents. At the federal level, after all, female suffrage was granted in 1971, about half a century later than in most other industrial states. Since the adjustment costs stemming from adverse market conditions were borne largely by a labor force politically too weak to protest, the decision to reduce employment sharply in the 1970s rested exclusively with the employers. The consequences of such weaknesses are illustrated by collective bargaining in the garment industry in the late 1970s. Concerns over job security, which the appreciation of the franc had created for many firms, severely circumscribed the unions' power. Modest wage increases were phased in over a five year period. The automatic indexation of wages and a thirteenth month's salary as an annual bonus, demands that the unions had won in earlier agreements, were rescinded in favor of periodic consultation and bargaining that take account of market conditions. Yet the absolute peace obligations, which prohibit all strike action for the duration of the contract, were retained.

The limits that weakness imposes on the unions are reinforced by the limited control of the employers' associations in textiles and garments over their memberships. This is particularly evident in the garment sector. Because of the industry's precarious economic position, its peak association, (Gesamtverband der Schweizerischen Bekleidungsindustrie, GSBI) emerged gradually between 1965 and 1972, and continued to consolidate itself throughout the 1970s. Yet despite the defensive convergence of the economic and political interests of all segments of the industry, only 330 of the 631 firms still operating in the late 1970s were members of the organization. Only 160 firms have signed the industry's standard collective bargaining agreement, and that relatively low figure includes 100 firms located in the canton of Tessin, the industry's greatest area of concentration, which had made the signing of such a contract a legal obligation.[43] In opposition to their own trade association many employers have been objecting since the late 1960s about contributing to a "Solidarity Fund" financed (at a modest level) equally by employers and employees, and disbursed at the level of the firm under strict supervision of the employers' organization. Since union members get their contributions rebated from the Solidarity Fund, employers fear that it will strengthen the position of the small number of organized workers at the plant level. One newspaper account observed in 1974 that "the employers' breach of an industry-wide collective bargaining agreement on such scale is probably unique in Switzerland."[44] Many firms that have not signed the contract offer similar or even higher benefits in plant-level bargaining; but many offer less. Under industry-wide collective agreements, social adjustment clauses protect employees in case of a firm's bankruptcy; they are at times written into plant-level agreements even though the necessary financial resources are absent. When firms do fail, workers, even though they can typically find new jobs, still bear many of the costs of adjustment in these plants.[45]

How can we explain the behavior of the unions? Union membership, low as it is, is heavily concentrated among Swiss male workers. The four unions engaged in collective bargaining in the textile industry, for example, represent 10 to 25 percent of the workforce, and only 10 percent in garments. This low level of unionization is explained by the fact that the workforce in these two industries consists largely of marginal labor, which is not easily organized. Two-thirds of the garment industry's workforce is foreign, as compared to one-half in the textile industry; four-fifths are women.[46] The unions' response was thus not industrial militancy but bargaining conducted in a spirit of social partnership intent on protecting the employment of the unionized, Swiss male workforce in the industry's economically viable core. This was not altogether irrational. Switzerland's tight labor market made worker militancy less necessary. Compared to an average of 85 percent in all industrialized countries, earnings in the Swiss textile industry measured in comparison to the average for all manufactures amounted to 93 percent, the highest figure in the industralized world and far greater than Austria's 70 percent.[47]

In the early stages of industrialization the adaptability of the Swiss textile industry in world markets had impressed the British Parliament so much that in 1835 it sent a commission to study the phenomenal success of this small but dangerous rival. Unrestrained pursuit of free trade, flexibility and adaptability in the face of new conditions, and willingness to live with the costs of change were the industry's secret then; they continue to be of great importance now.[48] Politics has not impeded shifts in factors of production; as one knowledgeable observer of the industry has written: "To sum up, Switzerland is still favorably situated as a work location, thanks to certain advantageous and special conditions, such as the close collaboration between public authorities and the Swiss Nationalbank, between employers and employees, between industry and the banking world as well as between the textile, machinery and chemical industries."[49]

The convergence of economic flexibility and political stability are thus constructed, and they are constructed by political means. The experience of Switzerland's textile industry illustrates the compatibility of liberal corporatism and economic change. The essence of corporatism lies in a narrowing of power inequalities that favors cooperation. It is a cooperation that does not spring from altruism, but from the calculation of the long-term advantages that derive from a business community that coheres. For example, the special assistance that Switzerland's financial community granted in support of export drives was a deliberate effort of the dominant part of the business community, the large corporations in industrial growth sectors and the banks (the beneficiaries of Switzerland's hard-currency policy), to lighten the burden on other parts of the business community (which shoulder the policy's heavy costs). These preferential credit provisions were not, it should be noted, granted altogether voluntarily. Producers of textiles and watches threatened to demand the establishment of a special, government-run export credit bank should the private banks, and in particular the large ones, fail to respond positively—as, in the end, they did.[50] The government also contributed a measure of political compensation. The different forms of assistance that it granted after 1975 were very inexpensive economically, and very valuable politically, in assuring the industry that it would not have to suffer the consequences of rapid economic change unassisted. Taken together, these different measures served the purpose of placating a sizable, though not dominant, segment of Swiss industry.

FIRMS IN TROUBLE (1): GLATTFELDEN

The characteristic features of Switzerland's liberal corporatism are illustrated when firms get into trouble. The closing of the weaving section of the Spinning and Weaving Company of Glattfelden and the dismissal of 100 mostly foreign, female workers in a workforce of 230, resembles the more than 200 instances of firm closings in Switzerland's textile and garment industries between 1976 and 1980.[51] As in Glattfelden, many firms were in the hard-pressed weaving segment of the industry; but in contrast to other firms the workers in Glattfelden had, by the standards of the Swiss textile industry, shown an unusual degree of militancy. In the slump of 1975, for example, they had successfully protested against the dismissal of 75 workers. They settled instead for working shorter hours and relinquishing the system of indexed wages. In 1979 they organized a successful one-hour warning strike to enforce the 44-hour work week specified in the industry's collective bargaining agreement over the objection of management, which had insisted on an extra half-hour per week. In the same year the workers also pressed management to bring the pay of 40 percent of the mostly foreign, female workforce up to the minimum wage stipulated in collective bargaining agreements.

The reasons for the closing of the company's weaving section included increasing international competition, declining demand, and lagging investments during the preceding decade. The investment funds necessary to regain competitiveness were simply too great for a medium-size firm. Profit in spinning had supported losses in weaving, and for fifteen years there had been no dividend payments. In 1975 the firm had stopped paying indexed wages, a bonus for working night shifts, and any wage after more than two days of sick leave. Nonetheless, the 1981 decision to lay off more than two-fifths of the company's employees came with unexpected suddenness. Without prior debate or consultation with the factory council, the unions, or the local political leadership, the company was to dismiss 100 workers on two weeks' notice. The lack of prior, timely consultation broke with both the letter of the collective bargaining agreement with the union and the spirit of the industry's system of social partnership. Management haste was perhaps due to the fact that by the middle of January the entire production of the company's spinning division for the year 1981 had already been sold, leaving the weaving division short of its traditional in-house orders. In brief, management had decided to restructure the business solely around its more profitable spinning operation before disclosing its decision to dismiss all of its weavers.

The company's decision was met with protest rallies organized during work hours on the factory floor and strongly worded demands by the unions. They gained a one-month delay in the workers' dismissal and a promise that all avenues to forestall the closing of the weaving section would be explored. The workers sought political allies outside the firm. They contacted the commune's council and demanded that all efforts be made to continue production at least over the summer. The local chapter of the Socialist Democratic Party and the union federation of the lower part of the canton of Zurich publicly backed the demands. The canton's economic ministry offered its good offices—but no subsidies—for reaching a satisfactory solution to the conflict. A public rally was organized, attended by most of the workers, union officials, politicians, and representatives of the Italian and Turkish emigrant organizations.

Apart from building a political alliance, the workers drew up, in the most general terms, a number of plans that they hoped would keep the weaving section open. These plans included the commune's purchase of the buildings and machinery, and its subsequent operation of the company; the formation of an independent company; a merger with other interested firms; product diversification; and the possible formation of a workers' cooperative. But all of these proposals had an air of unreality about them. The workers' solidarity committee lacked the all-important specific information on which to base their recommendations, and it did not command the expertise necessary to develop a concrete plan, which both the company and the employers' federation regarded as a precondition for serious negotiations. Furthermore, even under the best of circumstances the three-week deadline that management had set would have been exceedingly difficult to meet.

Of greater importance for many of the workers, the factory council, and the unions was their ability to work together with the company's director and the Federation of Employers in formulating a "social plan," the method by which dismissed workers in Switzerland are typically provided with a certain amount of protection against the hardships attending unemployment or relocation. Fortunately, economic conditions for the company were such that management's publicly proclaimed generosity, expressed in the language of paternalistic obligation toward dismissed workers, was no mere facade. Negotiations between the three unions directly affected, management, and the textile industry's employer organization produced a "social plan" that the company's workforce voted to accept. The plan made provisions for assisting the workers in their search for new jobs, for retraining those who needed it, making arrangements for moving, guaranteeing continuous insurance coverage and the right to live in company housing for another 15 months, transferring the workers' and the company's past contributions to the company pension fund to the new employer, and providing severance pay to workers according to their age and length of service with the company as well as their individual needs. In contrast to workers in other ailing firms, which declare bankruptcy only after they have used up all of the company's assets including, at times, the pension fund, in Glattfelden dismissed workers received substantial payments that fell within the range typical of the textile industry.[52] In addition, the 100 dismissed workers could choose among several hundred job openings that had been registered with the company within a few weeks of the lay-off decision. In Switzerland's privatized welfare state and tight labor markets, the loss of employment does not necessarily eliminate the material basis of a worker's existence.

But dismissal does impose severe hardships on the individual, including the prospect of moving one's family, leaving friends, and changing occupations. It is not atypical for the textile industry that in this instance, as in many others, most of the dismissed workers were Italian and Turkish women. Many of them had, over a period of years, begun the slow process of integrating themselves into a foreign milieu. For these workers the costs of disruption were especially high. The commune and its citizens also suffered greatly from the elimination of one hundred jobs, for no other major employer exists in the commune and many residents commute to neighboring Bülach or more distant Zurich to earn their livelihood. The commune's problems were, at least in part, of its own making. It had long previously sold all the commune land zoned for industrial use to the company, making Glattfelden a one-company town. Efforts to attract another firm to the commune had failed because the Glattfelden Company wanted no competition for the local pool of workers. Yet the company's contribution to the commune's total tax revenue was less than 2 percent, or $10,800 in 1980, about one-third less than in 1975.

The political lessons stressed by all who attended the final protest rally were the impotence of the workers, the factory council, the unions, and the commune; their lack of the information and expertise necessary for making realistic and viable proposals to counter management's decision; the necessity for a sharing of power inside the factory; and the need for building broader and stronger political alliances across ethnic and regional lines. These understandable lessons reflected the workers' great difficulty in opposing the prerogatives of management to hire and fire in a capitalist economy. They also underlined the difficulty of courting allies in a political setting that fosters fragmentation.

For a study of corporatism and economic change, however, Glattfelden teaches other lessons about adjustment. The firm had been ailing for a long time. In order to maintain employment levels in weaving, profits had long been allowed to suffer. The workers held their final rally after most of them had voted in favor of the social plan that their representatives had worked out with management. In discussing the consequences of the lay-off the factory council and the unions were fully involved in the deliberations and succeeded in extracting considerable benefits for the affected workers. Within the context of the Swiss textile industry in the late 1970s, the plan that workers, unions, and management drew up provided the workers with a considerable financial cushion to absorb some of the shock of job loss and to ease the transition to other employment. And, critically, all participants knew that alternative, well-paying jobs existed, not only as a statistical abstraction but in reality, with Swiss firms from near and far making concrete offers. When the Glattfelden Company failed, the logic of market developments was obeyed, not instantaneously according to strict criteria of profitability but with some delay and hesitation. Finally, the episode also mirrors the disjuncture between collective impotence and individual well-being so typical of Switzerland's liberal corporatism.

AUSTRIAN TEXTILES

Compared to textiles in other advanced industrial states, Austria's industry is still relatively large. Throughout the 1960s, for example, its employment remained virtually unchanged. And in the late 1960s the industry's decline was tempered by the Austrian economy's unprecedented boom. These fortuitous circumstances reflected Austria's position in the international economy: a mixture of relative economic backwardness (compared to Western Europe) and relative economic advancement (compared to Eastern Europe).

Foreign capital, especially in the relatively low-wage Eastern Austrian garment centers, prolonged favorable economic conditions and even expanded some capacity. Austria's Chamber of Labor found in the late 1970s that foreign investors most favored the textile and garment sectors, together with the electrical and paper industries.[53] Meanwhile, in the 1960s, Austria began to import foreign labor (primarily from Yugoslavia and Turkey). By the late 1970s, the proportion of foreign workers employed in textiles was greater than in any other Austrian industry: in 1978 12,500 workers, more than one-fifth of the industry's workforce, were foreigners.[54] Capacity expansion and relative labor abundance improved the industry's competitive position in international markets and enhanced its attractiveness in the domestic economy. Throughout the 1960s and early 1970s employment in the industry increased and the wages paid in textiles and garments narrowed the gap with wage rates paid in Austrian industry as a whole.[55]

Nonetheless, employment in textiles declined sharply in the 1970s. Austria's textile industry experienced nothing like the half million job losses and 3,500 closed factories that members of the European Communities claim to have suffered in the 1970s.[56] But, by Austrian standards, the decline in employment was very substantial. Indeed, between 1974 and 1979 the employment decline in textiles and garments was greater than in any other industrial sector and exceeded, by a wide margin, the decline for Austria's industry as a whole.[57] Between 1974 and 1978, production decreased by one-tenth; the number of firms also decreased sharply in the 1970s.

This decline in the industry's economic fortune was due in large measure to competition from foreign producers, especially in West Germany, Italy, Switzerland, and, in the case of garments, the Far East. But it is important to note that as late as 1979 only 5 percent of textiles and 12 percent of garments were imported from Asia. By 1980 textile imports exceeded exports by more than $193 million—in the garment industry the gap had increased to $262 million in 1979. The import gap, which had been evident since the late 1960s, was still widening.[58]

Austria has tried to live with economic change in recent years through a cautious mixture of trade liberalization and temporary subsidies. Throughout the postwar period Austria's gradual lowering of tariffs and quotas has been a source of potential tension with its commitment to a policy of full employment. By the mid-1970s Austria's policy of freeing trade with the European Communities, Comecon, and the less developed countries had progressed further than ever before. And the industrial sector most directly affected was textiles. Whatever the advantages for the Austrian economy as a whole, an increasing openness to the global economy was certainly inimical to the narrow interests of the textile industry.

In the late 1950s Austria was still adhering to a protectionist policy in the international economy and, in contrast to Switzerland and the

Scandinavian countries, virtually locked out textile imports from less developed countries. In 1962 the GATT pushed Austria toward liberalization by insisting that it double its import of cotton textiles over the next five years. In the same year the Long-Term Arrangement on Cotton Textiles shifted Austria's textile protection from the imposition of unilateral to the negotiation of bilateral trade restrictions. But Austria was reluctant to change; an UNCTAD report issued five years later (in 1967) singled the country out as the most conspicuous example of a developed market economy that had failed to liberalize its highly restrictive import quotas under the LTA.[59] In the late 1960s even the Swiss textile producers were complaining about several of Austria's protectionist policies.[60]

Austria's cautious attitude toward economic liberalization was also to be seen in the 1970s. In the early part of the decade Austria's average tariff rates on textile products were 16 percent, twice as high as in Switzerland and also substantially higher than in Sweden (12 percent) and the EC (10 percent).[61] Austrian textile tariffs have been occasional targets of criticism by members of the GATT.[62] Moreover, the Austrian government partially exempted its textile industry from the enlargement of the general trade preference granted to the less developed countries under GATT auspices. In the Tokyo Round agreement, signed in 1979, Austria's average tariff reduction in textiles was only about 10 percent, one-half of the Swiss cut and substantially below the even greater cuts made by Japan and the EC (25 percent), and the United States and Sweden (35 percent).[63] It is noteworthy, however, that despite Austria's cautious reliance on protectionism, government, bureaucracy, industry, and the unions eschewed explicit and unilateral measures of protection, for which laws prohibiting foreign dumping and assuring orderly market arrangements offered ample legal grounds.[64] Since Austrian politics typically operates not by administrative decree but by political consensus, these two laws have been used very sparingly.

Austria's attitude toward change as well as its political temperament are illustrated by its initial response to the serious difficulties that its stocking industry experienced in 1977. Imports from Israel, France, and Italy were selling at only a fraction of Austrian production costs, endangering five thousand jobs. Faced with mounting political pressures from both business and unions, the minister of Trade and Industry responded not with quotas or price quidelines but with a gentlemen's agreement with Austria's importers, which entitled them to import one inexpensive pair of stockings for every five domestically produced pairs. The results, however, were not encouraging: cheating was widespread, especially among Austria's big department store chains, several of them foreign-owned. The government subsequently introduced minimum import prices, but they proved equally unsuccessful. The big importers of stockings made sure that their foreign suppliers' bills reflected the administrative price and received credit for the difference between the administrative and the real price in foreign bank accounts. The Foreign Trade Ministry abolished the system in the fall of 1979 because, it claimed, price violations had been very rare. At the same time, as Austrian producers pointed out, imports had increased from 24 to 52 million pairs between 1977 and 1979 while domestic production had decreased from 76 to 60 million pairs.[65]

The ineffectiveness of these protectionist measures was not only due to importers. Some of the evidence suggests that Austria's textile industry itself is increasingly importing products that it can no longer produce competitively in Austria. Indeed, one large, ailing textile producer, eventually to be supported by government subsidies, had contracted for 35 million pairs of stockings from Romania over a period of five years in the mid-1970s. In a classic episode of shifting adjustment to change across national borders, Switzerland became one of Austria's favorite markets for selling its surplus stockings. Thus, as the case of Austrian stockings shows, protectionist policies are more easily monitored on paper than in reality. In this instance, as in others, the era of the "new protectionism" coincided with a continued expansion of international trade.

International trade negotiations at times afford other political opportunities for the Austrian government to regulate the pace of change. In the 1970s, within the framework of the Multi-Fiber Arrangement (MFA), the Austrian government negotiated voluntary export surveillance with eleven countries that were threatening Austria's textile producers, especially in uncompetitive low-cost, mass-production segments of the industry.[66] Outside the MFA, different producer organizations in the Austrian textile industry have themselves restricted imports by privately negotiating voluntary export restraints with Austria's Eastern trade partners, in the hope of making these countries purchase a larger share of Austrian production. Moreover, the Austrian government and industry openly favored a renewal of the Multi-Fiber Arrangement, along somewhat more liberal lines than those advocated by the large industrial states and, in particular, the EC. This renewal was a pragmatic way of defending a generally liberal trade order, from which Austria had greatly benefited, against the rising tide of protectionism, especially in the EC and the United States.

To say that the Austrians wanted a relatively liberal MFA is, however, a long way from saying that the Austrians favored free trade. Rather, the Austrian government preferred internationally negotiated limits on free trade such as the MFA to unilateral Austrian moves that might invite retaliation abroad. With the renewed MFA, Austrian policy in the late 1970s thus became more restrictive. For example, the illegal import of textiles and garments from the Far East under forged West German, Dutch, and Italian labels prompted the Austrian government to introduce a surveillance system of import declarations in twelve product categories, in the summer of 1977. These declarations had to be approved by the Ministry of Trade and Industry in Vienna before customs officials could permit foreign shipments to enter the Austrian market. According to one official, the ministry acts "promptly," "automatically," and "free of charge."

But as with stockings, political intervention in the textile trade runs up against the inefficiency of administrative supervision. Cheating, the Ministry of Trade and Industry reported, was soon widespread, and about two-thirds of the import declarations examined contained falsified data. Yet, according to one official in the Trade Ministry, the handful of officials in the provinces and in Vienna inspecting an avalanche of up to half a million declarations per year have just about the time needed for orderly filing.[67] With luck such an administrative system can pick out only a few of the most blatant instances of cheating, such as an import consignment of 70,000 shirts from Gambia (a country that lacks even a rudimentary capacity to produce shirts), or imports from Italy labeled "made in Hongkong."[68]

In general, then, trade restrictions through administrative intervention were ineffective in stopping certain kinds of imports. But they did create an early warning system, which registered shifting trade flows and provided the government with a basis for negotiating voluntary export restraint under the MFA with particular exporters in selected product categories. For example, in the spring of 1978, in an international climate of growing hostility toward Japan's export offensive, the Austrian government sensed an opportunity to improve its massive foreign trade deficit with Japan. Even though shirt imports from Japan had amounted to less than $30,000 in the last quarter of 1977, the Foreign Trade Ministry moved, in anticipation of a sharp increase in imported shirts, to open trade negotiations with

Japan. Trade in textiles was a pretext for raising broader questions of trade policy, such as the Austrian wish to become a more important supplier to Japan's automobile industry.[69]

On the other hand, in contrast to Switzerland, the Austrian government provided no special provisions, beyond its well organized system of trade representatives, to strengthen the industry's export capacity. Only very recently has the peak association of business, the Federal Economic Chamber, decided to go beyond the organization of occasional trade fairs as its major response to the industry's increasing involvement in foreign markets.[70] Favorable conditions in the international markets of the late 1960s and early 1970s had made exports the main stimulant of the industry's growth without special government support. In the early 1980s export-oriented segments of the Austrian textile industry, such as the embroidery industry in the Western province of Vorarlberg, were shipping abroad more than 90 percent of their highly specialized products, as compared to about two-thirds for the industry as a whole. But since it is a small country, Austria can exercise virtually no influence on developments in foreign markets, be they as momentous as the continuous depreciation of the dollar throughout most of the 1970s or as minor as the closing of Nigerian markets in 1977 (which affected Austria's exports of lace).[71] The industry's insistent demand for financing that would also cover production for exports was not heeded by the government. A special investment credit program (Investitionsmilliarde), allocated to all of Austrian industry in 1975 in an attempt to maintain aggregate demand in the face of shrinking export markets, excluded funds for the short-term credits that the textile industry badly needed. And the strong appreciation of the schilling pushed neither the government nor the banks to assist textile producers in export markets.

Foreign production, furthermore, is not an option that Austria's textile industry can pursue to counter the effects of appreciation. In sharp contrast to Swiss firms, Austria's garment manufacturers have strongly and consistently opposed foreign production on the grounds that it leads to a loss of jobs in Austria and confuses relations between industry and importers. The textile industry has not been quite so hostile. The relatively few applications from firms intending to open production facilities abroad are reviewed by the trade association of the textile industry within the Federal Economic Chamber and at times attract favorable rulings. But the issue of foreign production remains very controversial and is rarely discussed in public. Indeed, the government has explicitly ruled out state support for the foreign investment projects of those few adventurous textile firms which sought to strengthen profitability and growth by moving production abroad.[72]

The government has undertaken efforts to improve the domestic base of the textile industry; but it has faced great problems in doing so. In the abstract, Austria's policy is to encourage strongly interfirm cooperation and joint ventures; but, in practice, effective cooperation between firms requires financial links, and these are not easily forged.[73] In comparison to other industrial sectors relatively large family enterprises (such as Hämmerle, Rhomsberg, Getzner, Mäser, and Ganahl) have proud independent traditions to look back on. The prominent place of foreign firms in Austria's textile industry also tends to inhibit cooperation between firms. And, while the government has begun to recognize that an insufficient capital base is a serious weakness of the industry, and especially of its small and often more dynamic firms, the government's actions have contributed little to the infusion of new capital.[74] Austria's nationalized banks, furthermore, stood aloof until the late 1970s, having divested themselves of their holdings in the textile industry in the late 1950s.[75]

The Austrian government moved beyond ad hoc measures of partial relief only when the declining economic fortunes of the textile industry, especially in the Eastern part of the country, caused one notable collapse (Vöslau, which I examine in detail below) and endangered large numbers of jobs, threatening to undermine the government's full employment policy. In an effort to merge several of Austria's major, endangered textile producers into one large combine (Textilfusion-Ost), the government granted investment subsidies of $17.5 million in 1976–77, the beginning of an expensive but limited bail-out. In other words, policy amounted to little more than a government-initiated and supervised concentration of marginal producers, and limited subsidies in the interest of saving Austrian jobs. The government's defense of jobs was essentially a cushion, which delayed some of the impact of economic change, rather than a shield obstructing market developments.

The specialized, competitive, and export-oriented firms in the Western province of Vorarlberg, which accounted for just under one-half of the total production of the industry, were openly critical of the government's policy. Traditionally, most of these producers had existed only as cheap-labor subcontractors to higher-quality Swiss producers. But during the 1960s and 1970s many of them had regrouped and succeeded in firmly reestablishing their competitiveness in specialized market segments. Their strong preference was for different forms of cooperation between firms in the private sector, rather than industrial concentration under government sponsorship.[76] Furthermore, their economic problems differed radically from those of the industry in the Eastern parts of the country. As was true across the Swiss border, the most critical problem was the shortage of skilled workers, which increasingly prompted firms to cease bidding for foreign orders, to increase the share of imports relative to their own production, and to consider moving parts of their production facilities abroad and, to a limited extent, to Eastern Austria.[77] The regional decentralization of the industry and its different economic problems conjured up, for some observers, Austria's traditional partisan differences as well as regional conflicts between East and West.

But when the crisis spread to some of the larger family firms in Western Austria in 1981, it became clear that Austria's social corporatism extends equally to East and West, red and black. In the summer and fall of 1981 the threat of suddenly losing an additional 3,500 jobs prompted the chancellor to convene several "summit meetings" in his own office between leaders of industry, unions, and government.[78] The industry's traditional preference for cooperation clashed with the government's insistence on outright merger. But a first aid package of $2.5 million was nonetheless agreed on in the late autumn of 1981. It was financed, in equal parts, by the federal government, the provincial governments of Tyrol and Vorarlberg, and the two largest nationalized banks. At the cost of another $6.28 million, the federal government adopted in the spring of 1982 a program (Textillösung-West) that expressed a compromise between cooperation and merger. A holding company was created to disburse the funds for restructuring to firms in trouble. By the summer of 1983 the program was looking like a success. Employment in the affected firms had been cut by only one-third, rather than the one-half originally projected, the government had not increased its original financial commitment, and the firms were evidently heading back toward profitable operation. Because the rescue operation occurred in a politically conservative region, public controversy between business and government was greater than it had been a few years earlier in the East, and the role of the unions was smaller. But similar in both episodes was the logic by which the government sought to absorb severe economic shocks and thus to smooth the transition in an inevitably declining industry.

As early as the late 1970s the government's evident failure to halt the drastic decline in employment with its support of weak firms had led to a shift in policy aimed at a structural improvement of the industry. Rather than supporting ailing textile firms that threatened to close their doors, the federal government decided to fund 10 percent of the cost of new machinery between 1979 and 1983.[79] Subsequent lobbying by the garment and leather industries led to their inclusion in this subsidy program. Firms were eligible as long as they could prove that old machinery was simultaneously being scrapped and production capacity not expanded, and they could receive the subsidy in addition to other government programs facilitating investment. The government allocated a total of $6.18 million for each of the five years for the texile industry, $772,500 for the garment industry. Between 1979 and 1981 this government program affected investments totaling $125 million. In 1981 alone about 60 percent of the investment in machinery was thus subsidized in the textile industry, as compared to about 30 percent in garments.

This government aid reflected the political requirements of Austria's social partnership, as well as the government's intention to secure a viable future for the competitive core of the industry. Yet it should be stressed that the government did not adopt the program because of the political strength of the textile industry. For what is striking about the industry is its political weakness. Austria's textile industry lacks effective political representation in the business community and in the unions. In party councils and in Parliament its spokesmen are short on political imagination and influence.[80]

The government thus made a deliberate effort to compensate the textile industry for some of the economic losses it had sustained and to show through the choice of certain policies that it remained strongly committed to the industry as it confronted further economic changes. The costly, though temporary, subsidy programs adopted in the late 1970s illustrate the logic of the government's behavior. Although the industry's share in direct public subsidies declined from 20 percent in 1970 to 4 percent in 1975, the federal government, once it had grasped the magnitude of the economic crisis, did not hesitate to offer substantial resources.[81] After another two years the government concluded that its policy of heavily subsidizing a small number of large, uncompetitive firms had been a costly failure. Yet within a year it had committed itself to a differently conceived and organized program of assistance targeted not to uncompetitive large firms but to competitive small ones. These quick reorientations in policy, as well as the commitment of substantial amounts of capital, signaled to different segments of the industry the government's intention to assist firms in riding the crest of structural readjustment without seeking to override market pressures.

The subsidy policy of 1979 shows the spirit in which political compensation for economic change was granted. A firm had to send its application to the industry's association in the Federal Economic Chamber, which, after reviewing and approving it, presented it to the regular biweekly meetings of a special committee advising the Ministry of Trade and Industry. (In contrast to Switzerland the banks, whether private or public, were not entrusted with a screening of applications.) The deliberations of the advisory committee were based on data that did not permit careful evaluation of a firm's longer-term economic viability; indeed, it often proved impossible to establish the equivalence in terms of capacity between the new machinery for which investment subsidy was sought and the old machinery that was to be scrapped.[82] Similarly, other minor restrictions on firms receiving aid were difficult to enforce: the investment project should secure jobs in Austria, the bids of Austrian suppliers should be considered before those of foreign suppliers, and in times of economic crisis the firm should produce for domestic markets.[83]

In its review of applications, the committee acted quite perfunctorily. Although the program was inspired by Japan's selective industrial policy, it was in fact not selective—very few firms were denied support. Since the program did not address the industry's greatest weakness, in the areas of design and marketing, its political intent was plain. The government's policy to concentrate the ailing large firms of Eastern Austria had failed; this new program benefited a different segment of the industry, and a different region. The fact that government policy was having a hard time producing the intended economic results is less remarkable than that the government, on very short notice and under growing fiscal constraints, should have moved from the costly failure of an old policy to the costly experimentation with a new one, thus maintaining its support of the industry as a whole.

One reason for the government's flexibility in responding to crisis is that the organization of the country's political economy contains, and constrains, differences in sectoral interests. Austria's peak associations offer arenas in which the intense conflicts between different industry segments and industries can be aired without stalemating government policy. On the question of import restrictions, for example, the political opposition of Austria's importers, adversely affected by the adoption of import declarations and subsequent moves toward more protection such as the strict enforcement of Austria's textile label regulation after January 1979, led to heated discussions with the textile producers inside the peak association of business.[84] Several enraged importers were reported to have requested thousands of copies of the new forms when import declarations were introduced. Yet the great strength of Austria's peak associations lies precisely in the fact that contradictory interests are primarily managed through political bargains struck within the business community and adhered to by all firms and trade associations. Political bargaining within peak associations has made it unnecessary for the textile industry "to go public" in the search for new political solutions or political partners.

A similar process of containing political opposition to rapid economic change can be observed within the union movement. In the textile plants the rank and file typically favors protectionist policies to defend existing jobs. The central leadership of the trade union federation, on the other hand, sees its task as educating its membership about the benefits for Austria of open international markets. The task of mediating between these two conflicting views falls to the textile union, which adheres quite closely to the political stance of the central union leadership but welcomes flexibility when it comes to the imposition of temporary protectionist measures or subsidies to satisfy its membership.

In the 1970s, with declining employment and declining union membership, the union was weakened along with the industry as a whole.[85] The government attempted to provide political compensation and, through the granting of economic assistance, indicated that it remained strongly committed to full employment. Specific measures reaffirmed that commitment. In 1975 the government extended from three to seven months the period during which textile workers on short hours could receive special state support.[86] Partly as a result of this policy, in 1977 the industry had only eight hundred workers on short hours.[87] At the same time the Austrian government reaffirmed its legally sanctioned right to veto the lay-off of more than 10 percent of the workforce in any firm.

Under any circumstances it would be difficult for union leaders with a declining membership to mount a sustained attack on government policy, particularly since the government has needed no convincing that the loss of jobs should be compensated for as much as possible. The union favors a thorough modernization of the industry even at the risk of further reductions in employment. Its long-term objective does not lie in the defense of an ailing industry with low wages but in the narrowing of the 30 percent wage differential that in the late 1970s separated average wages in textiles from those in relative growth industries such as metals and engineering.[88] In the pursuit of this policy the union can rely on a workforce that is less unionized than in other industries. Nevertheless, the union's organization of 50 percent of the workforce in textiles and 42 percent in garments is much greater than across the Swiss border.

Austria's textile industry has undergone enormous changes in the 1970s. A cautious pursuit of free trade and a substantial, though limited, assistance of producers slowed the shift in factors of production without attempting to arrest it. The industry's troubles are by no means over. Change occurs so rapidly that the "healthy" segment of the industry in Western Austria was in the early 1980s experiencing more serious problems than the "sick" part in Eastern Austria. But Austrian industrialists and government officials are quite optimistic. Austria's textile industry will continue to be competitive in different market segments and, for the foreseeable future, will remain a medium-sized sector in the economy. In the process of slowing the economic change that is transforming the industry, government policies made it possible for all of those affected—workers and businessmen, interest group leaders and bureaucrats, elected officials and mass publics—to subscribe to the notion that living with large-scale economic change was tolerable as long as efforts were undertaken to compensate for it in both economic and political terms.

FIRMS IN TROUBLE (2): VÖSLAU

The spectacular failure of Austria's largest textile firm in the late 1970s illustrates the way social corporatism works when firms hit real trouble.[89] The 1975 merger of three large textile producers had been prompted by the fear of unemployment, a fear fed by serious deterioration in the economic conditions of one of Austria's oldest textile firms in Vöslau. In promoting the merger the government attempted to intervene actively in the process of industrial adjustment.

Preliminary debates about the concentration and rationalization of production in these firms had begun in the late 1960s; the idea remained dormant, however, during the prolonged economic growth of the years from 1968 to 1974. The sharp recession of the mid-1970s abruptly ended those favorable economic conditions, and, of the three companies that the government had singled out for the merger, the one in Vöslau had incurred losses of $3.21 million in 1974; a second was insolvent; and only the third was operating in the black. The merger was to unify most of the textile production in the Eastern provinces and to create a large, competitive firm with a turnover of about $60 million, a firm that could offer secure jobs to its 1,800 employess. The plan aimed to reduce, in the case of the Vöslau company alone, the number of products from 400 to 25 and would cut, with union approval, 700 jobs from the three companies' combined total of 2,500. The merger attracted support from the shareholders and managers, the union, private and nationalized banks, and the government. Yet, five years and $70 million later the government would admit that the company could not be saved.

The infusion of new capital was massive. As of 1 January 1976 the new company's capital base was strengthened through the conversion of $2.8 million of credits by Austria's largest nationalized bank, the Creditanstalt, and $1.1 million by Austria's best-known private bank, Schoeller, into company shares. Together with the Creditanstalt, Schoeller assumed majority control of the new company. Meanwhile the federal goverenment, for its part, made available through two of its investments funds the $7.5 million needed for investment in 1976–77 and agreed, at the insistence of the banks, to insure that amount through its loan and investment guarantee fund. In addition, the Ministry for Social Affairs contributed another $670,000 from Austria's labor-market funds. The reorganization plan thus left Austria's largest nationalized bank with a substantial direct investment in the new company and committed the federal government to finance and insure the company's investments for two years.

But those two years would dash initial bright hopes and expectations. Losses of $6 million in 1976 and more than $12 million in 1977 required the infusion of an additional $6 million in the summer of 1977. Twelve months later saw a further massive infusion, of more than $27.5 million, and the opening of additional credit lines. In tense negotiations involving the socialist finance minister, the director of the Creditanstalt, and the Schoeller representative (who, coincidentally, was also president of the Federation of Industry), the banks, primarily the Creditanstalt, agreed to further substantial investments and credit facilities while the government promised, after the necessary legislation had been approved by Parliament, to reimburse them for $9.6 million of credits on which the company had defaulted. As part of a package to save the firm, the union agreed to a halving of employment, from 1,600 to 800 by 1980.

During the next six months the distrust of relatively healthy textile firms in the Western province of Vorarlberg found expression in the determined opposition of the conservative ÖVP. It regarded an industrial policy that sought to defend jobs in ailing companies without granting similar assistance to other firms in the industry as arbitrary and imprudent. The government could not get Parliament to adopt legislation that would have provided additional capital, thereby preventing the banks from writing off an additional $6.9 million in bad debts.

In December 1978 the Vöslau company declared bankruptcy. According to the director of the Creditanstalt further subsidies, perhaps as much as $36 million, would have been necessary to keep the company afloat during the coming year. The SPÖ government could not continue to finance a company running up such enormous deficits while continuously cutting down on employment. All told, the government had lost about $70 million in its attempt to save a failing firm. At the same time, the nationalized Creditanstalt had become financially involved in the merger for primarily political reasons. Together with the government it was interested in setting an example in what was regarded at the time as an important experiment in industrial policy. But it ended up owning three-quarters of a bankrupt company that had defaulted on millions in loans.

The contrasts with Switzerland are clear. The redundancy of hundreds of workers was not left to the discretion of private management but instead galvanized political action at the highest level, triggered by the pressure of the unions, management, and a private bank—all of whom were interested in preserving the company's operation. In translating its political objectives into action the SPÖ government could rely on broad political support among industry and the unions, and command a wide array of financial instruments. But strong political intervention in rapidly changing markets proved to be commercially unviable and extremely costly; markets simply could not be overridden by political action. Even before it went bankrupt, the company had already eliminated more than one-third of its original workforce, and it was proposing an additional 50 percent cut. Thus the government's intervention was not so much a long-term policy of structural transformation as a tactically motivated attempt to compensate for rapidly deteriorating market conditions with increasing subsidies.

The failure of the firm, and the government's loss of $70 million in what turned out to be a futile defense of jobs in an exposed industrial sector, caused little political acrimony; the interested parties were either directly involved in decisions or were subsequently paid off. For example, concern for the subcontractors and workers adversely affected by the bankruptcy prompted the nationalized Creditanstalt, which had already lost millions of dollars, to spend an additional $4.5 million. And Austria's labor-market institutions were fully deployed to ease the transition of workers to new jobs. Similarly, in Switzerland the Glattfelden company's "social plan" provided for a range of services and financial assistance to dismissed foreign, female workers, at odds with the notion that the Swiss abuse an imported proletariat and that their method of adjustment is to let market developments take their course. In Switzerland, it is true, workers were fired at the sole discretion of management. But even though workers were not protected by strong unions, institutional procedures existed to prevent their becoming destitute. Furthermore, for years the managements of Glattfelden and Vöslau had sacrificed profits and dividends in the attempt to defend employment and in the hope of better times. Finally, full employment in both countries made for an easier adjustment in the textile industry. Questions of industrial adjustment cannot be separated from macroeconomic conditions that are politically shaped.

In both countries the textile industry suffered from the international liberalization that, to different degrees, Switzerland and Austria pursued in the 1970s. In the 1970s the reductions in the number of firms and the elimination of jobs were greater in Switzerland's textile industry than in Austria's. On the other hand, Austria's producers experienced higher rates of change than Swiss producers as measured by changes in the degree of import penetration and export orientation. Both countries were able to adjust flexibly, each in its own distinctive way. The major cost for Austria's more domestically oriented textile industry stemmed from growing liberalization; Switzerland's more internationally oriented textile industry suffered heavily from the appreciation of the Swiss franc and the ban on the import of foreign workers.

To aid domestic producers and protect employment, Switzerland granted temporary export aid while Austria practiced selective protection. The government's attempt to defend existing jobs in the textile industry points to the limits of the Austrian tolerance for change, as well as its inability to resist it. Neither the political ambition nor the financial resources deployed in the unsuccessful rescue mission at Vöslau in the mid-1970s would even exist a few years later. Yet the two cases, Vöslau and Glattfelden, and more general national policies in both Switzerland and Austria point to an important convergence in the 1970s: in different forms both countries compensate for economic change while living with it.

These two cases show how Switzerland and Austria converge in the three defining characteristics of democratic corporatism. First, Glattfelden and Vöslau underline the presence of an "ideology of social partnership" in both countries. The illustrations are numerous: business and unions created a new institutional arena for consultation in Switzerland; the views of unions and government were compatible in Austria; Switzerland's federal government silently accepted the consequences of economic change resulting from a harmonious accommodation of business and unions; and Austrian business acquiesced in the outcomes of a policy, agreed upon by the government and the unions, of slowing the pace of economic change. Second, peak associations of business proved very important in both countries in staging and resolving the intense political conflicts within and between industries. As a result, political conflicts within the business community did not immobilize the public agenda and government machinery. Furthermore, Austria's union was in a position to respond to the discontent of the rank and file. Finally, in their adjustment policies Switzerland and Austria converged in trying, in economic and political terms, to balance the losses the industry was forced to absorb. Economic and political objectives were, for example, inextricably linked in the export credit program organized by the Swiss banks and in the domestic assistance program provided by the Austrian government.

But the two cases also illustrate a divergence in the form that corporatism takes. In the Swiss case the banks play a more central role than the federal government. Moreover, the renewal of the commitment of business and unions to the principle of accommodation occurs at the sectoral level rather than at the political center. Thus, in general terms, Switzerland's liberal corporatism tends toward depoliticization and decentralization. In the Austrian case the federal government is more important than the banks, and the consensual relations between unions and government occur at the highest political levels. In general, then, Austria's social corporatism tends toward politicization and centralization. Despite their differences in form, however, both varieties of corporatism converge in compensating the textile industry, within limits, for some of the losses it incurred from rapid, adverse economic change. Switzerland and Austria have thus cultivated their capacities to "take a stitch in time" in mending their corporatist fabrics.

CHAPTER SIX

The Politics of Change in the
Steel and Watch Industries

Austria's steel and Switzerland's watch industries provide, like textiles, instructive ways of examining how corporatism deals with change. Although these four industries experienced different problems of adjustment, in the 1970s all of them faced serious challenges to their international competitiveness and sharp declines in their domestic prosperity. Their recent history shows that corporatism has the capacity to pacify those adversely affected by change. By seeking to compensate, within the limits of what international markets will permit, for the hardships of rapid economic change and by politically incorporating sectors in distress, Austria and Switzerland make politics a central part of their adjustment process.

The inclusionary characteristics of corporatism defuse opposition—defuse it so effectively that sectors in trouble do not go looking for allies to attack the foundations of Austrian and Swiss politics. Surprisingly, therefore, economic hardship becomes the occasion for relegitimizing and reinforcing corporatist arrangements; the point is particularly clear in steel and watches. These two industries occupy important positions in Austrian and Swiss politics and have traditionally enjoyed a strong place in international markets. When hundreds or thousands of workers face the loss of their jobs, and when millions or hundred of millions in investment capital are in danger of being written off as losses, corporatism shows how to mobilize consensus in crisis.

The steel industry illuminates traits typical of an intermediary goods industry of the Second Industrial Revolution, an industry that has experienced medium rates of economic growth in stable domestic markets and has only in recent years been exposed to serious import

competition from low-cost producers.[1] The industry is typically dominated by a few, frequently nationalized, large corporations, often
linked in cartel-like arrangements. Because it invented and patented
the oxygen-blast method of production, the Austrian steel industry
enjoyed, throughout most of the 1950s and 1960s, a position of market power characterized by a high degree of invulnerability. In the
1970s, Austria's steel industry increasingly began to produce for specialized market niches. Labor is typically well organized; and the corporations normally finance the industry's enormous investment
programs. But prolonged economic crises make these corporations
dependent on external sources of capital, and as a result their affairs
are often indirectly controlled or directly managed by the state bureaucracy. The centralization of the steel industry and its need for
stable markets typically encourage a political strategy of adjustment
focused on a longer-term sectoral transformation supplemented by
short-term attempts to export the costs of change. Formal cartel arrangements and orderly market arrangements are relatively easily
monitored in international markets and can become convenient ways
of deflecting economic pressure when cyclical and structural crises
coincide.

The watch industry exhibits the characteristics of a consumer goods
industry that mixes elements of the First, Second, and Third industrial revolutions. Until the mid-1970s it experienced high economic
growth in rapidly expanding markets. The industry is composed of
numerous small firms and a few large corporations that at times play
an important role in trade associations and national business federations. The dominant position that Switzerland's watch industry enjoyed in the world market gave it an unusual degree of international
market power, which was seriously challenged only by the introduction of electronic watches by Japanese and American competitors in
the 1970s. Despite the industry's fragmentation, skilled workers are
normally well organized because of their attachment to other, more
powerful unions. The investment needs of small firms and large corporations have until recently been typically met by retained earnings
or bank credits. Dependence on export markets prohibited exporting
the costs of change and encouraged industrial adjustment without
much government involvement.

A few summary statistics illustrate the specific features of the industries (see Table 4). Employment and the number of firms in Swiss
watches declined sharply in the 1970s while they remained stable or
slightly increased in Austrian steel. In terms of both the number of
firms and average firm size, Austria's steel industry is more central-

ized and concentrated than the Swiss watch industry. The export orientation of Austrian steel increased considerably in the 1960s and 1970s, though it did not remotely approach Swiss watches' dependence on world markets. At the same time, the Austrian steel market was increasingly opened to foreign producers. The growing share of

Table 4. The Swiss watch and Austrian steel industries

	Switzerland	Austria		
	Watches	Iron and metal works	Metal products	Engineering products and steel construction
Employment		*(thousands)*[a]		
1970	89	39	58	65
1980	47	39	63	79
Firms		*(number)*[b]		
1970	1177	14	504	423
1980	776	26	767	731
Average firm size (1980)		*(% of industry's employees)*[b]		
under 20	9	—	4	3
20–99	37	5	22	17
100–499	34	6	41	31
over 500	20	89	33	49
Research and development expenditures		*(% of total R and D)*[c]		
1969	3.6	0.2	5.8	10.7
1975	3.7	0.2	5.1	8.8
Export intensity		*(% of total production)*[c]		
1970	90–95	69	30	57
1980	90–95	66	37	61
Import penetration		*(% of total production)*[c]		
1970	5–10	29	35	76
1980	7–15	28	48	67

SOURCES:

a. Swiss figures are from Wirtschaftsförderung, *Artikeldienst,* 1 June 1981; Austrian figures are from Hans Wehsely, "Industriepolitik in den siebziger Jahren: Rückblick und Ausblick," *Österreichische Zeitschrift für Politikwissenschaft* 1981, no. 1: 30 (data are for 1969 and 1979).

b. Swiss figures are from *Statistisches Jahrbuch der Schweiz 1981* (Bern: 1982), pp. 154, 156, 160–61; Austrian figures are from *Statistisches Handbuch für die Republik Österreich 1981* (Vienna: 1982), pp. 312–14.

c. Austrian figures are from Beirat für Wirtschafts- und Sozialfragen, *Vorschläge zur Industriepolitik II* (Vienna: Ueberreuter, 1978), pp. 95, 103 (export and import data are for 1970 and 1977). Swiss figures are for line 4 from Silvio Borner et al., "Structural Analysis of Swiss Industry 1968–1978: Redeployment of Industry and the International Division of Labour" (Zurich: Industrial Consulting and Management Engineering Co., 1978), p. 71; for line 5 from Margret Sieber, *Die Abhängigkeit der Schweiz von ihrer internationalen Umwelt: Konzepte und Indikatoren* (Zurich: Huber Frauenfeld, 1981), p. 170; and for line 6, estimates based on data from interviews in Biel and Zurich, 1981.

imported watches or watch components in Swiss markets reflects a reorientation of that industry, which increasingly relies on foreign production and domestic assembly. Finally, the relative share of the two industries in the countries' total research and development budgets remained quite stable; but the figure for Austria is 4 to 5 times as large as the figure for Switzerland. This overview provides reference points for detailed examination of the two industries.

AUSTRIAN STEEL

The distinctiveness of Austria's steel industry since 1945 rests in the competitive advantages that it derived from a technological innovation in the early 1950s.[2] The L-D method of oxygen-blast steel production, named for Linz and Donawitz, gave Austria a technological lead that assured it of sizable advantages in steel production. The proportion of crude steel produced in Austria by modern equipment increased from 36 percent in 1954 to 49 percent in 1958, 62 percent in 1962, 67 percent in 1967, and 83 percent in 1978.[3] By 1967 only Japan and the Netherlands, which introduced the new technology on a commercial basis in 1957–58, could match Austria in the share of steel produced by the L-D method.

The cost advantages of the new technology were considerable, and capital costs in the construction of new facilities were about 25 to 30 percent below those of older technologies.[4] Austria's technological leadership brought other advantages; apart from the general strength that the steel industry derived from its cost effectiveness in the 1950s and 1960s, this process innovation was of considerable importance in the expansion of its steel construction and machinery production. And, since 70 percent of the subsequent expansion of the international steel industry occurred in steel produced with the L-D method, Austria also laid a solid foundation for exporting integrated steel mills. Between 1963 and 1968 the Voest built about one-third of all L-D steel plants that went into operation worldwide. These new plants outproduced Austria's steel industry by a factor of ten.[5]

Astonishing about these developments are the insignificant sums that Austria received from the export of a revolutionary technology. Indeed, Austria appears to have given away its technology virtually free in the 1950s and 1960s. Some of this largesse was involuntary. In the United States, for example, the Voest waged a protracted legal battle with American steel producers who claimed to have discovered, rather than imitated, the L-D technology. That case was eventually decided on procedural grounds against the Austrian company. As a result, the Voest collected not a single cent from licensing fees in the American market.

Negotiations with Japanese steelmakers are more revealing than the American episode. In 1956 Austria's Alpine-Montan (Oester-reichisch-Alpine Montangesellschaft) assigned to Nippon Kokan the rights to ownership or application of the new technology in Japan, gave it an exclusive license to use the patent rights or patent applications with right of sublicense in Japan, and committed itself to an unrestricted sharing of know-how, including all future improvements of the technology. In return Nippon Kokan paid the Austrian firm a total of $1.4 million, perhaps not insignificant in the 1950s, but a mere pittance judged by hindsight.[6] Thus policy greatly accelerated the spread of a technology that, in turn, would strengthen adverse market developments from which the Austrian steel industry suffered in the 1970s.

For some time, though, technological leadership reinforced the economies of scale created by the dramatic expansion of Austrian capacity under German occupation. The Marshall Plan and postwar reconstruction and rearmament provided market conditions favoring rapid expansion.[7] Indeed, so important was the nationalized steel industry in Austria's political economy that between 1948 and 1951 the Voest received one-third of Austria's total Marshall Plan aid of $1.4 billion.[8] The industry was thus able to reconstruct and expand its facilities with the most advanced technologies.

By about 1960, production and employment had increased massively in an industry that, after its initial funding by Marshall Plan aid, was largely self-financed and deeply enmeshed in international markets.[9] Thus, between the late 1950s and the late 1970s the export intensity of Austria's nationalized industry remained unchanged at about one-third of turnover; but the steel industry's leading producer, the Voest, was exporting two-thirds of its total turnover by the late 1970s.[10] As one measure of its importance, Austria's export surplus in steel and iron covered three-quarters of its import deficit in motor vehicles.

World demand became less buoyant in the 1960s, and the Austrian industry's eroding technological lead was mirrored in a 50 percent decline in profits between 1962 and 1966; hourly wages increased three times faster than productivity.[11] The industry's traditional structural disadvantages were revealed, prime among them the import of raw materials (virtually all of the necessary coking coal and two-thirds of the iron ore). Yet the post-1974 steel crisis was to have less drastic effects in Austria than elsewhere. Production cutbacks did occur between 1974 and 1976, eliminating 3,000 jobs through attrition and through the introduction of training courses for workers who otherwise would have been forced onto short hours.[12] But Austrian steel did remarkably well in absorbing lower demand for steel without massive lay-offs. All other steel-producing countries in the advanced industrial world lost far more jobs; and other industries, Austrian textiles for instance, had to absorb far greater job losses in the 1970s.

Industry leaders and government officials projected a continuing crisis in the European steel industry for the years 1980 to 1985 and planned to reduce employment, largely through attrition, by another 4,000. These projections were too optimistic: employment in the steel industry declined by 3,500 in 1981 alone. Nevertheless, between 1975 and 1981 one-third of European steel workers lost their jobs, compared to fewer than 10 percent in Austria.[13] The economic performance of the industry thus leads us back to a political analysis.

Politics pervades every nook and cranny of Austria's steel industry. Dominated first by Italian interests and later by the Thyssen combine, the steel industry during the interwar years had served the interests of foreign producers rather than those of the Austrian economy. After the war the nationalized industry was central to Austria's reconstruction, and the Austrian consensus on public ownership was never seriously shaken.[14] Yet the industry's very importance focused the intense conflict between Austria's two major political parties, the conservative ÖVP and the socialist SPÖ, over the proper role of the public sector in a capitalist market economy. These political conflicts, expressed as disagreements about what products the industry should manufacture, prevented a coherent policy of structural transformation through the 1960s.

Indeed, since 1945 Austria's steel industry has only experimented once with structural transformation. Facilitated by the government's temporary control over investment, the "iron and steel plan" of 1947–48 shaped both the reconstruction and expansion of Austria's heavily damaged industrial base and the development of complementary product lines in Austria's two largest steel firms, the Voest and Alpine-Montan. The steel plan to all intents and purposes eliminated competition between the two, even though initial American opposition prevented their full merger until 1973.[15] Yet this steel plan has remained the only instance in which the Austrian government was directly involved in planning a restructuring of the industry. Since the late 1940s policies have focused on the industry's organization and relation between corporate strategies and national policies with regard to prices, employment, and investment. But these policies taken together fall short of what one could legitimately call "structural transformation." Typically, the government has relied heavily on the steel industry to achieve economic and political objectives involving primarily the general economy.

Austria's political leadership recognized a potentially dangerous crisis in steel earlier than in textiles. The organizational reform of the industry in the late 1960s and early 1970s was prompted by growing concern over rationalizing Austria's industrial structure, expressed symbolically in the 1968 party programs of both the SPÖ and the ÖVP. Equally important, between 1966 and 1970 the ÖVP cabinet headed by Chancellor Klaus was intent on building a protective institutional shield around the nationalized industries, including steel, in the hope of removing them once and for all from direct political control—one of the socialists' major pillars of strength in the first two decades of the Second Republic. The 1970 law that established the Austrian Corporation for Industrial Administration as a holding company of Austria's vast nationalized sector mandated the concentration of different industries by the end of 1973, the year in which Austria's free trade agreement with the European Communities became effective. Despite the government's overwhelming presence in and pressure on the steel industry, the push for concentration spearheaded by both the ÖIAG and the Voest met with strong opposition.[16] Alpine-Montan, Austria's second largest steel producer, opposed the merger outright. Management and factory council jointly declared that the company "was opposed to the arbitrary decision of the owner of the industry," that is the state.[17] Differences in corporate strategies, regional conflicts, and opposition from the workers' councils fearing a loss of jobs explain the barely concealed split between Austria's two largest steel producers. Under the pressure of the free trade agreement, the first moves toward industrial concentration were made only in the very last months of the four-year period that Parliament had allowed for the purpose.[18] Conflict was equally intense when three smaller, nationalized firms producing specialty steels, Gebrüder Böhler, Schoeller-Bleckman Stahlwerke, and Steirische Gusstahlwerke, were also included in the merger. In 1975, though, these three nationalized producers, which had often been locked in fierce competition on foreign markets, were merged and incorporated in the Voest under the name United Specialty Steel Works (Vereinigte Edelstahlwerke, VEW).[19]

However, the imposition of a centralized institutional structure does not imply that the Austrian government could impose a structural transformation in response to changing markets. There exist, for example, no government directives: throughout the 1970s the nationalized steel industry conducted its business with virtually no direct interference from the government. Furthermore, because of determined opposition, in part from the nationalized steel industry, the ÖIAG only had the right to be "informed" about corporate strategy until 1981. Conflicts between the holding company and its subsidiaries were to be settled in ad hoc commissions. The industry's financial autonomy prevented the imposition of structural transformation policies by government bureaucrats. For example, in the area of research and development the Voest was generating 97 percent of necessary funding in the early 1970s within the company.[20] Furthermore, the Voest, Austria's largest company, has direct access to national and international capital markets to supplement investments financed through retained earnings.

When the steel industry did incur substantial losses, in the late 1970s, it received government subsidies. But the proportionate representation of both major parties on the boards of the ÖIAG and the Voest assured that the steel industry's novel financial dependence was politically managed not by bureaucratic intervention but by collaborative arrangements worked out by party leaders. In addition the 1970s saw local and regional elites, especially in Styria, intervening very effectively to defend existing jobs and uncompetitive small plants. Such territorial alliances were extremely complex: in Styria, for example, the ÖVP governed a province whose local councils were dominated by the SPÖ. The continuing divergence between the SPÖ and the ÖVP and, increasingly, between federal and local political leaders over the purpose of economic power prevented agreement on structural transformation, even when the industry was financially dependent on the government.

Similar impediments had operated in the 1960s. In the words of one senior civil servant in the Chancellery, "The ÖVP was not sufficiently strong to prevail with a general economic plan."[21] Thus political conflicts between the two major parties, played out in miniature in the industry's boardrooms, delayed the move from intermediary to final goods production and the development of new product lines in the Styrian segments of the industry.[22] The net effect of partisan conflict was to delay industrial adjustment, which the industry's declining competitive position in the 1970s would eventually make inevitable.

Thus, conflict between the major political parties and within the industry prevented direct political control. The government instead relied on Austria's large nationalized sector to shape the Austrian economy through indirect means. In a few conspicuous instances the government used its vast nationalized industries to accommodate strong political opponents. In the mid-1950s the Soviet Union received a substantial portion of output in return for granting Austrian sovereignty. In the same year the nationalized petroleum industry paid $11.5 million to farmers for a milk price support scheme.[23] But these instances were unusual. Over the next two decades the government would prefer to influence prices, investment, and employment in the economy by indirect means. The industry's cost effectiveness in the 1950s allowed low domestic steel prices that strengthened Austria's manufacturing industry in international markets. As the OECD concluded, "By charging low domestic prices for these raw materials and semi-finished goods, in accordance with the government's price policy, these industries made an important contribution to the stabilization of the general economic situation and to the favorable development of the—mostly privately owned—finished goods industries."[24]

The two major parties supported this general policy for different reasons. The ÖVP favored the policy's anti-inflation bias and its support of privately owned manufacturing; the SPÖ backed the policy because it cast the nationalized industries in the roles of benefactor of and model for the rest of Austria's industry. Although estimates vary between a low $7.75 million and a high of $31 million per year, there can be little doubt that the steel industry lost very considerable sums.[25] As recently as the early 1970s Austria's domestic prices were still well below those in the European Communities.

However, Austria's free trade agreement with the EC required the gradual increase of domestic prices to European levels.[26] This sharp reduction in the differential between domestic and world steel prices curtailed another policy illustrating the steel industry's strategic importance in the Austrian economy. Before 1945, when domestic prices were generally well above international price levels, Austrian steel producers had granted a special price rebate to domestic customers that processed crude steel and exported the manufactured products; in effect the steel industry provided an export subsidy for Austria's manufactured goods. The industry continued domestic rebates after 1945, when domestic prices were well below world market prices, an additional financial burden for the industry in fulfilling the government's general policy objectives. In the early 1960s price rebates amounted to about 10 percent of the price of steel and affected about 4 percent of Austrian exports.[27] In general, then, the government's postwar price policy amounted to requiring the steel industry to contribute to Austria's stabilization policy through diminished profits.[28]

In the 1970s the socialist government's commitment to full employment clearly predominated over the profit calculations of steel producers. As early as 1968, one year after the ÖIAG was established, a foreign consulting firm, Booz-Allen and Hamilton, concluded that the industry's labor force was too large.[29] But the prolonged boom of the Austrian economy in the late 1960s and early 1970s concealed that structural weakness. Since 1974 Austria's nationalized industries, and steel in particular, have been asked to contribute to full employment through corporate decisions that respond not only to the market place but also to general social objectives. In the 1970s the Voest-Alpine followed this long-established pattern; in particular, it was very careful in how and when it thinned the ranks of its workers. The company simply could not afford to neglect union and factory council demands, as well as the political preferences of the Chancellor and of his party.[30] The reason was political: management is accountable to a board of directors made up of government appointees, both socialist and conservative, and shop stewards from the industry.[31]

The presence of political forces strongly committed to full employment is only one part of the story; the other is management's explicit acknowledgment that its objectives have to concur with broader social objectives even when to do so diminishes profits. The investment rate in Austria's nationalized steel industry, in contrast to that in private industry, was high and steady in the critical recession years of 1975 and 1976, and, as mentioned before, the industry reduced its workforce by only a few thousands in the later 1970s.[32] This reduction was achieved through attrition rather than dismissal. Furthermore, plants used special in-service training programs financed by the federal Ministry for Social Affairs, to bridge work shortages without actually switching to short hours. In contrast to Austria's private industry, which reflects market developments quite directly, the steel industry (and nationalized industries more generally) thus tried to absorb the impact of the sharp economic decline of 1975 before filtering it gradually into the Austrian economy.

The industry accepted losses in productivity rather than in employment, even when this required selling below cost.[33] Profitability obviously suffered, and the costs have been very sizable—between 1975 and 1981 the Voest-Alpine incurred total losses of more than $400 million and in 1980 and 1981 dragged Austria's whole nationalized sector into deficit. Nevertheless, the Austrian government managed, until the end of the 1970s, to stay clear of granting direct subsidies. In the words of Chancellor Kreisky, "A government has to value equally all workers and employees."[34] Instead, losses were covered through financial measures taken within the ÖIAG. Essentially, the costs were borne by those nationalized firms and industries which operated profitably: simply, oil profits paid for steel losses. But in 1981 the losses of Austria's two largest steel producers skyrocketed, and the government decided to step in with financial guarantees and interest subsidies totaling $375 million; an additional $375 million were granted in 1982, and the government was prepared to pay substantial subsidies thereafter. The ÖIAG raised that sum on capital markets, and the federal government paid some of the interest directly from its budget. Compared to the 1970s this was a new level of support, designed to protect employment.[35]

The political commitment to full employment has been complemented since 1974 by large-scale investments in modernization and rationalization. Between 1975 and 1979 the Voest invested about $1.2 billion without government subsidies. Likewise, the ÖIAG received no direct government subsidies and raised the capital it needed on open markets with government guarantees. But the massive losses that the Voest sustained during the prolonged crisis since 1975 gave it some leverage to extract partial support, from both the ÖIAG and the government, for its $1.13 billion investment program for the years 1978 to 1983. In a time of escalating budget deficits, the government's financial contribution took the form of direct interest subsidies, as well as renunciation of its claim to a nominal dividend from the ÖIAG.[36]

These substantial infusions of capital are one of the reasons why Austria's steel industry fared comparatively well in the 1970s. One million tons of obsolete furnace capacity was scrapped between 1975 and 1980. The proportion of continuous casting in Austria's total steel production stood at 58 percent in 1981, compared to 60 percent in Japan and 20 percent in the United States.[37] Most importantly, modernization has accelerated the Voest-Alpine's shift from the production of unprocessed steel to manufactured goods, including high-pressure pipes and containers, oil refineries, dams, ships, utility poles, engineering products, and integrated steel mills. Taken together, these new product lines constitute 40 to 45 percent of the company's total production in 1980, a higher percentage than for any other West European steel producer. The company hopes to raise the proportion to 60 percent by 1990. Because its steel industry is so modern, Austria's subsidies per ton of steel cost only $3.33 compared to $41.63 in the rest of Western Europe.[38]

Good contacts with Austria's Eastern European trade partners are of considerable advantage in the move to high-value-added products. In 1981, for example, Austria signed a contract with the Soviet Union for the delivery of 800,000 tons of seamless oil pipes valued at $880 million. An order of this size required investments of about $69 million in the Voest's pipe-rolling mill in Kindberg (Styria). In the growing division of labor in international steel markets Austria's steel industry is thus well on the way to concentrating on finished products while leaving the necessary inputs to other countries that enjoy lower wage levels and better locations on the world's main seaways.

In meeting the rising tide of foreign competition, Austria is looking to policy measures that will strengthen its steel industry's competitive position. In 1981 more than 70 percent of the Voest's output was sold abroad. Eastern trade continues to be of great importance; large contracts, such as a $1.3 billion agreement concluded in 1980 to produce a major steel plant in the German Democratic Republic, can be secured only when the government provides generous credit facilities and subsidized interest rates. Meanwhile, foreign aid to less developed countries has been used to increase the market for Austrian products, thus strengthening domestic production and employment. This affinity between nationalized industries and economic aid is reflected in the very organization of the state bureaucracy. The bureau in charge of economic aid was eventually located in the section dealing with the problems of Austria's nationalized industries.[39]

International markets are thus sources of both opportunities and constraints. Austria's steel policy should be viewed within the broader context of its relations with the EC and the spread of protectionism in global steel markets since the mid-1970s. Since 1977 Austria has been an indirect beneficiary of some protectionist arrangements worked out between the EC and non-European steel producers. And the adoption of the EC's minimum import price system has helped to contain the losses that Austria's industry sustained in the early 1980s.[40] But European protectionism also has some costs. The tight supervision and restriction of steel imports from non-European sources leaves Austria still vulnerable to illegal imports, primarily from Italian producers, who count on Austria's impotence in bringing about effective sanctions. And in the early 1980s, as a bystander rather than a participant, Austria has been drawn into the bitter conflicts between the North American and the European steel industries.

The Austrian steel industry is also looking to diversification for, although foreign production has no appeal, foreign capital and foreign technological know-how do. When the managers of Austria's nationalized steel industry became firmly convinced in the late 1970s that the deep international steel recession was not cyclical but structural, they moved aggressively to diversify away from steel. Their intention was to create new sources of corporate growth and, more important, of employment, especially in Styria, by inducing foreign producers to locate research centers and production facilities for integrated circuits in Austria on a joint-venture basis. Aware of their vulnerability to low-cost countries, Austrian officials are careful in insisting on the sharing of integrated circuit know-how. In 1979 Siemens decided to locate a research and development center next to its components facility in Villach; the center is operated jointly with the ÖIAG. About 50 percent of the center's research and development expenditures will be subsidized by public funds. In 1981 the steel industry concluded joint-venture agreements with IBM for the construction of two plants in Upper Austria and Styria; and it signed an agreement with American Microsystems for research and development and the production of electronic components for the European market in a new plant to be constructed in Styria, at a cost of $50 million. Top management of Austria's nationalized industries, including steel, is now committed to a diversification that looks to the electronics industry and foreign know-how in order to counterbalance the inevitably shrinking steel industry.

The nationalized steel industry is so large that how it has met adverse economic change cannot be viewed apart from Austria's political economy as a whole. The country's flexibility of response to change results from three main features: heavy investment in technological innovation and modernization; the government's reliance on the steel industry to effect change in the Austrian economy at large without pursuing structural transformation; and close cooperation between government and unions predicated on a productive use of labor and full employment, without defending every single job threatened by adverse economic change. In sum, the industry has been used to compensate for economic developments deemed undesirable for the Austrian economy as a whole. Austria has fashioned its own recipe for dealing with the steel crisis of the 1970s and 1980s: as Oskar Grünwald says, "Close cooperation between the management of the undertakings, representatives of the workpeople, and the state remains our best hope for overcoming all the difficulties we shall encounter along the way."[41] The most successful champion of the sport of body-building in the 1970s, Austria's Arnold Schwarzenegger, summarized the secret of his success in a book bearing the title *Pumping Iron,* in a way aptly describing the political formula that brought Austria's steel industry so successfully through the turbulent 1970s: "The better you get, the less you run around showing off as a muscle guy."[42]

FIRMS IN TROUBLE (3): THE VEW

As a nationalized subsidiary of the Voest-Alpine with a 1981 turnover of $660 million, 16,500 employees, a worldwide sales organization, and numerous foreign subsidiaries, the United Specialty Steel Company (VEW) is Austria's second-largest industrial corporation.[43] Since the company exports about 80 percent of production, it was severely affected by the appreciation of the schilling in the 1970s and the worldwide steel crisis that began in 1975, the very first year of VEW's operation after the merger of three previously independent producers. Assuming at the time that the steel crisis was cyclical rather than structural, the new company focused its energies in 1975–77 on consolidating its administration and foreign sales organizations. Massive losses, totaling more than $45 million in three consecutive years, resulted from a policy that sought to protect employment by maintaining high capacity utilization while selling at substantial losses.

Saddled with geographically dispersed, overlapping, and often uncompetitive production sites scattered throughout Styria and Lower Austria, the VEW management hoped that its parent company, the Voest, or the ÖIAG would cover the inevitable losses once its own financial reserves had been depleted, until the "steel cycle" started to turn up. As the VEW's losses continued to mount, both the Voest and the ÖIAG became increasingly opposed to management's policy. But the management viewed the obvious option, closing plants, as unattractive. It is true that Austria's Law for Joint Stock Corporations (Aktiengesetz) guarantees the freedom of management in the nationalized industries to lead companies without political interference. But that freedom does not exist in the area of labor relations; management cannot simply renounce its commitment to full employment. Furthermore, in the short and medium term a continuation of operations at great loss was no more expensive to the company than the very high costs of lay-offs, especially in the area of workmen's compensation. Since many of the unprofitable production sites were located in areas where no alternative sources of employment existed, it was considered socially undesirable and, between 1975 and 1977, economically unnecessary to restructure the company's operations.

Mounting losses urged more drastic steps in 1978. Considering the rapid deterioration of the company's financial base, management decided that a sharp cut in costs had become inevitable. Three alternative plans were put to the factory council: dismissal of 2,000 workers; short hours for 5,500; or a wage cut. Rejecting all three, the council agreed, after long, arduous negotiations, to a package that involved a hiring freeze, restrictions on overtime pay, a decrease in the retirement age, and ten unpaid vacation days per worker per year; it was estimated that these steps would generate savings of about $17 million for the company. One year later, with no improvement in sight, management proposed a second package of cost-cutting measures totaling $24 million, which included a very substantial cut (40 percent) in the firm's generous fringe benefits. Again, after long and tough negotiations, the workers accepted a modification of this proposal. This time, however, and more insistently than before, management pressed the issue of dismissing up to 1,000 workers at one production site, Judenburg. But the workers and the factory council refused to yield and, in somewhat more guarded language, the chancellor himself, in parliamentary speeches, public debates, and numerous visits to the area, opposed layoffs until suitable new jobs could be created in the region. Judenburg became a symbol of democratic socialism's political responsibilities in a capitalist society to provide employment opportunities for all citizens.

The VEW undertook three special investment programs, in 1977, 1978, and 1981, aimed at securing jobs through raising profitability. The "Medium-Term Program for Structural Adaptation" of 1978, for example, was to cost about $275 million over a period of five years and was expected to increase annual revenues after 1983 by $34 million. Since the company had used up all of its financial reserves between 1975 and 1977, the necessary funds came from a variety of public sources: $27.5 million from the Voest, $69 million from the federal government, government guarantees for an additional $34.5 million in bank credits, and subsidized interest rates as part of the government's general $138 million investment subsidization program of 1978. VEW management and government officials had become convinced that the time for drastic action had arrived. "Economic summit meetings," well publicized in the press, prepared the ground for the announcement of an expensive modernization program that was to bring the company back into the black.

But market conditions in 1978 pushed company losses to new unexpected heights. Between 1978 and 1980 the losses added up to $142 million as compared to $47 million between 1975 and 1977. For 1981–83 losses were expected to amount to about one-third of a billion dollars. The company began to suffocate under the burden of interest charges on what was, by 1981, an accumulated debt of $1 billion. Indeed interest payments accounted for 80 to 90 percent of total losses in the late 1970s. By 1981 an infusion of capital on a massive scale, to reduce the relative share of interest payments, had become essential for the company's survival. The VEW's third structural reform plan in four years was backed by a "grand coalition" of all three parties in Parliament, which unanimously approved a subsidy of $250 million in 1981 even though no one knew whether total payments to the company could be restricted to this sum. The provincial government of Styria, where most of the VEW's production sites are located, committed an additional $12.5 million. Across all partisan lines and levels of government there was basic consensus that, in a country as small as Austria, a company as large as the VEW simply could not be permitted to stop operating.

The recognition of an acute crisis in 1981 also provoked a VEW decision to start working short hours and to consider lay-offs. In October 1980, 2,600 workers were put on short hours; the number was increased to 4,000 in January 1981. In the spring of 1981, a foreign consulting firm, Booz-Allen and Hamilton, from whom the government had commissioned an independent assessment, recommended the dismissal of 4,000 workers over several years in the interest of maintaining the company's long-term viability. (The same consulting company, ironically, had made very similar recommendations in the late 1960s, as noted above. But at that time, business conditions had been too good for the report to be accepted.) Using the 1981 report, management decided to recommend the lay-off of only 1,700 workers; they based their decision in part on a different assessment of the company's structure and strategy, and in part on the socially responsible employment policy to which company officials adhered.

The factory council fought the decision tooth and nail. In a series of meetings, including repeated meetings of the "Economic Council" (Wirtschaftskonferenz) presided over by the chancellor and attended by the key actors in Austria's system of social and economic partnership, the total number of layoffs was gradually diminished from 1,700 to 750. Between September 1980 and December 1981, to be sure, management could point to a cut in employment reaching almost 4,000, just what the foreign experts had recommended. But outright dismissals were rare, the overwhelming number being accounted for by early retirements, natural attrition, and a shift of workers to the Voest (which had received an enormous contract for steel pipes from the Soviet Union). In fact this contract helped save a substantial number of jobs in Judenburg and thus made possible the factory council's consent to a reduced number of job cuts.

Inevitably, it appears, changes in global markets in the 1980s over which Austria has no control will force further cuts in employment. The VEW had 22,000 employees in the mid-1970s, 19,000 in 1980, and 15,000 in 1983. By the late 1980s employment may dip below 10,000. A government committed to the goal of full employment regards as its prerogative the political management of this economic retrenchment. It wants at all costs to avoid unilateral actions by either management or workers. During the SPÖ's 1982 party congress, Chancellor Kreisky reiterated this prerogative, in a stern warning directed at both management and workers. "Life is not simple for capitalists. They can't simply decide how many employees they should fire. . . . We certainly didn't hand them a check for more than $200 million just so they could. I think they will still have to come and bargain with us, the government." And the chancellor admonished militant union officials "not to lead workers out of the factories. . . . Those who believe that work stoppages can secure jobs are mistaken. It is very possible for factories that have been shut down never to reopen."[44]

Both the company and the government sought to counter the social impact of the reduction in employment that eventually proved unavoidable. The VEW, for instance, made available an emergency fund of $1 million for particular hardship cases to the mayors of the communes most directly affected. Workers on short hours were entitled to a special allowance from Austria's labor-market administration, an allowance that could amount to as much as half the worker's standard wage. Those workers retiring a year earlier than the legally established age were entitled to a compensation payment of up to 80 percent of their last month's wage for an additional twelve months.

In addition, plans were drawn up for a basic reorganization of those segments of the industry located in Upper Styria. Since the unemployment effect of a plant closing is geographically concentrated and often devastating, the plan envisages low-cost credits and loans for job creation, and the structural improvement of selected plants whose products are potentially competitive. The program will receive funding estimated at about $28 million, but it remains to be seen whether this effort at structural improvement will fare any better than the costly and ultimately futile subsidization of uncompetitive textile firms in Eastern Austria. Confronted by a prolonged economic crisis the government has, in the case of steel, not yet swayed from its commitment to full employment at growing cost.

The magnitude of losses in capital and employment suffered in this case should be measured, in part, against those in other steel-producing countries in Western Europe. Like West Germany, Austria only followed the general trend toward government subsidization in 1981. Compared to the massive subsidies in Belgium, Britain, France, and Italy, the level of support in Austria has to date been extremely modest. Furthermore, unlike its West German neighbor and all other West European steel producers, Austria has so far managed to avoid massive lay-offs. Indeed, the VEW's ratio of loss over turnover was favorable by international standards, even though its personnel costs were by those same standards extremely high.

At the same time, the case of the VEW illustrates a distinctive rigidity in decision making that accompanies the ability to reach consensus in crises. The reason lies in an intricate and enduring web of political ties that link workers, management, and politicians. The VEW's supervisory board of twenty-four consists of eight members of the management of the Voest, the parent company, eight representatives of the factory council, and eight politicians drawn from political parties at the federal and provincial levels. SPÖ control of the company is assured: in 1981, all but one of the twenty-five members of the central workers' council were elected from the SPÖ list; four of the eight politicians represented the SPÖ, and, atypical among Austria's nationalized industry, a majority of the VEW's management team could be counted as SPÖ supporters. Moreover, because its representatives hold one-third of the seats on the supervisory board and are also represented on the board's presidium, the factory council can effectively veto any management decision. Finally, the struggle over the question of employment was from the very beginning a politically charged affair within the company, both because prominent provincial and local political leaders were sitting on the supervisory board and because high-level conflicts within the nationalized industries (between the ÖIAG and the Voest on the one hand and the VEW on the other) led to the involvement of the chancellor and the minister of Finance. The factory council combined with prominent politicians on the supervisory board to leave VEW management weak, uncharacteristically so when compared to the management of other nationalized firms. That weakness has politicized all important company decisions on questions of employment and investment, and it has impaired the

VEW's ability to adjust more rapidly to changing market conditions. Because it is in this respect an anomaly, the case of the VEW thus illustrates how fine a balance of power needs to be struck between political choice and economic change.

Within the broader context of Austrian politics it is perhaps to be expected that the prolonged attempt to save the VEW centered around government efforts to protect employment at almost all costs. Rapidly deteriorating market conditions pushed one of Europe's strongest producers of specialty steel to the brink of bankruptcy. Two aspects of this episode point to important commonalities with the Swiss process of industrial adjustment and hence deserve to be underlined. The numerous attempts to restructure the firm before 1981 did not resemble a plan for the medium and long terms; instead, they looked like highly politicized bargains involving management, the workers, and the country's political leadership.

Furthermore, in a potentially explosive setting, the SPÖ leadership and the unions managed to involve workers at the grassroots as well as political elites at the summit in a continuous process of tough bargaining. It is therefore not surprising that in the late 1970s Austria's system of social and economic partnership has in effect recreated itself at the local level, in the two provinces most affected by the steel crisis, Styria and Upper Austria. The VEW is central both as actor and as medium in the extension of Austria's corporatist arrangements from the federal to the provincial level. Economic rationalization is constrained (but not eliminated) by the constant need to recreate politically the basis of consensus. Everyone in Austria, including the parliamentary opposition and the provincial ÖVP leadership, knows that a company as big as the VEW has to be saved; its insolvency would have disastrous consequences for Styria and for broad segments of the Austrian economy. As in Switzerland, economic adjustment follows the logic of a corporatist bargain.

SWISS WATCHES

Since only one-tenth of the value of the final product is imported, watches typify the modern alchemy of Swiss industry. Indeed, with the exception of a modest cyclical downturn in 1957–58, the industry prospered until the mid-1970s. Employment and production increased and, compared to the textile industry, profits were high in an industry that succeeded in identifying its product as the very acme of precision. During the 1970s, however, Switzerland's share of global production declined, its share of world exports sharply diminished, employment in the industry was halved, and the number of firms was reduced by one-third.[45] Yet at the beginning of the 1980s, after living for half a decade with a structural crisis greater than any other in its history, the industry still enjoyed a more dominant position in international markets than did any other industrial sector in any small European state.

Since the industry exports more than 95 percent of its production, it has always been subject to extreme fluctuations. But only the conditions of the 1930s were sufficiently severe to provoke the legal codification of the industry.[46] With exports, production, and employment decreasing dramatically, the federal government stepped in to save the industry: it made membership in various cartels compulsory and affected the merger of the main producers of components. It went so far as to assume partial ownership of the General Swiss Watch Corporation (Allgemeine Schweizerische Uhrenindustrie Aktiengesellschaft, ASUAG), the predominant firm, which in the mid-1970s was still producing about three-quarters of the industry's components. In an attempt to reduce competition between literally thousands of watchmakers, the government prohibited firms from moving among different segments of the industry. Finally, it slowed the spread of technology to foreign competition by tightly supervised prohibitions on the export of know-how, tools, machinery, and components.[47]

The liberalization of international trade relations in the 1950s and 1960s set the stage for a dramatic expansion of the industry, as well as for pressures for the government's eventual withdrawal. Successive rounds of GATT tariff reductions were essential to the industry's worldwide growth of sales, especially in the late 1960s. By the end of 1966 all tariffs on watch products had been eliminated among members of the European Free Trade Association.[48] In 1967 President Johnson finally reduced by one-half the 65 percent tariff rate on watches and watch products that the United States had imposed in 1954.[49] But even these substantial tariff reductions were only one aspect of international liberalization. In 1965 the watch industry settled a ten-year-old antitrust suit with the U.S. government, ending all Swiss export restrictions on shipments of components to U.S. producers. In the same year, Switzerland's producers of inexpensive watches on their own accord liberalized restrictions impeding the export of watch movements. Moreover, the growing liberalization of components trade encouraged some foreign producers in the late 1960s to locate production facilities in Switzerland, where they could take advantage of a skilled and then relatively inexpensive labor force and an industrial culture that had developed watchmaking to artistic levels of perfection.

This liberalization was accompanied by the government's gradual withdrawal from the industry.[50] Under the "Watch Statute" of 1951, government supervision of this cartelized industry was intended to preserve decentralization in the face of economic change. The renewal of a revised statute in 1961 instead focused on enhancing competitiveness through gradual relaxations of regulations concerning price, production, supply, and demand. Only the export of components and know-how remained tightly controlled, and a new system of quality control was introduced. This cautious move toward liberalization split the industry deeply, indeed so deeply that it did not contribute to the preparation of the legislation.[51] By 1971, however, virtually all segments of the industry agreed with the federal government that, with the sole exception of mandatory quality control, the time had come to lift all remaining regulations and restrictions. To complete its disengagement, the government chose not to participate in the 1972 restructuring of the industry's largest firm, the ASUAG, thus reducing its shareholdings from 38 percent in 1971 to 8 percent in 1978.[52] By 1976, the Swiss government had become not indifferent but impartial to the industry.[53] In the growth and decline of products, firms, or industry segments, market pressure rather than state policy was to be the decisive force. Thus it was only logical that in 1983 the banks rather than the federal government would engineer the merger of a de facto bankrupt ASUAG with the number two firm in the industry.

Like Austrian steel, Swiss watches confronted the postwar international economy from a position of market dominance, but unlike the case of steel that dominance depended on market share rather than technological innovation. If anything, dominance led to a neglect of technological developments with uncertain commercial value. For example, in the 1950s the industry ignored the revolutionary advances that a Swiss engineer, Max Hetzel, had made in the development of electronic watches. As a consequence, in the late 1960s, a subsidiary of the ASUAG was forced to sign a cross-license agreement with the American producer Bulova, which had recognized the commercial implications of the new technology.[54] Two further licensing agreements with American corporations (Eurosil and Hughes) were concluded in the mid-1970s, when the burgeoning mass production of electronic chips made it important for the Swiss watch industry to gain access to rapidly changing know-how in chip production.[55]

Imitation of foreign innovations was, however, only one among several responses once industry leaders recognized—about ten years late—the adverse effects the electronic watch would have on its dominant position in world markets. In an unprecedented bold move the major producers collaborated in 1962 in the founding of a "Center for Electronic Watches," which, by the end of the decade, had spent $7 million in research and development. Annual investment in research and development increased from $700,000 in the late 1950s to $7 million in the late 1960s, and about $60 million in the late 1970s.[56] As a result of this determined reaction, Swiss producers had by 1970 caught up in the technological race with foreign competitors on several dimensions and were ahead on several others. At a cost that would eventually surpass $7 million, a consortium of firms created a new production site in 1970 for the early generation of electronic watches.[57] The industry thus reacted flexibly to its earlier mistakes as well as to changes in market conditions.

In the 1970s the industry repeated its experience of the 1950s and 1960s. The commercial introduction of the first "solid-state" digital watch in 1972 ended reliance on traditional watch-making skills and opened the market to American semiconductor firms looking for new applications for their technology. Enjoying the inflationary boom of the early 1970s Swiss firms missed the enormous competitive threat that the drastic decline in the cost of electronic watches would bring over the next several years. They also failed to recognize the enormous appeal of the new product for the North American mass market.

A study completed in 1965 had predicted that electronic watches would capture no more than 10 percent of the world market by 1985.[58] Industry leaders did not revise that estimate until 1974–75; by 1977 the industry was estimating that electronic watches would capture between one-half and two-thirds of the world market in the early 1980s. Because of their late start, Swiss producers lost market share that they would not be able to recoup in the 1980s; in 1976 less than 10 percent of Switzerland's total watch production was in electronic watches.[59] But the industry's all-out effort to master the new technology and introduce new products paid off very rapidly. Most important and most risky was the decision to produce electronic chips in Switzerland, a gamble that paid off handsomely against considerable odds. By 1979 the two largest producers in the industry generated about 60 and 40 percent, respectively, of turnover in electronic watches.[60] Thus, as in the 1960s, the industry reacted quickly.

The difference between initiating and reacting to market changes is one of the fundamental reasons why Switzerland's dominant position in world markets eroded so quickly in the 1970s. As ASUAG president Peter Renggli noted in 1978, "The mechanical watch was successful until the recession of the mid-1970s. There was simply no reason to switch over to the production of electronic watches since we could hardly fulfill our orders for mechanical watches. Why should we have chosen to compete against ourselves with electronic products?"[61] This reluctance to initiate change has been typical of the Swiss industry. Back in the 1960s, for example, Switzerland's components producers had created prototypes and the production capacity to mass-produce competitive brand-name watches, but manufacturers and assemblers had shown no interest. As a result the Swiss industry lost sizable market shares to Timex and Seiko, the two largest producers worldwide, and never developed a Swiss brand-name product.[62]

The crisis of the 1970s was not only of the industry's own making. The watch industry suffered more than any other industrial sector from the appreciation of the Swiss franc across the decade. Like the textile industry, the watch industry blamed its serious economic difficulties on Switzerland's hard-currency policy.[63] Like the textile industry, it offered far-reaching and detailed proposals for political intervention in international capital markets. And like the textile industry, it was resoundingly defeated; its proposals cut so deeply against the liberal grain of Switzerland's strategy that they did not even receive a serious hearing. In a situation of grave crisis the president of the Swiss Watch Chamber (Schweizerische Uhrenkammer), the industry's peak association, argued in 1978 that "the real question is whether authorities want to preserve a Swiss watch industry of significant size or whether they are willing to have this sector suffer the fate, for example, of the textile industry."[64]

In losing its fight over foreign-exchange policy the Swiss watch industry stood united in its opposition to the government and to Switzerland's financial community. But on virtually all other issues, different industry segments fought one another with great intensity. For example, in the early 1970s between 10 and 30 percent of the market value of a watch depended on the image of high craftsmanship. Thus the government made obligatory a quality control system for those products that were to be designated "Swiss made."[65] This regulation worked to the disadvantage of a sizable segment of the industry, which produced just under one-half of the total volume (about 15 percent of the value) of watch exports in 1969. In the late 1960s these producers were attracted to foreign sourcing of components and foreign production; they were intent on meeting Japanese and American competition in the low-cost segments of world markets. But obligatory quality control strengthened the main producer of components, the ASUAG, as well as the hundreds of small manufacturers and assemblers of high-quality watches. Legalizing quality control and supervising the designation "Swiss made" became necessary because the conflict within the industry ran very deep—so deep, in fact, that it would resurface ten years later in debate about the policy's extension.[66]

Political conflicts over the major issues of the 1970s—industrial concentration and direct foreign investment—were reinforced rather than hindered by the complex system of thirty-five branch organizations expressing the interests of different segments of a horizontally organized industry.[67] Because the peak association, the Swiss Watch Chamber, represents the industry's economic interests in Swiss politics, it has stayed neutral in the industry's bitter conflicts. Meanwhile, the government's gradual withdrawal compelled the association representing small manufacturers and assemblers of high-quality watches, the Fédération horlogère (FH) to transform itself from an occupational group enforcing government regulations, such as the allocation of export permits, to a modern service organization.[68] That reorganization permitted direct membership by individual firms for the first time. For the benefit of its numerous small member firms, the FH in the 1960s developed a worldwide system of information, training, and repair centers located in thirty strategic markets, especially in Third World countries, where, as its contribution to Switzerland's development aid, it has trained about 1,500 watch repairmen. The FH has seen as one of its particular mandates the coordination and concentration of investment projects in the areas of research and development, production and sales. At the same time, it has been the industry's most vociferous, though unsuccessful, spokesman in opposing the government's hard-currency policy and the moves of other industry segments toward concentration and direct foreign investment, which constitute the most serious threat to small producers in the 1980s.

The extreme decentralization mirrored in over 10,000 trade names and more than 100,000 styles of watches was a residue of the government's legal enforcement of industry segmentation *(compartimentage)* for thirty years. It provided a second issue that differentially affected the industry's numerous segments. On the average Japan produced, under each brandname, 6 million watches in the 1970s compared to fewer than 100,000 in Switzerland.[69] The industry's fragmentation between high- and low-priced watches, between manufacturers and assemblers, and between final producers and producers of components inhibited dynamic firms from moving between market segments and prevented specialization in selected products with large production runs.

The late 1960s and the 1970s provide some evidence that international and domestic liberalization was bringing about industrial concentration. Between 1965 and 1974 the very small firms with fewer than ten employees largely vanished, and many mergers took place.[70] Most importantly, in 1971 the ASUAG decided to change from a financial to an industrial holding company by moving from its traditional preserve of component production to the production of watches. Against the determined opposition of its own customers, the hundreds of small assemblers represented by the FH, the ASUAG organized seven relatively large and well-known firms in a new subdivision, the General Watch Corporation (GWC).[71]

But all of these corporate mergers affected organizational blueprints rather than production runs. Because the statutes of the ASUAG, written in the 1930s, direct it to maintain and further the interest of the whole industry rather than that of particular segments, the full benefits of increasing market pressure on small producers could not be realized; the firms that had merged in the GWC did not receive the benefit of preferential prices and retained virtually all of their former autonomy.[72]

The industry's economic crisis after 1975 and, in particular, the appreciation of the Swiss franc in 1978 and 1979, provided a greater impetus toward industrial concentration than did liberalization in the early 1970s. Most of the important measures were taken by the ASUAG. In 1978 it moved to assume full ownership and tighter control over its largest subsidiary.[73] It also decided to concern itself less with its statutory mandate to look after the prosperity of the whole industry. From now on, it announced, it wanted to be viewed simply as another large watch manufacturer, free to take advantage of the benefits of vertical integration and corporate reorganization into different profit centers.[74] This shift in corporate philosophy was reflected in its decision to move production abroad, to export technology, and to sell component parts to foreign producers. Most important the ASUAG decided to exploit its monopolistic market position as the supplier of three-quarters of the industry's components and assume control over the price structure, profit margins, and marketing of hundreds of small producers. Strong opposition by the small manufacturers, including a veto by the FH representative in the ASUAG's board of managers, had blocked the company's initial move in that direction in 1971. The FH voiced the same opposition with similar intensity in 1978, but to no avail.[75] Among others, the federal government came out in public to support the shift in corporate strategy, which is likely to transform the structure of the industry fundamentally in the 1980s.[76]

The various fractures within the industry made watches unique among Switzerland's major industries for its belated turn toward the internationalization of production.[77] In the interest of securing Swiss production and Swiss jobs, direct foreign investment was legally banned in the 1930s. The concerted effort to maintain world market shares through domestic production extended to the industry's employment policy within Switzerland. Perhaps through a fear a strengthening competitors abroad, the watch industry employed a proportion of foreign workers that, while sizable, was less than the average for all Swiss industry.[78]

The liberalization of the international economy led to a rapid dismantling of Switzerland's export restraints. Yet even when the last export restrictions on components were lifted in 1971, a move that the ASUAG unsuccessfully opposed, the industry did not seize the initiative to move abroad despite its gradual loss of market share. Since as late as 1975 the ASUAG owned only one production facility in the Third World, it attempted to meet cheaper imports through further automation rather than through direct foreign investment. Indeed, automation was one of the reasons why in the 1970s Switzerland remained relatively competitive in the production, though not in the assembly, of components. Switzerland's second-largest watch producer did acquire minority participation in two American producers, the Sheffield Watch Corporation and Hamilton.[79] But like the ASUAG it too did not seriously consider moving production permanently abroad.

Thus the industry failed to initiate changes under favorable market conditions; but it moved quickly to internationalize its operations once it absorbed the full shock of 1975. In 1974–75 watch exports declined by more than 20 percent, compared to 8 percent for Swiss industrial exports and only 5 percent for exports of textiles and garments.[80] A survey commissioned by the government concluded, in 1977, "that there exists a pressing and relatively great danger of losing further jobs in Switzerland through the redeployment of production sites abroad."[81] The ASUAG substantially reoriented corporate strategy in 1978, increasingly shifting to the production of watch components for export as well as to production and assembly in low-cost countries. Prominent among the reasons for this reorientation

223

were the hope of countering the adverse effects of Switzerland's hard-currency policy and of high domestic wages, large protected markets in the Third World, and the extension of tariff reductions to the developing countries under the GATT's Generalized System of Preferences. In addition to a Mexican plant already in operation, production facilities were planned for India, Brazil, and Nigeria, as well as several production sites in the Far East, especially Hong Kong.[82] By 1979, although still heavily weighted toward foreign sales rather than foreign production, the industry already had one-fifth of its employees working abroad.[83] In the same year, one-third of Swiss watches were assembled abroad, and more than one-half of the Swiss watches manufactured at home relied on parts or components produced abroad.[84]

Even though the ASUAG aims to keep the major share of its production in Switzerland and to cultivate its special relationship with Swiss assemblers, it now operates under market pressures forcing outcomes less favorable for the Swiss industry. This is reflected in the changing composition of watch exports. In the late 1970s the relative share of finished watches declined while the number of components for foreign assembly increased sharply.[85] With costs rising very rapidly, the ASUAG had little choice: it needs large markets among foreign watch producers in order to finance its research and development. Within a few years most of the inexpensive Swiss watches were being produced in the Far East.[86] The reorientation of the watch industry on the issue of foreign production occurred in record time. Whether it occurred fast enough for the ASUAG remains an open question. The company reported a loss of $73 million in 1982. In a desperate attempt to save the two largest firms in the watch industry, Switzerland's two largest banks forced the ASUAG to merge with the number two firm in the spring of 1983.

The crisis of the latter 1970s, dramatic by most standards, was not of sufficient severity to prompt large-scale government intervention. Instead, the government seized the opportunity to develop its embryonic regional policy, tailoring it primarily to the needs of the watch industry.[87] (That it was watches rather than textiles which spurred this political development is only one measure of the watch industry's traditionally greater prominence in Swiss politics.) The government's 1978 Program concerning Financial Help for Economically Threatened Regions mainly focused on the "watch cantons" in the Jura. Under certain conditions, firms in these cantons became eligible for subsidies and loan guarantees of private investment projects that promised diversification and innovation.[88] The industry benefited from its location at the fault line of one potential earthquake in Swiss politics, the movement to establish an independent canton of the Jura. But it also benefited from the regional concentration of the watch industry. From the government's vantage point, framing assistance in regional rather than sector-specific terms had a triple advantage: it was receptive to the regional movement in the Jura, it made other industries such as textiles also eligible for assistance, and it prevented its being dragged back into an industry from which it had only extricated itself in 1971.[89] Furthermore, Switzerland's slow process of reaching consensus gave maximum play to market pressures. Three-and-a-half years elapsed between the initial formation of a study group in the winter of 1975 and the first selection of regions eligible for special assistance in May 1979. Although most of the regions targeted for special assistance were located in Switzerland's "watch cantons," true to the character of Switzerland's corporatism they also included three regions relying heavily on textiles and metals.[90]

The government's program was modest. At the insistence of the metalworkers and watchmakers union, the initial plan had focused on the creation of a parapublic corporation to provide substantial low-interest loans and financial guarantees.[91] Received critically by the peak association of business, this provision was eventually dropped for more modest low-interest subsidies. Besides expecting a modest financial contribution from applicants in support of industrial readjustment, the federal government would rely on the banks to screen firms with a competitive future, and close collaboration between the banks and the cantonal and federal governments established the criteria for eligibility and selection. (In the spring of 1983 it would be a consortium of banks that would force a merger of the two largest firms in the industry, making it clear that Switzerland's process of industrial adjustment was organized by the banks rather than by the government.)

Many firms in the watch industry were considering liquidation rather than investment, and so the program was modestly used. In the first two years of operation the government funded forty-six projects that met the criteria of innovation and diversification. The average project size was $2 million, and of the roughly one thousand jobs thus created or saved about half were in the watch industry.[92] Meanwhile, other government programs were also offering modest levels of assistance. Under the provisions of Switzerland's employment stabilization program, for example, 164 firms in the watch industry unfroze about $33 million of previous profits and received a total of

225

about $10.8 million of federal, cantonal, and local tax subsidies for additional investment projects.[93]

Furthermore, the government responded to the industry's crisis, with little public notice, by stimulating further development of the already considerable technological capabilities in the field of electronics to maximum advantage, both for the watch industry and for industry more generally. The Program for the Alleviation of Economic Difficulties contains a $28 million subsidy for research and development in the electronic components of watches; between 1979 and 1982 the government carried one-third of the program's costs. The financial size of the program, the insistence on cooperative research and compatible components, and the absence of other restrictions are as noteworthy as the hoped-for effect of permanently enlarging the staff and financial outlays of the industry's research and development laboratories. This aid reinforces a number of far-reaching cooperative projects in the private sector, and it reflects the growing gap between the escalating costs of research and development and the sharply declining assets of the industry.[94] Despite Switzerland's traditional aversion to government involvement in economic affairs, this instance of government involvement is likely to continue.

Furthermore, as in the case of textiles, government and banks tried to alleviate the plight of the watch industry through a variety of financial measures: among them, the extension of Export Risk Insurance to consumer goods industries in March 1975; the agreement between the Nationalbank and the large commercial banks to provide inexpensive export credits in April 1975; the agreement between the Nationalbank and the watch and textile industries concerning foreign exchange risks for exporters in October 1976; and the agreement between the Nationalbank and the Swiss Banking Association (Schweizerische Bankiersvereinigung) of December 1978, designed to strengthen all of Switzerland's exporters. Although the watch industry welcomed the help that it received, most firms hesitated to take advantage of these benefits. The provision for inexpensive export credits of April 1975 was eventually used by about 20 percent of watch firms and only benefited about 10 percent of the industry's total export sales between 1975 and 1980. Although the system of guaranteed exchange rates was better understood, only one-third of firms relied on it, covering about 20 percent of total export sales.[95]

Knowledgeable officials estimate that the industry lost about $560,000 a day between 1975 and 1980, a total somewhere between $840 million and $1.2 billion.[96] Between 1975 and 1977 subsidized payments from Export Risk Insurance to the watch industry came to about $4 million.[97] While estimating the capital base of an industry is a tricky business, a plausible guess is that the industry lost about half of its capital in the 1970s. Thus, while the cushion for future setbacks had shrunk drastically, it had not vanished by 1980; the industry's assets still amounted to about three times the $840 million in bank loans outstanding in that year.[98] Considering these losses, the industry itself judges that, without massive bank credits, it will not be in a position to undertake the enormous investment programs required in the 1980s.[99] The collapse of export markets in 1982 prompted numerous bankruptcies and massive infusions of capital from Swiss banks hoping to save the industry's number one firm, the ASUAG. The watch industry now depends on the very supporters of the hard-currency policy that weakened its position in the 1970s.

In the early 1970s neither industry nor government was concerned over the consequences of technological change for employment.[100] In 1972 *Business Week* predicted that the new digital watches and intense foreign competition would cause the industry's work force to decline to under 50,000; nobody in Switzerland took the prediction seriously. Five years later, both the government and the FH agreed in separate reports that the industry's employment would probably be under 38,000 by 1985. The collapse of the world watch market in 1982, and a one-third decline in the number of exported watches, reduced employment to this level by 1983. Thus the employment consequences of the crisis of the 1970s and early 1980s have been as serious as those of 1873–75, 1920–22, and 1929–34. The legacy of the 1930s in the watch cantons was unemployment provisions that were, by and large, more extensive than those elsewhere in Switzerland. Still, with more than one hundred fifty different unemployment schemes operating in the watch industry, coverage was variable and on the whole inadequate.[101]

The 50 percent decline in employment in the 1970s was to undermine permanently the political prominence that the industry had traditionally enjoyed in Swiss politics. In 1931, for example, industry leaders handed over to the Federal Council a petition with 56,000 signatures protesting the export of watch components.[102] In 1961 the industry was still capable of convincing the general public that it was necessary to continue the system of government regulation; by a margin of two-to-one the Watch Statute was approved by referendum. By the late 1970s the industry had shrunk so much that it could no longer organize the national electorate.

As part of the metalworkers union (SMUV), the watchmakers un-

227

ion did little to bring the employment question to the fore. Although workers are better organized in watches than in textiles, they have remained uninvolved in debates about the sharp reduction in the industry's workforce. This has followed from the SMUV's general exclusion from questions of manpower policy and vocational training for the watch industry. Such issues are to a large extent the prerogative of public (communal) fulltime schools, in which the unions are not represented.[103] In the first half of the 1970s the SMUV had succeeded in securing an early warning system for lay-offs, and limited provisions for adjustment assistance and on-the-job retraining.[104] But after 1975, the union concentrated on the development of proposals for emergency relief. As in the 1930s, union and employers cooperated closely in an atmosphere of crisis. But in the late 1970s the union was unsuccessful in its half-hearted opposition to the sharp reduction in employment and the growing attraction of foreign production.[105] The union waited as late as the fall of 1982 before organizing a public demonstration to dramatize the social consequences of the crisis in watches.

The union's programmatic concern with job security offers a striking contrast to the drastic reduction in the industry's workforce. As in the last major recession of 1957–58, when 12,000 workers lost their jobs, the union chose to do no more than to organize, on a case-by-case basis, an orderly retreat. In 1975 it formulated employment guidelines that, with the agreement of the business community as the union's "social partner," established a careful ranking of types of workers—the old, foreign workers, and women—who should be laid off first.[106] Despite massive lay-offs, collective bargaining proceeded throughout the late 1970s without strikes and in an orderly fashion. Controversies were resolved by arbitration, and, since union officials agreed with the employers on the essential strategy for the industry, the relations between employers and union officials remained "excellent."[107] Their agreement is solidified by the union's participation in the informal discussions that the FH organizes for the benefit of different segments of the industry.

Although it has lost its preeminent position in world markets, Switzerland's watch industry continues to rank ahead of all of its foreign competitors in both world production (about 96 million watches in 1981) and exports. Yet the sharp decline in the volume of watch exports in 1982 illustrates that Switzerland's watchmakers have lost the mass market for watches to their Asian competitors. More important for the future of the watch industry is, therefore, a second set of statistics. For watches priced above $225, Switzerland's share in the world market is 85 percent, as compared to 5 percent for inexpensive watches. Switzerland's position remains very strong in those market segments where profits are high and demand is relatively inelastic.[108] Among the competing technologies of the electronic age, Switzerland's watchmakers have chosen a combination of tradition and modernity, of mechanical and electronic watchmaking, suited to their unrivaled tradition of craftsmanship. In 1979 Switzerland produced one-quarter of all the quartz watches worldwide but only 1 percent of all digital watches, the initial preserve of American semiconductor firms.[109] This choice reflects the fact that industries are social and political institutions as well as instruments for the creation of profit and wealth. Switzerland's preeminence in this particular industry dates back to 16th century politics and Calvin's ban on jewelry, but not on watches, in the city of Geneva. Profitable, high-quality watch making prospers in a European atmosphere featuring the indispensable "soft" elements of technology including design, jewel production, and jewel cutting. Switzerland's traditional watchmakers regard a $10 watch by Texas Instruments with the same disdain that the People's Republic of China reserves for Taiwan: it won't last long. Swiss watchmakers lack the short time horizon and short-term profit orientation that make it so easy for Americans to open and close firms or segments of industrial sectors.

But Swiss watchmakers also have a keen commercial instinct. They know that luxury watches, though highly profitable, will not assure them of a market share sufficient to maintain the industry's competitive strength. As a social and political institution, the watch industry in Switzerland needs to be both preserved and altered. In a small open economy, industry, union, and government recognize that shifts in factors of production cannot be obstructed in the medium or long term. Instead, they cultivate a capacity to react quickly to economic changes. Industrial adjustment can therefore be understood, in David Landes's phrase, as a "cultural and social as well as an economic phenomenon."[110] Only time will tell whether the clock will continue to tick in support of the horological fame that the Swiss have enjoyed for so long.

FIRMS IN TROUBLE (4): THE SSIH

To all intents and purposes the second-largest watch manufacturer, the Swiss Watch Corporation (Société suisse pour l'industrie horlogère, SSIH), went bankrupt in 1980–81.[111] The SSIH is hardly typical of the average small watch manufacturer. It is a holding company with twenty-seven subsidiaries arranged around the two flagships of this fifty-year-old watch empire, Omega and Tissot. For the Swiss these two quality watches are as close to their sense of national identity and collective worth as a Cadillac is for the average American. Yet the SSIH is typical of the industry in that its demise typified the fate of hundreds of watch firms in the 1970s. Its rescue, at least for the time being, by a consortium of Swiss banks is, of course, atypical of the fate of the average firm; but it illustrates with particular clarity how the process of industrial adjustment is organized in times of crisis.

The reasons for the economic decline of the SSIH resembled those affecting the entire watch industry. An undervalued franc and an overvalued dollar created conditions favorable to what would turn out to be the SSIH's ill-fated move into low-price watches in the late 1960s. Throughout the 1970s the company sustained heavy losses from low-cost producers in Asia. Like some of its successful Japanese and American competitors the SSIH could command a worldwide distribution and sales system, but this sales network insulated production from changes in consumer demand and tended to encourage production for inventory rather than for sales. Although bulging inventories had to be written down at considerable cost more than once in the 1970s, disaster was postponed until 1980. Instead of following the industry's change to a new generation of thin watches, Omega, in particular, continued to produce watches about 2.5 millimeters thicker than the new "slim line" look. The result was a very sharp drop in sales and rapidly increasing inventories. Although large, the SSIH had spread its financial and management resources very thin because it tried to cover all market segments and all stages of production while at the same time attempting to diversify away from watchmaking. Finally, like the rest of the industry, the SSIH had been adversely affected by developments in the 1970s: the sharp appreciation of the Swiss franc, the rapid move toward electronic watches, and new competition.

Between 1974 and 1979 turnover declined, and employment dropped from 7,300 to 5,500. The situation had, in fact, become quite precarious as early as 1977 when, after three years of uninterrupted losses totaling close to $40 million, the banks refused further credits. But the infusion of new capital and management by Silber-Hegner, a Zurich trading company, gave the SSIH a new though, as it turned out, short lease on life. In 1980 turnover and employment declined by another 10 percent, and the SSIH registered a loss on the year of $36 million, considerably more than its total capital. So sudden an appearance of massive losses signaled that the company's hidden assets had finally been used up.

Remarkable about this drastic turn for the worse was the utter surprise with which the news was greeted. Rumors had begun flying inside the industry in the summer of 1980. They intensified in October 1980, after the SSIH refused to comply with an industry-wide arbitration committee's instruction to pay a cost-of-living bonus, totaling $3.6 million, due to its workers. When four of Switzerland's big banks, together with two smaller cantonal ones, declared in December 1980 their intention to provide additional credit lines to overcome the SSIH's latest liquidity crisis, it dawned on everyone that the company's capital base would have to be totally restructured and strengthened through an infusion of new capital.

The plan that was eventually approved included the following provisions. First, stocks previously valued at $35 million were written down to $175,000, 5 percent of their previous value. Second, through converting $49 million of their credits to long-term capital, the six banks increased the new capital base of the company to $51 million. Third, the six banks and other financial institutions, including some foreign banks, agreed to write off credits totaling $51 million. And fourth, the six banks agreed to open additional credit lines totaling over $51 million. All told, in the biggest financial restructuring in Switzerland's postwar corporate history, the banks committed $175 million.

In the spring of 1983 the SSIH's future would become inextricably mixed with that of the ASUAG, which had suffered disastrous losses in 1982. A merger was brought about by the Swiss Bank Corporation and the Union Bank of Switzerland, which, together with six other Swiss banks, hoped to save these two industrial giants through further rationalization of their production and the infusion of $300 million in new capital. The early 1980s thus gave credence to the old stock market adage that "the first loss is always the smallest." It is likely that in the years ahead the newly formed company will require sizable additional infusions of capital and special credit facilities.

The banks' decision to bail out the SSIH was only partly based on commercial considerations. Since they had entered far-reaching financial commitments for many years, the banks had a choice between writing off more than $100 million as permanent losses (and in the process probably facing law suits charging negligence in their financial oversight) and committing additional funds in the hope of saving the company. More importantly, broader social and political considerations weighed heavily in the banks' decision. With more than 2,000 subcontractors and 5,000 workers directly threatened by the SSIH's default, keeping the company afloat was a matter of prime political importance. Rumors of a possible takeover of the SSIH by Switzerland's Japanese competitors pushed in the same direction. In fact, the government made no public appeal. Private consultations sufficed to reinforce the plain fact, backed by a sense of duty, that only Switzerland's financial community commanded the resources necessary to tackle so large a job.

Having once strayed from the narrow path of market rationality in defense of social order and the industry's long-term economic interest, the banks will continue to confront uncomfortable choices in the gray area between the logic of the market and the logic of the state. The banks' initial decisions predictably favored a further rationalization and concentration of operations, and, by 1983, a full merger with the ASUAG in which the banks also exercised some influence. But the future will demand a continuing choice between two options. One is a financial strategy intent on maximizing bank profits (or minimizing losses) irrespective of the consequences for employment, regional development, and the industry's long-term growth. The other is an industrial strategy that seeks to strengthen the technological and market strength of the company and takes a long-term attitude that includes industry-wide concern and, almost inevitably, further substantial infusions of capital. Switzerland's position in international markets and the logic of Swiss politics prompted the banks and the major stockowners to assume virtually all of the SSIH's massive losses rather than risk a chain reaction of bankruptcies. And there continue to exist strong resistance against a narrow financial strategy and pressures toward a broader industrial strategy, perhaps with some additional political help from cantonal and federal governments. In times of crisis Switzerland's banks rather than the government are charged with developing a policy of industrial adjustment.

Two features of this episode deserve to be underlined because they point to important characteristics in the adjustment process in both Switzerland and Austria. Adverse economic changes were plainly met with a stop-and-go policy. Short-run adjustments, like those in 1977 and 1981, predominated over any clear, long-term planning effort involving the SSIH in relation to other producers and segments of the watch industry and in relation to its regional economic setting. Furthermore, like the crisis of the watch industry at large, the crisis of the SSIH has prompted no political debate or unrest of any significance. At first the sizable hidden assets of the SSIH permitted it to absorb very large losses over several years. Later everybody in Switzerland accepted without debate that the SSIH could not be permitted to go under, for it would force hundreds of other bankruptcies and thousands of redundancies. Like the case of the Spinning and Weaving Company of Glattfelden, this episode illustrates the predominantly private nature of Swiss adjustment; but in contrast to it, the sheer size of the SSIH facilitated a large-scale mobilization of resources unthinkable for smaller firms situated in industrial sectors and regions less central to Switzerland's overall economic prosperity. Switzerland met the impact of ineluctable market changes in an ad hoc fashion, which, to date, has proved effective in absorbing large economic changes without any apparent political stress.

COMPARISONS

These two cases confirm what the textiles cases have already suggested: Austria and Switzerland converge in the three characteristics that define democratic corporatism. An ideology of social partnership is prominent in the adjustment process of both steel and watches; it is to be found in the compatibility of the views of union and government in Austria; in the amicable relations between unions and business in Switzerland; and in the acquiescence of Austria's business community to the consequences of a policy that seeks to slow the pace of economic change. Second, as in textiles, centralized institutions are important. The peak association of Swiss business defended Switzerland's hard-currency policy against the united opposition of the watch industry. On all other issues, the extreme fragmentation of the watch industry intensified the conflicts between different industry segments and thus afforded the federal government and other sectors of Swiss business the luxury of not having to confront an industry demanding policy change with one voice. In Austria, a centralized trade union was so effective in insisting on full employment that other choices were neither entertained by the government nor debated by the business community. Finally, in their adjustment policies both Austria and Switzerland attempted to compensate hard-pressed industries in both economic and political terms for some of the losses they were forced to absorb. For example, both economic and political calculations prompted the defense of employment in Austria's steel industry and the limited subsidy program that the Swiss government developed primarily in response to the watch industry's crisis.

These two cases also illustrate the differences in form that democratic corporatism can take. In the Swiss case the role of the federal government is subordinate to that of the business community and the market. Moreover, the accommodation between unions and business sectors does not require central coordination but occurs at the level of the sector. Both features reveal the depoliticization and decentralization that characterize Switzerland's liberal corporatism. In the Austrian case political involvement in industry is much greater and the adjustment to market developments is explictly framed in political terms. Furthermore, the consensual relations between the government and the unions occur at the political center. These two features point to the politicization and centralization that distinguish Austria's social corporatism. But despite these differences in institutional form, liberal corporatism and social corporatism converge in providing economic and political compensation in times of rapid, adverse economic change.

The four industries on which I have focused—Swiss textiles, Austrian textiles, Austrian steel, and Swiss watches—allow some rather wider reflections on what corporatism, in its variants, does, and what it does not do. The four industries were deliberately selected for their large differences on a number of dimensions, among them the source of economic change, the process of internal differentiation, the character of the typical economic actor, and the political organization of the industry as well as its political connection with other sectors. Thus we can be reasonably confident that convergences in strategy and structure are not artifacts of the method of selection.

All four cases illustrate the flexible adjustment that follows from democratic corporatism rather than the logic of either market or state. Remarkable is the strong commitment to free trade despite limited subsidies in Switzerland, and the inability or unwillingness to fashion sectoral policies of transformation despite large subsidies in Austria. Although committed to free trade, Switzerland did not simply accept adverse economic change. Swiss banks protected, to some extent, the exporters of watches and textiles against the appreciation of the franc; the government fashioned a modest program of assistance for the watch industry, especially targeted to an indigenous capacity for producing electronic components; and the banks intervened massively to forestall the collapse of the SSIH and the ASUAG. Despite intervention in textiles and steel, the Austrian government did not transform industrial sectors. Small textile firms in Western Austria flourished as the large Eastern segment of the industry was receiving massive subsidies. In textiles, political disengagement after a costly and futile effort at intervention was possible without major ramifications. But disengagement from the core of Austria's nationalized industries and the socialist stronghold in the Austrian economy, the steel industry, which suffers from structural depression in world markets, would be much more difficult. The crucial test for the country's political tolerance for the consequences of adverse economic change will probably occur only in the coming years. Acknowledging this possible exception, we can still conclude that the economic decline of these four industries in the 1970s did not breed either policies of protection or of structural transformation.

Like those of the United States and Britain, Switzerland's government lacks the instruments for intervening selectively in the economy; but, in contrast, it shies away from exporting the costs of change to others through protection. Though Austria's government, even more than those of Japan and France, controls the instruments for economic intervention, it does not try to preempt the costs of change through a policy of structural transformation. In slowing the pace of change through a policy of deficit spending, Austria borrows against its own future; Switzerland, on the other hand, would be hard pressed without the cushion provided by its foreign workforce. Switzerland and Austria have chosen to live with the costs of change.

Austria's and Switzerland's adjustment to economic change absorbs political conflict. Institutions in both countries reveal, in the area of industrial policy, multiple links between industry, banks, government, and the unions. The difference between the two countries lies in the fact that Switzerland tends toward depoliticization, decentralization, and institutional connections in the private sector organized around the pivotal position of the large banks; while Austria tends toward politicization, centralization, and institutional links in the public sector organized around the major interest groups and the government. These institutional links are essential guarantors for the political capacity to tolerate high rates of change. They help in organizing the political debates and marshalling the troops for a strategy of industrial adjustment that in both countries is reactive and continuous rather than active and sporadic, and which seeks to contain political realignments in response to the changing position of particular industries in world markets. Since this feature of the adjustment process is easily overlooked, the political consequences of economic change that might be imaginable but cannot, in practice, be observed deserve to be spelled out in somewhat greater detail.

One could think of the textile, steel, and watch industries as different arenas for the formation of political coalitions between different industrial sectors, coalitions that press for particular policies of industrial adjustment. Their demands may point to ways of coping with the costs of change that may or may not be consonant with Switzerland's or Austria's political strategy and domestic structure.[112] Technological change and changes in competitive position in international markets continuously create and recreate cycles of innovation, maturation, and imitation in different industries. In the international division of labor each industrial product cycle has its political correlate. The central political characteristic of economic growth and decline in particular industrial sectors such as textiles, steel, or watches is the redefinition of that sector's interest, normally articulated in political terms by its dominant firms and trade associations. In some instances a few major firms in critically important sectors may succeed in creating a political coalition that imposes its definition of interest on that of the national interest. What is good for Switzerland's General Watch Corporation or Austria's United Steel Works may, indeed, be good for Switzerland or Austria. Under different circumstances, in an attempt to create political barriers to economic change, major firms or trade associations in hard-pressed sectors may seek to increase their strength through political alignments with labor unions whose existence is threatened by widespread unemployment. Between these poles of "international liberalism" and "national socialism" there exists a wide variety of possible political coalitions advocating different strategies of adjustment. A political alignment between major firms in critically important sectors often constitutes a country's dominant political force, which defines the long-term objectives of a political strategy. A political coalition among numerous weak firms and labor unions in marginal sectors may extract only short-term economic relief for particular segments of an industry. Thus, political coalitions that result from economic changes lead to outcomes that may be as broad as the characteristics of a political regime and as narrow as a particular set of adjustment policies.

Political realignment between industrial sectors has its corollary, at a lower level of abstraction, in political realignment within sectors. Laura Tyson and John Zysman have argued persuasively that industrial sectors are statistical artifacts with their own political reality.[113] Within that broad cluster of economic activities and products that we subsume under the label of textiles, or steel, or watches, is a bewildering array of real-life experiences, from cottage-style production of clothing by women working at home to fully-automated textile mills producing industrial fabrics; from old-fashioned, open-hearth furnaces to modern, integrated steel mills; from the craftsmanship that goes into the production of a high-quality mechanical watch in a mountain cottage to the assembly of the components of electronic watches in a modern factory down in the valley. As a result of these variations, changing political coalitions, which create the condition for advocating new political strategies of industrial adjustment, occur within industrial sectors as well as between them. In their preference for letting market rather than state institutions shape economic outcomes and for bearing rather than rejecting the costs of change, competitive firms do not fundamentally differ in their political alignments and preferences from competitive sectors. Some sectors or sector segments generate political pressures and create political capabilities for absorbing economic change; others resist it.

Whether we analyze the formation of coalitions between sectors or within them, we might expect the political coalitions and political choices in different industries to reflect the changes in the international division of labor. But Swiss and Austrian politics are remarkable because they very severely constrain the building of alternative political coalitions to challenge existing institutions and policies. In Austria the textile industry did not regroup politically but relied instead on a collaborative management of change. That collaboration was sufficiently strong to bridge the different preferences of textile producers in the Eastern and the Western parts of the country. In Switzerland the textile industry regrouped politically in response to crisis. In the interest of more effective political representation in federal politics the industry imposed on itself a greater degree of centralization, and it further reinforced its collaborative arrangements with the textile unions at the sectoral level. The political response was essentially to recreate, at a sectoral level, those political arrangements which characterize Switzerland at large.

This ability to constrain the formation of alternative political coalitions is also to be found in Austria's steel and Switzerland's watch industries. Here realignment took the form of an economic regrouping; in the 1970s it occurred somewhat earlier in steel than in watches. Since the steel industry occupies a pivotal position in Austria's nationalized sector, and in its domestic structure more generally, political realignments involving a formation of coalitions between or within sectors would, by definition, have transformed Austrian politics. But the nationalized steel industry was the prime instrument by which Austria's government sought to maintain full employment; no serious political conflicts arose. The conflicts between the different firms in the nationalized sector— the VEW, Voest-Alpine, and the ÖIAG—over subsidies and investments were articulated and resolved at the highest political level, the cabinet and the chancellery. In contrast, the regrouping within the Swiss watch industry involved intense political conflicts. When concentration and direct foreign investment were seriously entertained as strategic options, in the late 1970s, the institutional organization of all stages of production of the deeply segmented watch industry made it probable for conflicts within the industry to dominate over the search for political allies outside. As a consequence, the fundamental restructuring of the industry, which is now underway, has remained politically encapsulated. In this industry, as in textiles, no attempts were made to create new political coalitions between industry segments or to seek new political allies in other industrial sectors. Furthermore, the formation of such coalitions is quite improbable in the foreseeable future. The watch industry will increasingly depend on good relations with Swiss banks even though the banks' defense of the appreciation of the franc contributed greatly to the industry's decline. On this point, relations between the Austrian government and its steel industry offer a parallel. Through its policy of charging below-market prices in the 1960s the industry became financially more dependent on the government in the 1970s and 1980s.

Both countries accept, within broad limits, the force of market pressures and react to these pressures in a flexible manner. Neither country seriously attempts to shift the costs of change to other countries through protectionist measures. And neither country seeks to preempt the costs of change through a deliberate and long-term structural transformation. Furthermore, both countries have been able politically to absorb very large economic changes without much controversy and without a fundamental questioning of existing political institutions and practices. Groups that might have benefited from other policies were politically contained and accommodated within existing domestic structures. That accommodation requires trade-offs between economic efficiency and political compensation. In its industrial adjustment Switzerland exhibits more of the former, Austria more of the latter. For this reason, as hallmarks of democratic corporatism the political concessions to disadvantaged actors made in "capitalist" Switzerland are as noteworthy as the responsiveness to changing market conditions in "socialist" Austria.

CHAPTER SEVEN

Conclusion

Austria and Switzerland are two great success stories. They have shared an economic prosperity and a political stability that contribute to pervasive self-satisfaction among their citizens, and to a mixture of astonishment and admiration among foreigners. Despite their exposed positions in the international economy, Austria and Switzerland can point to remarkable achievements in the crisis-ridden 1970s. They managed to achieve inflation and unemployment rates that were among the lowest in the industrial states. In terms of per capita income, in the late 1970s Switzerland was one of the richest countries in the world; and Austria could look back on a decade of economic growth significantly surpassed only by Japan. Americans, spellbound by Japan as Number One and perhaps by West Germany as Number Two, have failed to notice that diminutive Austria and Switzerland have also avoided the troubles that beset the American Gulliver.

COMPARISONS

It is perhaps understandable that the Swiss and the Austrians have been more aware of each other's achievements than have others less intimately acquainted with this particular corner of the world. But the two countries often pose riddles to each other. At one moment they appear to be united by history and divided by geography. The very next moment they are united by geography and divided by history. These blurred images baffle not only outsiders but the Swiss and the Austrians themselves. Still, the most obvious comparisons lie across their common border.

239

Switzerland has its share of "Austrians," located mostly on the Left; and Austria has its native "Swiss," mostly on the Right. Geographic proximity and a confusing blend of similarities and differences have made these two countries acutely aware of each other. As the *Economist's* reporter noted, "Even the courteous Austrians turn a little bitchy when comparing themselves with their Swiss neighbours. The two countries are too similar in size . . . and international positions, and two different in history and domestic political complexion, to do otherwise."[1] Grating to the Swiss, on the other hand, is the fact that Austria is a Number Two which, to the Swiss eye, is not trying all that hard. Economically, Switzerland and Austria epitomize the difference between rich and poor cousins. But through its political strategy Austria has reinforced the potential for higher rates of economic growth that derives from its position of relative economic backwardness. As the *Economist* predicts, "Economically Austria will probably never be another Switzerland, but, if inflation can be contained, it will not be lagging all that far behind it."[2]

In their own distinctive way, the Swiss retain a hidden curiosity about Austria. The director of the Swiss intelligence service's top secret operations was suspended in late 1979 after a subordinate sent to spy on Austrian army maneuvers was arrested by the Austrian police. This unsuccessful search for information freely available to Swiss and other foreign observers provided a comic interlude in Swiss-Austrian relations; but comedies are linked to reality. The Swiss are secretly a bit confounded by their neighbors' success. And they resent Austria's shameless copying of their own strategy—combining political neutrality with economic profitability by attracting international organizations and foreign capital. Vienna's new United Nations complex is a symbol of Austria's "virtuous competition" with Switzerland; and Austria's recent bank legislation in many ways exceeds the assurances of anonymity and underbids the level of taxation that foreign capital has traditionally enjoyed in Switzerland.

Generally speaking, though, Austria regards Switzerland as more of a model than the other way around. This fixation can be attributed to the important role that permanent neutrality along Swiss lines has played as a guarantor of the sovereignty of the Second Republic.[3] The Moscow Memorandum of 15 April 1955, the Austrian State Treaty of 15 May 1955, and the Declaration of Permanent Neutrality by the Austrian Parliament of 26 October 1955 provide the cornerstones of Austria's statehood. In Austria, as in Switzerland, permanent neutrality means armed neutrality. Both countries are located between the northern and southern wings of NATO; both have good relations with West and East; both are members of the group of nonaligned states; and, for reasons of their permanent neutrality, neither is a full member of the European Communities.

But the very fact that Austria has modeled its neutrality after Switzerland's points to important differences. As Anton Pelinka has written, "The Swiss neutrality is an old one, based on an international treaty and on a multilateral consensus, expressed by a formal agreement between the great powers. The Austrian neutrality is a new one, based on a national, domestic, unilateral law and on a multilateral consensus, expressed only by an informal agreement between the great powers."[4] Because of these differences, the political interpretation of the concept of neutrality is broader and less contentious in Switzerland than in Austria. Switzerland spends considerably more on national defense than Austria does—as a share of its national budget in the 1970s, almost five times as much.[5] And because Switzerland's armed forces are organized along the lines of a militia, the strength of the Swiss mobilized army as a proportion of the population is four times that of Austria.[6] How could it be otherwise? In Switzerland there has only been one army since the beginning of the nineteenth century; peace and neutrality have been coterminous. Austria, on the other hand, has been defeated in war twice, and the republican army that has existed since 1955 is the fifth army claiming Austria's allegiance in the twentieth century. That Austria spends so little on a defense that emulates the Swiss model is plausible, both historically and psychologically, but it also contributes to the Swiss perception of Austrian irresponsibility. By and large, though, such critical attitudes resemble private family quarrels. Political relations between the two countries are free of tension, and disdain for the political life across the border is balanced by an appreciation of the neighbors' real accomplishments during the past generation.

IMPLICATIONS

Comparing countries is a tricky business. Like other peoples, the Swiss and the Austrians are skeptical of foreigners' abilities to discover things about their societies that are both important and true. To them their own institutions and ideologies necessarily remain shrouded in mystery. Peter Bettschart has captured this attitude: "An Austrian trade union official once characterized the Joint Commission as an institution which you do not have to explain to an Austrian and which you cannot explain to a foreigner. The same is true of Swiss federalism."[7] Comparison, moreover, may do to countries what caricature does to people. It runs the risk of overemphasizing or underplaying features that to the nonspecialist appear equally prominent. In offering this analysis I therefore accept the risk of incurring that mixture of general disapproval and studied indifference which the Austrians and Swiss reserve for foreigners who do not fully understand.

Indeed, the risk is the greater in this instance because some of my arguments cut against the grain of notions widely held, and not only in these two countries. In their local variants of corporatism, Switzerland and Austria provide fertile soil for capitalism and for democracy. They thus both challenge reactionary and radical critiques of modern society. A liberal strategy relying on private sector initiatives and favoring social stability, Switzerland shows, can create conditions under which individual liberty and national autonomy are maintained; and a socialist strategy, Austria shows, does not necessarily lead to structural dependency and immiseration. But Switzerland also belies a view from the Left, which holds that capitalism and democracy are antithetical; and Austria invalidates a view from the Right, which stipulates that democracy and socialism are in unrelenting tension. The restraints that liberal corporatism imposes on the unilateral exercise of power limits the extent of capitalist hegemony in Switzerland—despite the political predominance of the business community and despite the strong electoral influence of the conservative Alpine cantons. Similar restraints in Austria's social corporatism have impeded the growth of socialist hegemony—despite the electoral successes of the SPÖ in the 1970s, despite a powerful, centralized union movement, and despite the government's vast industrial holdings. What holds for Austria holds for Switzerland as well: since crisis has been redefined as normality, not much ever changes. "The old wheeling and dealing, under the unholy trinity [of unions, business, and the government bureaucracy], goes on as before."[8]

Although corporatism restrains the exercise of power in both countries, Switzerland and Austria differ in their political strategies—how they adapt as well as how they compensate for change. Switzerland adheres to a far-reaching strategy of global adaptation marked by a consistent pursuit of liberal objectives in, for example, the areas of trade, foreign investment, and relations with developing countries. Switzerland has invested a greater proportion of productive capital abroad than any other industrial state. At the same time, more than any other country Switzerland relies on its foreign labor force as a buffer against changes in world markets. Switzerland also imposes numerous restrictions on the government's modest efforts at compensation. It limits public expenditures and has largely resisted the temptation to create a publicly funded social welfare state. Austria, by contrast, has been more hesitant and restrained about international liberalization, and has accorded the government somewhat greater prominence. It lacks significant production facilities abroad and imports fewer foreign workers than Switzerland. Instead, Austria favors public compensation and national adaptation. It subsidizes domestic investment extensively and pursues an active labor-market policy designed to ensure full employment. Austria has large public expenditures and a generous social welfare system that relies heavily on public funding, and it features the most far-reaching and stable incomes policy anywhere in the industrial world today.

Economists have offered two major remedies for the economic ills of our times. Switzerland exemplifies the neoliberal prescription: to strengthen capitalism through unrestricted market competition. Austria is the very model of the neo-Keynesian remedy: politically to modify the logic of markets to fit the social requirements of capitalist expansion. Applied to the economic situation of the advanced industrial states, these two answers amount to a reduction or a restructuring of the role government plays in domestic markets. These two answers, furthermore, are often viewed as addressing the topic of unfettered international trade; neoliberalism seems to support it, neo-Keynesianism to oppose it. According to this view, Switzerland's global adaptation suggests that neoliberalism is incommensurate with capitalism's mercantile past. Austria's national adaptation, on the other hand, suggests that neo-Keynesianism retains its ties with socialism's autarchic instincts.

But such an inference may be premature. Switzerland's policy in the 1970s consisted of fiscal frugality and deliberate deflation conducted in the name of economic rationalization and export competitiveness. If adopted by other states, this policy would lead to an international race to pay for expensive oil through the accumulation of current-account and balance-of-payments surpluses. As an ever-greater proportion of world trade occurs between advanced industrial states, in this contemporary form of social darwinism one country's surplus aggravates another's deficit. The recent history of trade relations between Japan and the United States suggests that trade competition substantially increases conflict in the global economy and tends to undermine its liberal foundations.

In contrast, Austria financed economic growth through borrowing in highly liquid international markets; it bought prosperity on credit.

When OPEC countries ran substantial balance-of-payments surpluses and OECD countries substantial deficits, such a policy, were it to be adopted by other states, offered the prospect of international cooperation within the limits of what creditors regarded as prudent levels of indebtedness. As long as economic growth is sufficiently high to keep the relative debt burden in check, financial limits imposed by the creditors' demands are not stringent. But when economic growth falters and the relative debt burden increases rapidly, the threat of default and the closing of capital markets impose harsh limits. In the 1970s Austria exemplified the former possibility, Poland the latter. Until the early 1980s the fear that Austria was borrowing too heavily to finance its prosperity was unfounded. Budget deficits and the national debt did increase sharply in the 1970s, as the Austrian government was adamant in defending full employment, but Austria's linking of the schilling to the deutsche mark limited the extent of deficit financing. Since the late 1970s Austria's political leadership has explicitly acknowledged these limits. Year in year out, throughout the 1970s and early 1980s, the OECD reported that government deficits and government borrowing in Austria were relatively low by international standards. Viewed from this perspective, the experience of capitalist Switzerland and socialist Austria suggests that neoliberal remedies may encourage national neomercantilism and international conflict, while, within limits, neo-Keynesian prescriptions foster global liberalism and international cooperation.[9]

The differences between Switzerland's strategy and Austria's reflect differences in domestic structures: social coalitions, policy networks, and policy process. In Switzerland an internationally oriented business community, including both industry and finance, enjoys substantial political advantages over a nationally oriented business community and a divided Left. In Austria a united and politically strong Left has much greater influence over policy; it finds itself in partial competition with a business community that is nationalized and oriented to domestic rather than to international markets. In both countries these social coalitions are organized in concentrated interest groups that interact uninterruptedly in a policy process that also involves the state bureaucracy and political parties. Both policy networks continuously reaffirm and modify a consensual domestic structure that fuses interest groups, political parties, and government bureaucracies in a corporatist system of politics. The difference between the Swiss and Austrian variants of corporatism is the difference between a depoliticized, private, and decentralized liberal corporatism, on the one hand, and a politicized, public, and centralized social corporatism, on the other.

Similarities and differences in strategy and structure have been revealed in detail in the four cases of political adaptation to industrial change. In the case of textiles Switzerland's policy was marked by a willingness to bear the costs of change. Temporary support was extended for export financing, and very selective and limited financial relief measures were adopted at the height of the industry's crisis. Austria's adjustment policy, by contrast, stressed limited protection, less extensive support for exports, and temporary, massive domestic subsidies to protect employment. In the case of Swiss watches the government's political disengagement from the industry proceeded without interruption during the industry's crisis-ridden 1970s. The government's very limited and very belated aid left the industry largely to its own devices (as well as to the intervention of Swiss banks). Austria, finally, adjusted not in but through the nationalized steel industry that looms so large in its economy. In the 1970s this facilitated the defense of full employment, a strategy reinforced, in the late 1970s, by Austria's adoption of the protectionist policies of the European Communities on which its steel industry depends for markets.

These four cases illustrate how corporatism deals with change. While the industries in both countries experienced adverse economic change, politics either did not impede a shift in the factors of production or did so in a manner that contributed politically to a flexible adjustment policy. Although the Swiss textile and watch industries were primarily forced to adjust through the institution of the market, they were also aided by a special effort of Switzerland's banks and the federal government to assist producers in a limited way. In Austria's textile and steel industries, on the other hand, adjustment to economic change depended heavily on the actions of the government rather than the banks. But in the case of textiles the government very quickly learned that it lacked the resources to override market forces. And in the steel industry, the government chose a substantial reduction in capacity and modernization while trying to minimize the impact on employment. In all four cases the awareness of the need to be competitive and of the force of market developments was prominent. Thus Austria and Switzerland are distinctive in that they calibrate the requirements of economic flexibility with those of political stability. Switzerland encourages economic flexibility while making some political concessions. Austria organizes policy around political concessions without neglecting the requirements of flexibility. In linking flexibility with stability, both countries have chosen to live with the costs of change.

Liberal capitalism and democratic socialism are historically rooted structures that offer distinct strategies for the economic problems of our time. It is a notable irony that liberals and Marxists tend fundamentally to agree that industrialization and modernization are great levelers of differences between advanced industrial societies. While liberals focus on the logic of markets and Marxists on the logic of capitalist exploitation, both argue that modern society is shaped by technology and the social relations it engenders. In contrast, this book's view of Switzerland and Austria emerges from another body of research, which contends that economic viability and political legitimacy can be secured in many ways, and that these ways are fundamentally shaped by history and politics. At the same time, though, this book also argues that economic openness and international vulnerability have forced a significant convergence in strategy and structure. To put matters boldly, *contra* liberalism I have argued that in looking at political adjustments to economic change one should distinguish between a market-driven process of change and market change. Markets are embedded in political contexts that must be analyzed in their own right as they affect the success or failure of particular strategies of adjustment. *Contra* Marxism I have argued that in the case of Switzerland and Austria, international vulnerability and economic openness have led to a partial redefinition of divisive class interests in terms of a more encompassing national interest. And *contra* statism I have shown that the national interest cannot be stipulated abstractly, but that it emerges from distinctive corporatist structures.

But this book also challenges the liberal, statist, and Marxist paradigms as they apply to international politics. The economic success and political autonomy that Switzerland and Austria have enjoyed since World War II provide both partial confirmation and unresolved puzzles for the three paradigms. The strength of the liberal analysis lies in its confirmation by the consciously liberal strategy that small European states pursue in the international economy, and the favorable economic outcomes that accord with liberal predictions. Statists point to a favorable constellation in the international state system since 1945 that has permitted small European states to maintain their sovereignty and political autonomy. Combining both insights, Marxists argue that an era of prosperity and peace has provided the small European states with a permissive international context. Common to all three interpretations is the assumption that international markets, the international state system, and global capitalism are the main determinants of political strategies. All three thus flirt with determinism, viewing international forces as decisive in shaping national choice. All three presume either a loss of political autonomy in the era of international interdependence or the irrelevance of domestic needs. They thus tend to shortcircuit an examination of domestic structures. Yet as I have shown, these structures are of critical importance in mediating between the international setting and the national response, of making the requirements of the first compatible with the requirements of the second. Indeed, the pervasiveness of corporatism in Austria and Switzerland, and its durability across the last four decades, have been shaped by this interaction of domestic and international forces.

CONFLICT AND CHANGE

Switzerland's liberal capitalism and Austria's democratic socialism embody a corporatist politics that, notwithstanding past prosperity and consensus, must live with conflict and change. Austrians are increasingly aware that a prolonged downturn in the fortunes of the German Federal Republic, or the international economy in general, would threaten their ability to fund full employment and thus would generate political pressures not known since 1945.[10] The loss of the socialists' absolute majority in Parliament as well as the resignation of Chancellor Kreisky in April 1983 signified to all that Austrian politics is not immune to crisis. And, across the border, Switzerland's consistent policy of deflation and diminishing rates of upward social mobility are generating, for the first time in decades, social tensions that many Swiss hesitate to acknowledge because they intersect in unpredictable ways with the already uneasy juxtaposition of plebiscitarian politics, interest-group bargaining, and rule by emergency decree. Up to a point that we do not recognize until it is too late, economic crisis, this book has argued, reinforces rather than undermines the corporatist arrangements of Austria and Switzerland. As in all forms of politics, corporatism harbors its own political contradictions. In Switzerland's liberal capitalism and Austria's democratic socialism, these political contradictions involve both domestic and international politics.

Austria's domestic policy network incorporates all potential sources of opposition, thus assuring the policy process of a high degree of continuity and consensus. But in contrast to the Swiss experience, the far-reaching transformation in Austria's economic structure was accomplished in a very centralized manner. The difference between the few who arrange the consensus and the many who merely accept it, though not unique to Austria, is the most probable source of tension and change in the long term.[11] The insignificance to date of wildcat strikes and the acquiescence of union members in the indirect election of union officials are only two signals of a possible demobilization of the unions' grassroots support and a delegitimation of their leadership.[12] It is by no means imminent, but if the character of Austria's labor movement were to change in reaction to further concentration of political power in times of economic crisis, it would have profound consequences for Austria's social and economic partnership. On the side of business, the possibilities for change are both less remote and less far-reaching. Small, private firms, in particular, insist that a substantial decline in investments and profits during the 1970s has endangered their viability, and thus the most dynamic sector of the Austrian economy. Whether Austria's hard-currency policy and high indirect labor costs impair the competitiveness of Austrian businesses has been a source of animated political debate, conducted in the language of economic statistics. Unfavorable economic conditions could easily intensify the modest political pressures that thousands of small and medium-sized firms now exert in the Federal Economic Chamber.

Large-scale transformations within the peak associations of labor and business are less likely than a more gradual divergence of interest. Austrian white-collar unions, now so prominent, have adopted a more aggressive stance than blue-collar unions on questions of collective bargaining, social policy, and economic redistribution. Moreover, the political implications of more decentralized forms of work, which have only become technologically possible in recent years, may also pose severe problems for the central union. Furthermore, the Federal Economic Chamber is now encountering opposition from a more self-confident, liberal, and strident segment of the business community, primarily located in Western Austria. And the strains on Austria's centralized consensus building become apparent when it meets unaccustomed challenges from below—illustrated, for example, by the country's political fission over nuclear power. But these potential sources of disaffection from Austria's economic miracle should not be overstated. Austria's potent system of political institutions encourages participation—indeed, one large-scale comparative study concludes that Austria has a "more politicized organization system than that found elsewhere."[13] It is only a slight exaggeration to say that there are few indications of dramatic changes in the relation between the omnipotence of Austria's organizations and the impotence of the organized.

Like Austria, Switzerland is subject to change generated by its internal political contradictions. On questions of political economy Switzerland's policy network incorporates all important political actors, thus assuring the policy process of both continuity and consensus. To the pragmatic political bargaining so distinctive of Swiss politics, the institution of direct democracy offers both reinforcement and relief. Centralized bargains are reinforced by major actors' strategically deployed threats to leave the table and resolve the issue at the polls. But these bargains have been challenged in the last decade, and with increasing frequency, by issue-specific coalitions. Since it provides for effective citizen participation, Switzerland's domestic structure appears less brittle than Austria's when confronted with such challenges as the antinuclear movement. And, with its nationally oriented business community decisively weakened by the long tradition of liberal economic policy and its Left devoid of a socialist vision, Switzerland is probably less vulnerable to large-scale political changes than is more centralized Austria.

The weakness of and potential threat to Switzerland's durable government by consensus lies neither in its transformation by a disaffected, impotent citizenry nor in a radical restructuring of its peak associations. Weakness and threat are, rather, to be found in Switzerland's extremely low tolerance for disorder, protest, and political change. The wave of spontaneous youth protests that spread in 1980 from the familiar scenery of Frankfurt, Berlin, and Amsterdam to Zurich, as well as other Swiss cities, brought to the surface an illiberal undercurrent in the country's politics.[14] A small, disaffected segment of Swiss youth, unwilling to articulate any specific demands, demonstrated with increasing violence against the frozen contours of Switzerland's political scenery with the slogan "Melt the ice pack!" Switzerland's tight-knit relations between state and society, and the delicate balance between competing interests, do not easily accommodate dissent. This is particularly true when dissent undermines Switzerland's legend of tranquil sanity in a turbulent world, a legend central to its comparative advantage in the international economy. "When the city trembles, the banks quake." Asked just how important were a few broken windows, a banker who was not amused by the demonstrations gave a reply that he felt most of his compatriots would endorse: "In Switzerland," he said, "a few broken windows are a great deal indeed."[15]

But for Switzerland, as for Austria, the major source of change lies neither in contradictions between social sectors nor in tensions inherent in political and social institutions. Today developments in the international economy are forcing change upon Switzerland. All advanced industrial states, large and small, initially reacted to the crisis of the 1970s largely in terms congruent with their domestic structures of power and well-tested strategies. Switzerland was no exception. Throughout the turbulent 1970s it primarily preserved its stability through a strategy of global adaptation. But on questions of employment, in particular, Switzerland today has a thinner cushion to absorb future economic shocks than it did in the early 1970s. The few systematic studies dealing with Switzerland's future view structural unemployment as a major problem in the next two decades, and foreign-exchange policies in support of exports as a potentially major stimulus for generating jobs. Switzerland is condemned to export.[16] The acceleration of Switzerland's openness to the international economy in the 1970s has made the nation more sensitive and vulnerable to developments in the global economy without corresponding increases in the international coordination of policy. This is likely to reinforce the tendency to supplement private initiatives with emergency action by the Swiss government.

The domestic and international strains that Switzerland can anticipate in the middle and latter 1980s raise some questions about the durability of the corporatist institutions and political practices that perpetuate Switzerland's consensual politics. Are these institutions and practices the consequence or the precondition of economic prosperity and social stability? The Swiss prefer not to think about future contingencies arising from their great dependence on unpredictable world markets. The problems Switzerland confronted in the international economy in the 1970s were the problems of success: the management of monetary stability in a world of inflation and the viability of an export industry undermined by the appreciation of the franc. But the economic consequences of the second sharp increase in oil prices, in 1979, suggest that even Switzerland may not be totally immune to the problems that have bedeviled most other industrial states since the first oil shock of 1973-74: adverse terms of trade, sharply growing trade deficits, a weak currency, and increasing inflationary pressures. But it is easy to forget that in the 1970s Switzerland lived through a crisis whose economic proportions exceeded that of the 1930s. Displacing the costs of unemployment largely onto a foreign workforce ameliorated the political consequences of economic adversity. Crisis conditions and the appearance of normality are more closely intertwined in small industrial states than in large ones. There is little in the record of the past half-century to suggest that the Swiss will not draw closer together in the center of their small boat as the waters they sail get choppier.

For Austria, as for Switzerland, the major source of change lies in developments in the international economy. Austria can maintain its policy of high investment and high growth in the 1980s only if it develops a broad-gauged export offensive in world markets. In contrast to the 1970s, a Keynesian policy of deficit spending in the 1980s will probably generate less domestic growth. The import content of consumer demand markedly increased in the 1970s. Projected over the medium term, this trend jeopardizes Austria's employment- and investment-oriented policy; as one perceptive journalist notes, "Too much of any extra income pumped out through a wider budget deficit flows out into payment for imports."[17] Austria's growing internationalization will put additional burdens on the strategy of domestic adaptation that the country favored in the 1960s and 1970s. The search for responses to these additional burdens has already divided Austria's governing Socialist Party.[18] The majority views Austria's current balance-of-payments problems as the result of cyclical growth in consumer demand for foreign goods and of the rising import bill for fuel, which can only be paid for through a determined export offensive. A minority sees in the current crisis a secular shift toward import dependence in both the consumer and the investment goods sectors, a shift reinforced by the increasing costs of energy that may eventually require selective import controls.

Since the evidence supports both these and other interpretations, the SPÖ's veneer of political compromise has not yet worn as thin as might be expected under harsher economic conditions. But if Austria were to act on either of these two interpretations in the years ahead, the consequences for its domestic structure would be important. The liberal strategy would push Austria toward a more decisive state capitalism based on the bureaucracy's selective intervention in specific industrial sectors. The neomercantilist strategy would move Austria toward a rejuvenation of its economic and social partnership as well as an improvement of the capital base and investment climate for small and medium-sized firms. Although the whole debate originated within the Socialist Party, moves in either of these two directions would have profound consequences for the ÖVP and its ancillary interest groups. The political representatives of big business appear more favorable toward the liberal strategy (and the support of big business it entails) than the Federal Economic Chamber, which, as the spokesman for small and medium-sized firms, favors more aggressive nontariff barriers. The strength of liberal and protectionist currents in the large industrial states lends some credence to the claims of both factions. But the political possibilities and limits of change are largely preprogrammed by the logic of Austria's domestic structures.

The domestic and international tensions that Austria faces in the 1980s call into question the durability of institutions and political practices that have perpetuated Austria's overarching consensus. The head of Austria's Economic Research Institute, for example, observed in 1981 that "Austria's social consensus is going to be sharply tested in the next few years."[19] Is a stable politics the consequence or the precondition of economic growth? Austrians are deeply divided on this subject.[20] Admitting that it is impossible to give a clear and confident answer, the interpretation of Austrian politics developed in this book points to the importance of the political preconditions for economic growth and consensus formation.[21] This was certainly true in the late 1940s, as Andrew Schonfield noted: "The need for some formula which would allow the parties to collaborate actively in the national interest became urgent when the country faced severe economic strains immediately after the war."[22] A similar strengthening of domestic consensus in times of economic adversity occurred in the 1950s. And the adoption of a hard-currency policy, coupled with wage restraint and generous social welfare in the 1970s, began at a moment "when the Austrian small-country sense of aloneness in a difficult world could be energetically invoked."[23] Were the present prolonged recession in the world economy to intensify, Austria would be one of the few industrialized countries with a solution in store: growing unemployment would be combated through a shorter workweek and a cut in real wages. For, as the *Financial Times* observes, "The spectre of recession . . . is bound to strengthen the pressures for cooperation."[24] The OECD admiringly observed in 1981 that "in summary Austria's economic performance compares favorably with that of most other countries. The most important factor in this has been the continuous dialogue between the social partners and the government on income determination in the context of broader economic management and social progress."[25]

Austria struggles hard to find the proper balance between national autonomy and international interdependence. Under the chancellorship of Bruno Kreisky, Austria pursued a decade-long policy of active neutrality. In close cooperation with like-minded countries, Austria sought to strengthen detente by keeping on good terms with both the United States and the Soviet Union; to develop good relations with

Italy and Yugoslavia over problematic issues such as the South Tyrol and the Slovenes in Carinthia; to facilitate international peace keeping in the United Nations by supporting the Austrian secretary-general and an Austrian contribution to the UN emergency force; and to mediate political conflicts, especially in the Middle East. This list illustrates that, in contrast to Switzerland, Austria heavily tilts the balance between interdependence and autonomy toward the former. The two countries' attitudes toward military defense and international institutions point up the difference. Convinced of the inefficacy of a military force tied neither to NATO nor to the Warsaw Pact, Austria spends a bare minimum on national defense. And the public controversies over Austria's defense posture in the 1970s revealed widespread uncertainty over the necessity of a strong army. Such uncertainty does not exist in Switzerland.

Conversely Austria, even more than Switzerland, seeks to attract international institutions as diplomatic deterrents to foreign threats. Political interdependence is thus an essential ingredient in Austria's national autonomy. Skeptics never cease asking whether the United Nations commands more divisions than the pope; but, at a cost of $700 million, Vienna has become the third UN city, after New York and Geneva. Since 1979 a complex of office buildings on the banks of the Danube has housed 3,500 employees from various international agencies, for the token rent of one schilling a year. In addition Vienna houses the headquarters of OPEC; it serves as a conduit for Eastern European and Soviet emigrés; and it is the clearinghouse for most private business deals between East and West. It hosts about 250 companies and even more representative offices concerned with East-West trade, as well as 35 agencies for East European firms.[26] And because it trains diplomats from 49 countries, including five Communist ones, the Diplomatic Academy of Vienna is unique among the world's government-sponsored foreign service schools.[27] The fact that an Austrian national was twice elected secretary-general of the United Nations, an organization Switzerland has not yet joined, illustrates the different balances between interdependence and autonomy that Vienna and Bern have struck.

"Neutrality and universality" is the official maxim informing Switzerland's political strategy abroad. It expresses the country's deep ambivalence toward the outside world. Unlike Austria, Switzerland has valued national autonomy more highly than international interdependence. Switzerland's armed neutrality is grounded in widely shared perceptions of what is in the country's national interest, and, indeed, Swiss prosperity today derives in part from its ability to avoid armed conflict since 1815. Switzerland's militia system makes it literally a nation in arms, one that does not question the need or value of constant military preparedness. "In the Eye of the Hurricane" between 1939 and 1945, Switzerland interned 77,000 soldiers and suffered 6,500 violations of its sovereign space.[28] In the 1970s frugal Switzerland spent twice as much of GNP as Austria did on military defense. National defense is favored by the country's geography—even the casual tourist is impressed by the constant and visible military preparedness of this peaceful Alpine fortress. And the national defense rests on an indigenous armaments industry that assures the country of a considerable amount of independence from foreign suppliers and, in addition, earns substantial export revenues. The Swiss believe, as Jane Kramer told *New Yorker* readers, that "their Army and their Alps, and not the convenience of an open Switzerland, are what protect them."[29]

But the wish for political autonomy that Switzerland expresses today goes well beyond its military implications. It provides, for example, a rationale for keeping international organizations at arm's length.[30] Today Switzerland has not yet joined the United Nations, because it is still engaged in the preliminaries of domestic consensus formation. For a variety of reasons, all rooted in economic interest, it has refused to join the International Monetary Fund, the World Bank, and the Group of Ten as a full-fledged member. Full membership in the GATT became effective only in 1966, after Switzerland had, under strong prodding from its agricultural lobby, won a permanent exemption from free trade in agriculture. The president of the Nationalbank, Leo Schürmann, argued that "we are willing to take the political and economic risk of standing alone; but we are also willing to exploit the opportunities which it offers."[31] This perhaps overdramatizes the risks. A Swiss journalist more recently wrote that "We still play the honest if slightly stupid farmer as a facade behind which we can engage in our cunning financial deals. We live off the fact that people often forget to include Switzerland among the major industrial states."[32] For example, Switzerland's legalistic application of internationally negotiated export restraints on sensitive nuclear technologies indicates an energetic export strategy. Switzerland, it could therefore be argued, follows the opportunistic strategy of a free rider, unwilling to pay the full political cost of the institutional infrastructure for a secure, liberal, international economy.[33]

But this is only one side of the ledger. The other side records the inevitable and deep entanglement of Switzerland with the outside world, especially in economic affairs. In fact, Switzerland's foreign policy seems to have become largely coterminous with its foreign economic policy.[34] Switzerland simply cannot afford to keep apart from the international community. It cooperates with all the technical agencies of the United Nations. In the World Bank, the IMF, and the Group of Ten, it holds a fully recognized status as observer and, for example, since 1978–79 has been actively involved in stabilizing the value of the dollar and the exchange rate between the franc and the deutsche mark. Switzerland has, in recent years, joined organizations like the International Energy Agency and is inching toward joining the United Nations.

Like the other advanced industrial states, both small and large, Switzerland and Austria confront the dilemma of how to balance their quest for autonomy with the fact of interdependence. The emphasis of Austria's democratic socialism on adaptation at home and of Switzerland's liberal capitalism on adaptation abroad is in basic contradiction with the balance these two states have struck between autonomy and interdependence. Austria finances its export support system abroad, and it agreed grudgingly to an international agreement regulating the credit terms of export trade in 1978. Switzerland finances its export offensive at home, and it refused to sign that international agreement. The government spares no expense in luring foreign firms to Austria. In Switzerland the business community has erected private fences against foreign take-overs. Austria imports innovations from others and liberally exports its own technological innovations, as in steel. Switzerland produces its innovations at home and controls their outflow, at times strictly, as in the case of watches. Austria ties the value of its currency to that of another state. Switzerland lets its currency float freely. In general terms, then, widely accepted interpretations of the celebration of markets in liberal Switzerland and of the pursuit of state intervention in socialist Austria do not capture the political choices these two countries have made to balance autonomy with interdependence. What has been said of Austria applies as well to Switzerland: both countries have "managed to pursue an economic policy that has been both evidently successful and remarkably independent."[35] The consequences of that policy for Switzerland's and Austria's domestic politics are potentially far-reaching. Will Switzerland continue to rely on a mixture of political improvisation and rule by emergency decree, or will it choose domestic reform of its institutions? Will Austria continue to rely on its system of economic and social partnership, or will it choose more forceful state intervention? In both cases the argument of this book points to the first answer, to continuity, rather than to the second, that of change. Switzerland lives contentedly with the contradictions that arise from its insistent pursuit of political autonomy and the industrious reaping of the fruits of economic interdependence. And Austria acquiesces in the tensions that stem from combining its growing political entanglement with the world with the remnants of economic insularity.

These tensions and contradictions are mirrored in the metaphors with which the Austrians and the Swiss interpret the reality they experience. If Austrians have a national characteristic, it is to be cynical toward prosperity and cheerful about adversity. Hence the Austrian saying, "The situation is hopeless but not serious." In their attempts to match continued domestic stability and prosperity with increasing international turbulence and adversity, Austrians are beginning to ask themselves whether their country is what the pope in 1971 called "an island of the blessed," or whether it is, as the New Left argues, a system of peripheral capitalism. Two of the three answers one hears most often in Austria—"Something must happen" and "Nothing can be done"—capture the contradiction that the country experiences in the contemporary global economy. The resolution of that contradiction lies in the third answer—"We'll have to muddle through" (man wird sich durchwursteln).

Like the Austrians, the Swiss are also quite aware of the tensions with which they live. Herbert Lüthy expresses it well: "We seem to be in a state of self-contradiction. Our desire to maintain our position in the economic race is constantly at variance with our political urge to stay as we are, or rather as we were."[36] One metaphor that recurs in the debates about Switzerland's strategy in the international economy stresses the need to fight with pikes equal in length to those of foreign competitors (mit gleich langen Spiessen fechten). The reference is to a special kind of pike, the halberd, a piece of military hardware that centuries ago made Swiss mercenaries feared throughout Europe. Deployed offensively it did to the head of a well-armored opponent what a modern can opener does to a can, and from a safe distance. Handled defensively, the halberd permitted Swiss troops to move shoulder to shoulder, forming an unassailable hedgehog that relied on collective movement. Today the Swiss face a world in which, with every forceful blow they strike, the shaft of the pike seems to shorten. The resolution of that contradiction lies in the confidence with which the Swiss use their political independence as a cover under which to reap the benefits of economic interdependence.[37]

Switzerland's and Austria's economic and political successes derive from their capacity to combine economic flexibility with political stability. A recent paper concludes that "Switzerland has managed to combine world dependence with a fair measure of domestic stability."[38] Similarly because of its corporatist arrangements, it has been argued that "the small and open Austrian economy has been able to show great flexibility in adjusting to changing world market conditions. Yet, this comparatively greater flexibility towards external change is only possible because of the system's internal rigidity."[39] Democratic corporatism offers a political avenue for mobilizing consensus on responses to economic change in societies that are dominated by international business in Switzerland and by a strong labor movement in Austria. In both countries such a consensus is essential for flexible strategies of adjustment that meet the economic requirements of openness and the political requirements of corporatism.

Democratic corporatism builds strong political links between the proponents of efficiency and those of equality; indeed, the corporatist formula for success is to restrain the unilateral exercise of power. This restraint is expressed in the narrowing of political inequalities to be found in both Switzerland and Austria. Their convergence in so many areas results not only from the economic pressures of international markets but from the political requirements of corporatist structures. In their policies and politics Austria and Switzerland do not strictly follow the logic of either market or state. Instead the Swiss rely on the corporatist formula to nurture capitalism in one country, while the Austrians continue down the corporatist path to build socialism in one world.

Notes

CHAPTER 1. *Introduction*

1. Any comparative analysis of Austria and Switzerland must build on Gerhard Lehmbruch's *Proporzdemokratie: Politisches System und politische Kultur in der Schweiz und in Österreich* (Tübingen: J. C. B. Mohr [Paul Siebeck], 1967). See also Murray Luck, ed., *Modern Switzerland* (Palo Alto, Calif.: SPOSS, 1978); Kurt Steiner, ed., *Modern Austria* (Palo Alto, Calif.: SPOSS, 1981); Walter S. G. Kohn, *Governments and Politics of the German-Speaking Countries* (Chicago: Nelson-Hall, 1980); Anton Pelinka, "Die österreichische Sozialpartnerschaft im internationalen Vergleich," *Österreichische Zeitschrift für Politikwissenschaft*, 1982, no. 3: 355–64; Edgar Grande and Werner Lang, "Zur politischen Steuerung kapitalistischer Ökonomien," ibid., pp. 341–54. This list should soon include as well a dissertation by Joachim Glasmeier, "Durchstaatlichung und Selbstorganisierung der Gesellschaft: Ein Systemvergleich von Macht und Herrschaft in Österreich und Schweiz" (Ph.D. diss. proposal, University of Göttingen, 1981).

2. Fritz W. Scharpf, "The Political Economy of Inflation and Unemployment in Western Europe: An Outline," discussion paper IIMV, Arbeitsmarktpolitik (Wissenschaftszentrum Berlin, IIM/LMP 81-21), p. 9.

3. Quoted in Jonathan Steinberg, *Why Switzerland?* (Cambridge: Cambridge University Press, 1976), p. 4.

4. Friedrich Engels, "The Civil War in Switzerland," in Karl Marx and Engels, *Collected Works*, vol. 6 (New York: International Publishers, 1976), p. 369.

5. Quoted in Peter Dürrenmatt, *Sonderfall oder Endstation: Die Schweiz im sozialistischen Zeitalter* (Zurich: Flamberg, 1979), p. 89.

6. Quoted in ibid., p. 109.

7. Max Beerbohm, *Yet Again* (New York: Knopf, 1951), p. 42.

8. Steiner, *Modern Austria*, p. xix.

9. Chris Cviic, "Their Own Kind of Miracle," *Economist*, 28 July 1973, Survey, p. 4.

10. *Der Spiegel*, 26 May 1980, p. 129.

11. Federal Press Department, Republic of Austria, "How Does Austria Do It? Reflections on the Austrian National Day," 26 October 1981.

12. Albert C. Hunod, *The Industrial Development of Switzerland* (Cairo: National Bank of Egypt, 1954), p. 10.

13. Emil Küng, *The Secret of Switzerland's Economic Success* (Washington D.C.: American Enterprise Institute, 1978), and Fritz Leutwiler *Swiss Monetary and Exchange Rate Policy in an Inflationary World* (Washington D.C.: American Enterprise Institute, 1978).

14. U.S. Congress, Joint Economic Committee, *Austrian Incomes Policy: Lesson for the United States*, 97th Cong., 1st sess., 2 June 1981.

15. Sven W. Arndt, *The Political Economy of Austria* (Washington D.C.: American Enterprise Institute, 1981); "Making a Miracle Is Hard Work," *Wall Street Journal*, 6 October 1981, p. 23.

16. Uwe Kitzinger, "The Austrian Election of 1959," *Political Studies* 9 (June 1961): 119. See also Leland G. Stauber, "Roads to Democratic Socialism in America: Lessons from the Market-Planning Experience in Austria" (Southern Illinois University at Carbondale, n.d., mimeo).

17. Christian Smekal, "Korreferat zu 'Budgetpolitik in der Schweiz,' " in *Budgetpolitik in der Bundesrepublik Deutschland, in der Schweiz und in Österreich* (Vienna: Zentralsparkasse und Kommerzialbank, 1980), p. 58.

18. *World Business Weekly*, 6 July 1981, p. 27.

19. See Konrad W. Stamm, *Die guten Dienste der Schweiz: Aktive Neutralitätspolitik zwischen Tradition, Diskussion und Integration* (Bern: Lang, 1974).

20. Hugo is quoted in J. R. DeSalis, *Switzerland and Europe: Essays and Reflections* (London: Wolff, 1971), p. 69. A very broad and detailed survey of the historical experience from which we derive our divergent perceptions of Switzerland is contained in Karl W. Deutsch and Herbert Weilenmann, "Switzerland: Exception or Example?" (Harvard University, Cambridge, Mass., n.d., mimeo).

21. Peter J. Katzenstein, "The Last Old Nation: Austrian National Consciousness since 1945," *Comparative Politics* 9 (January 1977): 147–71; and *Disjoined Partners: Austria and Germany since 1815* (Berkeley: University of California Press, 1976).

22. Sarah Hogg, "A Small House in Order," *Economist*, 15 March 1980, Survey, p. 8.

23. Kurt Steiner, *Politics in Austria* (Boston: Little, Brown, 1972), p. vii.

24. James Bryce, *Modern Democracies*, 2 vols. (New York: Macmillan, 1921); André Siegfried, *Switzerland: A Democratic Way of Life* (London: Cape, 1950).

25. Herbert Lüthy, *Die Schweiz als Antithese* (Zurich: Arche, 1969), p. 14, and Lüthy, "Has Switzerland a Future? The Dilemma of the Small Nation," *Encounter* 19 (December 1962): 27.

26. Jane Kramer, "A Reporter in Europe: Zurich," *New Yorker*, 15 December 1980, p. 130.

27. *World Business Weekly*, 17 March 1980, p. 31.

28. Quoted in "Their Own Kind of Miracle," Survey, p. 10.

29. *Economist*, 15 March 1980.

30. Paul Lewis, "The Austrian Economy Is a Strauss Waltz," *New York Times*, 22 March 1981, p. 8F.

31. Andrew Shonfield, *Modern Capitalism: The Changing Balance of Public and Private Power* (London: Oxford University Press), p. 195.

32. The next two paragraphs condense material discussed at greater length in my *Small States in World Markets: Industrial Policy in Europe* (Ithaca: Cornell University Press, forthcoming). The main studies of corporatism include Philippe C. Schmitter and Gerhard Lehmbruch, eds., *Trends toward Corporatist Intermediation* (Beverly Hills, Calif.: Sage, 1979). Suzanne D. Berger, ed., *Organizing Interests in Western Europe* (Cambridge: Cambridge University Press, 1981). Gerhard Lehmbruch and Philippe C. Schmitter, eds., *Patterns of Corporatist Policy-Making* (Beverly Hills, Calif.: Sage, 1982). Francis G. Castles, ed., *The Impact of Parties* (Beverly Hills, Calif.: Sage,1982).

33. Lehmbruch, *Proporzdemokratie*, p. 15. In this discussion I draw from pp. 15–26.

34. Leo Panitch, "Recent Theorizations of Corporatism: Reflections on a Growth Industry," *British Journal of Sociology* 31 (1980): 161–87.

35. For example, John D. Stephens, *The Transition from Capitalism to Socialism* (London: Macmillan, 1979), pp. 112–28; Harold L. Wilensky, *The "New Corporatism," Centralization, and the Welfare State* (Beverly Hills, Calif.: Sage,1976), and Wilensky, "Leftism, Catholicism, and Democratic Corporatism: The Role of Political Parties in Recent Welfare State Development," in Peter Flora and Arnold J. Heidenheimer, eds., *The Development of Welfare States in Europe and America* (New Brunswick, N.J.: Transaction, 1981), pp. 345–82.

36. Michele Salvati and Giorgio Brosio, "The Rise of Market Politics: Industrial Relations in the Seventies," *Daedalus* (Spring 1979), p. 50.

37. The Netherlands provides similar, though less extreme, analytical problems. See, for example, Stephens, *Transition from Capitalism to Socialism,* p. 124; Norbert Lepszy, *Regierung, Parteien und Gewerkschaften in den Niederlanden: Entwicklung und Strukturen* (Dusseldorf: Droste, 1979); Erwin Zimmermann, "Entwicklungstendenzen des Korporatismus und die Industriepolitik in den Niederlanden," in Klaus Armingeon et al., *Neokorporatistische Politik in Westeuropa,* Diskussionsbeiträge 1/1983 (University of Constance, Sozialwissenschaftliche Fakultät, 1983), pp. 107–33; Steven B. Wolinetz, "Neo-Corporatism and Industrial Policy in the Netherlands" (paper prepared for the annual meeting of the Canadian Political Science Association, University of British Columbia, Vancouver, B.C., 6–8 June 1983).

38. Hanspeter Kriesi, *Entscheidungsstrukturen und Entscheidungsprozesse in der schweizer Politik* (Frankfurt: Campus, 1980), pp. 377–78, 689–90. Hanspeter Kriesi, "The Structure of the Swiss Political System," in Lehmbruch and Schmitter, *Patterns of Corporatist Policy-Making,* pp. 155–57.

39. Peter J. Katzenstein, ed., *Between Power and Plenty: Foreign Economic Policies of Advanced Industrial States* (Madison: University of Wisconsin Press, 1978).

40. Schmitter and Lehmbruch, *Trends toward Corporatist Intermediation.*

41. Peter Katzenstein, "Introduction: Domestic and International Forces and Strategies of Foreign Economic Policy," in Katzenstein, *Between Power and Plenty,* p. 19.

42. Ronald Dore, *British Factory—Japanese Factory: The Origins of National Diversity in Industrial Relations* (Berkeley: University of California Press, 1973); Alexis de Tocqueville, *The Old Regime and the French Revolution* (Garden City, N.Y.: Doubleday, 1955).

43. Barbara Stuckey, "Das Babbage-Prinzip der Internationalisierung der industriellen Produktion: Strukturwandel in den Industrieländern," in Silvio Borner, ed., *Produktionsverlagerung und industrieller Strukturwandel* (Bern: Haupt, 1980), pp. 52–53.

CHAPTER 2. *Social Democracy in Austria*

1. Wilhelm Hankel, *Prosperity amidst Crisis: Austria's Economic Policy and the Energy Crunch* (Boulder, Colo.: Westview, 1981). See also Bernd Marin, ed., *Wachstumskrisen in Österreich*, 2 vols. (Vienna: Braumüller, 1979); Anton Kausel, "Die österreichische Wirtschaft ist kerngesund," *Quartalshefte*, 1979, no. 1: 11–34; Erich Spitäller, "Incomes Policy in Austria," *IMF Staff Papers* 26 (1973): 191–99; Austria Federal Press Department, Vienna, "Austria's Economy—A European Example," 26 October, 1981; *Austrian Information* 33, 1 (1980): 1; 32, 6 (1979): 8; 31, 6 (1978): 2–3, 6; *News from Austria*, 12 May, 1981, p. 3, and 5 December 1980, p. 3; Organization for Economic Cooperation and Development *(OECD)*, *Economic Surveys: Austria* (Paris: 1971), pp. 6–11; and Heinz Handler and Jan Stankovsky, "How to Prolong Economic Stability: Austria's Position at the Beginning of the Eighties," *Austria Today* 1981, no. 2: 47–53.

2. Alexander Gerschenkron, *An Economic Spurt That Failed: Four Lectures in Austrian History* (Princeton: Princeton University Press, 1977).

3. Jack Barbash, *Trade Unions and National Economic Policy* (Baltimore: Johns Hopkins University Press, 1972), p. 45; Alexander Vodopivec, *Die Dritte Republik: Machtstrukturen in Österreich* (Vienna: Molden, 1976), p. 41; and Anton Pelinka, *Gewerkschaften im Parteienstaat: Ein Vergleich zwischen dem Deutschen und dem Österreichischen Gewerkschaftsbund* (Berlin: Duncker & Humblot, 1980), pp. 54–60, 183–84. More generally see Fritz Klenner, *Die österreichischen Gewerkschaften: Vergangenheit und Gegenwartsprobleme*, 3 vols. (Vienna: Verlag des Österreichischen Gewerkschaftsbundes, 1951, 1953, 1979); Franz Traxler, *Evolution gewerkschaftlicher Interessenvertretung: Entwicklungslogik und Organisationsdynamik gewerkschaftlichen Handelns am Beispiel Österreich* (Vienna: Braumüller, 1982); Werner Lang, *Kooperative Gewerkschaften und Einkommenspolitik: Das Beispiel Österreichs* (Frankfurt: Lang, 1978); Fritz Klenner, *The Austrian Trade Union Movement* (Brussels: International Conference of Free Trade Unions, 1956); Gertrud Neuhauser, "Die verbandsmässige Organisation der österreichischen Wirtschaft: Systematische Gesamtdarstellung," in Theodor Pütz, ed., *Verbände und Wirtschaftspolitik in Osterreich* (Berlin: Duncker & Humblot, 1966), pp. 19–20; and *Arbeit und Wirtschaft* 1981, no. 5: 6–8.

4. Vodopivec, *Die Dritte Republik*, pp. 49–50.

5. Thomas Lachs, *Wirtschaftspartnerschaft in Österreich* (Vienna: Verlag des Österreichischen Gewerkschaftsbundes, 1976), p. 81.

6. Manfred W. Wenner, Lettie M. Wenner, and Eugene V. Flango, "Austrian and Swiss Judges: A Comparative Study," *Comparative Politics*, 10 (July 1978): 499–518.

7. Oskar Grünwald and Herbert Krämer, *Die verstaatlichte österreichische Metallindustrie* (Frankfurt: Europäische Verlagsanstalt, 1966), pp. 102–3, 105.

8. Kurt L. Shell, *The Transformation of Austrian Socialism* (Albany: State Uni-

versity of New York, 1962), p. 66. Cf. Fritz Klenner, "Der Österreichische Gewerkschaftsbund," in Pütz, *Verbände und Wirtschaftspolitik*, pp. 468–69.

9. Shell, *Transformation of Austrian Socialism*, pp. 58–71; Vodopivec, *Die Dritte Republik*, p. 44.

10. Barbash, *Trade Unions*, p. 46; Klenner, "Der Österreichische Gewerkschaftsbund," pp. 446–47.

11. Pelinka, *Gerwerkschaften im Parteienstaat*, pp. 126–27; Fritz Klenner, *Die österreichischen Gewerkschaften: Eine Monographie* (Vienna: Verlag des Österreichischen Gewerkschaftsbundes, 1967), p. 208.

12. Barbash, *Trade Unions*, p. 55; Lang, *Kooperative Gewerkschaften*, pp. 199–200.

13. Lang, *Kooperative Gewerkschaften*, p. 200; Pelinka, *Gewerkschaften im Parteienstaat*, pp. 60–63; and Vodopivec, *Die Dritte Republik*, pp. 45–46, 51, 56.

14. Pelinka, *Gewerkschaften im Parteienstaat*, pp. 70, 86; Anton Pelinka, "Österreich—Mitbestimmung von oben: Zur Funktion von Zentralisation und Gewerkschaftsdemokratie," *Journal für Sozialforschung* 21, 2 (1981): 161–68; and Erich Andrlik, "The Organized Society: A Study of 'Neo-corporatist' Relations in Austria's Steel and Metal Processing Industry" (Ph.D. diss., M. I. T., 1983), pp. 196–241.

15. Melanie A. Sully, "The Socialist Party of Austria," in William E. Paterson and Alastair H. Thomas, eds., *Social Democratic Parties in Western Europe* (New York: St. Martin's 1977), pp. 218–23; Dennison I. Rusinow, "Notes toward a Political Definition of Austria," Parts I–V *AUFS Reports*, March–July 1966, especially Parts II and III; and Vodopivec, *Die Dritte Republik*, pp. 151–72.

16. Pelinka, *Gewerkschaften im Parteienstaat*, pp. 104, 108, 195; Shell, *Transformation of Austrian Socialism*, pp. 41–42, 62–63.

17. Rusinow, "Notes," Parts I and III, discusses the situation in the 1960s when the SPÖ had less firm a grasp on the levers of power.

18. Rupert Zimmermann, *Verstaatlichung in Österreich: Ihre Aufgaben und Ziele* (Vienna: Verlag der Wiener Volksbuchhandlung, 1964), pp. 82, 106, 129–35; Rusinow, "Notes," Part IV, pp. 17–18; and Ferdinand Lacina, *The Development of the Austrian Public Sector since World War II* (University of Texas at Austin, Institute of Latin American Studies, Office for Public Sector Studies, Technical Papers Series no. 7, 1977), p. 23.

19. Shell, *Transformation of Austrian Socialism*, pp. 62, 189–231.

20. Eric Schiff, *Incomes Policies Abroad, Part II: France, West Germany, Austria, Denmark* (Washington, D.C.: American Enterprise Institute, 1972), p. 32; E. März, E. Weissel, and H. Reithofer, "Die Kammern für Arbeiter und Angestellte (Arbeiterkammern)," in Pütz, *Verbände und Wirtschaftspolitik*, pp. 409–10; and Günther Chaloupek and Hannes Swoboda, "Sozialpartnerschaft und Wirtschaftsentwicklung in den fünfziger Jahren," *Österreichische Zeitschrift für Politikwissenschaft* 1975, no. 3: 333–44.

21. Lang, *Kooperative Gewerkschaften*, pp. 77–83; Klenner, *Die österreichischen Gewerkschaften*, p. 182; Barbash, *Trade Unions*, pp. 49, 51; and OECD, *Economic Surveys: Austria* (Paris: 1974), p. 20.

22. OECD, *Economic Surveys: Austria* (Paris: 1971), p. 11.

23. *Austrian Information* 34, 2–3 (1981): 6; Hankel, *Prosperity amidst Crisis*, pp. 56, 69.

24. Egon Matzner, *Wohlfahrtsstaat und Wirtschaftskrise: Österreichs Sozialisten*

suchen einen Ausweg (Hamburg-Reinbek: Rowohlt, 1978), pp. 10–11, 44–125; Günther Chaloupek and Herbert Ostleitner, "Einkommensverteilung und Verteilungspolitik in Österreich," in Heinz Fischer, ed., *Das politische System Österreichs,* (Vienna: Europa Verlag, 1974) pp. 453–67; Elisabeth Merth, "Die Schichtung der persönlichen Einkommen in Österreich," *Quartalshefte* 1974, no. 2: 45–57; Hannes Suppanz, "Einkommensverteilung in Österreich," *Journal für angewandte Sozialforschung* 20, 3–4 (1980): 40–45; Robert J. Flanagan, David W. Soskice, and Lloyd Ulman, *Unionism, Economic Stabilization, and Incomes Policies: European Experience* (Washington, D.C.: Brookings, 1983), pp. 77–78; Klenner, *Die österreichischen Gewerkschaften,* 3: 2728–29; Günter Chaloupek, "Die Verteilung der persönlichen Einkommen in Österreich: I. Die hohen Einkommen," *Wirtschaft und Gesellschaft* 3, 1 (1979): 9–22, and "II. Die Arbeitsverdienste," ibid., 4, 2 (1978): 191–208; and Michael Wagner, "Einkommensverhältnisse," in Marina Fischer-Kowalski and Josef Bucek, eds., *Lebensverhältnisse in Österreich: Klassen und Schichten im Sozialstaat* (New York: Campus, 1980), pp. 427–46.

25. Pelinka, *Gewerkschaften im Parteienstaat,* pp. 73–81, 119–20.

26. Sarah Hogg, "A Small House in Order," 15 March 1980, Survey, p. 11.

27. Then Deputy Chancellor Hannes Androsch as quoted in *Arbeiterzeitung,* 9 January 1977.

28. Reprinted in Zimmermann, *Verstaatlichung in Österreich,* p. 84.

29. Rusinow, "Notes," Part IV, p. 16; Zimmermann, *Verstaatlichung in Österreich,* 107; and Lacina, *Development of the Austrian Public Sector,* p. 20.

30. *New York Times,* 12 October 1975, business sec. p. 3.

31. Ewald Nowotny, "Verstaatlichte und private Industrie in der Rezession: Gemeinsamkeiten und Unterschiede," *WISO* 2 (May 1979): 77, 83, 89, 92–93. On the basis of slightly different statistical data the same point is made in Ferdinand Lacina, "Development and Problems of Austrian Industry," in Kurt Steiner, ed., *Modern Austria* (Palo Alto, Calif.: SPOSS 1981), p. 166.

32. Hogg, "A Small House in Order," Survey, p. 10.

33. Wolfgang Schmitz, "Diskussionsbeitrag," in *Budgetpolitik in der Bundesrepublik Deutschland, in der Schweiz und in Österreich* (Vienna: Zentralsparkasse und Kommerzialbank, 1979), p. 69; Ernst Gehmacher, "Der Beamte im sozialen Wandel," in Günter Engelmayer, ed., *Die Diener des Staates: Das bürokratische System Österreichs* (Vienna: Europa Verlag, 1977), p. 139.

34. Feliz Butschek, "Full Employment during Recession" in Sven W. Arndt, *The Political Economy of Austria* (Washington, D. C.: American Enterprise Institute for Public Policy Research, 1982), p. 106; August Andrae Clemens and Hubert Büchel, "Die Entwicklung der öffentlichen Personalbestände und Personalausgaben in Österreich, der Bundesrepublik Deutschland und der Schweiz seit 1950," in Werner Clement and Karl Socher, eds., *Empirische Wirtschaftsforschung und monetäre Ökonomik: Festschrift für Stephan Koren zum 60. Geburtstag* (Berlin: Duncker & Humblot, 1979), pp. 18–19.

35. Egon Matzner, "The Future of the Welfare State: Towards a New Pattern of State Intervention," International Institute for Management (Wissenschaftszentrum Berlin, 80-74, 1980), pp. 5–6.

36. Schmitz, "Diskussionsbeitrag," p. 69.

37. Butschek, "Full Employment during Recession," pp. 105–6; Johann Wösendorfer, *Arbeitsmarktpolitik: Beurteilungskriterien für das Arbeitsmarktför-*

derungsgesetz (Linz: Österreichisches Institut für Arbeitsmarktpolitik, University of Linz, 1980), pp. 38, 63, 77, 103, 120, 124.

38. Federal Press Department, Republic of Austria, "Employment for Young People," 1981.

39. OECD, Manpower and Social Affairs Committee, "Report to the Council of the Working Party on Migration" (Paris, 4 April 1980, mimeo), p. 7.

40. Wösendorfer, *Arbeitsmarktpolitik*, pp. 38–39.

41. Butschek, "Full Employment during Recession," pp. 110–12.

42. *News from Austria* 26 May 1981, p. 3.

43. Gunther Tichy, "Theoretische und praktische Probleme der österreichischen Staatsverschuldung," *Quartalshefte* 1975, no. 2: 24, 27–28; Adolf Nussbaumer, "Die Grenzen der Staatsverschuldung," *Quartalshefte*, 1976, no. 4: 22–24; and Stephan Koren, "Change and Tradition in the Economic Development of Austria," in Kurt Steiner, ed., *Tradition and Innovation in Modern Austria* (Palo Alto, Calif.: SPOSS, 1982), pp. 84–85.

44. OECD, *Economic Surveys: Austria* (Paris: 1963), pp. 12, 15–16.

45. D. Bös and B. Genser, "Die finanzpolitische Entwicklung in Österreich 1975–1978," *Finanzarchiv*, N.F. 37, 4 (1979): 485–510.

46. *Österreich Bericht* no. 113 (1983): 2. *Economic Surveys: Austria* (Paris: 1976), pp. 22–35.

47. Nussbaumer, "Grenzen der Staatsverschuldung," p. 23. It should be noted that the Austrian figure remains low by international standards. The per capita public debt in Switzerland is $6,000, twice as high as Austria's. See OECD, *Economic Surveys: Austria* (Paris: 1977), p. 41; *Austrian Information* 33, 8 (1980): 1, and 34, 2–3 (1981): 7.

48. *Jahrbuch der österreichischen Wirtschaft 1976/1: Tätigkeitsbericht der Bundeswirtschaftskammer* (Vienna: Bundeskammer der Gewerblichen Wirtschaft, 1977), p. 23.

49. OECD, *The 1978 Tax/Benefit Position of a Typical Worker in OECD Member Countries* (Paris: 1979), pp. 21–22.

50. Manfred G. Schmidt, "Wohlfahrtsstaaliche Politik unter bürgerlichen und sozialdemokratischen Regierungen" (University of Constance, 1980, mimeo), p. 218. See also David R. Cameron, "On the Limits of the Public Economy" (Paper prepared for the annual meeting of the American Political Science Association, New York, September 1981), p. 5A.

51. OECD, *Economic Surveys: Austria* (Paris: 1978), p. 28; Helmut H. Haschek, "Trade, Trade Finance, and Capital Movements," in Arndt, *Political Economy of Austria*, pp. 176–98; and Hankel, *Prosperity amidst Crisis*, pp. 36, 51–54.

52. *New York Times*, 15 July 1979, sec. 3, p. 2; "The Austrian Lesson in Economic Harmony," *Euromoney*, May 1979 (Supplement).

53. *News from Austria* 4 November 1980, p. 3.

54. Helmut Frisch, "Macroeconomic Adjustment in Small Open Economies," in Arndt, *Political Economy of Austria*, p. 51; Peter Hull Kristensen and Jørn Levinsen, *The Small Country Squeeze* (Roskilde, Denmark: Roskilde University Center, Institute of Economics, Politics and Administration, 1978), pp. 17, 20.

55. Stephan Koren, "Changes in International Economic Policy and Their Impact on Austria (Stanford, Calif., 1980, mimeo), p. 22.

56. OECD, *Public Expenditure Trends* (Paris: 1978), pp. 14–15. An overview is given in Rudolf Strasser, "Social Policy since 1945: Democracy and the Welfare State," in Steiner, *Modern Austria,* pp. 301–20.

57. Peter Flora, Jens Alber, and Jürgen Kohl, "Zur Entwicklung der westeuropäischen Wohlfahrtsstaaten," *Politische Vierteljahresschrift* 18, 4 (1977): 736–39, 767.

58. Harold L. Wilensky, *The "New Corporatism," Centralization, and the Welfare State* (Beverly Hills, Calif.: Sage, 1976), p. 11; *Public Expenditure on Income Maintenance Programmes* (Paris: 1976), pp. 17, 20; Harold L. Wilensky, *The Welfare State and Equality: Structural and Ideological Roots of Public Expenditure* (Berkeley: University of California Press, 1975), p. 122; Max Horlick, *Supplemental Security Income for the Aged: A Comparison of Five Countries* (U.S. Department of Health, Education and Welfare, Social Security Administration, Office of Research and Statistics, DHEW Publication no. (SSA) 74–11850, Staff Paper no. 15), p. 64; Alois Brusatti, Karl Gutkas, and Erika Weinzierl, *Österreich 1945–1970: 25 Jahre Zweite Republik* (Vienna: Österreichischer Bundesverlag, 1970), pp. 215–17, 241–44, 264–67, 283–86, 314–17.

59. Giovanni Vasella, "Arten und Ansätze der Familienzulage der EWG-Staaten, Grossbritanniens, Österreichs und der Schweiz," *Schweizerische Zeitschrift für Sozialversicherung* 1969, no. 4: 274.

60. Flanagan, Soskice, and Ulman, *Unionism,* pp. 54–55; Hogg, "A Small House in Order," Survey, pp. 14–15.

61. OECD, *The Tax/Benefit Position of Selected Income Groups in OECD Member Countries 1972–1976* (Paris: 1978), pp. 20–21, 94.

62. Horlick, *Supplemental Security Income,* p. 29. In Scandinavia these rates vary between two-thirds and three-quarters in the mid-1970s. See Gösta Esping-Andersen and Walter Korpi, "From Poor Relief to Institutional Welfare States: The Development of Scandinavian Social Policy" (Stockholm: Swedish Institute for Social Research, 30 September 1981), Table 5.

63. Horlick, *Supplemental Security Income,* p. 36; see also ibid., pp. 13, 34.

64. Ibid., p. 64.

65. Wilensky, *Welfare State and Equality,* p. 9.

66. *Austrian Information* 34, 2–3 (1981): 1, reporting an OECD study.

67. *Das Recht der Arbeit* 29, 4–5 (October 1979), pp. 344–46; Vereinigung Österreichischer Industrieller, *Mittelfristiges Industrieprogramm* (Vienna, 1974), p. 20; OECD, *Public Expenditure on Income Maintenance,* pp. 36, 57; and Robert Holzmann, "Wachstumskrise und Pensionsversicherung," in Marin, *Wachstumskrisen in Österreich?* vol. 2: *Szenarios,* pp. 157–82.

68. OECD, *Economic Surveys: Austria* (Paris, 1971), p. 34; Schiff, *Incomes Policies Abroad, Part II,* p. 31; Lang, *Kooperative Gewerkschaften,* p. 105; Bernd Marin, *Die Paritätische Kommission: Aufgeklärter Technokorporatismus in Österreich* (Vienna: Braumüller, 1982), pp. 136–37, 147–50; *Austrian Information* 34, 4 (1981): 1, 7; Lachs, *Wirtschaftspartnerschaft in Österreich,* pp. 49–50; and Neuhauser, "Die verbandsmässige Organisation der österreichischen Wirtschaft," pp. 105–6.

69. Ewald Nowotny et al., *Studien zur Wettbewerbsintensität in der österreichischen Wirtschaft,* Schriftenreihe des Ludwig Boltzmann Instituts für Wachstumsforschung (Vienna: Österreichische Nationalbank, 1978), p. 7.

70. Hanspeter Hanreicher, "Der Wettbewerb—ein vernachlässigtes Gebiet

sozialwissenschaftlicher Forschung," *Wirtschaftspolitische Blätter* 23, 2 (1976): 98. See ibid., p. 99, for a list of goods where markets do not function. See also Lang, *Kooperative Gewerkschaften*, p. 105, and Schiff, *Incomes Policies Abroad*, p. 33.

71. Flanagan, Soskice, and Ulman, *Unionism*, p. 61; Karl Korinek, "Das System der Preisregelung in Österreich," *Wirtschaftspolitische Blätter* 22, 4 (1975): 76.

72. Flanagan, Soskice, and Ulman, *Unionism*, p. 47.

73. Hans Wehsely, "Nichtagrarische Marktordnungen: Überblick über Wettbewerbsbeschränkungen in Österreich," *Wirtschaftspolitische Blätter* 25, 2 (1978): 92.

74. Nowotny et al., *Studien zur Wettbewerbsintensität*, p. 72, notes 38–40.

75. Wehsely, "Nichtagrarische Marktordnungen," p. 94.

76. Ibid., pp. 43, 62; OECD, *Economic Surveys: Austria* (Paris: 1973), p. 27.

77. Nowotny et al., *Studien zur Wettbewerbsintensität*, pp. 356–57.

78. OECD, *Economic Surveys: Austria* (Paris: 1971), p. 6.

79. Frisch, "Macroeconomic Adjustment," p. 46.

80. Kurt Steiner, *Politics in Austria* (Boston: Little, Brown, 1972), p. 298; Klenner, "Der österreichische Gewerkschaftsbund," pp. 437–501.

81. Klenner, "Der österreichische Gewerkschaftsbund," pp. 444–45; Lang, *Kooperative Gewerkschaften*, pp. 202–4; Pelinka, *Gewerkschaften im Parteienstaat*, pp. 64–67, 187, 189; and Vodopivec, *Die Dritte Republik*, pp. 47–49.

82. Lang, *Kooperative Gewerkschaften*, p. 205.

83. Klenner, *Die österreichischen Gewerkschaften*, p. 173; Flanagan, Soskice, and Ulman, *Unionism*, p. 80, note 42.

84. Flanagan, Soskice, and Ulman, *Unionism*, p. 60.

85. Barbash, *Trade Unions*, pp. 56–57.

86. *World Business Weekly*, 17 March 1980, p. 32; Hogg, "A Small House in Order," Survey, p. 15.

87. Quoted in "The Austrian Lesson in Economic Harmony," p. 29.

88. Flanagan, Soskice, and Ulman, *Unionism*, p. 53.

89. *Austrian Information* 34, 2-3 (1981): 5, quoting the latest OECD report.

90. Quoted in Barbash, *Trade Unions*, p. 50.

91. Flanagan, Soskice, and Ulman, *Unionism*, p. 72.

92. Quoted in *Jahrbuch der österreichischen Wirtschaft 1976/1*, p. 19.

93. OECD, *Economic Surveys: Switzerland* (Paris: 1972), pp. 49–50.

94. Hogg, "A Small House in Order," Survey, p. 8.

95. Rusinow, "Notes," Part IV, p. 3.

96. Ibid., p. 10; Lacina, *Development of the Austrian Public Sector*, p. 11.

97. Lacina, *Development of the Austrian Public Sector*, p. 8. See also Anton Tautscher, *Die österreichische Wirtschaftsordnung* (Salzburg: Pustet, 1971), p. 101; Christian Smekal, *Die verstaatlichte Industrie in der Marktwirtschaft: Das österreichische Beispiel* (Cologne: Heymanns, 1963), pp. 33–34; Steiner, *Politics in Austria* p. 85; and OECD, *Economic Surveys: Austria* (Paris, 1963), p. 23. In general see also Edmond Langer, *Les nationalisations en Autriche* (The Hague: Nijhoff, 1964); Andrlik, "The Organized Society," pp. 174–95; and Leopold Wallner, "Staatskapitalismus in Österreich," *Politische Studien* 14 (May-June 1963): 299–311. *Österreichische Zeitschrift für Politikwissenschaft* 1981, no. 4, is a special issue devoted to nationalized industry in Austria.

98. Rusinow, "Notes," Part IV, p. 9; Andrew Shonfield, *Modern Capitalism:*

The Changing Balance of Public and Private Power (London: Oxford University Press, 1965), p. 193; Nowotny, "Verstaatlichte und private Industrie," p. 74; and OECD, *The Industrial Policy of Austria* (Paris, 1971), pp. 65–66, 73–74. Definitional ambiguities of the term "public sector" are discussed in Albert Lauterbach, *The Austrian Public Sector in International Perspective: A Socio-Historical Evaluation* (University of Texas at Austin, Institute of Latin American Studies, Office for Public Sector Studies, Technical Papers Series no. 14, 1978), note 1; Christof Gaspari and Hans Millendorfer, *Prognosen für Österreich: Fakten und Formeln der Entwicklung* (Vienna: Verlag für Geschichte and Politik, 1973), pp. 114–15.

99. Oskar Grünwald, "Austrian Industrial Structure and Industrial Policy" in Arndt, *Political Economy of Austria*, p. 136.

100. Hogg, "A Small House in Order," Survey, p. 8. See also Nowotny, "Verstaatlichte und private Industrie," p. 74, and Beirat für Wirtschafts- und Sozialfragen, *Vorschläge zur Industriepolitik* (Vienna: Ueberreuter, 1970), p. 24.

101. Ferdinand Lacina, "Zielsetzung und Effizienz verstaatlichter Unternehmen," *Wirtschaft und Gesellschaft* 4, 2 (1978): 143–54; Herbert Durstberger, "Versuch einer Anwendung von Konzentrationsmassen in Österreich," *Quartalshefte* 1968, no. 3: 69–83.

102. Tautscher, *Die österreichiche Wirtschaftsordnung*, p. 101; Manfred Drennig, "Vermögensverteilung in Österreich—ihre politische Relevanz," in Fischer, *Das politische System Österreichs*, p. 481.

103. Volker Bornschier, *Wachstum, Konzentration und Multinationalisierung von Industrieunternehmen* (Frauenfeld: Huber, 1976), p. 206.

104. United Nations, *Transnational Corporations in World Development: A Reexamination* (New York: U.N. Economic and Social Council, 1978), pp. 287–312. The two firms are numbered 170 and 320, respectively.

105. Karl Socher, "Die öffentlichen Unternehmen im österreichischen Banken- und Versicherungswesen," in Wilhelm Weber, ed., *Die Verstaatlichung in Österreich* (Berlin: Duncker & Humblot, 1964), p. 400, and ibid., pp. 347–411; Hogg, "A Small House in Order," Survey, p. 8; Oskar Grünwald, "Die Beteiligungsgesellschaften der verstaatlichten Grossbanken," in Weber, *Verstaatlichung in Österreich*, pp. 477–96; and Felix Spreitzhofer, "Wer dominiert die österreichische Wirtschaft?" in Fischer-Kowalski and Bucek, *Lebensverhältnisse in Österreich*, p. 334.

106. Socher, "Die öffentlichen Unternehmen," pp. 393–400.

107. *Monatsberichte* 33, 2 (February 1960): 69.

108. *Die Presse,* 17 March 1973.

109. *Die Presse,* 9 March 1977. See also Evelyn Klein, "Österreichs Kapitalexport in der Zweiten Republik," *Österreichische Zeitschrift für Politikwissenschaft,* 1978, no. 3: 305–20.

110. *ÖIAG-Journal* 1979, no. 3: 3–4; Klein, "Österreichs Kapitalexport," pp. 312–14; Lauterbach, *The Austrian Public Sector,* p. 2; and OECD, *The Aims and Instruments of Industrial Policy: A Comparative Study* (Paris: 1975), p. 24.

111. Haschek, "Trade, Trade Finance and Capital Movements," pp. 194–95.

112. "Austrian Lesson in Economic Harmony," pp. 3, 10, 12–13, 17.

113. Bornschier, *Wachstum von Industrieunternehmen* p. 206; United Nations, *Multinational Corporations in World Development* (New York: U.N. Department of Economic and Social Affairs, 1973), p. 173; M. Dillinger, O. Höll, and H.

Kramer, "The State and International Economic Power: The Case of Austria" (discussion paper prepared for the ECPR workshop "The State and International Economic Power," Louvain, Belgium, 8–14 April 1976), pp. 16–21; and Otmar Höll and Helmut Kramer, "Österreich im internationalen System 1955–1975: Datenzusammenstellung, Teil I" (Vienna, Institut für Höhere Studien, 1976), pp. 17–19.

114. OECD, *Economic Surveys: Austria* (Paris, 1977), p. 27, note 23.

115. *Monatsberichte* 26 (June 1953): 194–96; 26 (September 1953): 276–90; 27 (February 1954, Supplement 24); 34 (October 1961): 431–36; 35 (January 1962): 40–43; 36 (November 1963): 416–22. See also Curtis E. Harvey, "A Case Study of the Adaptation of a Small National Economy's Industry to International Competition: Austria" (Ph.D. diss., University of Southern California, 1963), pp. 106, 264–66; Fritz Breuss, *Komparative Vorteile im österreichischen Aussenhandel* (Vienna: Verlag der österreichischen Akademie der Wissenschaften, 1975), pp. 220–21.

116. Franz Nemschak, *Liberalisierung und Zollpolitik in Österreich,* "Vorträge und Aufsätze" no. 8 (Vienna: Österreichisches Institut für Wirtschaftsforschung, 1954). Jan Stankovsky, "Austria's Foreign Trade: The Legal Regulations of Trade with East and West," *Journal of World Trade Law* 3 (1969): 611–12, describes preferential imports especially of investment goods. See also *Monatsberichte* 26 (June 1953): 195; 34 (October 1961): 435; 35 (January 1962): 41; 48 (July 1975): 314.

117. Gerard Curzon, *Multilateral Commercial Diplomacy: An Examination of the Impact of the General Agreement on Tariffs and Trade on National Commercial Policies and Techniques* (London: Michael Joseph, 1965), pp. 161, 240.

118. Hans Mayrzedt, *Multilaterale Wirtschaftsdiplomatie zwischen westlichen Industriestaaten als Instrument zur Stärkung der multilateralen und liberalen Handelspolitik* (Bern: Lang, 1979), p. 389.

119. Gardner C. Patterson, *Discrimination in International Trade: The Policy Issues 1945–1965* (Princeton: Princeton University Press, 1966), p. 293, note 42.

120. Gerald and Victoria Curzon, "The Management of Trade Relations in the GATT," in Andrew Shonfield, ed., *International Economic Relations of the Western World 1959–1971,* vol. 1: *Politics and Trade* (London: Oxford University Press, 1976), pp. 209–10. Curzon and Curzon note that "there is no evidence at all that the United States abused its dominant power position to force concessions from Austria" (p. 210). At the same time this episode illustrates that U.S. decision makers did not hesitate to use their power.

121. U.S. Senate, Committee on Finance, Subcommittee on International Trade, *MTN Studies 5: An Economic Analysis of the Effects of the Tokyo Round of Multilateral Trade Negotiations on the United States and the Other Major Industrialized Countries* (Washington, D.C.: 1979), pp. 38, 44, 48.

122. *Jahrbuch der österreichischen Wirtschaft 1976/1.*

123. Egon Matzner, *The Trade between East and West: The Case of Austria* (Stockholm: Almqvist & Wiksell, 1970). There are also numerous articles and reports in the *Monatsberichte* of the Österreichische Institut für Wirtschaftsforschung.

124. *Wiener Zeitung,* 21 February 1976; *World Business Weekly,* 5 May 1980, p. 24; and United Nations, *Transnational Corporations: A Reexamination,* p. 283.

125. Hans Naef, *Die Handelsbeziehungen der Schweiz zu den Zentralplan-*

wirtschaften von 1954–1968 (Zurich: Juris, 1971), pp. 58–59, 64, 117, 134, 151.

126. On the traditional orientation of Austria to Western Europe see Peter J. Katzenstein, *Disjoined Partners: Austria and Germany since 1815* (Berkeley: University of California Press, 1976), pp. 199–218; M. Koch, "Contemporary Austrian Foreign Policy: Elite Attitudes concerning Consensus and Decision-making" (Ph.D. diss., Brandeis University, 1972), pp. 183–88.

127. *Die Presse,* 19 April 1975; *Neues Volksblatt,* 17 April 1976; and *Wiener Zeitung,* 5 June 1976.

128. *News from Austria,* 26 May 1981, p. 3; Jan Stankovsky, "Austria's Trade with Eastern Europe in the 1980s: Deficits and Brisk Demand for Financing," Österreichische Länderbank, *Economic Bulletin* 7/8 (July–August 1980): 8.

129. Länderbank, *Economic Bulletin* 7/8 (July–August 1980).

130. *Die Presse,* 4 November 1975 and 9 January 1976; *Österreichische Textil-mitteilungen,* 3 October 1975.

131. *New York Times,* 26 January 1979, pp. Al, D4; Hogg, "A Small House in Order," Survey, pp. 16, 22; and Klein, "Österreichs Kapitalexport," pp. 309–10.

132. Stankovsky, "Austria's Foreign Trade," *Internationale Wirtschaft,* 12 July 1974.

133. Karl Aiginger, "Die Eigenkapitalausstattung der Industrie in makroökonomischer Sicht," *Quartalshefte* 1976, nos. 1–2: 38; Gunther Tichy, "Probleme der Eigenkapitalknappheit und Ansätze zu ihrer Überwindung: zum Thema dieses Heftes," ibid., p. 6; Peter Swoboda et al., "Zum Verschuldungsgrad und zur Verschuldungsstruktur der österreichischen Industrieunternehmen," *Wirtschaftspolitische Blätter* 23, 1 (1976): 27–28; Claus J. Raidl, "Aufgaben einer modernen Industriepolitik," in Andreas Khol and Alfred Stirnemann, eds., *Österreichisches Jahrbuch für Politik 1978* (Munich: Oldenbourg, 1979), pp. 436–37; Beirat für Wirtschafts- und Sozialfragen, *Vorschläge zur Industriepolitik II* (Vienna: Ueberreuter, 1978), pp. 24, 26–27; "Investitionspolitik und Investitionsfinanzierung in Österreich," *Wirtschaft und Gesellschaft* 7, 2 (1981); and Ferdinand Lacina, "Ausbau oder Umbau der steuerlichen Investitionsförderung?" *Wirtschaft und Gesellschaft* 2, 3 (1976): 9–25.

134. *News from Austria,* January 1980, p. 3.

135. Gerhard Lehner, "Wirtschaftsförderung als Instrument des wirtschaftspolitischen Kompromisses," *Wirtschaftspolitische Blätter* 23, 2 (1976): 78; *News from Austria,* January 1980, p. 3.

136. Investment programs of the federal government only (Lehner, "Wirtschaftsförderung," pp. 80–81).

137. Helmut Dorn, "Zur Vorgeschichte der Kapitalbeteiligungsgesellschaften in Österreich," *Wirtschaftspolitische Blätter* 25, 3 (1978): 119. A somewhat lower estimate is given by Hankel, *Prosperity amidst Crisis,* p. 75.

138. Haschek, "Trade, Trade Finance and Capital Movements," p. 194. Estimates vary considerably depending on the source. For the years 1960 to 1976 see Klenner, *Die österreichischen Gewerkschaften,* 3: 2102–3. See also Oskar Grünwald and Ferdinand Lacina, *Auslandskapital in der österreichischen Wirtschaft* (Vienna: Europa Verlag, 1970); Eckard P. Imhof, "Ausländische Investitionen in Österreich im Rahmen eines internationalen Vergleichs unter besonderer Berücksichtigung der Direktinvestitionen" (Ph.D. diss., University of Vienna, 1960); Wiener Arbeiterkammer, *Das Eigentum an den*

österreichischen Kapitalgesellschaften (Vienna: Vorwärts, 1962); P. Schaposchnitschenko, "Stille Invasion des westdeutschen Kapitals in Österreich," *Deutsche Aussenpolitik* 11 (December 1966): pp. 1468–75; and Fritz Diwok, *Die Bedeutung des Auslandskapitals für Österreichs Wirtschaft* (Vienna: Verlag für Geschichte und Politik, 1959). In addition, since the early 1970s Austria's National Bank has regularly monitored the role of foreign investment in Austria.

139. OECD, *Interim Report of the Industry Committee*, p. 13; OECD, *The Aims of Industrial Policy* (Paris: 1975), p. 115. See also "Austrian Industrial Development," *Financial Times*, 29 August 1975, pp. 9–11; Vereinigung Österreichischer Industrieller, *Zur Wirtschaftspolitik*, 2d ed. (Vienna: 1975), p. 30.

140. Hogg, "A Small House in Order," Survey, pp. 3–22.

141. Quoted in H. Peter Dreyer, "Austria Opening Door to Larger Foreign Investors," *Austrian Information* 34, 2–3 (1981): 2. See also Beirat für Wirtschafts- und Sozialfragen, *Vorschläge zur Industriepolitik*, 2:9.

142. "Austrian Lesson in Economic Harmony," p. 25.

143. Grünwald, "Austrian Industrial Structure," p. 136; Lacina, "Development and Problems of Austrian Industry," p. 160. See also *Information über Multinationale Konzerne* 1979, no. 1: 1; ibid., 1979, no. 3: 3; *World Business Weekly*, 22 October 1979, p. 51; and J. Peischer, "Auslandskapital in Österreich: Neue Studie der Nationalbank," *Informationen über Multinationale Konzerne* 1981, no. 2:3–6. Higher figures are given for 1969 (24 percent) and 1975 (37 percent) in Haschek, "Trade, Trade Finance and Capital Movements," p. 194. The higher figures report total direct and indirect investment rather than direct investment in industry.

144. "Liste der grössten ausländisch beherrschten Unternehmen Österreichs," *Informationen über Multinationale Konzerne* 1980, no. 4: 27. Fourteen of the top fifty firms were foreign-owned.

145. United Nations, *Transnational Corporations: A Reexamination*, pp. 265, 273–74; United Nations, *Multinational Corporations in World Development*, p. 167; Gerd Junne and Alua Nour, *Internationale Abhängigkeiten, Fremdbestimmung und Ausbeutung als Regelfall internationaler Beziehungen* (Frankfurt: Athenäum, 1974), p. 90; and Rudolf Kohlruss, "30 Jahre verstaatlichte österreichische Elektroindustrie," *ÖIAG Journal* 2 (August 1976): 22–23.

146. *Information über Multinationale Konzerne* 1981, no. 2: 4.

147. Eduard März, *Österreichs Wirtschaft zwischen Ost und West: Eine sozialistische Analyse* (Vienna: Europa Verlag, 1965), pp. 62–63; Zimmermann, *Verstaatlichung in Österreich* pp. 92–93; Lacina, *Development of the Austrian Public Sector*, pp. 15–16; Stephan Koren, "Sozialisierungsideologie und Verstaatlichungsrealität in Österreich," in Weber, *Die Verstaatlichung in Österreich*, p. 251; and Grünwald and Krämer, *Die verstaatlichte österreichische Metallindustrie*, pp. 73–80.

148. Herwig Kainz, "Produktpolitik der österreichischen Kraftfahrzeugindustrie" (Diplom, Vienna Hochschule für Welthandel, 1972); Helmut Krackowizer, "Die österreichische Kraftfahrzeug-Industrie, ihre volkswirtschaftliche Bedeutung und ihre wirtschaftlichen Probleme" (Ph.D. diss., University of Innsbruck, 1952).

149. *Arbeiterzeitung*, 14 August 1977 and 24 August 1971; *Kurier*, 17 June 1971.

150. *World Business Weekly,* 17 March 1980, p. 34.

151. Building on a long tradition of subcontracting in the late 1970s about 100 Austrian firms exported more than $231 million of components to the European automobile industry. See Federal Press Department, Republic of Austria, e/1980, p. 2; see also Lacina, "Development and Problems," pp. 161–62.

152. *World Business Weekly,* 3 March 1980, p. 13, 26 May 1980, p. 13, and 17 March 1981, pp. 34–35; *Der Spiegel,* 21 April 1980, p. 137; and *New York Times,* 9 July 1979, p. D5.

153. OECD, *Regional Problems and Policies in OECD Countries,* vol. II: *UK, Belgium, Netherlands, Norway, Finland, Spain, Austria, Germany, Canada, Switzerland* (Paris: 1976), p. 126; "Austrian Lesson in Economic Harmony," p. 33; and Hogg, "A Small House in Order," Survey, pp. 18–19.

154. Österreichische Länderbank, *Economic Bulletin* 4 (April 1981): 2; "The Strains in Consensus," *World Business Weekly,* 9 March 1981, p. 35.

155. *Der Spiegel,* 10 July 1978, pp. 95–96; Federal Press Department, Republic of Austria, "Austria's Economy—A European Example," 26 October 1980.

156. The Boston Consulting Group, *A Framework for Swedish Industrial Policy* (Stockholm: Departementens Offsetcentral, 1979), Appendix 9, p. 7.

157. Spitäller, "Incomes Policy in Austria," p. 171.

158. Rusinow, "Notes," Part I, p. 2; Herbert P. Secher, "Representative Democracy or 'Chamber State': The Ambiguous Role of Interest Groups in Austrian Politics," *Western Political Quarterly* 13 (December 1960): 890–909.

159. Karl Ucakar, "Die Entwicklung der Interessenorganisationen," in Fischer, *Das politische System Österreichs,* p. 400.

160. Lauterbach, *The Austrian Public Sector,* pp. 3–4.

161. Pütz, *Verbände und Wirtschaftspolitik;* Secher, "Representative Democracy"; and Adolf Stirnemann, *Interessengegensätze und Gruppenbildungen innerhalb der Österreichischen Volkspartei* (Vienna: Institut für Höhere Studien, October 1969).

162. Shonfield, *Modern Capitalism,* p. 193.

163. März, Weissel, and Reithofer, "Kammern für Arbeiter und Angestellte," pp. 393–436.

164. Secher, "Representative Democracy," p. 895.

165. Barbash, *Trade Unions,* p. 48.

166. März, Weissel, and Reithofer, "Kammern für Arbeiter und Angestellte," p. 426; Theodor Pütz, "Die Bedeutung der Wirtschaftsverbände für die Gestaltung der österreichischen Wirtschaftspolitik," in Pütz, *Verbände und Wirtschaftspolitik,* pp. 188, 196–97.

167. Pelinka, *Gewerkschaften im Parteienstaat,* p. 187.

168. Ibid., pp. 65, 189; Klenner, *Die österreichischen Gewerkschaften,* 3: 2258–63.

169. John P. Windmuller, "Concentration Trends in Union Structure: An International Comparison," *Industrial and Labor Relations Review* 35 (October 1981): 43–57. See also Franz Traxler, "Organisationsform des ÖGB und 'Wirtschaftspartnerschaft': Organisationsstrukturelle Bedingungen kooperativer Gewerkschaftspolitik," *Wirtschaft und Gesellschaft* 7, 1 (1981): 29–52.

170. Rainer Minz, "Stichwort Österreich," in Fischer-Kowalski and Bucek, *Lebensverhältnisse in Österreich,* p. 11.

171. Johannes Koren and Manfred Ebner, eds., *Österreich auf einem Weg: Handelskammern und Sozialpartnerschaft im Wandel der Zeit* (Graz: Leopold Stocker, 1974); *Jahrbuch der österreichischen Wirtschaft 1976/1*, pp. 233–57; and Max Mitic and Alfred Klose, "Die Handelskammerorganisation in Österreich," in Pütz, *Verbände und Wirtschaftspolitik*, pp. 505–8, 513–15, 521.

172. *The Economic Chambers of Austria* (Vienna: Bundeskammer der Gewerblichen Wirtschaft, 1979), p. 4.

173. Ibid., p. 9; Secher, "Representative Democracy," pp. 894, 902–6; Koren and Ebner, *Österreich auf einem Weg;* and Mitic and Klose, "Handelskammerorganisation in Österreich," pp. 505–6, 519–20.

174. Mitic and Klose, "Handelskammerorganisation in Österreich," p. 513.

175. Alfred Klose, *Ein Weg zur Sozialpartnerschaft: Das österreichische Modell* (Munich: Oldenbourg, 1970), p. 81.

176. Franz Geissler, "Die Bundeskammern," in Koren and Ebner, *Österreich auf einem Weg,* p. 30, and Herbert Reiger, "Die Basis der Arbeit der Handelskammern," in ibid., pp. 207–12; Mitic and Klose, "Handelskammerorganisation in Österreich," pp. 521, 524–25.

177. Walter Riener, "Organisierte Interessen in Österreich," in *Organisierte Interessen in Europa* (Osnabrück: Fromm, 1966), p. 61.

178. Rusinow, "Notes," Part I, p. 10.

179. Secher, "Representative Democracy," p. 905. Although Secher refers here to the 1950s, this quotation captures Austrian politics in the 1970s as well.

180. Engelmayer, *Die Diener des Staates;* R. Kneucker, "Austria: An Administrative State. The Role of Austrian Bureaucracy," *Österreichische Zeitschrift für Politikwissenschaft* 1973, no. 2: 95–127; Raoul F. Kneucker, "Public Administration: The Business of Government," in Steiner, *Modern Austria,* pp. 261–78; Heinrich Neisser, "Die Rolle der Bürokratie," in Fischer, *Das politische System Österreichs,* pp. 233–70; and Eva Kreisky, "Zur Genesis der politischen und sozialen Funktion der Bürokratie," in ibid., pp. 181–231.

181. Wilensky, *The Welfare State and Equality,* pp. 10–11.

182. Gehmacher, "Der Beamte im sozialen Wandel," pp. 150–51.

183. Gerhard Lehmbruch, "Liberal Corporatism and Party Government," in Philippe Schmitter and Lehmbruch, eds., *Trends toward Corporatist Intermediation* (Beverly Hills, Calif.: Sage, 1979), p. 173.

184. U.S. Congress, Joint Economic Committee, *Austrian Incomes Policy: Lesson for the United States,* 97th Cong., 1st sess., 2 June 1981, p. 11.

185. Mitic and Klose, "Handelskammerorganisation in Österreich," p. 563.

186. Lachs, *Wirtschaftspartnerschaft in Österreich,* pp. 80–81.

187. OECD, *Industrial Policy of Austria,* p. 45.

188. Gerhard Lehner and Karl Wohlmuth, "Stabilisierungspolitik in Österreich: Eine Konfrontation mit dem deutschen Stabilitätsgesetz," *Quartalshefte* 1969, nos. 2-3: p. 68.

189. OECD, *Indusrial Policy of Austria,* p. 66.

190. Siegfried Hollerer, *Verstaatlichung und Wirtschaftsplanung in Österreich (1946–1949)* (Vienna: Verband der Wissenschaftlichen Gesellschaften Österreichs, 1974), p. 2.

191. Rusinow, "Notes," Part IV, p. 5; Zimmermann, *Verstaatlichung in Österreich,* p. 78.

192. Koren, "Sozialisierungsideologie in Österreich," p. 96.

193. OECD, *Industrial Policy of Austria,* p. 72.

194. Ibid., pp. 70–73; OECD, *Aims and Instruments of Industrial Policy,* pp. 23–24.

195. Koren, "Sozialisierungsideologie in Österreich," p. 105, describes the 1960s.

196. See the recommendations in Beirat für Wirtschafts- und Sozialfragen, *Vorschläge zur Industriepolitik,* pp. 33–36.

197. Wolfgang Hobl, "Die Reform der verstaatlichten Buntmetallindustrie in Österreich: In Erfüllung der Forderungen des ÖIG-Gesetzes" (Diplom, Vienna, Wirtschaftsuniversität, 1975); Steiner, *Politics in Austria,* pp. 83–90; and Brusatti, Gutkas, and Weinzierl, *Österreich 1945–1970,* pp. 210–14, 252–56, 289–303.

198. Koren, "Sozialisierungsideologie in Österreich," p. 335, offers a similar assessment for the late 1950s.

199. Rusinow, "Notes," Part IV, pp. 11–12.

200. *Economic Chambers of Austria;* Tautscher, *Österreichische Wirtschaftsordnung,* pp. 54–80; Ucakar, "Entwicklung der Interessenorganisationen"; and Pütz, *Verbände und Wirtschaftspolitik.*

201. Chris Cviic, "Their Own Kind of Miracle," *Economist,* 28 July 1973, Survey, p. 19.

202. Marin, *Die Paritätische Kommission;* Schiff, *Incomes Policies Abroad,* Part II, pp. 29–42; OECD, *Aims and Instruments of Industrial Policy,* pp. 33–34; Lachs, *Wirtschaftspartnerschaft in Österreich;* Pütz, "Bedeutung der Wirtschaftsverbände," pp. 65–134; Hannes Suppanz and Derek Robinson, *Prices and Incomes Policy: The Austrian Experience* (Paris: OECD, 1972); Klose, *Ein Weg zur Sozialpartnerschaft;* Ewald Nowotny, "Das System der 'Sozial- und Wirtschaftspartnerschaft' in Österreich—Gesamtwirtschaftliche und einzelbetriebliche Formen und Effekte," *Die Betriebswirtschaft* 38 (1978): pp. 273–85; "Die Preiskontrolle der Paritätischen Preis-Lohn Kommission," *Monatsberichte* 37 (May 1964): 173–78; Institut für Angewandte Sozial- und Wirtschaftsforschung, ed., *Zur Paritätischen Kommission für Preis- und Lohnfragen* (Vienna: Jupiter, 1966); Dieter Bichlbauer and Anton Pelinka, *Wissenschaftliche Politikberatung am Beispiel der Paritätischen Kommission* (Vienna: Institut für Gesellschaftspolitik, n.d.); Wilhelm Braun, *Die Paritätische Kommission: Einkommenspolitik in Österreich* (Cologne: Deutscher Industrieverlag, 1970); Johann Farnleitner, *Die Paritätische Kommission: Institution und Verfahren* (Eisenstadt: Prugg, 1974); and Dieter Bichlbauer, "Zur Paritätischen Kommission," *Österreichische Zeitschrift für Politikwissenschaft* 1974, no. 3: 295–311.

203. *Austrian Incomes Policy,* p. 4.

204. Marin, *Die Paritätische Kommission,* pp. 63–64, 140.

205. Murray Edelman, *National Economic Planning by Collective Bargaining: The Formation of Austrian Wage, Price, and Tax Policy after World War II* (Urbana: University of Illinois, 1954); Chaloupek and Swoboda, "Sozialpartnerschaft in den fünfziger Jahren."

206. Spitäller, "Incomes Policy in Austria," pp. 181–83, has a useful summary table.

207. Lachs, *Wirtschaftspartnerschaft in Österreich,* pp. 40–42; Lang, *Kooperative Gewerkschaften,* p. 100.

208. Lehmbruch, "Liberal Corporatism," pp. 150–51, 173. See also Egon

Matzner, "Sozialpartnerschaft," in Fischer, *Das politische System Österreichs,* p. 433.

209. The Raab-Boehm Agreement of 1957 and the Raab-Benya Agreement of 1961, which led first to the creation of the commission and subsequently to the enlargement of its jurisdiction, are clearer illustrations of this bilateralism than one finds today. The government and the state bureaucracy are now more involved in the preliminary negotiations between interest groups.

210. Lachs, *Wirtschaftspartnerschaft in Österreich,* p. 46; Spitäller, "Incomes Policy," pp. 186–88; and Neuhauser, "Verbandsmässige Organisation," pp. 90–94.

211. Marin, *Die Paritätische Kommission,* p. 140; Spitäller, "Incomes Policy," p. 184; and Neuhauser, "Verbandsmässige Organisation," p. 91.

212. Marin, *Die Paritätische Kommission,* pp. 136–40; Gerhard Lehmbruch, "Consociational Democracy, Class Conflict, and the New Corporatism" (paper prepared for the IPSA Round Table, Jerusalem, 9–13 September 1974), p. 4.

213. Spitäller, "Incomes Policy," p. 189; Schiff, *Incomes Policies Abroad,* Part II, p. 32; and März, Weissel, and Reithofer, "Kammern für Arbeiter und Angestellte," pp. 409–410.

214. Neuhauser, "Verbandsmässige Organisation," pp. 90–94; Spitäller, "Incomes Policy," p. 183; and Lachs, *Wirtschaftspartnerschaft in Österreich,* pp. 42–46.

215. Between 1955 and 1970 wage drift in the Austrian industry amounted to 20–30 percent. See Lachs, *Wirtschaftspartnerschaft in Österreich,* pp. 185, 193. Between 1966 and 1976 it varied between 30 and 35 percent. See Marin, *Die Paritätische Kommission,* p. 168.

216. Klose, *Ein Weg zur Sozialpartnerschaft,* pp. 54–67; Lachs, *Wirtschaftspartnerschaft in Österreich,* pp. 68–73; Lang, *Kooperative Gewerkschaften,* pp. 39–43; Riener, "Organisierte Interessen," pp. 77–81; "Ein neuer Stil in der Wirtschaftspolitik? Zum Beirat für Wirtschafts- und Sozialfragen," *Wirtschaftspolitische Blätter* 10, 6 (1963): 269–94; "Probleme und Aufgaben des Wirtschaftsbeirates," *Wirtschaftspolitische Blätter* 11, 6 (1961): 378–430; *Vernunft in Arbeitswelt und Wirtschaft: Die Wirtschafts- und Sozialpartnerschaft in Österreich* (Vienna: Bundespressedienst, 1973); and Manfred Majer, "Der Beirat für Wirtschafts- und Sozialfragen: Problematik einer neuen Institution" (Ph.D. diss., University of Innsbruck, 1965).

217. Marin, *Die Paritätische Kommission,* pp. 292–300; Pütz, "Bedeutung der Wirtschaftsverbände," p. 198; and Helmut Kramer, "Mittelfristige Wirtschaftsprognosen in Österreich—Möglichkeiten und Unmöglichkeiten," *Quartalshefte* 1969, no. 1: 5.

218. Erhard Fürst, "Die holländische Planung: Vorbild für Österreich," *Quartalshefte* 1969, no. 1: 99; Bernd Marin, *Politische Organisation Sozialwissenschaftlicher Forschungsarbeit: Fallstudie zum Institut für Höhere Studien* (Vienna: Braumüller, 1978); and Kramer, "Mittelfristige Wirtschaftsprognose."

219. Bernd Marin, "'Freiwillige Disziplin'? Preiskontrolle ohne autonome Sanktionspotenzen—Österreichs Paritätitische Kommission," *Wirtschaft und Gesellschaft* 7, 2 (1981): 161–97; Schiff, *Incomes Policies Abroad,* p. 34; and Lachs, *Wirtschaftspartnerschaft,* pp. 62–65.

220. Marin, *Die Paritätische Kommission,* pp. 92–126; Lachs, *Wirtschaftspart-*

nerschaft, pp. 53–57, 61–62; Spitäller, "Incomes Policy," p. 179; and Neuhauser, "Verbandsmässige Organisation," pp. 99, 101, 106.

221. OECD, *Economic Survey: Austria* (Paris: 1962), p. 16.

222. Lachs, *Wirtschaftspartnerschaft,* p. 38.

223. Quoted in Flanagan, Soskice, and Ulman, *Unionism,* p. 82. See also *Jahrbuch der österreichischen Wirtschaft* 1976, no. 1: 48; Maria Szecsi, "Social Partnership in Austria," in Steiner, *Modern Austria,* pp. 195–97.

224. *Jahrbuch der österreichischen Wirtschaft 1980: Statistiken* (Vienna: Bundeskammer der Gewerblichen Wirtschaft, 1980), pp. 34–35, 51–52.

225. For positive evaluations see Flanagan, Soskice, and Ulman, *Unionism;* Schiff, *Incomes Policies Abroad,* Part II; OECD, *Economic Survey: Austria* (Paris: 1971), pp. 7, 33–35; ibid., 1972, pp. 22–23, 38–39; and ibid. 1973, pp. 41–44. For critical evaluations in the early 1960s see ibid., 1963, pp. 19–20; Koren, "Sozialisierungsideologie in Österreich," pp. 136–38.

226. Spitäller, "Incomes Policy," p. 186.

227. The point is made well for an earlier time period by Edelman, *National Economic Planning,* pp. 20–22, 62–63.

228. Lachs, *Wirtschaftspartnerschaft,* p. 87.

229. *Vernunft in Arbeitswelt und Wirtschaft,* pp. 22–23; Michael Pollak, "Vom Konflikt- zum Kompromissverhalten. Die Sozialpartnerschaft als Sozialisationsmittel politischen Handelns," *Austriaca: Cahiers universitaires d'information sur l'Autriche* (November 1979): 373, 375; Lang, *Kooperative Gewerkschaften,* p. 82; and Lachs, *Wirtschaftspartnerschaft,* p. 89.

230. *Vernunft in Arbeitswelt und Wirtschaft,* p. 20.

231. Pollak, "Vom Konflikt- zum Kompromissverhalten"; Marin, *Die Paritätische Kommission.*

232. *World Business Weekly,* 17 March 1980, p. 32.

233. Pollak, "Vom Konflikt- zum Kompromissverhalten," p. 384; Bernd Marin, "Neuer Populismus und 'Wirtschaftspartnerschaft.' 'Neokorporatistische' Konfliktregelung und ausserinstitutionelle Konfliktpotentiale in Österreich," *Österreichische Zeitschrift für Politikwissenschaft* 1980, no. 2: 157–76.

234. On the historical causes see Koren and Ebner, *Österreich auf einem Weg,* pp. 215, 227–33; Lachs, *Wirtschaftspartnerschaft,* p. 32; and Pollak, "Vom Konflikt- zum Kompromissverhalten," p. 369. In general see Fischer, *Das politische System Österreichs;* Steiner, *Modern Austria;* Anton Pelinka and Manfried Welan, *Demokratie und Verfassung in Österreich* (Vienna: Europa Verlag, 1971); Karl-Heinz Nassmacher, *Das österreichische Regierungssystem: Grosse Koalition oder alternierende Regierung?* (Cologne: Westdeutscher Verlag, 1968); Reinhold Knoll and Anton Mayer, *Österreichische Konsensusdemokratie in Theorie und Praxis: Staat, Interessenverbände, Parteien und die politische Wirklichkeit* (Vienna: Böhlaus), 1976; Gerald Schöpfer, ed., *Phänomen Sozialpartnerschaft: Festschrift für Hermann Ibler zum 75. Geburtstag* (Vienna: Böhlaus, 1980); Felix Kreissler and Michel Cullin, *L'Autriche contemporaine* (Paris: Armand, 1971); Ernst Wimmer, *Sozialpartnerschaft aus marxistischer Sicht* (Vienna: Globus, 1979); and Chaloupek and Swoboda, "Sozialpartnerschaft in den fünfziger Jahren," pp. 333–34. The *Österreichische Zeitschrift für Politikwissenschaft* has devoted special issues to the topic of social partnership in 1974, no. 3, and 1982, no. 3. See also Peter Gerlich, *Parlamentarische Kontrolle im politischen System: Die Verwaltungsfunktion des Nationalrates in Recht und Wirklichkeit* (New York: Springer, 1973); Peter Gerlich and Helmut Kramer, *Abgeordnete in der*

Parteiendemokratie: Eine empirische Untersuchung des Wiener Gemeinderates und Landtages (Munich: Oldenbourg, 1969); Peter Pulzer, "The Legitimizing Role of Political Parties: The Second Austrian Republic," *Government and Opposition* 3 (Winter 1968): 324–44; and Gerhard Lehmbruch, "Das Modéll der Sozialpartnerschaft," *Die Republik* 4 (March 1971): 19–25.

235. Dieter Bös, "Machtproportionen in den paritätischen Organen," *Berichte und Informationen,* 10 October 1969, pp. 1–4; Gerhard Lehmbruch, "Das politische System Österreichs in vergleichender Perspektive," *Österreichische Zeitschrift für öffentliches Recht* 22 (1971): 35–36.

236. Lachs, *Wirtschaftspartnerschaft,* p. 34.

237. Gerhard Botz, "Politische Gewalt und industrielle Arbeitskämpfe in Wirtschaftskrisen," in Marin, *Wachstumskrisen in Österreich,* 2: 277. At the same time the relative number of wildcat strikes has declined by only one-half. See Lang, *Kooperative Gewerkschaften,* p. 102.

238. Alfred Klose, "Die Sozialpartnerschaft als Konfliktregelungssystem," in Schöpfer, *Phänomen Sozialpartnerschaft,* pp. 75–86.

239. Andrlik, "The Organized Society," pp. 144–45.

240. Anton Pelinka, *Modellfall Österreich? Möglichkeiten und Grenzen der Sozialpartnerschaft* (Vienna: Braumüller, 1981), pp. 34–35, 38.

241. Rodney P. Stiefbold, "Segmented Pluralism and Consociational Democracy in Austria: Problems of Political Stability and Change," in Martin Heisler, ed., *Politics in Europe: Structures and Processes in Some Postindustrial Democracies* (New York: McKay, 1974), pp. 123, 173; *Vernunft in der Arbeitswelt,* pp. 19, 21.

242. Frederick Engelmann and Mildred A. Schwartz, "Austria's Consistent Voters," *American Behavioral Scientist* 18 (September–October 1974): 97–110; Rudolf Steininger, *Polarisierung und Integration: Eine vergleichende Untersuchung der strukturellen Versäulung der Gesellschaft in den Niederlanden und in Österreich* (Meisenheim am Glan: Anton Hain, 1975); Sidney Verba, Norman H. Nie, and Jae-on Kim, *Participation and Political Equality: A Seven-Nation Comparison* (Cambridge: Cambridge University Press, 1978); G. Bingham Powell and Lynda W. Powell, "The Analysis of Citizen-Elite Linkages: Representation by Austrian Local Elites," in Sidney Verba and Lucian Pye, eds., *The Citizen in Politics: A Comparative Perspective* (Stamford, Conn.: Greylock, 1978), pp. 195–217; G. Bingham Powell Jr., "Incentive Structures and Campaign Participation: Citizenship, Partisanship, Policy and Patronage in Austria" (Conference on political participation, Leiden University, Leiden, The Netherlands, 17–22 March 1972); Powell, "Political Cleavage Structure, Cross-pressure Processes, and Partisanship: An Empirical Test of the Theory," *American Journal of Political Science* 20 (February 1976): 1–23; Powell and Rodney P. Stiefbold, "Anger, Bargaining, and Mobilization as Middle-range Theories of Elite Conflict Behavior: An Empirical Test," *Comparative Politics* 9 (July 1977): 379–98; and Joseph John Houska Jr., "The Organizational Connection: Elites, Masses, and Elections in Austria and the Netherlands" (Ph.D. diss., Yale University, 1979).

243. Data for the 1960s and 1970s can be found in Sully, "The Socialist Party of Austria," pp. 218–19, and in Vodopivec, *Die Dritte Republik,* p. 140. See also Andrlik, "The Organized Society," pp. 126–27.

244. Uwe Kitzinger, "The Austrian Election of 1959," *Political Studies* 9 (June 1961): 123.

245. Rodney P. Stiefbold, "Elites and Election in a Fragmented Political System," in Rudolf Wildenmann, ed., *Sozialwissenschaftliches Jahrbuch für Politik*, vol. 4 (Munich: Olzog, 1975), pp. 119–227.

246. Wolfgang Rudzio, "Entscheidungszentrum Koalitionsausschuss: Zur Realverfassung Österreichs unter der Grossen Koalition," *Politische Vierteljahresschrift* 12 (1971): 87–118.

247. Neisser, "Rolle der Bürokratie," p. 241.

248. Gehmacher, "Der Beamte im sozialen Wandel," p. 145.

249. Rusinow, "Notes," Part I, p. 9.

250. Heinz Fischer, "Beamte und Politik," in Engelmayer, *Diener des Staates*, pp. 109–110; Pelinka and Welan, *Demokratie und Verfassung*, pp. 180–83.

251. Klenner, *Die österreichischen Gewerkschaften*, 3: 2066–73; *Vernunft in Arbeitswelt und Wirtschaft*, pp. 19–21. For illustrations drawn from the 1950s and 1960s see Szecsi, "Social Partnership," pp. 193–94.

252. Johann Farnleitner, "Prepared Remarks" (Delivered at the conference on "The Political Economy of Austria," American Enterprise Institute for Public Policy Research, Washington, D.C., 1–2 October, 1981).

253. Spitäller, "Incomes Policy," p. 180.

254. Pollak, "Vom Konflikt- zum Kompromissverhalten," pp. 377–79.

255. Lachs, *Wirtschaftspartnerschaft*, pp. 7, 34–35.

256. Lehmbruch, "Liberal Corporatism and Party Government."

257. Lachs, *Wirtschaftspartnerschaft*, pp. 74–87.

258. *Der Spiegel*, 11 August 1980, pp. 84–85.

259. Dorothy Nelkin and Michael Pollak, "The Politics of Participation and the Nuclear Debate in Sweden, the Netherlands, and Austria," *Public Policy* 25 (Summer 1977): 333–57; Pollak, "Vom Konflikt- zum Kompromissverhalten," p. 383; and *New York Times*, 31 August 1980, p. A15.

260. OECD, *Gaps in Technology: Comparisons between Member Countries in Education, Research and Development, Technological Innovation, International Economic Exchanges* (Paris: 1970), p. 198; Otmar Höll and Helmut Kramer, "Kleinstaaten im internationalen System: Endbericht" (Vienna, December 1977, mimeo), pp. 66, 68, 72.

261. Kristensen and Levinsen, *Small Country Squeeze*, p. 151; Gaspari and Millendorfer, *Prognosen für Österreich*, p. 89. In general see OECD, *Reviews of National Science Policy: Austria* (Paris: 1971); *Neue Technologien und Produkte für Österreichs Wirtschaft* (Vienna: Zentralsparkasse and Kommerzialbank, 1979).

262. Gaspari and Millendorfer, *Prognosen für Osterreich*, pp. 85–86; Höll and Kramer, "Kleinstaaten," p. 60; Lacina, *Development of the Austrian Public Sector*, p. 21; Beirat für Wirtschafts- und Sozialfragen, *Vorschläge zur Industriepolitik*, pp. 59–69, 86–87; and Beirat für Wirtschafts- und Sozialfragen, *Vorschläge zur Industriepolitik*, 2: 78.

263. Gaspari and Millendorfer, *Prognosen für Österreich*, p. 86.

264. Ibid., pp. 86–87; Höll and Kramer, "Kleinstaaten," pp. 63, 65; Otmar Höll, *Austria's Technological Dependence: Basic Dimensions and Current Trends* (Laxenburg: Institute for International Affairs, 1980), p. 10; Karl Vak, "The Competitiveness of the Austrian Economy," in Arndt, *Political Economy of Austria*, pp 172–73; and *News from Austria*, 23 June 1980, p. 7.

265. OECD/DSTI, "Science Resources" Unit, *Science Resources Newsletter* 2 (Spring 1977): 1; A. Nussbaumer, "Financing the Generation of New Science and Technology," in B. R. Williams, ed., *Science and Technology in Economic*

Growth (New York: Wiley, 1973), p. 177; Gaspari and Millendorfer, *Prognosen für Österreich*, pp. 86–87; and Höll and Kramer, "Kleinstaaten," pp. 52, 68.

266. Quoted in *Austrian Information* 30, 3 (1977): 3.

267. Anton Kausel, "The Austrian Economy: A Macroeconomic Analysis," *Austrian Information* 32, 4–5 (1979): 5–6.

268. OECD, *Gaps in Technology*, p. 205; Höll, *Austria's Technological Dependence*, pp. 45–46; and Breuss, *Komparative Vorteile im österreichischen Aussenhandel*, p. 143.

269. Höll, *Austria's Technological Dependence*, p. 44.

270. Gaspari and Millendorfer, *Prognosen für Österreich*, p. 86.

271. *Oberösterreichische Nachrichten*, 12 April 1973; Beirat für Wirtschafts- und Sozialfragen, *Vorschläge zur Industriepolitik*, 2: 78.

272. Bernhard Kamler, "Elektroindustrie: Mehr Forschung, Spezialisierung und Kooperation," *Die Industrie*, 3 January 1972, pp. 7–10.

273. OECD/DSTI, "Science and Technology Indicators" Unit, *Science Resources Newsletter*, Winter 1977/78, pp. 5–6; *Oberösterreichische Nachrichten*, 12 April 1973; and *Die Presse*, 24 June 1977.

274. *Oberösterreichische Nachrichten*, 12 April 1973.

275. *Wochenpresse*, 8 November 1972.

276. Mayer, "Foreign Workers," pp. 99–101; *Gastarbeiter: Wirtschaftliche und soziale Herausforderung* (Vienna: Europa Verlag, 1973); Beirat für Wirtschafts- und Sozialfragen, *Möglichkeiten und Grenzen des Einsatzes ausländischer Arbeitskräfte* (Vienna: Ueberreuter, 1976); Ernst Gehmacher, "Foreign Workers as a Source of Social Change," in Richard Rose, ed., *The Dynamics of Public Policy: A Comparative Analysis* (Beverly Hills, Calif.: Sage, 1976), pp. 157–76; and Österreichisches Institut für Wirtschaftsforschung, *Monatsberichte* 35 (May 1962): 232–36; ibid., 36 (November 1963): 411–15; ibid., 47 (April 1974): 214–24.

277. OECD, "Report on Migration," p. 4.

278. OECD, *Economic Surveys: Austria* (Paris: 1970), pp. 19–25, and ibid., 1974, pp. 47–51; ibid., 1976, pp. 43–44.

279. *Monatsberichte* 26 (September 1953): 278.

280. Peter J. Katzenstein, "Trends and Oscillations in Austrian Integration Policy since 1955: Alternative Explanations," *Journal of Common Market Studies* 14 (December 1975): 171–97; Edward E. Platt, "Political Factors Affecting the Austrian Government's Decision to join EFTA" (Ph.D. diss., University of Connecticut, 1967); M. Dillinger et al., "Die europäische Integration und Österreich," *Österreichische Zeitschrift für Politikwissenschaft* 1976, no. 1: 65–87; and Thomas O. Schlesinger, *Austrian Neutrality in Postwar Europe: The Domestic Roots of a Foreign Policy* (Vienna: Braumüller, 1972), pp. 92–111.

281. Bruno Rossmann, "Exportförderung in Österreich," *Wirtschaft und Gesellschaft* 1982, no. 1: 57–78; Helmut Haschek, *Exportförderung, Finanzierungen und Garantien: Internationaler Vergleich und österreichische Praxis* (Vienna: Molden, 1976); and Haschek, "Exportförderung in Österreich," in *Exportförderung in der Bundesrepublik Deutschland, in der Schweiz und in Österreich* (Vienna: Zentralsparkasse and Kommerzbank, 1979), pp. 46–65.

282. Helmut H. Haschek and Ernst Löschner, *Zwanzig Jahre Exportfinanzierung 1960–1980* (Vienna: Österreichische Kontrollbank, March 1981), p. 34; Helmut Haschek, letter to the author, 22 March 1981.

283. *Der Österreich-Bericht*, 4 August 1983, p. 2. Haschek, letter of 22 March 1981.

284. Haschek and Löschner, *Zwanzig Jahre.*
285. Cviic, "Their Own Kind of Miracle," Survey, p. 14.
286. Koch, "Contemporary Austrian Foreign Policy," pp. 206–7, 256–60; *Die Presse,* 19 April and 25 October 1975, 16 April 1976; Josef G. Maier, "Die Entwicklung der Exportförderung durch die Aussenhandelsstellen" (Diplom, Vienna, Hochschule für Welthandel, 1976); Erich Staringer, "Die Ausfuhrförderung in Österreich," *Quartalshefte* 1967, no. 1: 67–75; and *Die Presse,* 18 March 1975. It should be noted, though, that the technological sophistication of this foreign trade system is to some extent misleading. Computer printouts are only a partial remedy for the traditional weakness of Austrian firms in the area of marketing and aggressive salesmanship.
287. *News from Austria,* 2 September 1980, p. 4.
288. *Der Spiegel,* 4 August 1980, pp. 104–7; *New York Times,* 15 March 1981, p. 20. The contrast with Switzerland could not be greater. See Anton Pelinka, "Defense Policy and Permanent Neutrality" (Paper prepared for the annual conference of the Committee on Atlantic Studies, Wingspread, Racine, Wisconsin, September 1979), p. 12.

CHAPTER 3. *Liberal Capitalism in Switzerland*

1. See Emil Küng, *The Secret of Switzerland's Economic Success* (Washington, D.C.: American Enterprise Institute, 1978); Fritz Leutwiler, *Swiss Monetary and Exchange Rate Policy in an Inflationary World* (Washington, D.C.: American Enterprise Institute, 1978); S. Borner et al., *Structural Analysis of Swiss Industry 1968–1978: Redeployment of Industry and the International Division of Labor* (Zurich: Industrial Consulting and Management Engineering Co., August 1978); Organization for Economic Co-operation and Development (OECD), *Public Expenditure Trends* (Paris: 1978); *OECD Economic Surveys: Switzerland* (Paris: 1978 and 1980); *New York Times,* 25 July 1979, p. D8; *Lage und Probleme der schweizerischen Wirtschaft: Gutachten 1977/78* (Bern: Eidgenössisches Volkswirtschaftsdepartment und Schweizerische Nationalbank, 1978), 1: 118; Norman Crossland, "The Everlasting League," *Economist,* 3 February 1979, Survey, p. 23; "Euer Friede ist faul und erlogen, wenn. . . . SPIEGEL-Report über das politische und gesellschaftliche System der Schweiz," *Der Spiegel,* 2 August 1971, pp. 72–86; Sarah Hogg, "A Small House in Order," *Economist,* 15 March 1980, Survey, p. 8; *Austrian Information* 32,6 (1979): 8; and *World Business Weekly,* 4 February 1980, p. 51, and 21 July, p. 24.
2. Rudolph G. Penner, "Paradise Is in the Alps," *New York Times,* 11 October 1981, p. F3.
3. Volker Bornschier, *Wachstum, Konzentration und Multinationalisierung von Industrieunternehmen* (Frauenfeld: Huber, 1976), p. 206. Bornschier estimates foreign production as 200 percent of direct foreign investment (p. 551).
4. This is the suggestive title of Thomas Horst's *At Home Abroad: A Study of the Domestic and Foreign Operations of the American Food-Processing Industry* (Cambridge, Mass.: Ballinger, 1974).
5. Jürg Niehans, "Benefits of Multinational Firms for a Small Parent Economy: The Case of Switzerland," in Tamir Agmon and Charles P. Kindleberger, eds., *Multinationals from Small Countries* (Cambridge: MIT Press, 1977), pp. 37–38.

6. Ibid., p. 2.

7. United Nations, *Transnational Corporations in World Development: A Re-Examination* (New York: U.N. Economic and Social Council, 1978), p. 238.

8. Walter A. Jöhr, *Finanzplatz Schweiz kontra Exportwirtschaft? Fakten und Überlegungen zum Wechselkursproblem unseres Landes* (Zurich: Vereinigung für Gesunde Währung, 1976), p. 17.

9. Ibid., p. 30.

10. *Die Schweiz im Zeichen des harten Frankens* (Zurich: Schweizerische Kreditanstalt, 1978), p. 20; Leutwiler, *Swiss Monetary and Exchange Rate Policy* p. 6; and Max Iklé, *Switzerland: An International Banking and Finance Center* (Stroudsbourg, Penn.: Dowden, Hutchinson & Ross, 1972), pp. 146–47.

11. Schweizerischer Handels- und Industrie-Verein, *Jahresbericht des Vororts an die Delegiertenversammlung: 107. Vereinsjahr* (n.p., n.d.), p. 37. See also Niehans, "Benefits of Multinational Firms," p. 5, and François Höpflinger, *Das unheimliche Imperium: Wirtschaftsverflechtung in der Schweiz* (Zurich: Eco, 1978), p. 15. There is some uncertainty about this estimate since we do not know how much of Switzerland's direct foreign investment is really disguised indirect investment by larger countries, in particular the United States. See United Nations, *Transnational Corporations: A Reexamination,* p. 41, and Gilles Y. Bertin, "France as Host to Small-country Foreign Investment," in Agmon and Kindleberger, *Multinationals from Small Countries,* pp. 84–85.

12. Höpflinger, *Das unheimliche Imperium,* p. 15; Bornschier, *Wachstum von Industrieunternehmen,* pp. 342, 398.

13. Bornschier, *Wachstum von Industrieunternehmen,* p. 206. In general see Silvio Borner, ed., *Produktionsverlagerung und industrieller Strukturwandel* (Bern: Haupt, 1980). See also Peter C. Meyer, "Switzerland: Small State and Big Business" (Paper prepared for the ECPR workshop on "The State and International Economic Power," Louvain, Belgium, April 1976), p. 5.

14. Bornschier, *Wachstum von Industrieunternehmen,* p. 206.

15. Niehans, "Benefits of Multinational Firms," pp. 5–7, and Höpflinger, *Das unheimliche Imperium,* pp. 25, 27. See also John M. Geddes, "Nestlé Seeking Market Balance," *New York Times,* 27 March 1980, pp. D1, D5.

16. Silvio Borner, "Ist der Standort Schweiz für einen Industriebetrieb, insbesondere für die Textilindustrie, noch richtig?" *Mitteilungen über Textilindustrie: Mittex* 10 (October 1979): 375; *World Business Weekly,* 25 May 1981, p. 37; Urs Haymoz, *Finanzplatz Schweiz und Dritte Welt* (Basle: Z-Verlag, 1978), pp. 23, 38–39, 74–88; and Vital Gawronski, "Entwicklungsländer auf dem Weg ins Industriezeitalter: Auswirkungen aus internationaler und aus schweizerischer Sicht," *Mitteilungsblatt für Konjunkturfragen* 36, 3 (1980): 63, 65.

17. Niehans, "Benefits of Multinational Firms," p. 6.

18. Ibid., p. 8.

19. Antoine Basile, *Commerce extérieur et développement de la petite nation: Essai sur les contraintes de l'exiguité économique* (Geneva: Droz, 1972), p. 199.

20. Niehans, "Benefits of Multinational Firms," p. 2; Jonathan Steinberg, *Why Switzerland?* (Cambridge: Cambridge University Press, 1976), p. 141.

21. Ulrich Frey, ed., *Schweizer Dokumentation für Politik und Wirtschaft,* 6 vols. (Bern: 1969–), "Investitionsrisikogarantie"; Gottfried Berweger, *Investition und Legitimation: Privatinvestitionen in Entwicklungsländern als Teil der schweizerischen Legitimationsproblematik* (Diessenhofen: Rüegger, 1977), p. 77. In 1973

total financial commitments under the Investment Risk Guarantee equaled about 1 percent of the sums committed under the Export Risk Guarantee; see Handels- und Industrie-Verein, *Jahresbericht 1977/78*, p. 59.

22. Fritz Leutwiler, *Die Schweiz als internationaler Finanzplatz: Wachstum in Grenzen* (Zurich: Schweizerischer Handels- und Industrie-Verein, 1977), p. 16; *World Business Weekly*, 4 May 1981, pp. 49–50; and Martin Ungerer, *Finanzplatz Schweiz: Seine Geschichte, Bedeutung und Zukunft* (Vienna: Econ, 1979). Some of the darker sides of Swiss banking are discussed in Jean Ziegler, *Switzerland: The Awful Truth* (New York: Harper, 1977), pp. 39–60, and in Christian Dorninger, "Finanzplatz Zürich—über jeden Verdacht erhaben?" *Informationen über Multinationale Konzerne* 1981, no. 2: 6–10.

23. "International Insurance—Swiss Style," *Economist*, 18 July 1970, Survey, p. xxviii.

24. Jöhr, *Finanzplatz Schweiz kontra Exportwirtschaft?* p. 13; Höpflinger, *Das unheimliche Imperium*, p. 163; Meyer, "Switzerland: Small State and Big Business," p. 8; and *World Business Weekly*, 7 July 1980, p. 33.

25. R. A. Jeker, *Die schweizer Banken in den achziger Jahren* (Zurich: Crédit Suisse, 1979), p. 17.

26. Robert Metz, "Swiss Defense on Takeovers," *New York Times*, 9 April 1980, p. D6.

27. Berweger, *Investition und Legitimation*, p. 209.

28. *Die Schweiz im Zeichen des harten Frankens*, p. 20; Höpflinger, *Das unheimliche Imperium*, p. 163; Robert Holzach, *Banken und Strukturpolitik* (Aargau: Aargauische Industrie- und Handelskammer, 1977), pp. 7–8; Meyer, "Switzerland," p. 9; and *Lage und Probleme der schweizerischen Wirtschaft: Gutachten 1977/78* (Bern: Eidgenössisches Volkswirtschaftsdepartment und Schweizerische Nationalbank, 1978), 1: 48–49, 215.

29. Bornschier, *Wachstum von Industrieunternehmen*, p. 445. Based on different data and methods of computation, other sources report higher figures for 1938 and lower ones for 1972–73. See, respectively, Amilio Albisetti, "Die Banken," in *Strukturwandlungen der schweizerischen Wirtschaft und Gesellschaft: Festschrift für Franz Marbach zum 70. Geburtstag* (Bern: Stämpfli, 1962), p. 201; Hans C. Binswanger and Reinhardt Büchi, "Aussenpolitik und Aussenwirtschaftspolitik," in Alois Riklin, Hans Haug, and Hans C. Binswanger, eds., *Handbuch der schweizerischen Aussenpolitik* (Bern: Haupt, 1975), p. 708; and *Euromoney*, May 1979, p. 13.

30. B. Beedham and G. Lee, "Even in Paradise," *Economist*, 22 February 1969, Survey, p. xii.

31. Meyer, "Switzerland," pp. 8–9. It is, however, very likely that the growth of international lending will slow in the 1980s; see *World Business Weekly*, 1 December 1980, p. 50.

32. Robert B. Cohen, "Structural Change in International Banking and Its Implications for the U.S. Economy" (Draft paper submitted to the Special Study on Economic Change of the Joint Economic Committee, U.S. Congress, 22 July 1980), pp. 3, 5.

33. Susan Strange, "Still an Extraordinary Power: America's Role in a Global Monetary System," in Raymond E. Lombra and Willard E. Witte, eds., *Political Economy of International and Domestic Monetary Relations* (Ames: Iowa State University Press, 1982), p. 85.

34. Alfred Bosshardt, *Aussenhandels-, Integrations- und Währungspolitik aus*

schweizerischer Sicht (Zurich: Schulthess, 1970), pp. 330–32; Ernst Jordi, "Krisennot und Teuerung aus sozialdemokratischer Perspektive," in Egon Tuchtfeldt, ed., *Schweizerische Wirtschaftspolitik, zwischen Gestern und Morgen: Festgabe zum 65. Geburtstag von Hugo Sieber* (Bern: Haupt, 1976), p. 210; and Hermann Maurer, *Die schweizerische Wechselkurspolitik nach dem Zweiten Weltkrieg (1945–10.5, 1971)* (Bern: Lang), 1972.

35. *Neue Zürcher Zeitung,*2 March, 14 May, and 20 June 1970.

36. *Die Schweiz als Kleinstaat in der Weltwirtschaft* (St. Gallen: Fehr'sche Buchhandlung, 1945), pp. 296–97, 283–84; Hans Vogel, "Die Schweiz und die Schichtung des internationalen Systems, untersucht anhand ihrer asymmetrischen Handelsbeziehungen," *Annuaire suisse de science politique,* 1974, pp. 124–25.

37. Holzach, *Banken und Strukturpolitik.*

38. Berweger, *Investition und Legitimation,* pp. 209–10; Steinberg, *Why Switzerland?* p. 141; Ziegler, *Switzerland: The Awful Truth,* p. 108; and Peter Rusterholz, "Power Structures in the Swiss Economic System" (Paper presented to the ECPR workshop on "Interorganizational Networks," Brussels, 17–21 April 1979).

39. The quotation is from W. A. Jöhr and F. Kneschaurek, "Study of the Efficiency of a Small Nation—Switzerland," in E. A. G. Robinson, ed., *Economic Consequences of the Size of Nations: Proceedings of a Conference Held by the International Economic Association* (London: Macmillan, 1960), p. 58. See also Guntram Rehsche, *Schweizerische Aussenwirtschaftspolitik und Dritte Welt: Ziele und Instrumente. Exportförderung kontra Entwicklungspolitik* (Adliswil: Institut für Sozialethik, 1977), pp. 8–9; Arnold Koller, "Entwicklungstendenzen der Wirtschafts- und Sozialpolitik der CVP," in Tuchtfeldt, *Schweizerische Wirtschaftspolitik,* p. 152.

40. OECD, *Reviews of National Science Policy: Switzerland* (Paris: 1971), p. 55.

41. Alexandre Jetzer, "L'activité de la Commission des Cartels dans l'optique du commerce et de l'industrie," in *Wettbewerbspolitik in der Schweiz: Festgabe zum 80. Geburtstag von Fritz Marbach* (Bern: Haupt, 1972), p. 44; Hans Huber, "Rückblick auf die 'neuen' Wirtschaftsartikel der Bundesverfassung," and Walter R. Schluep, "Schweizerische Wettbewerbspolitik zwischen Gestern und Morgen," both in Tuchtfeldt, *Schweizerische Wirtschaftspolitik,* pp. 69–70 and 95–130.

42. Dusan Sidjanski, "Interest Groups in Switzerland," *Annals of the American Academy of Political Science* no. 413 (May 1974): 112; Josua Werner, *Die Wirtschaftsverbände in der Marktwirtschaft* (Zurich: Polygraphischer Verlag, 1957), pp. 53, 55, 60, 104.

43. Gerhard Winterberger, *Das Bild der Industrie in der Öffentlichkeit* (Zurich: Schweizerischer Handels- und Industrie-Verein, 1972), pp. 6–7.

44. Richard Senti, "Die Schweiz und die Europäischen Gemeinschaften," in Senti, ed., *Die Schweiz und die internationalen Wirtschaftsorganisationen* (Zurich: Schulthess, 1975), pp. 125–27.

45. Hans Mayrzedt, *Multilaterale Wirtschaftsdiplomatie zwischen westlichen Industriestaaten als Instrument zur Stärkung der multilateralen und liberalen Handelspolitik* (Bern: Lang, 1979), p. 389.

46. Österreichisches Institut für Wirtschaftsforschung, "Österreich, Schweiz, Schweden: Ein Wirtschaftsvergleich," *Monatsberichte* 37 (October 1964, Supplement 77): 8.

47. U.S. Department of Commerce, Bureau of International Commerce, "Foreign Trade Regulations of Switzerland," *Overseas Business Reports* OBR 69–22 (June 1969): 1.

48. U.S. Senate, Committee on Finance, Subcommittee on International Trade, *MTN Studies 5: An Economic Analysis of the Effects of the Tokyo Round of Multilateral Trade Negotiations on the United States and the Other Major Industrialized Countries* (Washington D.C.: 1979), p. 38.

49. William R. Cline et al., *Trade Negotiations in the Tokyo Round: A Quantitative Assessment* (Washington, D.C.: Brookings, 1978), pp. 74, 121, 142. The interest of Swiss negotiators in mediating the conflict between the United States and the European Community can, no doubt, be attributed to the uncomfortable position in which they found themselves in the earlier Kennedy Round negotiations of tariff reductions; see E. H. Preeg, *Traders and Diplomats: An Analysis of the Kennedy Round of Negotiations under the GATT* (Washington, D.C.: Brookings, 1970), pp. 65–67; Karin Kock, *International Trade Policy and the GATT 1947–1967* (Stockholm: Almqvist & Wiksell, 1969), p. 103; and U.S. Senate, Committee on Finance, *MTN Studies*, p. v.

50. *Der Spiegel*, 26 June 1978, p. 122. See also Margret Sieber, "Die Entwicklung der schweizerischen Aussenbeziehungen in der Nachkriegszeit: 1948–1978," *Kleine Studien zur Politischen Wissenschaft* no. 208 (Zurich: Forschungsstelle für Politische Wissenschaft of the University of Zurich, 1981); corresponding figures for Austria varied between 25 and 51 percent in 1964, 1968, and 1972; see Renate Rottensteiner, "Die Willensbildung in der österreichischen Aussenpolitik," in Heinz Fischer, ed., *Das politische System Österreichs* (Vienna: Europaverlag, 1974), p. 378.

51. P. R. Jolles, quoted in Binswanger and Büchi, "Aussenpolitik und Aussenwirtschaftspolitik," pp. 694–95. A similar view was expressed by Switzerland's foreign minister, Pierre Aubert; see the interview in *Der Spiegel*, 26 June 1978, pp. 118–23.

52. Crédit Suisse, *Bulletin* 86 (Spring 1980): 20; Ziegler, *Switzerland: The Awful Truth* p. 28; Hans Naef, *Die Handelsbeziehungen der Schweiz zu den Zentralplanwirtschaften von 1945–1968* (Zurich: Juris, 1971); and Stefan Masu, *La coopération économique des pays de l'Est avec la Suisse: Roumaine* (Geneva: Institut universitaire des hautes études internationales, 1975).

53. For general background see numerous articles in Riklin, Haug, and Binswanger, *Handbuch;* R. Büchi and K. Matter, eds., *Schweiz-Dritte Welt: Solidarität oder Rentabilität?* (Zurich: Schulthess, 1973); Franz Bluntschli, *Zu den Beziehungen zwischen schweizerischer Aussenwirtschafts- und Entwicklungspolitik: Versuch einer Klärung und Orientierung im bestehenden Weltwirtschaftssystem* (Adliswil: Institut für Sozialethik, 1980); Rudolf Höhn, *Der schweizerische Aussenhandel mit der Dritten Welt 1972–1978: Struktur, Erklärungsversuche und entwicklungspolitische Bedeutung* (Adliswil: Institut für Sozialethik, 1980); Hugo Aebi and Bruno Messerli, eds., *Die Dritte Welt und Wir* (Bern: Haupt, 1980); and Haymoz, *Finanzplatz Schweiz.*

54. Alexander Melzer, "Die Schweiz und die internationalen Wirtschaftsorganisationen der Dritten Welt," in Senti, *Die Schweiz und die internationalen Wirtschaftsorganisationen*, pp. 156, 161–63; *Neue Zürcher Zeitung*, 15 December 1975; 8 December 1976; and 3 June 1977, 9 May 1976 and 8 December 1976.

55. *Zehnter Bericht zur Aussenwirtschaftspolitik*, 8 February 1978, p. 25; Österreichische Länderbank, *Economic Bulletin*, September 1980, pp. 7–8; and

Helmut Kramer, "Österreich und die Dritte Welt: Am Beispiel der österreichischen Entwicklungshilfe," *Österreichische Zeitschrift für Politikwissenschaft* 7, 3 (1978): 321–40.

56. Paul R. Jolles, *Die Schweiz in den Bestrebungen nach Neuordnung der internationalen Wirschaftsbeziehungen* (Zurich: Schweizerischer Handels- und Industrie-Verein, 1977), p. 21; Jolles, "Beurteilung der Pariser Nord-Süd-Konferenz aus schweizerischer Sicht" (Paper presented at the Generalversammlung der Freiburgischen Handels- und Industriekammer, 16 June 1977); and Jolles, "Die Schweiz in den Nord-Süd Beziehungen," *Documenta* 5 (1976): 17–24. See also *Neue Zürcher Zeitung*, 3 and 6 June 1977; Anselm Skuhra, "Austria and the New International Economic Order: A Survey" (Paper prepared for the ECPR Joint Session workshop on "The Western Response to the New International Economic Order," Florence, 24–29 March 1980), p. 10.

57. United Nations, *Transnational Corporations: A Reexamination*, p. 27.

58. Berweger, *Investition und Legitimation*, pp. 11, 98.

59. Schweizerische Kreditanstalt, *Bulletin* 86, 8–9 (1980), p. 8.

60. *Neue Zürcher Zeitung*, 19 March 1977.

61. *Botschaft des Bundesrates an die Bundesversammlung über einen Beitrag an die Schweizerische Zentrale für Handelsförderung*, 26 February 1975, p. 14. Melzer, "Die Schweiz und die internationalen Wirtschaftsorganisationen," p. 167.

62. Max Pfister, *Die Sonderstellung der Schweiz in der internationalen Wirtschaftspolitik: Aussenwirtschaftspolitik 1945–1959* (Winterthur: Keller, 1971), pp. 247, 232–34. In the late 1950s impending negotiations between Switzerland and the General Agreement on Tariffs and Trade (GATT) made the tactical argument for temporary increases compelling even to free-traders.

63. *World Business Weekly*, 24 December 1979, p. 32.

64. Iklé, *Switzerland*, p. 32; *Wall Street Journal*, 20 May 1982, p. 34.

65. Jöhr, *Finanzplatz Schweiz kontra Exportwirtschaft?* p. 10. Guido A. Keel, "L'influence des groupes d'intérêt politiques sur la politique étrangère Suisse," in Riklin et al., *Handbuch*, p. 298, gives somewhat higher figures.

66. For a brief overview see André Jäggi and Margret Sieber, "Interest Aggregation and Foreign Economic Policy: The Case of Switzerland" (Paper prepared for the ECPR workshop on Interest Groups and Governments, Florence, 25–30 March 1980), pp. 25–44; Peter Bettschart, "Exportförderung in der Schweiz," in *Exportförderung in der Bundesrepublik Deutschland, in der Schweiz und in Österreich: Ergebnisse eines Symposiums vom 9. Oktober 1979 veranstaltet von der Zentralsparkasse und Kommerzbank* (Vienna: Zentralsparkasse und Kommerzbank, 1979), pp. 27–45.

67. *Die Schweiz als Kleinstaat in der Weltwirtschaft*, p. 301.

68. Borner et al., *Structural Analysis*, p. 162. A good schematic overview of different export support policies is given in Rehsche, *Schweizerische Aussenwirtschaftspolitik und Dritte Welt*, pp. 38–41.

69. *Zehnter Bericht zur Aussenwirtschaftspolitik*, p. 45; Bernard Küffer, "Die kollektive Exportwerbung; Dargestellt am Beispiel der gesamtschweizerischen Fremdenverkehrs-, Uhren- und Käsewerbung im Ausland" (Ph.D. diss., University of Bern, 1959), pp. 53–60, 167–72.

70. *Zehnter Bericht*, p. 44; Rehsche, *Schweizerische Aussenwirtschaftspolitik und Dritte Welt*, p. 65; *Finanz und Wirtschaft*, 21 July and 11 September 1976; *Neue*

Zürcher Zeitung, 6 March 1976; Albert Weitenauer, "Aussenpolitik und Aussenwirtschaft: Ausblick auf ein gemeinsames Ziel," *Schweizer Monatshefte* 57 (1977): 713–26; and Schweizerischer Handels- und Industrie-Verein, *Jahresbericht 1976/77,* pp. 29–30.

71. Peter J. Katzenstein, "Domestic Structures and Political Strategies: Austria in an Interdependent World," in Richard Merritt and Bruce Russett, eds., *From National Development to Global Community* (London: Allen & Unwin, 1981), pp. 257–59.

72. Interview, Zurich, 1978.

73. *Botschaft über einen Beitrag an die Schweizerische Zentrale für Handelsförderung,* p. 11. Norway is missing from the group of small states. Among the large advanced industrial states British export subsidies amounted to $76 million. This figure deviated significantly from the $51 million average for the other three European powers.

74. Binswanger and Büchi, "Aussenpolitik," pp. 733–35; Rehsche, *Schweizerische Aussenwirtschaftspolitik und Dritte Welt,* pp. 14–17; Schweizerischer Handels- und Industrie-Verein, *Jahresbericht 1976/77,* pp. 64–66; and Hermann Hofer, "Die Exportrisikogarantie (ERG) als Instrument der Exportförderung," in Willy Linder and Kurt Braendle, eds., *Volkswirtschaft der Schweiz: Dokumentation,* 2d ed. (Zurich: Sozialökonomisches Seminar, University of Zurich, 1978), 2: 231–41.

75. *Finanz und Wirtschaft,* 10 December 1975.

76. Borner et al., *Structural Analysis,* p. 37.

77. Hans-Balz Peter, "Schweizerische Ausfuhr nach Südafrika und Exportrisikogarantie," *Entwicklungsstudien* Paper 19 (Adliswil: Institut für Sozialethik, December 1977), pp. 4–5.

78. *Die Welt,* 12 June 1961; Schweizerischer Handels- und Industrie-Verein, *Jahresbericht 1977/78,* pp. 57–58; Borner et al., *Structural Analysis,* p. 38; Paul R. Jolles, *Die Schweiz in Spannungsfeld der Welthandels-, Währungs- und Rohstoffprobleme* (Zurich: Schweizerischer Handels- und Industrie-Verein, 1975), p. 19; and Helmut Haschek, letter to the author, 22 March 1982.

79. *Neue Zürcher Zeitung,* 10 January 1970; Peter, "Ausfuhr nach Südafrika," p. 5.

80. Helmut Haschek, letter to the author, 22 March 1982; Schweizerischer Handels- und Industrie-Verein, *Jahresbericht 1976/77,* p. 64, *1979/80,* p. 56, *1980/81,* p. 51. In sharp contrast, three-quarters of Switzerland's trade with South Africa is covered by this insurance scheme; see Peter, "Ausfuhr nach Südafrika," p. 1.

81. Borner et al., *Structural Analysis,* p. 39; Schweizerischer Handels- und Industrie-Verein, *Jahresbericht 1976/77,* pp. 28–29; and Gerhard Winterberger, *Die Zusammenarbeit von Staat und Privatwirtschaft bei der Exportförderung* (Zurich: Schweizerischer Handels- und Industrie-Verein, 1976), pp. 13–14.

82. *Die Schweiz im Zeichen des harten Frankens,* p. 13.

83. Rehsche, *Schweizerische Aussenwirtschaftspolitik und Dritte Welt,* p. 63.

84. OECD, *Economic Surveys: Switzerland* (Paris: 1979), p. 30.

85. Naef, *Die Handelsbeziehungen der Schweiz,* p. 86.

86. André Siegfried, *Switzerland: A Democratic Way of Life* (London: Cape, 1950), pp. 68–69.

87. In its trade with West Germany Switzerland's innovation lead is, by this

measure, only three to six times as large; see Crédit Suisse, *Bulletin* 86 (Spring 1980): 20.

88. Felix Streichenberg, *Forschung und volkswirtschaftliches Wachstum unter besonderer Berücksichtigung schweizerischer Verhältnisse* (Bern: Lang, 1968), pp. 114–23. See also OECD, *National Science Policy: Switzerland;* Wolf Linder, Beat Hotz, and Hans Werder, *Planung in der schweizerischen Demokratie* (Bern: Haupt, 1979), pp. 287–312.

89. Volker Ronge, "Spätkapitalismus ohne Politisierung: Forschung und Forschungspolitik in der Schweiz," *Projekt Staat und Ökonomie,* Forschungsbericht 3/77 (Starnberg: 1977), p. 6; *Neue Zürcher Zeitung,* 24 January 1967.

90. Schweizerischer Handels- und Industrie-Verein, *Forschung und Entwicklung in der schweizerischen Privatwirtschaft: Bericht zur Erhebung des Vororts im Jahre 1976* (Zurich: n.d.), pp. 4, 18; Streichenberg, *Forschung,* p. 135.

91. Streichenberg, *Forschung,* p. 120.

92. "Österreich, Schweiz, Schweden," p. 13.

93. Streichenberg, *Forschung,* p. 135; Hubertus G. Tschopp, *Entwicklungstendenzen der Inlandsnachfrage nach Industriegütern in der Schweiz* (Winterthur: Schellenberg, 1973), p. 29; Schweizerischer Handels- und Industrie-Verein, *Forschung und Entwicklung,* pp. 17, 24; and OECD, *National Science Policy: Switzerland,* p. 34. Experts estimate that about one-third of the research and development expenditures are financed by foreign firms.

94. Tschopp, *Entwicklungstendenzen,* p. 29; Schweizerischer Handels- und Industrie-Verein, *Forschung und Entwicklung,* p. 17. The proportion has declined from three-quarters to two-thirds since the late 1960s.

95. Christopher Hughes, *Switzerland* (New York: Praeger, 1975), pp. 178–79; Eric Schiff, *Industrialization without National Patents: The Netherlands 1869–1912, Switzerland 1850–1907* (Princeton: Princeton University Press, 1970).

96. Schweizerischer Handels- und Industrie-Verein, *Jahresbericht 1977/78,* pp. 48–53.

97. Bornschier, *Wachstum von Industrienunternehmen,* p. 454.

98. OECD, *The Research System: Comparative Survey of the Organization and Financing of Fundamental Research* (Paris: 1973), 2: 32–33.

99. *Helvetas Partnerschaft* 20, 79 (March 1980): 8. It should be noted that about one-half of Switzerland's technology exports are not of Swiss origin, but reflect the tax incentives that lure patent corporations (*Patentverwertungsgesellschaften*) to locate in Switzerland.

100. Berweger, *Investition,* pp. 61–62. For different though roughly comparable estimates see Lorenz Stucki, *Das heimliche Imperium: Wie die Schweiz reich wurde* (Bern: Scherz, 1969), p. 339, and Bornschier, *Wachstum von Industrieunternehmen,* p. 402.

101. For general discussions see Kenneth R. Libbey, "The Socialist Party of Switzerland: A Minority Party and Its Political System" (Ph.D. diss., Syracuse University, 1979); François Masnata, *Le Parti Socialiste et la tradition démocratique en Suisse* (Paris: Armand Colin, 1963); Ural Ayberk and Jean-Noël Rey, "Le mouvement syndical dans une société industrielle: Exemple de la Suisse" (Paper prepared for the ECPR Joint Session workshop, Trade Unions and the Political System, Brussels, 17–21 April 1979); François Höpflinger, *Industrie-Gewerkschaften in der Schweiz: Eine soziologische Unter-*

suchung (Zurich: Limmat, 1976); and Höpflinger, *Die anderen Gewerkschaften: Angestellte und Angestelltenverbände in der Schweiz* (Zurich: Econ, 1980).

102. Dieter Greuter, *Der schweizerische Metall- und Uhrenarbeiter-Verband und die Industriegewerkschaft Metall für die Bundesrepublik Deutschland: Ein Vergleich* (Berlin: Duncker & Humblot, 1972), p. 58; *Die Gewerkschaften in der Schweiz: Wesen und Struktur Einst und Jetzt* (Bern: Schweizerische Arbeiterbildungszentrale, 1970), pp. 40, 42–43; and *Die Gewerkschaften in der Schweiz* (Bern: Unionsdruckerei, 1975), pp. 11–12, 15.

103. Höpflinger, *Industrie-Gewerkschaften in der Schweiz*, p. 120.

104. François Höpflinger, "Zum Organisationsgrad bei Angestellten: Daten und Argumente," *Gewerkschaftliche Rundschau* 1979, no. 5: 151; Jürg K. Siegenthaler, "Labor and Politics: Switzerland" (American University, Washington, D.C. n.d. mimeo), pp. 27–28; "Gewerkschaften- und Angestelltenverbände," in Frey, ed., *Schweizer Dokumentation*, p. 2; Crossland, "The Everlasting League," Survey, p. 11; and Jürg K. Siegenthaler, *Die Politik der Gewerkschaften: Eine Untersuchung der öffentlichen Funktionen schweizerischer Gewerkschaften nach dem Zweiten Weltkrieg* (Bern: Francke, 1968), p. 15. For earlier estimates see Jean Meynaud, *Les organisations professionnelles en Suisse* (Lausanne: Payot, 1963), pp. 15–17.

105. Jürg K. Siegenthaler, "Decision-making in Swiss Labor Unions," *Proceedings of the 22nd Annual Meeting of the Industrial Relations Research Association* (Madison, Wisc.: n.d.), p. 195.

106. Libbey, "The Socialist Party," p. 151.

107. Ibid., pp. 155–56. On the politics of the Swiss Left see also Hansueli von Gunten and Hans Voegeli, *Das Verhältnis der Sozialdemokratischen Partei zu andern Linksparteien in der Schweiz (1912–1980)* (Bern: Verlag für politische Bildung, 1980).

108. Siegenthaler, "Labor and Politics," pp. 13–15.

109. Libbey, "The Socialist Party," p. 138. On parliamentary activities see Siegenthaler, "Labor and Politics," p. 29.

110. Höpflinger, *Industrie-Gewerkschaften*, pp. 62–96.

111. Raimund Germann and Andreas Frutiger, "Les experts et la politique," *Revue suisse de sociologie* 4 (June 1978): 110. See also Germann and Frutiger, "Role Cumulation in Swiss Advisory Committees" (Paper prepared for the ECPR workshop on "Interest Groups and Governments," Florence, 25–30 March 1980), pp. 8, 10, 16, for essentially the same conclusion for the years 1970–77.

112. Erich Gruner, *Die Parteien in der Schweiz* (Bern: Francke, 1969), p. 189.

113. Roland Ruffieux, "The Political Influence of Senior Civil Servants in Switzerland," in Mattei Dogan, ed., *The Mandarins of Western Europe: The Political Role of Top Civil Servants* (New York: Wiley, 1975), p. 242.

114. *New York Times*, 5 June 1979, p. D4.

115. OECD, *Economic Surveys: Switzerland* (1972), pp. 49–52.

116. Gerhard Winterberger, *Politik und Wirtschaft* (Bern: Berner Handelskammer, 1970), p. 3.

117. E. Wüthrich, *Verbände und Politik* Bern: Schweizerischer Metall- und Uhrenarbeiter-Verband, 1963), p. 15.

118. OECD, *Economic Surveys: Switzerland* (1979), p. 24.

119. Heidi Schelbert, "Stabilisierungspolitik in kleinen offenen Volkswirtschaften: Das Beispiel Schweiz," *Schweizerische Zeitschrift für Volkswirtschaft und*

Statistik 115, 3 (1979): 280; Hans Schaffner, "Konstanten der schweizerischen Wirtschaftspolitik," *Arbeitgeberpolitik in der Nachkriegszeit 1948 bis 1967* (Zurich: Zentralverband schweizerischer Arbeitgeber-Organisationen, 1968), p. 91; and Egon Tuchtfeldt, *Wachstumprobleme der schweizerischen Volkswirtschaft,* Kieler Vorträge, no. 40 (Kiel: Institut für Weltwirtschaft, 1965), pp. 6, 8–12.

120. *World Business Weekly,* 2 June 1980, p. 24. In 1980 only 10,000 new work permits were issued, despite a severe labor shortage. OCED, *Economic Surveys: Switzerland* (1979), p. 15; OECD, Manpower and Social Affairs Committee, "Report to the Council of the Working Party on Migration" (Paris, 4 April 1980, mimeo), p. 15.

121. Ernst Schwarb, "Arbeitsmarkt und Fremdarbeiterpolitik," in *Arbeitgeberpolitik,* p. 215; Iklé, *Switzerland,* p. 46.

122. *Die Schweiz im Zeichen des harten Franken,* p. 9; *Lage und Probleme der schweizerischen Wirtschaft,* 1: 115; Schweizerischer Gewerkschaftsbund, *Tätigkeitsbericht 1975–1977* (n.p.: n.d.), p. 63; and OECD, *Economic Surveys: Switzerland* (1976), pp. 16–19.

123. *World Business Weekly,* 2 June 1980, p. 24.

124. Küng, *Secret of Switzerland's Economic Success,* p. 2.

125. Lester C. Thurow, "Inflation: We're Fighting Yesterday's War," *New York Times,* 21 October 1979, Section F, p. 16.

126. Höpflinger, *Industrie-Gewerkschaften,* pp. 106–19; Jürg K. Siegenthaler, "Current Problems of Trade Union-Party Relations in Switzerland: Reorientation versus Inertia," *Industrial and Labor Relations Review* 28 (January 1975): 276; and René Riedo, *Das Problem der ausländischen Arbeitskräfte in der schweizerischen Gewerkschaftspolitik von 1945–1970* (Bern: Lang, 1976).

127. Höpflinger, *Industrie-Gewerkschaften,* p. 117; Hughes, *Switzerland,* p. 170. The proportion of foreign workers in the Christian union is about 15 percent. The only exceptions are the construction unions, which organize foreign workers in large numbers; but the construction industry was hit hardest by the deflationary policies that the Swiss pursued in the 1970s and has thus suffered the greatest job attrition. There exist no precise figures on the unionization of foreign workers. One paper cites a survey according to which 15 percent of the foreign workers in Zurich are unionized. A second paper cites a unionization figure of 20 percent for foreign workers and 30 percent for Swiss workers in the mid-1970s. See, respectively, Dietrich Thränhardt, "Ausländische Arbeiter in der Bundesrepublik, in Österreich und der Schweiz," *Neue Politische Literatur* 20, 1 (1975): 77, and Mark J. Miller, "The Political Impacts of Foreign Labor: A Reevaluation of the European Experience" (Paper prepared for the International Studies Association convention, 20–22 March 1980, Los Angeles), p. 21.

128. Höpflinger, *Industrie-Gewerkschaften,* p. 116. See also *New York Times,* 6 April 1981, p. A2.

129. Thränhardt, "Ausländische Arbeiter," p. 82.

130. "Österreich, Schweiz, Schweden," p. 12. This statistical lag is to some extent the result of the character of Switzerland's education system. Many Swiss engineers do not receive an academic but a semi-academic, vocational training in Switzerland's excellent Higher Technical Institutes (Höhere Technische Lehranstalten). These are not reported as universities. The statistical lag is also widened by the prominent role that the research laboratories of the large corporations play in the training of technical cadres.

131. Meyer, "Switzerland," p. 21; *Neue Zürcher Zeitung,* 24 January 1967; and OECD, *National Science Policy: Switzerland,* pp. 89–90, 92.

132. Arnold Saxer, *Die soziale Sicherheit in der Schweiz,* 4th ed. (Bern: Haupt, 1977), pp. 244–69; Hans Peter Tschudi, "Die Entwicklung der schweizerischen Sozialversicherung seit dem Zweiten Weltkrieg," *Schweizerische Zeitschrift für Volkswirtschaft und Statistik,* 112, 3 (1976): 312; and William M. Yoffee, *International Social Security Agreements: Totalization, Equality of Treatment and Other Measures to Protect International Migrant Workers* (Washington, D.C.: U.S. Department of Health, Education, and Welfare, 1973).

133. Max Holzer, "Die Schweiz und die Europäische Sozialcharta," *Schweizerische Zeitschrift für Sozialversicherung* 1968, no. 4: 252–53.

134. Ziegler, *Switzerland: The Awful Truth,* p. 121.

135. Mark J. Miller, "French and Swiss Seasonal Workers: Western Europe's Braceros" (Paper presented at the 1980 Europeanist Conference, sponsored by the Council for European Studies, Washington, D.C.), p. 13 and note 49.

136. Kurt Mayer, "Foreign Workers in Switzerland and Austria," *European Demographic Bulletin* 2 (1971): 97; Hans-Joachim Hoffman-Nowotny and Martin Killias, "Switzerland," in Ronald E. Krane, ed., *International Labor Migration in Europe* (New York: Praeger, 1979), pp. 45, 47, 57.

137. *New York Times,* 6 April 1981, p. A2.

138. *Neue Zürcher Zeitung,* 3 November 1975. A similar episode with less drastic cuts is reported in *Neue Zürcher Zeitung,* 25 August 1967. The 1975 cut was later reconsidered; the contribution of the federal government was gradually being increased in the late 1970s and regained the 1974 level in the early 1980s.

139. Gerhard Winterberger, *Die Erhaltung der Wettbewerbskraft der schweizerischen Wirtschaft* (Zurich: Schweizerischer Handels- und Industrie-Verein, 1976), pp. 12–14. See also Max Weber, *Geschichte der schweizerischen Bundesfinanzen* (Bern: Haupt, 1969); Josef Stofer, "Ein Erklärungsversuch der wachsenden Staatstätigkeit in der Schweiz" (Ph.D. diss., University of Freiburg/Switzerland, 1971); Hans Müller-Bodmer, Alfred Meier, Heinz Hauser, and Max Rössler, *Die Einnahmen und Ausgaben von Bund, Kantonen und Gemeinden* (Bern: Haupt, 1973); Hans Letsch, *Öffentliche Finanzen und Finanzpolitik in der Schweiz* (Bern: Haupt, 1972); and OECD, *Economic Surveys: Switzerland* (1974), pp. 34–47.

140. Walter Wittmann, *Reform des schweizerischen Subventionswesens* (Zurich: Schweizerische Bankgesellschaft, 1978), p. 3; Schweizerischer Gewerkschaftsbund, *Tätigkeitsbericht 1972, 1973, 1974* (n.p.: n.d.), p. 80; Kurt Schiltknecht, "Economic Policy in Switzerland," in *Economic Policy in West Germany, Switzerland, and Austria: Readings from the Symposium held at the Z-Bank/Zentralsparkasse on November 23, 1978* (Vienna: Zentralsparkasse der Gemeinde Wien, 1979), pp. 38–39; and Yann Richter, "Nach dem 20. Mai," *SKA-Bulletin* 85 (May–June 1979): 3.

141. OECD, *Public Expenditure Trends,* p. 14. The comparative analysis of Swiss public expenditure is impaired by discontinuities in the statistical data. Due to a technical redefinition in the OECD data, public expenditures declined by more than 4 percent in 1968. See G. Warren Nutter, *Growth of Government in the West* (Washington, D.C.: American Enterprise Institute, 1978), pp. 84–85. For statistical data see also *Lage und Probleme der schweizerischen Wirtschaft: Gutachten 1977–1978,* 1: 80–81; Paolo Urio, "Parliamentary

Control over Public Expenditures in Switzerland," in David L. Coombes, ed., *The Power of the Purse: A Symposium on the Role of European Parliaments in Budgetary Decisions* (New York: Praeger, 1975), pp. 313–38; and George A. Codding Jr., "Financing a Federal Government: The Swiss Example," *German Studies Review* 2 (February 1979): 63–87.

142. OECD, *Economic Surveys: Switzerland* (1980), p. 38.

143. Silvio Borner-Barth, "Budgetpolitik in der Schweiz," in *Budgetpolitik in der Bundesrepublik Deutschland, in der Schweiz und in Österreich* (Vienna: Zentralsparkasse und Kommerzialbank, 1979), pp. 7, 16–17.

144. Manfred G. Schmidt, "Wohlfahrtsstaatliche Politik unter bürgerlichen und sozialdemokratischen Regierungen" (University of Constance, October 1980, mimeo), p. 173.

145. *Die Arbeitsbeschaffungsprogramme 1975/76: Schlussbericht des Bundesamtes für Konjunkturfragen* (Bern: Bundesamt für Konjunkturfragen, 1980); Peter Schwarz and Ernst-Bernd Blümle, "Öffentliche Betriebe in der Schweiz: Bemerkungen zu ihrer betriebswirtschaftlichen Behandlung, ihren Formen und ihrer Bedeutung," *Zeitschrift für öffentliche und gemeinswirtschaftliche Unternehmen* 3, 3 (1980): 309–31.

146. These figures are conservative because they refer only to direct effects. Estimates of the multiplier (2.0) given in the report appear, however, to be quite high.

147. "Arbeitsbeschaffungsreserven der privaten Wirtschaft: Die Arbeitsbeschaffungsaktion 1975/76 im Rückblick," *Mitteilungsblatt für Konjunkturfragen* 37, 1 (1981): 2–5.

148. Peter Tschudi, "Der schweizerische Sozialstaat: Realität und Verpflichtung," in Tuchtfeldt, *Schweizerische Wirtschaftspolitik*, pp. 133, 138–39, 143; Kurt Sovilla, "Die schweizerische Sozialversicherung," in *Arbeitgeberpolitik*, pp. 195–96, 207; and Saxer, *Die soziale Sicherheit*, pp. 98–106. For comparative material see William C. Greenough, *Pension Plans and Public Policy* (New York: Columbia University Press, 1976).

149. Schweizerischer Metall- und Uhrenarbeitnehmer-Verband, *Geschäftsbericht 1973, 1974, 1975* (n.p.: SMUV, n.d.), p. 313. Slightly different figures are given in Hans Peter Tschudi, "Die Altersvorsorge auf der neuen Verfassungsgrundlage," in *Schweizerische Zeitschrift für Sozialversicherung* 1974, no. 3: 172.

150. Max Frischknecht, "Der Entwurf zu einem Bundesgesetz über die obligatorische berufliche Vorsorge," *Schweizerische Zeitschrift für Sozialversicherung* 1976, no. 2; 73–98; Tschudi, "Die Entwicklung der schweizerischen Sozialversicherung," p. 323; and Schweizerischer Metall- und Uhrenarbeitnehmerverband, *Geschäftsbericht 1973, 1974, 1975*, p. 373. Zentralverband Schweizerischer Arbeitgeber-Organisationen, *Jahresbericht 1980: 73. Berichtsjahr* (n.p.: n.d.), pp. 62–70.

151. Victor Ziegler, *Die Auswirkungen der betrieblichen Versicherungs- und Fürsorgeeinrichtungen auf die Faktoren des volkswirtschaftlichen Wachstums in der Schweiz* (Zurich: Keller, 1967), pp. 22–23; Saxer, *Soziale Sicherheit*, p. 105; and Alfred Maurer, "Wechselwirkungen zwischen Sozialversicherung und Volkswirtschaft," *Schweizerische Zeitschrift für Sozialversicherung* 1969, no. 3: 188.

152. Jean François Aubert, *So funktioniert die Schweiz: Dargestellt anhand einiger konkreter Beispiele*, 2d ed. (Muri/Bern: Cosmos, 1981), p. 95.

153. Linder and Braendle, *Volkswirtschaft der Schweiz*, 1: 401; Hans Werder,

Die Bedeutung der Volksinitiative in der Nachkriegszeit (Bern: Francke, 1978), p. 61, note 54.

154. Rainer E. Gut, *Entwicklungstendenzen der Züricher Börse* (Zurich: Schweizerische Kreditanstalt, 1977), p. 4.

155. J. Steiger, *Zweite Säule: Sozialwerk oder Geschäft?* (Zurich: Limmat, 1977), pp. 31–32.

156. Ziegler, *Auswirkungen der Fürsorgeeinrichtungen*, pp. 26, 93–94. Linder and Braendle, *Volkswirtschaft der Schweiz*, 1: 401.

157. Ernst Heissmann, *Blick über die Grenzen: Die betriebliche und staatliche Altersversorgung in 20 Ländern* (Wiesbaden: Verlag Arbeit und Alter, 1963), p. 54; Linder and Braendle, *Volkswirtschaft der Schweiz*, 1: 402.

158. Karl Hartmann, *Subsidiarität und Föderalismus in der schweizerischen Sozialpolitik* (Winterthur: Schellenberg, 1971), p. 79; Gut, *Entwicklungstendenzen*, p. 5; and A. Schaefer, *The Banks in a Time of Challenge* (Zurich: Union Bank of Switzerland, 1975), p. 10. A major portion of private insurance is now taken out in the form of life insurance; see Wilhelm Bickel, *Die Volkswirtschaft der Schweiz: Entwicklung und Struktur* (Aarau: Sauerländer, 1973), pp. 352–53, 359. The relative share of individual savings in total public and private, institutional and individual payments has declined from about 50 percent at the end of World War II to 44 percent in the mid-1960s, to 30 percent in the 1970s. See Hans Wyss, "AHV, Quo Vadis?" *Schweizerische Zeitschrift für Sozialversicherung* 1969, no. 3: 179–80.

159. "International Insurance—Swiss Style," Survey, p. xxxvi; "Not All Cake and Chocolate," *World Business Weekly*, 25 May 1981, p. 45. In 1979 the average family spent 14.6 percent of its income on insurance, 12.8 percent on food, and 12.6 percent on leisure and education.

160. OECD *Public Expenditure Trends*, pp. 42–45; Harold L. Wilensky, *The "New Corporatism", Centralization, and the Welfare State* (Beverly Hills, Calif.: Sage, 1976), p. 16; Schweizerischer Handels- und Industrie-Verein, *Jahresbericht 1977/78*, p. 35; and *Social Security in Ten Industrial Nations* (Zurich: Union Bank of Switzerland, 1977) pp. 26, 32.

161. *Social Security in Ten Industrial Nations*, p. 28. Japan is not included in this sample of countries. See also Walter Hess, *Ökonomische Aspekte der sozialen Sicherung: Eine Untersuchung über die umverteilungs-, konjunktur- und wachstumspolitische Bedeutung des Sozialversicherungshaushaltes unter besonderer Berücksichtigung der schweizerischen Verhältnisse* (Bern: Haupt, 1975), pp. 161–62.

162. OECD, *Public Expenditure Trends*, p. 22.

163. In general see Saxer, *Soziale Sicherheit;* Edwin Schweingruber, *Sozialgesetzgebung der Schweiz: Ein Grundriss*, 2d ed. (Zurich: Schulthess, 1977); Georg Macciacchini, *Ökonomische und finanzwirtschaftliche Aspekte der schweizerischen Sozialversicherung* (Winterthur: Keller, 1966); Tschudi, "Der schweizerische Sozialstaat"; Sovilla, "Die schweizerische Sozialversicherung"; and Siegenthaler, *Die Politik der Gewerkschaften*, pp. 51–78.

164. Peter Flora in collaboration with Jens Alber and Jürgen Kohl, "On the Development of the Western European Welfare States," *Historical Indicators of the Western European Democracies*, Report no. 5 (Mannheim: 1976), pp. 27–28. The index consists of the weighted average of the percentage of the labor force covered by the four main insurance schemes. See also David Collier and Richard E. Messick, "Prerequisites versus Diffusion: Testing Alternative Ex-

planations of Social Security Adoption," *American Political Science Review* 69 (December 1975): 1299–1315.

165. Wilensky, *The "New Corporatism,"* p. 11. Unfortunately Switzerland is not covered by the OECD, *Public Expenditure on Income Maintenance* (Paris: OECD, 1976).

166. Max Horlick, *Supplemental Security Income for the Aged: A Comparison of Five Countries* (U.S. Department of Health, Education and Welfare, Social Security Administration, Office of Research and Statistics, DHEW Publication no. (SSA) 74-11850, Staff Paper no. 15, 1973), p. 72.

167. Wittmann, *Reform des schweizerischen Subventionswesens*, p. 21; Crossland, "The Everlasting League," Survey, p. 14; Tschudi, "Die Entwicklung der schweizerischen Sozialversicherung," pp. 313, 316; *Social Security in Ten Industrial Nations*, p. 27; and Tschudi, "Die Altersvorsorge auf der neuen Verfassungsgrundlage," p. 176.

168. Gradual improvements in the public plan, especially in the second half of the 1960s, roughly equalized the importance of the public and the private pillars of Swiss social security. Only with the sharp expansion of public pensions in 1973 when, following a referendum, benefits almost doubled from one year to the next, did the relative importance of private pensions fall to about 60 percent of public pensions. For the 1950s and 1960s see Ziegler, *Die Auswirkungen der betrieblichen Versicherungs- und Fürsorgeeinrichtungen*, pp. 29–31; Wyss, "AHV, Quo Vadis?" pp. 173–74. For the late 1960s see ibid., pp. 179–80; Hans Wyss, "AHV und Pensionskassen," *Schweizerische Zeitschrift für Sozialversicherung* 1970, no. 3: 167; and Saxer, *Soziale Sicherheit*, p. 105. For the mid-1970s see Schweizerischer Handels- und Industrie-Verein, *Jahresbericht 1976–77*, p. 34; *Sozialversicherung in der Schweiz*, IVW, Beiträge zur Sicherheitsökonomik, 1 (St. Gallen, 1977), p. 10; and Aubert, *So funktioniert die Schweiz*, p. 101. A somewhat different estimate is given in Frischknecht, "Entwurf zu einem Bundesgesetz," p. 259.

169. *Lage und Probleme der schweizerischen Wirtschaft*, p. 360.

170. *Social Security in Ten Industrial Nations*. This comparison is based on both public and private pension plans. These data are biased in favor of Switzerland because they are drawn from only one rich canton, Zurich. See also Willy Schweizer, *Die wirtschaftliche Lage der Rentner in der Schweiz* (Bern: Haupt, 1980), 1: 144, 146.

171. Schweingruber, *Sozialgesetzgebung der Schweiz*, p. 31.

172. Karl Meyer, *Verbände und Demokratie in der Schweiz* (Olten: Dietschi, 1968), p. 45; Sidjanski, "Interest Groups in Switzerland," p. 105; and Bundesamt für Industrie, Gewerbe und Arbeit, *Verzeichnis schweizerischer Berufs- und Wirtschaftsverbände*, 13th ed. (Bern: Verlag des Schweizerischen Handelsamtsblattes, 1974). See also Hanspeter Kriesi, "Collaborative Relationships in Swiss Politics: Interest Associations and the Federal Government" (Paper prepared for the Special Session on "Voluntary Groups in Modern Society— Current Transnational Research Issues," IX World Congress of Sociology, Uppsala, Sweden, August 1978); Peter Heintz, "Die Interessenartikulation durch Verbände in der Schweiz" (Paper prepared for the international colloquium on Pre- and Extra-Parliamentary Solution of Conflicts in Industrial Democracies, Zurich, Forschungsstelle für Politische Wissenschaft, December 1977).

173. Jürg Steiner, *Gewaltlose Politik und kulturelle Vielfalt: Hypothesen entwick-elt am Beispiel der Schweiz* (Bern: Haupt, 1970), p. 127; Steiner, *Amicable Agreement versus Majority Rule: Conflict Resolution in Switzerland* (Chapel Hill: University of North Carolina Press, 1970), p. 110; and Klaus Schumann, *Das Regierungssystem der Schweiz* (Cologne: Heymanns, 1971), pp. 127–28.

174. Christopher Hughes, *The Parliament of Switzerland* (London: Cassell, 1962), p. 34.

175. Ibid., p. 34; Bernhard Wehrli, *Aus der Geschichte des Schweizerischen Handels- und Industrie-Vereins: Zum hundertjährigen Bestehen des Vororts* (Erlenbach-Zurich: Rentsch, 1970); and Wehrli, *The Vorort: A Leading Voice of Swiss Business* (Zurich: Swiss Federation of Commerce and Industry, 1975). Unfortunately no detailed case studies examine the role of the Swiss Federation of Commerce and Industry in the policy process. Hanspeter Kriesi of the University of Zurich is currently conducting research on this question.

176. Wehrli, *Aus der Geschichte*, p. 98.

177. Wehrli, *Aus der Geschichte*, pp. 104–5.

178. *Gewerkschaften in der Schweiz* (1975), pp. 42–43.

179. Siegenthaler, *Politik der Gewerkschaften*, p. 155.

180. Greuter, *Der schweizerische Metall-Verband*, p. 141; Siegenthaler, *Politik der Gewerkschaften*, pp. 65, 158–70.

181. Höpflinger, *Industrie-Gewerkschaften*, pp. 48, 82–83; Greuter, *Der schweizerische Metall-Verband*, p. 41.

182. *Gewerkschaften in der Schweiz* (1970), pp. 40–43; Siegenthaler, *Politik der Gewerkschaften*, pp. 80–81, 160–62; and Höpflinger, *Industrie-Gewerkschaften*, p. 92.

183. Siegenthaler, *Politik der Gewerkschaften*, pp. 90, 49.

184. *Gewerkschaften in der Schweiz* (1970), pp. 24–25; Siegenthaler, *Politik der Gewerkschaften*, pp. 21–33.

185. Ulrich Klöti, *Die Chefbeamten der schweizerischen Bundesverwaltung* (Bern: Francke, 1972), p. 144; F. Höpflinger and G. Geser, "'Active' and 'Passive' Innovations in Swiss Public Administration" (University of Zurich, n.d., mimeo); and Jürg Steiner, "Politische Prozesse," in Steiner, ed., *Das politische System der Schweiz* (Munich: Piper, 1971) pp. 130, 154.

186. Beedham and Lee, "Even in Paradise," Survey, p. 5.

187. Klöti, *Chefbeamten*, p. 10. This fusion of function expresses a more general lack of staff-line distinctions characteristic of Swiss organizational structures; see H. Geser and F. Höpflinger, *Vier kantonale Verwaltungen im Vergleich* (Zurich: Soziologisches Institut, University of Zurich, 1977), p. 3. See also Thomas A. Baylis, "Collegial Leadership in Advanced Industrial Societies: The Relevance of the Swiss Experience," *Polity* 13 (Fall 1980): 33–56; Schumann, *Das Regierungssystem der Schweiz*, pp. 178–234.

188. Harold E. Glass, "Consensual Politics, Class and Dissatisfaction in Switzerland: The Importance of Institutions," *Kleine Studien zur Politischen Wissenschaft* no. 80 (Zurich: Forschungsstelle für Politische Wissenschaft, University of Zurich, 1976): 27.

189. Geser and Höpflinger, *Vier Verwaltungen*, pp. 1–2; Klöti, *Chefbeamten*, p. 152; Schumann, *Das Regierungssystem der Schweiz*, pp. 202–6; Willy Bretscher, "Das Verhältnis von Bundesversammlung und Bundesrat in der Führung der auswärtigen Politik," *Jahrbuch der Schweizer Vereinigung für*

Politische Wissenschaften 6 (1966): 7–27; and Armin Daenike, "Die Rolle der Verwaltung in der schweizerischen Aussenpolitik," ibid., pp. 61–74.

190. Hanspeter Kriesi, *Entscheidungsstrukturen und Entscheidungsprozesse in der schweizer Politik* (Frankfurt: Campus, 1980), p. 35. The numbers changed from 14,000 in 1940 to 29,600 in 1945, 21,000 in 1950, and about 32,000 in 1976.

191. Meynaud, *Les organisations professionnelles en Suisse*, p. 313, as quoted in Ruffieux, "Political Influence of Senior Civil Servants," p. 250.

192. Germann and Frutiger, "Role Cumulation in Swiss Advisory Committees," pp. 1–3.

193. OECD, *Public Expenditure Trends*, p. 90. This picture is consistent with another cross-national study of economic policy; see Gottfried Berweger and Jean-Pierre Hoby, "Typologien für Wirtschaftspolitik" (Sociology Institute, University of Zurich, mimeo, 1978), pp. 6–8.

194. Gerhard Winterberger, *Probleme der schweizerischen Wirtschaftspolitik* (Bern: Stämpfli, 1957), p. 18; Ilké, *Switzerland;* and Tuchtfeldt, *Wachstumprobleme der schweizerischen Volkswirtschaft,* p. 13. On the restrictions imposed on Switzerland's monetary and fiscal policy see respectively OECD, *Economic Surveys: Switzerland* (1966), pp. 22–27, (1970), pp. 41–44.

195. Hans Schaffner, *Dauer und Wandel in der schweizerischen Wirtschaft* (Zurich: Schweizerischer Handels- und Industrie-Verein, 1970), p. 9.

196. Winterberger, *Probleme der Wirtschaftspolitik,* p. 49.

197. See, for example, *New York Times,* 5 June 1979, pp. D1, D4; Crossland, "The Everlasting League," Survey p. 28; *World Business Weekly,* 5 May 1980, p. 52; and Cohen, "Structural Change in International Banking," p. 70.

198. *New York Times,* 5 June 1979, p. D4.

199. *Wall Street Journal,* 27 April 1982, p. 31.

200. Iklé, *Switzerland,* p. 34; George A. Codding, *The Federal Government of Switzerland* (Boston: Houghton Mifflin, 1965), p. 135.

201. Steinberg, *Why Switzerland?,* p. 156.

202. Leonhard Neidhart, *Plebiszit und pluralitäre Demokratie: Eine Analyse der Funktion des schweizerischen Gesetzesreferendums* (Bern: Francke, 1970), pp. 313–19; Schumann, *Das Regierungssytem der Schweiz,* pp. 250–52.

203. Kriesi, *Entscheidungsstrukturen und Entscheidungsprozesse,* pp. 108–13, 177–232, 247, 263–64, 335–38, 359, 437, 574, 587–682; Beat Hotz, *Politik zwischen Staat und Wirtschaft: Verbandsmässige Bearbeitung wirtschaftlicher Probleme und die daraus resultierenden Konsequenzen für die Aktivitäten des Staates im Falle der Schweiz* (Diessenhofen: Rüegger, 1979); Linder, Hotz, and Werder, *Planung in der schweizerischen Demokratie;* Marjorie Mowlam, "The Impact of Direct Democracy on the Influence of Voters, Members of Parliament and Interest Group Leaders in Switzerland" (Ph.D. diss., University of Iowa, 1977), pp. 51–53; Werder, *Die Bedeutung der Volksinitiative,* p. 39; Beat Hotz and Hans Werder, "Bedingungen Politischer Planung in der Schweiz," *Annuaire suisse de science politique* 16 (1976): 79, 88–93; Walter Buser, "Fallen die Entscheide im Vorverfahren der Gesetzgebung?" *Documenta Helvetica* 1976, no. 1: 10–15; Hanspeter Kriesi, "Interne Verfahren bei der Ausarbeitung von Stellungnahmen in Vernehmlassungsverfahren," *Annuaire suisse de science politique* 19 (1979): 233–58; Georges Guggenheim, "Das Vernehmlassungsverfahren im Bund: Eine statistische Untersuchung 1970–1976," *Kleine*

Studien zur Politischen Wissenschaft nos. 142–143 (Zurich: Forschungsstelle für Politische Wissenschaft, University of Zurich, 1978); and André Jaeggi, "Between Parliamentary Weakness and Bureaucratic Strength: Interest Representation in Swiss Foreign Relations" (Paper prepared for the ECPR workshop on "Interest Representation in Mixed Polities," Lancaster, 29 March–4 April 1981).

204. Germann and Frutiger, "Role Cumulation," pp. 1–3.

205. Erich Gruner, *Politische Führungsgruppen im Bundesstaat* (Bern: Francke, 1973), p. 11.

206. Bobby Gierisch, "Interest Groups in Swiss Politics" (Institute of Sociology, University of Zurich, 1974, mimeo), p. 76. A partial updating that confirms this conclusion can be found in Mowlam, "Impact of Direct Democracy," p. 78.

207. Erwin Ruchti, *Wirtschaftspolitische Ketzereien: Kritische Anmerkungen zur schweizerischen Wirtschaftspolitik* (Bern: Haupt, 1976), p. 19.

208. Mowlam, "Impact of Direct Democracy," pp. 83–84.

209. Meynaud, *Organisations professionnelles en Suisse*, p. 312.

210. Germann and Frutiger, "Role Cumulation," pp. 1–3. The cumulation of roles is particularly common on politicized issues and questions of economic policy. See also Germann and Frutiger, "Les experts et la politique," pp. 99–127.

211. Gierisch, "Interest Groups," pp. 29, 75, 121; Sidjanski, "Interest Groups," p. 107.

212. Gierisch, "Interest Groups in Switzerland," p. 121; Siegenthaler, *Politik der Gewerkschaften*, p. 137. A similar tendency is also observable in political parties; see Steiner, *Gewaltlose Politik*, pp. 125–26.

213. The institution of direct democracy is considered by some students to be one important reason why Switzerland should not be thought of as a consociational system. See, for example, Brian Barry, "[Review Article:] Political Accommodation and Consociational Democracy," *British Journal of Political Science* 5 (October 1975): 481–90. On the referendum in general see Schumann, *Das Regierungssystem der Schweiz*, pp. 235–62; Jean-François Aubert, "Switzerland," in David Butler and Austin Ranney, eds., *Referendums: A Comparative Study of Practice and Theory* (Washington, D.C.: American Enterprise Institute, 1978), pp. 39–66. See also Roland Ruffieux et al., *La démocratie referendaire en Suisse au XXe siècle*, vol. 1: *Analyse de cas* (Fribourg: Éditions universitaires Fribourg, Suisse, 1972).

214. Neidhart, *Plebiszit und pluralitäre Demokratie*, pp. 247–319; Berweger, *Investition*, pp. 218–19; Erich Gruner, *Regierung und Opposition im schweizerischen Bundesstaat* (Bern: Haupt, 1969), pp. 12–15; and Gerhard Lehmbruch, "Konkordanzdemokratie im politischen System der Schweiz," *Politische Vierteljahresschrift* 9 (1968): 455.

215. Kriesi, *Entscheidungsstrukturen und Entscheidungsprozesse*, pp. 656–57.

216. Computed from data in Aubert, "Switzerland," pp. 50–64.

217. Aubert, "Switzerland," pp. 45, 50–64. See also Steinberg, *Why Switzerland?* p. 56; Benjamin R. Barber, *The Death of Communal Liberty: A History of Freedom in a Swiss Mountain Canton* (Princeton: Princeton University Press, 1974), p. 227; Schumann, *Das Regierungssystem der Schweiz*, pp. 236, 241–43; and Alois Riklin, *Stimmabstinenz und direkte Demokratie* (Zurich: Schweizerischer Aufklärungsdienst, 1979).

218. Gierisch, "Interest Groups," p. 50.

219. Kriesi, *Entscheidungsstrukturen und Entscheidungsprozesse*. See also Werder, *Bedeutung der Volksinitiative*, p. 10; Aubert, "Switzerland," pp. 50–64; and Benno Homann, "Direct Democracy: Towards a New Theory Based on Recent Developments in Switzerland" (Paper prepared for the ECPR workshop on "Referenda as New Forms of Participation," Lancaster, 29 March–4 April 1981).

220. Libbey, "The Socialist Party," pp. 195–97; Schumann, *Das Regierungssystem der Schweiz*, p. 240. Spokesmen of the far right thus reject Switzerland's concordance system and are ardent supporters of the referendum democracy. See Kriesi, *Entscheidungsstrukturen und Entscheidungsprozesse*, pp. 668–69.

221. Werder, *Bedeutung der Volksinitiative*, pp. 10, 22, 26, 30, 32, 35–56, 65, 97.

222. Ibid., pp. 46–48; Ruchti, *Wirtschaftspolitische Ketzereien*, pp. 23, 38–39; Neidhardt, *Plebiszit und pluralitäre Demokratie*, p. 294; and Kurt Nüssli and Erwin Ruegg, "Ziele und Massnahmen in den Richtlinien der Regierungspolitik 1975–1979," *Kleine Studien zur Politischen Wissenschaft* nos. 131–132 (Zurich: Forschungsstelle für Politische Wissenschaft, 1978), pp. 14, 30–38. A more general treatment of this theme can be found in Raimund E. Germann, *Politische Innovation und Verfassungsreform: Ein Beitrag zur schweizerischen Diskussion über die Totalrevision der Bundesverfassung* (Bern: Haupt, 1975).

223. Baylis, "Collegial Leadership," p. 14.

224. Margret Sieber and Hans Werder, "Environmental Politics in Switzerland: Do Plebiscitary Rights Matter?" (Paper prepared for the ECPR workshop on "Environmental Politics and Policy," Lancaster, 29 March–4 April 1981).

225. Steiner, "Politische Prozesse," p. 133.

226. Lehmbruch, "Konkordanzdemokratie," pp. 444, 446; Gruner, *Regierung und Opposition*, pp. 21, 40; Steiner, "Politische Prozesse," p. 138; Erich Gruner, "100 Jahre Wirtschaftspolitik: Etappen des Interventionismus in der Schweiz," *Schweizer Zeitschrift für Volkswirtschaft und Statistik* 100, 1–2 (1964): 58–59, 66–67; and Gierisch, "Interest Groups," pp. 75, 80, Appendix; Schumann, *Das Regierungssystem der Schweiz*, pp. 132–45. Good summaries of case studies of Swiss public policy can be found in Neidhart, *Plebiszit und pluralitäre Demokratie*, pp. 247–319; Sidjanski, "Interest Groups in Switzerland," pp. 106–15; Siegenthaler, *Politik der Gewerkschaften*, pp. 34–106; Steiner, *Gewaltlose Politik*, pp. 149–260; and Steiner, "Politische Prozesse," pp. 129–62.

227. Paul Hofmann, "The Swiss Malaise," *New York Times Sunday Magazine*, 8 February 1981, p. 59.

228. Kriesi, *Entscheidungsstrukturen und Entscheidungsprozesse*, p. 688.

229. Gierisch, "Interest Groups," pp. 117, 120, 138, 141, 144.

230. Jürg Steiner, "Conclusion: Reflections on the Consociational Theme," in Howard R. Penniman, ed., *Switzerland at the Polls* (Washington D.C.: American Enterprise Institute, 1983), p. 168.

231. Höpflinger, *Das unheimliche Imperium*, p. 28; Ziegler, *Switzerland: The Awful Truth*, pp. 25–26, 137–39.

232. Quoted in *Wall Street Journal*, 20 October 1981, p. 27.

233. Kriesi, *Entscheidungsstrukturen und Entscheidungsprozesse*, pp. 529–32.

234. Hughes, *Parliament of Switzerland,* p. 34.

235. Kriesi, *Entscheidungsstrukturen und Entscheidungsprozesse,* pp. 31–32, 309, 358, 410.

236. Jürg Steiner, draft of "Conclusion: Reflections on the Consociational Theme," manuscript, p. 4. See also Adolf Gasser, "Der freiwillige Proporz im kollegialen Regierungssystem der Schweiz," *Politische Studien* 165 (January–February 1966): 269–76.

237. Steiner, *Amicable Agreement.*

238. Steiner, "Conclusion," p. 170. See also Jürg Steiner and Robert H. Dorff, *A Theory of Political Decision Modes: Intraparty Decision Making in Switzerland* (Chapel Hill: University of North Carolina Press, 1980).

239. Höpflinger, *Industrie-Gewerkschaften,* pp. 90–93; *Gewerkschaften in der Schweiz* (1970), pp. 40–43; R. Inglehart and D. Sidjanski, "Dimensions gauche-droit chez les dirigeants et électeurs suisses" *Revue française de science politique* 24 (October 1974): 994–1025; Alan B. Reed, "Parties and Integration in Switzerland" (Ph.D. diss., University of Texas at Austin, 1971); and Richard S. Katz, "Dimensions of Partisan Conflict in Swiss Cantons" (Paper prepared for the annual meeting of the American Political Science Association, New York, 3–6 September 1981).

240. Peter J. Katzenstein, "Economic Dependency and Political Autonomy: The Small European States in the International Economy" (Cornell University, November 1978, mimeo), table 6; Arend Lijphart, *Democracy in Plural Societies: A Comparative Exploration* (New Haven: Yale University Press, 1977), pp. 72–74; and Henry H. Kerr Jr., *Switzerland: Social Cleavages and Partisan Conflict* (Beverly Hills, Calif.: Sage, 1974), pp. 25–26.

241. Jeffrey Obler, Jürg Steiner, and Guido Dierickx, *Decision-Making in Smaller Democracies: The Consociational "Burden"* (Beverly Hills, Calif.: Sage, 1977), p. 8; and Steiner and Obler, "Does the Consociational Theory Really Hold for Switzerland?" in Milton J. Esman, ed., *Ethnic Conflict in the Western World* (Ithaca: Cornell University Press, 1977), pp. 322–25.

242. Steiner and Obler, "Consociational Theory," p. 334; Kenneth McRae, "Introduction," in McRae, ed., *Consociational Democracy: Political Accommodation in Segmented Societies* (Toronto: McClelland & Stewart, 1974), pp. 21–23; Val R. Lorwin, "Segmented Pluralism: Ideological Cleavages and Political Cohesion in the Smaller European Democracies," in ibid., p. 121; Lijphart, *Democracy in Plural Societies,* pp. 72–73, 77, 79, 82, 84, 89–97; Obler, Steiner, and Dierickx, *Decision-Making,* pp. 11–12; Kerr, *Social Cleavage,* pp. 7, 14, 16; Arend Lijphart, "Religious vs. Linguistic vs. Class Voting: The 'Crucial Experiment' of Comparing Belgium, Canada, South Africa, and Switzerland," *American Political Science Review* 72 (June 1979): 442–58.

243. Steiner, *Gewaltlose Politik,* pp. 283–86. The only exceptions are the relatively close links between the unions and the parties of the Left. See also Gerhard Lehmbruch, *Proporzdemokratie: Politisches System und politische Kultur in der Schweiz und in Österreich* (Tübingen: Mohr, 1967), p. 33; Lijphart, *Democracy in Plural Societies,* pp. 60, 104; Kenneth D. McRae, "The Structure of Political Cleavages and Political Conflict: Reflections on the Swiss Case" (Paper prepared for the ECPR/CES Workshop on Contemporary Switzerland, Geneva, 19–24 June 1975), pp. 10–11; and Harold E. Glass, "Subcultural Segmentation and Consensual Politics: The Swiss Experience" (Ph.D. diss., University of North Carolina at Chapel Hill, 1975).

244. Jürg Steiner, "The Principles of Majority and Proportionality," in McRae, ed., *Consociational Democracy*, p. 95; Lehmbruch, *Proporzdemokratie*, p. 37; and Kerr, *Social Cleavages*, pp. 27, 30.

245. Steiner, *Gewaltlose Politik*, p. 228; Lijphart, *Democracy in Plural Societies*, pp. 89–97, especially pp. 91, 94.

246. André Jaeggi, Victor Schmid, and Bruno Hugentobler, "Die Chefbeamten des EPD: Eine Untersuchung zur Personalstruktur," *Kleine Studien zur Politischen Wissenschaft* no. 133 (Zurich: Forschungsstelle für Politische Wissenschaft, 1978), p. 2; Gierisch, "Interest Groups," p. 48; Gruner, *Politische Führungsgruppen*, p. 10; Schumann, *Das Regierungssystem der Schweiz*, pp. 145–78; and Paolo Urio, "Parliamentary Control over Public Expenditure in Switzerland"; Forschungszentrum für Schweizerische Politik, "Miliz- und Berufsparlament" (Bern, 1972).

247. Gruner, *Die Parteien in der Schweiz*, pp. 172–74; Schumann, *Das Regierungssystem der Schweiz*, pp. 145–78; Hans-Peter Hertig, *Partei, Wählerschaft oder Verband? Entscheidungsfaktoren im eidgenössischen Parlament* (Bern: Francke, 1980); Anton Pelinka and Manfried Welan, *Demokratie und Verfassung in Österreich* (Vienna: Europaverlag, 1971), p. 101; and Karl-Heinz Nassmacher, *Das österreichische Regierungssystem: Grosse Koalition oder alternierende Regierung* (Cologne: Westdeutscher Verlag, 1968), pp. 53–54.

248. Gierisch, "Interest Groups," p. 24; Steiner, "Die politischen Prozesse," p. 130; Gruner, *Politische Führungsgruppen*, p. 70; Meyer, *Verbände und Demokratie*, pp. 82–83; Schumann, *Das Regierungssystem der Schweiz*, p. 156; and Gruner, "100 Jahre Wirtschaftspolitik," p. 88.

249. Erwin Bucher, "Historische Grundlegung: Die Entwicklung der Schweiz zu einem politischen System," in Steiner, *Das politische System der Schweiz*, p. 50; Gierisch, "Interest Groups," p. 53; and Steiner, "Die politischen Prozesse," pp. 122–23, 144.

250. Lijphart, *Democracy in Plural Societies*, p. 84; Lehmbruch, *Proporzdemokratie;* and Roger Girod, "Switzerland: Geography of the Swiss Party System," in McRae, ed., *Consociational Democracy*, pp. 207–25. The only notable exception is the weak alliance between the unions and the parties of the Left. Yet at least 100,000 union members do not vote for the parties of the Left and union representation in Parliament is a low 15 percent of the total number of parliamentarians. See Siegenthaler, *Politik der Gewerkschaften*, pp. 139–41, and Schumann, *Das Regierungssystem der Schweiz*, pp. 61–131.

251. Steiner, *Gewaltlose Politik*, p. 75; Gruner, *Politische Führungsgruppen*, p. 10; and Steinberg, *Why Switzerland?* p. 79. Historical statistics on the outcomes of different referenda types are given in Sidjanski, "Interest Groups in Switzerland," p. 111; in Gruner, *Politische Führungsgruppen*, p. 12; in Gierisch, "Interest Groups," p. 50; and in Harold E. Glass, "Consensus and Opposition in Switzerland: A Neglected Consideration," *Comparative Politics* 10 (April 1978): 370–71.

252. Steinberg, *Why Switzerland?* p. 80.

253. Steiner and Obler, "Consociational Theory," p. 334; Gierisch, "Interest Groups," pp. 26, 28–29; Steiner, *Gewaltlose Politik*, pp. 285–86; Glass, "Consensual Politics, Class and Dissatisfaction," pp. 3, 15–16, 18; and Glass, "Consensus and Opposition."

254. OECD, *Economic Surveys: Switzerland* (1980), p. 38.

255. *Lage und Probleme der schweizerischen Wirtschaft*, 1: 118. More generally

see Otto E. Sattler, *Die Arbeitslosenversicherung in einem marktwirtschaftlichen System: Dargestellt am Beispiel der Schweiz* (Zurich: Schulthess, 1973); Kurt Sovilla, "Neuordnung der Arbeitslosenversicherung," *Schweizerische Zeitschrift für Sozialversicherung* 1975, no. 2: 115–33; and Saxer, *Soziale Sicherheit*, pp. 208–18.

256. Schweizerischer Metall- und Uhrenarbeitnehmer-Verband, *Geschäftsbericht 1973, 1974, 1975*, pp. 393–94; *World Business Weekly*, 2 June 1980, p. 24.

257. *World Business Weekly*, 2 June 1980, p. 24, and 22 June 1981, p. 42.

258. Steinberg, *Why Switzerland?* pp. 44–45; Hughes, *Switzerland*, pp. 115, 170–73; and Ulrich J. Hossli, "Die Beziehungen der Sozialparteien in der schweizerischen Maschinen- und Metallindustrie, mit besonderer Berücksichtigung der Friedensvereinbarungen von 1937/1954" (Ph.D. diss., University of Basel, 1958).

259. See the estimates in *Schweizerische Arbeiterbewegung: Dokumente zu Lage, Organisation und Kämpfen der Arbeiter von der Frühindustrialisierung bis zur Gegenwart* (Zurich: Limmat, 1975), pp. 400–402; in Siegenthaler, *Politik der Gewerkschaften*, p. 145; and in Höpflinger, *Industrie-Gewerkschaften*, p. 58.

260. Höpflinger, *Industrie-Gewerkschaften*, p. 206; Siegenthaler, *Politik der Gewerkschaften*, p. 86; *Gewerkschaften in der Schweiz: Wesen und Struktur Einst und Jetzt* (Bern: Schweizerische Arbeiterbildungszentrale, 1975), pp. 20, 86; and Crossland "The Everlasting League," p. 11. In Switzerland in the 1960s and 1970s collective bargaining agreements that stipulated more than minimal standards of compensation might be extended to all workers in a particular industry; this lessened the incentives of workers to join local unions. The number of workers covered by contracts that included an extension of a collective agreement roughly doubled between 1960 and 1979 from 138,000 to 250,000. This now constitutes more than a third of all workers covered by industry-wide agreements, especially those working in very small firms. This development may thus contribute to the political demobilization of workers, which constitutes the greatest challenge to Switzerland's industrial unions. See Höpflinger, *Industrie-Gewerkschaften*, pp. 198–99; Hossli, "Beziehungen der Sozialparteien," p. 86; and Charbel Ackermann and Walter Steinmann, *Historische Aspekte der Trennung und Verflechtung von Staat und Gesellschaft in der Schweiz: Die Genese der Verschränkung* (Zurich: Institut für Orts-, Regional-, und Landesplanung, Forschungsprojekt "Parastaatliche Verwaltung", July 1981), pp. 118–19.

261. Siegenthaler, "Current Problems of Trade Union—Party Relations," p. 273.

262. Schweizerischer Gewerkschaftsbund, *Tätigkeitsbericht 1972, 1973, 1974*, p. 25, and *Tätigkeitsbericht 1975, 1976, 1977* (n.p., n.d.), p. 27. Siegenthaler, *Politik der Gewerkschaften*, pp. 112, 129–30.

263. Siegenthaler, *Politik der Gewerkschaften*, pp. 92–93, 129–130, 202, 204, 209, 210.

264. Wüthrich, *Verbände und Politik*, pp. 9, 19; *Arbeiterbewegung*, p. 308; Höpflinger, *Industrie-Gewerkschaften*, pp. 181, 191, 195; and Siegenthaler, *Politik der Gewerkschaften*, pp. 142–43.

265. The political developments are discussed well in Ackermann and Steinmann, *Historische Aspekte der Trennung und Verflechtung*, pp. 136–46; Hotz, *Politik zwischen Staat und Wirtschaft*, pp. 323–46; Aubert, *So funktioniert die Schweiz;* and Clive Loertscher and Georges Piotet, "Corporatist Patterns in

Swiss Economic Policies in the Immediate Post-war II Period" (Paper prepared for the ECPR Joint Session, Grenoble, 6–12 April 1978).
266. Quoted in Hotz, *Politik zwischen Staat und Wirtschaft*, p. 131.
267. Beedham and Lee, "Even in Paradise," Survey, p. vi.
268. Robert L. Heilbroner, *Business Civilization in Decline* (New York: Norton, 1976).

CHAPTER 4. *Democratic Corporatism in Austria and Switzerland*

1. Adolf Stirnemann, *Interessengegensätze und Gruppenbildungen innerhalb der Österreichischen Volkspartei: Eine empirische Studie* (Vienna: Institut für Höhere Studien und Wissenschaftliche Forschung, 1969), especially pp. 46–47, 74; Erich Andrlik, "The Organized Society: A Study of 'Neo-Corporatist' Relations in Austria's Steel and Metal Processing Industry" (Ph.D. diss., M.I.T., 1983), pp. 127–29.
2. Bernd Marin, *Die Paritätische Kommission: Aufgeklärter Technokorporatismus in Österreich* (Vienna: Braumüller, 1982), pp. 101–4, 106–7. See also Bernd Marin, "Freiwillige Disziplin? Preiskontrolle ohne autonome Sanktionspotenz—Österreichs Paritätische Kommission," *Wirtschaft und Gesellschaft* 7, 2 (1981): 161–97.
3. Anton Pelinka, *Modellfall Österreich? Möglichkeiten und Grenzen der Sozialpartnerschaft* (Vienna: Braumüller, 1981), pp. 40–42; *Der Österreich-Bericht: Presseübersicht* 25 March 1982, p. 1.
4. Uwe Kitzinger as quoted in Andrew Shonfield, *Modern Capitalism: The Changing Balance of Public and Private Power* (London: Oxford University Press, 1965), p. 194.
5. Ferdinand Lacina, *The Development of the Austrian Public Sector since World War II* (University of Texas at Austin, Institute of Latin American Studies, Office for Public Sector Studies, Technical Papers Series no. 7, 1977), pp. 12–17; Christian Smekal, *Die verstaatlichte Industrie in der Marktwirtschaft: Das österreichische Beispiel* (Cologne: Heymanns, 1963), pp. 23, 27, 40–45; Rupert Zimmermann, *Verstaatlichung in Österreich: Ihre Aufgaben und Ziele* (Vienna: Verlag der Wiener Volksbuchhandlung, 1964), pp. 69–114; Dennison I. Rusinow, "Notes toward a Political Definition of Austria, Part IV," *AUFS Reports* (June 1966): 5–8, 13–14; Stephan Koren "Sozialisierungsideologie und Verstaatlichungsrealität in Österreich," in Wilhelm Weber, ed., *Die Verstaatlichung in Österreich* (Berlin: Duncker & Humblot, 1964), pp. 79–110, 334; Oskar Grünwald and Herbert Krämer, *Die verstaatlichte österreichische Metallindustrie* (Frankfurt: Europäische Verlagsanstalt, 1966), pp. 23–31; and Alexander van der Bellen, "The Control of Public Enterprises: The Case of Austria," *Annals of Public and Co-operative Economy* 52, 1–2 (January–June 1981): 73–96.
6. Koren, "Sozialisierungsideologie," p. 91.
7. United Nations, Economic Commission for Europe, *Economic Survey of Europe 1959*, Part 3, chap. 5, p. 35. In the 1960s, for example, of the 89 members of the board of directors and chairmen of the board surveyed in one study only two were nonpartisan. This clear partisan division of positions of economic power made it possible for another study to calculate that in the 1960s in Austria's nationalized industries, firms dominated by the ÖVP had 67,000 employees as compared to 53,000 for those dominated by the SPÖ.

See, respectively, Christof Gaspari and Hans Millendorfer, *Prognosen für Österreich: Fakten und Formeln der Entwicklung* (Vienna: Verlag für Geschichte und Politik, 1973), p. 117, and Smekal, *Die verstaatlichte Industrie*, p. 55.

8. Rusinow, "Notes," Part IV, p. 20.

9. Ibid., pp. 20–21. See also Organization for Economic Co-operation and Development (OECD), *The Industrial Policy of Austria* (Paris: 1971), pp. 69–71.

10. Quoted in Rusinow, "Notes," Part IV, p. 20.

11. Lacina, *Development of the Austrian Public Sector,* p. 16.

12. Erich Andrlik, "Labor-Management Relations in Austria's Steel Industry" (San Francisco, May 1982, mimeo), pp. 12–13; Andrlik, "The Organized Society," p. 190.

13. See, for example, *Kurier,* 22 May 1976; *Arbeiterzeitung,* 11 May 1977.

14. "The Austrian Lesson in Economic Harmony," *Euromoney,* supplement (May 1979).

15. Karl Socher, "Die öffentlichen Unternehmen im österreichischen Banken- und Versicherungssystem," in Weber, ed., *Verstaatlichung in Österreich,* p. 446; Lacina, *Development of the Austrian Public Sector,* p. 12; and Van der Bellen, "The Control of Public Enterprises," pp. 84–87.

16. See Socher, "Die öffentlichen Unternehmen," p. 381, and Lacina, *Development of Austria's Public Sector,* p. 13; Socher, "Die öffentlichen Unternehmen," pp. 437–39, 451, and 385–88.

17. Socher, "Die öffentlichen Unternehmen," pp. 444–45, 454.

18. Edmond Langer, "Nationalisations in Austria," *Annals of Public and Cooperative Economy* 35 (1964): 115–63.

19. Sarah Hogg, "A Small House in Order," *Economist,* 15 March 1980, Survey, p. 3.

20. With former Finance Minister Androsch joining the Creditanstalt as its new head in 1981, it is at least conceivable that "this equitable system of political color coding may be summarily dismissed." See *World Business Weekly,* 8 December 1980, p. 50.

21. Socher, "Die öffentlichen Unternehmen," p. 372. See also pp. 370–73, 381–82.

22. "The Austrian Lesson," p. 9. See also *Austrian Information* 30, 5 (1977): 2.

23. Beirat für Wirtschafts- und Sozialfragen, *Vorschläge zur Industriepolitik* (Vienna: Ueberreuter, 1970), pp. 33–36.

24. OECD, *Policies for the Stimulation of Industrial Innovation: Country Reports* (Paris: 1978), vol. 22, pp. 24–25.

25. Ibid., p. 23. See also *Branchenindikatoren: Studie erstellt vom Österreichischen Institut für Wirtschaftspolitik im Auftrag des Bundesministeriums für Handel, Gewerbe und Industrie* (Vienna: Bundesministerium für Handel, Gewerbe und Industrie, 1973).

26. *Die Presse,* 8 June 1976; *Jahrbuch der österreichischen Wirtschaft 1976/1: Tätigkeitsbericht der Bundeswirtschaftskammer* (Vienna: Bundeswirtschaftskammer, 1977), pp. 30–34.

27. Professor Seidel, as quoted in a congressional hearing: U.S. Congress, Joint Economic Committee, *Austrian Incomes Policy: Lesson for the United States,* 97th Cong., 1st sess., 2 June 1981 (Washington, D.C., 1981), p. 6.

28. Quoted in "The Austrian Lesson," p. 23.

29. *Die Gewerkschaften in der Schweiz: Wesen und Struktur Einst und Jetzt* (Bern:

Schweizerische Arbeiterbildungszentrale, 1970), p. 26; *Die Gewerkschaften in der Schweiz* (Bern: Unionsdruckerei, 1975), pp. 19–20; and Dieter Greuter, *Der schweizerische Metall- und Uhrenarbeiter-Verband und die Industriegewerkschaft Metall für die Bundesrepublik Deutschland: Ein Vergleich* (Berlin: Duncker & Humblot, 1972), pp. 77, 194.

30. See E. Wüthrich, *Verbände und Politik* (Bern: Schweizerischer Metall- und Uhrenarbeiter-Verband, 1963), p. 19.

31. Ibid., p. 20.

32. Hans Werder, *Die Bedeutung der Volksinitiative in der Nachkriegszeit* (Bern: Francke, 1978), pp. 61–64; Jürg K. Siegenthaler, "Labor and Politics: Switzerland" (American University, Washington, D.C., n.d., mimeo), pp. 13–15.

33. Greuter, *Schweizerischer Metall-Verband*, p. 66. See also Marco de Nicolo, *Die Sozialpolitik des schweizerischen Gewerkschaftsbundes (1860–1960)* (Winterthur: Keller, 1962).

34. François Höpflinger, *Industrie-Gewerkschaften in der Schweiz: Eine soziologische Untersuchung* (Zurich: Limmat, 1976), pp. 122–24; Karl Meyer, *Verbände und Demokratie in der Schweiz* (Olten: Dietschi, 1968), pp. 87–88.

35. Hanspeter Kriesi, *Entscheidungsstrukturen und Entscheidungsprozesse in der Schweizer Politik* (Campus: Frankfurt, 1980), p. 316; Bobby M. Gierisch, "Interest Groups in Swiss Politics" (Sociological Institute, University of Zurich, 1974, mimeo), pp. 119–23, 139–42, 153; Dusan Sidjanski, "Interest Groups in Switzerland," *Annals of the American Academy of Political Science* 413 (May 1974): 105; and Marjorie Mowlam, "The Impact of Direct Democracy on the Influence of Voters, Members of Parliament and Interest Group Leaders in Switzerland" (Ph.D. diss., University of Iowa, 1977), p. 78.

36. Jürg Steiner, "Conclusion," in Howard R. Penniman, ed., *Switzerland at the Polls* (Washington, D.C.: American Enterprise Institute, 1983), pp. 173–74.

37. Mowlam, "Impact of Direct Democracy," pp. 80, 148–49; Kriesi, *Entscheidungsstrukturen und Entscheidungsprozesse*, p. 359.

38. Mowlam, "Impact of Direct Democracy," pp. 56–57; Werder, *Bedeutung der Volksinitiative*, pp. 22, 46–48, 66–67; and Klaus Schumann, *Das Regierungssystem der Schweiz* (Cologne: Heymanns, 1971), p. 247.

39. Greuter, *Schweizerischer Metall-Verband*, p. 108; Kenneth R. Libbey, "The Socialist Party of Switzerland: A Minority Party and Its Political System" (Ph.D. diss., Syracuse University, 1969), pp. 147–48; and Jürg Siegenthaler, *Die Politik der Gewerkschaften: Eine Untersuchung der öffentlichen Funktionen schweizerischer Gewerkschaften nach dem Zweiten Weltkrieg* (Bern: Francke, 1968), pp. 55–60.

40. OECD, *Economic Surveys: Switzerland* (1978), pp. 42–43; Jürg K. Siegenthaler, "Current Problems of Trade Union-Party Relations in Switzerland: Reorientation versus Inertia," *Industrial and Labor Relations Review* 28 (January 1975): 272; and Schweizerischer Gewerkschaftsbund, *Tätigkeitsbericht 1972, 1973, 1974* (n.p., n.d.), pp. 26–27.

41. Libbey, "Socialist Party," pp. 191–218; Kenneth R. Libbey, "Initiatives, Referenda and Socialism in Switzerland," *Government and Opposition* 5 (Summer 1970): 307–26; Mowlam, "Impact of Direct Democracy," pp. 141–42; and Kriesi, *Entscheidungsstrukturen und Entscheidungsprozesse*, p. 107.

42. Mowlam, "Impact of Direct Democracy," pp. 63, 148–50, 178.

43. Kriesi, *Entscheidungsstrukturen und Entscheidungsprozesse*, passim.

44. Ibid., pp. 410, 577.

45. Ibid., pp. 517–18, 578, 652–53, 675, 693.

46. Ibid., p. 377.

47. Ibid., pp. 414, 578.

48. Ibid., pp. 621–26.

49. Ibid., 663–65.

50. Ibid., pp. 579, 695–96. See also Höpflinger, *Industrie-Gewerkschaften,* p. 120; Harold E. Glass, "Consensual Politics, Class and Dissatisfaction in Switzerland: The Importance of Institutions," *Kleine Studien zur Politischen Wissenschaft* no. 80 (Zurich: Forschungsstelle für Politische Wissenschaft, University of Zurich, 1976), pp. 16, 18; and Autorenkollektiv, *Krise: Zufall oder Folge des Kapitalismus? Die Schweiz und die aktuelle Wirtschaftskrise. Eine Einführung aus marxistischer Sicht* (Zurich: Limmat, 1976).

51. Siegenthaler, "Current Problems of Trade Union-Party Relations," p. 278; Schweizerischer Gewerkschaftsbund, *Tätigkeitsbericht 1972, 1973, 1974,* p. 29.

52. Kriesi, *Entscheidungsstrukturen und Entscheidungsprozesse,* pp. 377–78, 689–90, 694–95.

53. Schumann, *Das Regierungssystem der Schweiz,* pp. 214–15, 225.

54. Roland Ruffieux, "The Political Influence of Senior Civil Servants in Switzerland," in Mattei Dogan, ed., *The Mandarins of Western Europe: The Political Role of Top Civil Servants* (New York: Wiley, 1975), pp. 245–47.

55. Peter Gaehler, "Les institutions suisses officielles et semi-officielles d'expansion économique à l'étranger" (Ph.D. diss., University of Paris, 1969), pp. 218–19; Gierisch, "Interest Groups," p. 49; Leonhard Neidhart, *Plebiszit und pluralitäre Demokratie: Eine Analyse der Funktion des schweizerischen Gesetzesreferendums* (Bern: Francke, 1970), pp. 301, 304, 315; Kriesi, *Entscheidungsstrukturen und Entscheidungsprozesse,* p. 88; and George J. Szablowski, "Central Agencies in Europe and Ottawa: A Comparative Analysis" (Paper prepared for the workshop on Smaller European Democracies and European-Canadian Comparisons, University of Western Ontario, 17–19 December 1979).

56. Raimund E. Germann and Andreas Frutiger, "Role Cumulation in Swiss Advisory Committees" (Paper prepared for the ECPR workshop on Interest Groups and Governments, Florence, 25–30 March 1980); André Jaeggi, "Between Parliamentary Weakness and Bureaucratic Strength: Interest Representation in Swiss Foreign Relations" (Paper prepared for the workshop on Interest Representation in Mixed Polities, Lancaster, 29 March–4 April 1981).

57. This paragraph is indebted to Irirangi Coates Bloomfield, "Public Policy, Technology and the Environment: A Comparative Inquiry into Agricultural Policy Approaches and Environmental Outcomes in the United States and Switzerland" (Ph.D. diss., Boston University, 1981), especially pp. 194, 221, 231, 235, 242, 249–50, 257. See also Dietrich Fischer, "Invulnerability without Threat: The Swiss Concept of General Defense," *Journal of Peace Research* 19, 3 (1982): 218–19.

58. Bloomfield, "Public Policy, Technology and the Environment," pp. 181–82.

59. Ibid., pp. 225, 232.

60. Benjamin R. Barber, *The Death of Communal Liberty: A History of Freedom in a Swiss Mountain Canton* (Princeton: Princeton University Press, 1974).

61. Paolo Urio, "Parliamentary Control over Public Expenditure in Switzerland," in David L. Coombes, ed., *The Power of the Purse: A Symposium on the Role of European Parliaments in Budgetary Decisions* (New York: Praeger, 1975), p. 319.

62. *Jahrbuch der österreichischen Wirtschaft 1976/1*, p. 110.

63. Kriesi, *Entscheidungsstrukturen und Entscheidungsprozesse*, p. 36.

64. *New York Times*, 1 February 1981, p. 13. See also *Der Spiegel*, 21 December 1981, p. 108.

65. Peter Bichsel, "Das Ende der schweizer Unschuld," *Der Spiegel*, 5 January 1981, p. 108.

66. Dietrich Thränhardt, "Ausländische Arbeiter in der Bundesrepublik, in Österreich und der Schweiz," *Neue Politische Literatur* 20, 1 (1975): 68–69; Hans-Joachim Hoffman-Nowotny and Martin Killias, "Switzerland," in Ronald E. Krane, ed., *International Labor Migration in Europe* (New York: Praeger, 1979), p. 49.

67. Mark J. Miller, "French and Swiss Seasonal Workers: Western Europe's Braceros" (Paper presented at the 1980 Europeanist Conference sponsored by the Council for European Studies, Washington, D.C.), p. 25; Hoffman-Nowotny and Killias, "Switzerland," p. 54.

68. Hoffman-Nowotny and Killias, "Switzerland," pp. 55–58.

69. Ibid., pp. 54, 61.

70. Bernhard Wehrli, *Aus der Geschichte des Schweizerischen Handels- und Industrie-Vereins: Zum hundertjährigen Bestehen des Vororts* (Erlenbach-Zurich: Rentsch, 1970), pp. 109–14; Hans Vogel, "Das Verhältnis von Staat und Wirtschaft in den schweizerischen Aussenbeziehungen," *Annuaire suisse de science politique* 16 (1976): 245–64; Vogel, *Die schweizerische Aussenwirtschaftspolitik: Domäne halbstaatlicher Verwaltungs- und Entscheidungsstrukturen* (Zurich: Institut für Orts-, Regional-, und Landesplanung, Forschungsprojekt "Parastaatliche Verwaltung," August 1981); and Dusan Sidjanski, "Les groupes de pression et la politique étrangère en Suisse," *Annuaire suisse de science politique* 6 (1966): 28–45.

71. Sidjanski, "Interest Groups in Switzerland," p. 109; Victor H. Umbricht, "Wirtschaftliche Aussenpolitik," *Schweizer Rundschau* 66, 4–5 (1967): 294.

72. Wehrli, *Geschichte des Industrie-Vereins*, pp. 18–19; Sidjanski, "Interest Groups in Switzerland," pp. 109–10; Norbert Kohlhase and Henri Schwamm, eds., *La négociation CÉE-Suisse dans le Kennedy Round* (Lausanne: Centre de recherches européennes, 1974), pp. 165–67; and Gottfried Berweger, *Investition und Legitimation: Privatinvestitionen in Entwicklungsländern als Teil der schweizerischen Legitimationsproblematik* (Diessenhofen: Ruegger, 1977), p. 244.

73. René M. W. Vogel, *Politique commerciale suisse* (Montreux: Leman, 1966), p. 349; Vogel, "Staat und Wirtschaft," p. 262; and Guntram Rehsche, *Schweizerische Aussenwirtschaftspolitik und Dritte Welt; Ziele und Instrumente. Exportförderung kontra Entwicklungspolitik* (Adliswil: Institut für Sozialethik, 1977), p. 65.

74. *Finanz und Wirtschaft*, 9 September 1976; *Neue Zürcher Zeitung*, 26 September and 16 December 1976.

75. Hans C. Binswanger and Reinhardt Büchi, "Aussenpolitik und Aussen-wirtschaftspolitik," in Alois Riklin, Hans Haug, and Hans C. Binswanger, eds., *Handbuch der schweizerischen Aussenpolitik* (Bern: Haupt, 1975), p. 701; Kohlhase and Schwamm, *Négociation CÉE-Suisse*, pp. 166–67; Sidjanski, "Interest Groups in Switzerland," p. 110; and Vogel, "Staat und Wirtschaft," pp. 262–63.

76. See the debate between Schwarzenbach and Jolles in *Neue Zürcher Zeitung*, 21 May and 29 May 1976.

77. Guido A. Keel, "L'influence des groupes d'intérêt politiques sur la politique étrangère suisse," in Riklin, Haug, and Binswanger, *Handbuch*, p. 313.

78. André Jäggi and Margret Sieber, "Interest Aggregation and Foreign Economic Policy: The Case of Switzerland" (Paper prepared for the ECPR workshop on Interest Groups and Governments, Florence, 25–30 March, 1980), p. 46.

79. Jane Kramer, "A Reporter in Europe," *New Yorker*, 15 December 1980, p. 140. See also Charles F. Schuetz, *Constitutional Change—Swiss Style* (Carleton University, Department of Political Science, Occasional Papers no. 9, Ottawa, April 1982).

80. Jörg P. Müller, *Gebrauch und Missbrauch des Dringlichkeitsrechts* (Bern: Haupt, 1977), p. 8; Schumann, *Das Regierungssystem der Schweiz*, pp. 175–78.

81. Sidjanski, "Interest Groups in Switzerland," p. 114.

82. Willy Linder and Kurt Braendle, eds., *Volkswirtschaft der Schweiz: Dokumentation* (Zurich: University of Zurich, Sozialökonomisches Seminar), 1: 193–94.

83. Müller, *Gebrauch und Missbrauch*, pp. 12, 15; Kriesi, *Entscheidungstrukturen und Entscheidungsprozesse*, p. 138; and Jaeggi, "Between Parliamentary Weakness and Bureaucratic Strength," p. 5, note 3.

84. Kriesi, *Entscheidungsstrukturen und Entscheidungsprozesse*, pp. 229, 247, 597–99, 614–17, 651–52.

85. John D. Stephens, *The Transition from Capitalism to Socialism* (London: Macmillan, 1979), p. 123.

86. Otto Bauer, *Die österreichische Revolution* (Vienna: Wiener Volksbuch-handlung, 1923), Part 4. See also Helmut Widder, *Parlamentarische Strukturen im politischen System: Zu Grundlagen und Grundfragen des österreichischen Regierungssystems* (Berlin: Duncker & Humblot, 1979), pp. 206–11, and Werner Lang, "Krisenmanagement durch Neokorporatismus," *Politische Vierteljahresschrift* 22 (April 1981): 23.

87. Beat Hotz, "Möglichkeiten und Grenzen kantonaler Wirtschafts-politik," *Annuaire suisse de science politique* 18 (1978): 183–210; Walter Steinmann, *Grundlagen, Träger, Entscheidungsprozesse und parastaatliche Aspekte der Wirtschaftsförderungspolitik* (Zurich: Institut für Orts-, Regional-, und Landesplanung, Forschungsprojekt "Parastaatliche Verwaltung," October 1980); Charbel Ackermann and Walter Steinmann, *The Representation of Private Actors in the Policy Implementation Process and the Implementation Structure* (Zurich: Institut für Orts-, Regional-, und Landesplanung, Forschungsprojekt "Parastaatliche Verwaltung," March 1981), pp. 14–23; Walter Hess, *Regional- und raumordnungspolitische Ziele und Massnahmen von Bund und Kantonen* (Bern: Haupt, 1979), pp. 34, 76–85, 147–49, 152–59; OECD, *Economic Survey: Switzerland* (1979), pp. 44–47; Wolf Linder, Beat Hotz, and Hans Werder, *Planung*

in der Schweizerischen Demokratie (Bern: Haupt, 1979), pp. 313–44; Heinz Hollenstein and Rudolf Loertscher, *Die Struktur- und Regionalpolitik des Bundes: Kritische Würdigung und Skizze einer Neuorientierung* (Diessenhofen: Rüegger, 1980); and Charbel Ackermann and Walter Steinmann, "Privatized Policy-Making: Administrative and Consociational Types of Implementation in Regional Economic Policy in Switzerland," *European Journal of Political Research* 10 (1982): 173–85.

88. Robert Holzach, *Banken und Strukturpolitik* (Aargau: Aargauische Industrie- und Handelskammer, 1977); R. A. Jeker, *Die schweizer Banken in den achtziger Jahren* (Zurich: Credit Suisse, 1979).

89. *World Business Weekly*, 4 February 1980, pp. 51–52, and 7 July 1980, p. 33; Peter Heseler, "Die Rolle der öffentlichen Banken in der Kreditwirtschaft der Schweiz," *Zeitschrift für öffentliche und gemeinwirtschaftliche Unternehmen* 3, 1 (1980): 12–26; and Walter Steinmann, *Die Entstehung öffentlicher und gemischtwirtschaftlicher Unternehmungen in der Schweiz* (Zurich: Institut für Orts-, Regional-, und Landesplanung, Forschungsprojekt "Parastaatliche Verwaltung," May 1980), pp. 13–20.

90. United Nations, *Transnational Corporations in World Development: A Reexamination* (New York: U.N. Economic and Social Council, Commission on Transnational Corporations, 1978), p. 238.

91. OECD, *Interim Report of the Industry Committee on International Enterprises* (n.p.: n.d.), p. 14.

92. United Nations, *Transnational Corporations: A Reexamination*, p. 176.

93. François Höpflinger, *Das Unheimliche Imperium: Wirtschaftsverflechtung in der Schweiz* (Zurich: Eco, 1978), pp. 80–81; Karl Arnold, "Defences to Takeovers: Switzerland," *International Business Lawyer* 8, 2 (1980): 41–43.

94. Robert Metz, "Swiss Defense on Takeovers," *New York Times*, 9 April 1980, p. D6.

95. Hans Wehsely, "Industriepolitik in den siebziger Jahren—Rückblick und Ausblick," *Österreichische Zeitschrift für Politikwissenschaft* 1981, no. 3: 34; Wolfgang C. Muller, "Economic Success without an Industrial Strategy: Austria in the 1970s," *Journal of Public Policy* 3 (February 1983): 119–30.

96. Hannes Androsch, "Die Rolle der österreichischen Wirtschaft in der arbeitsteiligen Weltwirtschaft der achziger Jahre," *ÖIAG Journal* 1 (April 1977): 3–5; Horst Knapp, "Spätherbst oder neuer Frühling: Informationen und Impressionen zur Industriepolitik," *Finanznachrichten*, 28 January 1977, pp. 1–8; and *Die Presse*, 27 January 1977. See also the informative article by Helmut Kramer, "Glanz und Elend der Strukturpolitik," *Die Industrie* 12 July 1974, pp. 5–7.

97. Anton Stanzel, "Vorstellungen staatlicher Strukturpolitik," *Wirtschaftspolitische Blätter* 25, 5 (1978): 69.

98. Interviews, Vienna, June 1981. See also *Österreich muss vorne bleiben: Entwurf für das SPÖ-Wirtschaftsprogramm* (Vienna: SPÖ, 1981), p. 6 and Wilhelm Hankel, *Prosperity amidst Crisis: Austria's Economic Policy and the Energy Crunch* (Boulder, Colo.: Westview, 1981), pp. 44, 66–68, 73–74.

99. It is estimated that this measure will subsidize a total of $2.75 billion over a period of five years. This would amount to about 18 percent of total and 90 percent of industrial fixed investment in 1977. See OECD, *Economic Surveys: Austria* (1978), p. 25.

100. See also above, chapter 2, notes 133–137. A lower ratio of 4:1 is

reported by Gunther Tichy, "Wie wirkt das österreichische System der Investitionsförderung?" *Quartalshefte* 1980, no. 1: 20.

101. Ernst Eugen Veselsky, "Möglichkeiten und Grenzen von Budgetprognosen in Österreich," *Quartalshefte* 1969, no. 1: 34–36; OECD, *Economic Surveys: Austria* (1970), pp. 43–47.

102. Quoted in Veselsky, "Möglichkeiten und Grenzen," p. 36.

103. Adolf Nussbaumer, "Die Grenzen der Staatsverschuldung," *Quartalshefte* 1976, no. 4: 22–24; OECD, *Economic Surveys: Austria* (1976), p. 24.

104. *Die Presse*, 31 August 1976.

105. *Wiener Zeitung*, 6 November 1974.

106. In 1975 that policy was changed to permit again the extension of short-term credits covering production periods; these credits were, however, granted at commercial rates and simply eased the liquidity problem of Austrian firms without strengthening their capital base. See *Die Presse*, 12 February 1975, and *Die Wirtschaft* 25 June 1975.

107. Nussbaumer, "Grenzen der Staatsverschuldung," p. 19; Gunther Tichy, "Theoretische und praktische Probleme der österreichischen Staatsverschuldung," *Quartalshefte* 1975, no. 2: 28; and Vereinigung Österreichischer Industrieller, *Zur Wirtschaftspolitik*, 2d ed. (Vienna: 1975), pp. 30–33.

108. Hankel, *Prosperity amidst Crisis*, p. 76. See also Erich Haas and Hans Wehsely, "Die direkte Investititonsförderung in Österreich 1948 bis 1978," *Wirtschaft und Gesellschaft* 3, 3 (1977): 245.

109. *Die Presse*, 14 December 1976; *Wochenpresse*, 3 August 1977; *Arbeiterzeitung*, 29 September 1976; *Salzburger Nachrichten*, 1 July 1977; and Jörg Schram, "Die Förderung der langfristigen Unternehmensfinanzierung durch Haftungen: Die Realisierung des EE-Fonds-Konzeptes," in Werner Clement and Karl Socher, eds., *Empirische Wirtschaftsforschung und monetäre Ökonomik: Festschrift für Stephan Koren zum 60. Geburtstag* (Berlin: Duncker & Humblot, 1979), pp. 225–34.

110. Helmut Dorn, "Zur Vorgeschichte der Kapitalbeteiligungsgesellschaften in Österreich," *Wirtschaftspolitische Blätter* 25, 3 (1978): 115–16; *Jahrbuch der österreichischen Wirtschaft 1977/1*, pp. 102–3.

111. *Die Presse*, 21 October and 11 December 1981.

112. Former State Secretary Veselsky quoted in Fritz Klenner, *Die österreichischen Gewerkschaften: Vergangenheit und Gegenwartsprobleme* (Vienna: Verlag des Österreichischen Gewerkschaftsbundes, 1979), 3: 2104.

CHAPTER 5. *The Politics of Change in the Textile Industry*

1. Gerhard Lehmbruch, "Introduction," in Gerhard Lehmbruch and Philippe C. Schmitter, eds., *Pattern of Corporatist Policy-Making* (Beverly Hills, Calif.: Sage, 1982), p. 27.

2. Organization for Economic Co-operation and Development (OECD), *Structural Problems of the Textile and Clothing Industry* (Paris: 1977). This is a useful, succinct survey of the problems of the industry and the policies of industrial states in the 1970s.

3. David B. Yoffie, "Adjustment in the Footwear Industry: The Consequences of Orderly Marketing Agreements," in John Zysman and Laura Ty-

son, eds., *American Industry in International Competition: Government Policies and Corporate Strategies* (Ithaca: Cornell University Press, 1983), pp. 328–32.

4. Vinod Kumar Aggarwal, "Hanging by a Thread: International Regime Change in the Textile-Apparel System, 1950–1979" (Ph.D. diss., Stanford University, 1981).

5. Alfred Bosshardt, Alfred Nydegger, and Heinz Allenspach, *Die schweizerische Textilindustrie im internationalen Konkurrenzkampf* (Zurich: Polygraphischer Verlag, 1959); Lukas A. Geiges, "Strukturwandlungen in der schweizerischen Textilindustrie: Eine historische und statistische Studie" (Ph.D. diss., University of Zurich, 1964); Hans Rudin, "Stand und Probleme der schweizerischen Wirtschaft: XXI. Die schweizerische Textilindustrie," *Wirtschaftspolitische Mitteilungen* 23 (December 1967); and Walter Bodmer, *Die Entwicklung der Schweizerischen Textilwirtschaft im Rahmen der übrigen Industrien und Wirtschaftszweige* (Zurich: Berichthaus, 1960).

6. Alfred Bosshardt and Alfred Nydegger, "Stand und Probleme der schweizerischen Wirtschaft: IX. Die schweizerische Textil- und Bekleidungsindustrie," *Wirtschaftspolitische Mitteilungen* 15 (October 1959): 4, 7; Kurt H. Fischer, "Konzentration und Kooperation in der schweizerischen Textilwirtschaft" (Ph.D. diss., University of Zurich [Winterthur: Schellenberg], 1969); and *Neue Zürcher Zeitung*, 17 June 1981.

7. The average for the garment industry in the 1970s is about 60 percent. See Gesamtverband der Schweizerischen Bekleidungsindustrie (GSBI), "Die Bekleidungsindustrie im Überblick: Eine permanente Dokumentation," (Zurich: May 1982), p. 16, and *Neue Zürcher Zeitung*, 18 June 1981.

8. Hans-Joachim Meyer-Marsilius, "Auswirkungen der Kooperations- und Konzentrationsbestrebungen der schweizerischen Textil- und Bekleidungsindustrien in der Praxis," *Deutschland-Schweiz* 19, 8 (1970): 453; *Neue Zürcher Zeitung*, 19 October 1968; *Wirtschaftsförderung*, Abenddienst, 30 November 1971, pp. B1, 652; and *Finanz und Wirtschaft*, 4 December 1971.

9. Bosshardt and Nydegger, "Schweizerische Textil- und Bekleidungsindustrie," p. 14; Interview, Zurich, June 1981. It is interesting to note that in the case of textiles Switzerland is only now approaching the level of international involvement that marked its operation before World War I.

10. GSBI, "Bekleidungsindustrie im Überblick," p. 13; Ulrich Albers, "Textilindustrie behauptet sich im internationalen Konkurrenzkampf," *Schweizerische Kreditanstalt Bulletin* 86 (December 1980), p. 16.

11. Industrieverband Textil, Verband der Arbeitgeber der Textilindustrie und Verein Schweizerischer Textilindustrieller, eds., *Textilindustrie 1980* (Zurich: April 1981), p. 45; *1976* (Zurich: April 1977), p. 41; and *1975* (Zurich: April 1976), p. 10.

12. *Neue Zürcher Zeitung*, 17 June 1981, p. 23; GSBI, "Bekleidungsindustrie im Überblick," p. 13.

13. GSBI, "Bekleidungsindustrie im Überblick," p. 10.

14. See, for example, *St. Galler Tagblatt*, 5 May 1973, and *Tages-Anzeiger*, 4 June 1977.

15. *Schweizerische Handels-Zeitung*, 1 November 1979; *Neue Zürcher Zeitung*, 18 October 1973; and *Finanz und Wirtschaft*, 10 December 1975.

16. *Zürcher Woche*, 24–25 January 1970, and *Textil-Revue*, 23 November 1967.

17. Ernst Nef, "Das Verbandswesen in der Textilindustrie," *Mitteilungen*

über Textilindustrie 2 (February 1969); *Textil-Revue* 18 October 1975; *Textil-Revue* 23 December 1968; *Basler Nachrichten,* 5 November 1970; and *Neue Zürcher Zeitung,* 3 November 1971, and 16 February 1977. See also Arnold Kappler, "Die Möglichkeiten kollektiver Exportpublizität der schweizerischen Textilindustrie, dargestellt am Beispiel der 'Exportwerbung für Schweizer Textilien'" (Ph.D. diss. University of St. Gallen [Winterthur: Schellenberg], 1973); Justus R. A. Hoby, "Der schweizerische Baumwollwaren-Export" (Ph.D. diss., University of Zurich, 1957); and Franz Adolf Tschan, "Die Aufgaben der Wirtschaftsverbände in der schweizerischen Textilwirtschaft" (Ph.D. diss., University of Bern, 1960).

18. *Neue Zürcher Zeitung,* 25 September 1961, and *Textil-Revue,* 9 February 1970.

19. *Neue Zürcher Zeitung,* 28 March 1972; *Textil-Revue,* 20 March 1972; and Kappler, "Möglichkeiten kollektiver Exportpublizität," pp. 31–32.

20. *Textilindustrie 1975,* p. 22, and *Textilindustrie 1979,* pp. 35–43.

21. VATI, "Volkswirtschaftliche Bedeutung und Struktur der schweizerischen Textilindustrie" (Zurich: n.d.), p. 4; *Textilindustrie 1979,* pp. 19–34.

22. Silvio Borner, "Ist der Standort Schweiz für einen Industriebetrieb, insbesondere für die Textilindustrie, noch richtig?" *Mitteilungen über Textilindustrie: Mittex* 10 (October 1979): 373–78; *Neue Zürcher Zeitung,* 19 October 1973; and Hans Rudin, "Die Konzentration in der Textilindustrie," *Neue Zürcher Zeitung,* 13 April 1970.

23. *Textilindustrie 1976,* p. 23.

24. *Krise, Zufall oder Folge des Kapitalismus? Die Schweiz und die aktuelle Wirtschaftskrise. Eine Einführung aus marxistischer Sicht* (Zurich: Limmat, 1976), p. 53.

25. Albers, "Textilindustrie," p. 16.

26. *Neue Zürcher Zeitung,* 19 October 1973.

27. *Textilindustrie 1977,* pp. 41–43.

28. *Textil-Revue,* 19 February 1979, pp. 231–32.

29. *Textil-Revue,* 13 August 1979, and *St. Galler Tagblatt,* 6 March 1959.

30. Firms in the textile and garment industries also became entitled to the limited tax subsidies of $600,000, which came with the investment of the $6 million of profits blocked under the employment stabilization program's provisions in prior years. "Arbeitsbeschaffungsreserven der privaten Wirtschaft: Die Arbeitsbeschaffungsaktion 1975/76 im Rückblick," *Mitteilungsblatt für Konjunkturfragen* 37, 1 (1981): 2–5.

31. *Textil-Revue,* 1 May 1978, p. 726.

32. Quoted in *Textil-Revue,* 25 June 1979, p. 916.

33. *Handelsblatt,* 20 February 1975; *Der Bund,* 9 September 1978; *Textilindustrie 1980,* pp. 15–26; and *Textilindustrie 1978,* pp. 26–31.

34. *Basler Nachrichten,* 9 October 1975; *Vaterland,* 2 November 1976; *Neue Zürcher Zeitung,* 28 January 1977; and *Handelsblatt,* 3 November 1977.

35. *Textil-Revue,* 26 June 1978; *Schweizerische Arbeitgeber-Zeitung* 26 (1978): 460. It is important to note that this arrangement did not require the private banks to incur such losses since they could have passed their losses on to the Swiss Nationalbank. But at the time interest rates were very low and the banks had excess liquid assets and apparently chose, for whatever reason, to carry the losses themselves. To the extent that the banks were carrying subsidized

credits into the era of high-interest rates in the early 1980s, their losses may have increased. However, this would affect only credits extended to Switzerland's investment goods industries that negotiate long-term contracts.

36. *Neue Zürcher Zeitung,* 17 February 1978; Schweizerischer Handels- und Industrie-Verein, *Jahresbericht 1977/78* (n.p.: n.d.), pp. 105–6.

37. *Textilindustrie 1975,* p. 15, and *1977,* p. 18.

38. *Textilindustrie 1975,* p. 14.

39. *Neue Zürcher Zeitung,* 9 September 1975; *Textilindustrie 1975,* pp. 16–22.

40. *Textil-Revue,* 25 June 1979, p. 916; *St. Galler Tagblatt,* 17 February 1979; and *Neue Zürcher Zeitung,* 4 November 1972. The privately organized export promotion system is described in *St. Galler Tagblatt,* 29 January 1976. In general see Kappler, "Möglichkeiten kollektiver Exportpublizität"; Hoby, "Der schweizerische Baumwollwaren-Export."

41. *Textilindustrie 1975,* p. 32; *1976,* p. 40; and *1977,* pp. 52–53.

42. *Tages-Anzeiger,* 10 November 1978.

43. *Tages-Anzeiger,* 13 March 1980, and *Basler Zeitung,* 23 May 1980.

44. *Berner Zeitung,* 11 December 1974. See also *Neue Zürcher Zeitung,* 28 February 1968. The situation has changed considerably if compared to 1957. Of the 24 collective bargaining agreements in the industry, 9 were concluded at the federal and 5 at the cantonal level. See Tschan, "Aufgaben der Wirtschaftsverbände," p. 114.

45. *Tages-Anzeiger,* 13 March 1980.

46. *Neue Zürcher Zeitung,* 24–25 May 1975, and *Textil-Revue,* 21 March, 1977. *Chemiefasern Textilindustrie* no. 4 (April 1981), pp. 264–66.

47. Robert Plant, *Industries in Trouble* (Geneva: International Labour Office, 1981), p. 49.

48. Borner, "Standort Schweiz," p. 373; *Mitteilungen über Textilindustrie: Mittex* 10 (October 1979), 373.

49. H. G. Meierhofer, "The Textile Industry Is out of the Doldrums," *Crédit Suisse Bulletin* 85 (Winter 1979/80): 16.

50. *Neue Zürcher Zeitung,* 23 December 1975; Guntram Rehsche, *Schweizerische Aussenwirtschaftspolitik und Dritte Welt: Ziele und Instrumente. Exportförderung kontra Entwicklungspolitik* (Adliswil: Institut für Sozialethik, 1977), p. 66; and Gerhard Winterberger, *Die Zusammenarbeit von Staat und Privatwirtschaft bei der Exportförderung* (Zurich: Schweizerischer Handels- und Industrie-Verein, 1976), p. 12.

51. This episode is reported in the following newspapers: *Volksrecht,* 23–24 January 1981; *Neue Zürcher Zeitung,* 31 January–1 February and 3 February 1981; *Tages-Anzeiger,* 10 February 1981; *Gewerkschaft Textil-Chemie-Papier,* 12 February 1981; *Neue Zürcher Zeitung,* 2 March 1981; *Tages-Anzeiger,* 2 March 1981; *Volksrecht,* 2 March 1981; *Neue Zürcher Zeitung,* 3 March 1981; *Volksrecht,* 3 March 1981; *Gewerkschaft Textil-Chemie-Papier,* 5 March 1981; *Volksrecht,* 17 March 1981; *Vaterland,* 1 April 1981; and *Tages-Anzeiger,* 6 May 1981.

52. *Textilindustrie 1980,* pp. 31–33.

53. *World Business Weekly,* 22 October 1979, p. 51; Josef Peischer, "Auslandseinfluss in der österreichischen Wirtschaft nimmt zu," *Informationen über Multinationale Konzerne* 1981, no. 2: 4. Only about 500 of the firms surveyed were joint-stock companies.

54. OECD, Directorate for Social Affairs, Manpower and Education, "Con-

tinuous Reporting System on Migration: SOPEMI 1979" (Paris: 1979), p. 30; *Gastarbeiter: Wirtschaftliche und soziale Herausforderung* (Vienna: Europa Verlag, 1973), pp. 18, 32.

55. Bundeswirtschaftskammer Vienna, *Pressedienst*, 23 July 1971; Handelskammer Niederösterreich, *Mitteilungen*, 18 September 1970; letter of the Österreichischer Arbeiterkammertag to the Ministry for Social Affairs, Vienna, 1 September 1972, p. 3; and *Jahrbuch der österreichischen Wirtschaft, 1973/2: Tätigkeitsbericht der Bundeswirtschaftskammer* (Vienna: Bundeskammer der Gewerblichen Wirtschaft, 1974), p. 180.

56. *Die Presse*, 19 July 1977.

57. Hans Wehsely, "Industriepolitik in den siebziger Jahren—Rückblick und Ausblick," *Österreichische Zeitschrift für Politikwissenschaft* 1981, no. 1: 31. Between 1971 and 1978 the total of 24,000 jobs lost in textiles and garments exceeded the loss in all other industrial sectors combined: *Der Kurier*, 30 January 1979. Between 1980 and 1982 it shrank further, from 45,000 to 39,000: *Wiener Zeitung*, 23 April 1983.

58. *Österreichische Textilindustrie im Jahre 1980* (Vienna: Fachverband der Textilindustrie Österreichs, June 1981), pp. 18–19; Vereinigung Österreichischer Industrieller, Vienna, *Pressedienst*, 12 November 1976; and Fachverband der Textilindustrie Österreichs, *Die österreichische Bekleidungsindustrie: Weissbuch 1980* (n.p.: n.d.) p. 30.

59. UNCTAD, *Nontariff Barriers: Study of the Origins and Operation of International Arrangements Relating to Cotton Textiles* (New Delhi, TD/20/Supp 3, October 1967), pp. 61–62, 65, 66. See also Gerard Curzon and Victoria Curzon, "The Management of Trade Relations in the GATT," in Andrew Shonfield, ed., *International Economic Relations of the Western World 1959–1971*, vol. 1: *Politics and Trade* (London: Oxford University Press, 1976), pp. 209–10, 263–64; Gerard Curzon, *Multilateral Commercial Diplomacy: The General Agreement on Tariffs and Trade and Its Impact on National Commercial Policies and Techniques* (London: Michael Joseph, 1965), p. 254; and Gardner C. Patterson, *Discrimination in International Trade: The Policy Issues 1945–1965* (Princeton: Princeton University Press, 1966), pp. 308, 311.

60. *Neue Zürcher Zeitung*, 15 December 1967.

61. Hans Mayrzedt, *Multilaterale Wirtschaftsdiplomatie zwischen westlichen Industriestaaten als Instrument zur Stärkung der multilateralen und liberalen Handelspolitik* (Bern: Lang, 1979), p. 501.

62. *Die Presse*, 8 January 1973, and *Wochenpresse*, 29 January 1975.

63. Institute of Developing Economies, Regional Development Unit, *The Textile Industry in Japan: Present Situation, Problems and Prospects* (Tokyo: Workshop on Comparative Advantage of Manufacturing Industries in Asian Countries, 11–18 December 1979), Appendix 9.

64. *Wochenpresse*, 29 January 1975. The *Jahrbuch der österreichischen Wirtschaft*, issued annually by the Bundeswirtschaftskammer, contains a useful summary of Austria's trade policy as it affects, among others, textiles and garments.

65. *Kurier*, 20 October and 12 December 1977; *Neue Zürcher Zeitung*, 8 November 1979.

66. *Die Presse*, 2 April 1974; *Wochenpresse*, 29 January 1975; *Parlamentskorrespondenz*, II-2564 der Beilagen zu den Stenographischen Protokollen des Nationalrates, XIV. Gesetzgebungsperiode; and *Die Presse*, 5 July 1979.

67. Interview, Vienna, 1981; *Die Wirtschaft,* 6 January 1981.
68. *Die Wirtschaft,* 6 January 1981 and 24 June 1980.
69. *Die Presse,* 21 March 1978.
70. *Textilindustrie 1980,* p. 18.
71. *Die Presse,* 4 April 1973; Austria Presse Agentur, *APA Konjunktur,* 17 July 1976.
72. *Wiener Zeitung,* 6 April 1976; *Frankfurter Allgemeine,* 17 October 1970.
73. This is one of the central conclusions of the report of an advisory commission of the government as well as the industrial sector legislation passed by Parliament in 1969. See Beirat für Wirtschafts- und Sozialfragen, *Vorschläge zur Industriepolitik* (Vienna: Ueberreuter, 1970).
74. *Die Presse,* 26 August 1970. In Austria's garment industry infusion of foreign investment, typically undertaken in response to temporary international wage differentials, had only a short-term character. See, for example, *Die Presse,* 5 September 1970; Michael Weber, "Die österreichische Textilindustrie und deren Probleme im Rahmen der Integration" (Masters thesis, Hochschule für Welthandel, Vienna, 1970), p. 148; and *Wochenpresse,* 29 January 1975.
75. Karl Socher, "Die öffentlichen Unternehmen im österreichischen Banken- und Versicherungssystem," in Wilhelm Weber, ed., *Die Verstaatlichung in Österreich* (Berlin: Duncker & Humbolt, 1964), pp. 409–10.
76. *Vorarlberger Nachrichten,* 19 March and 4 November 1976; Sarah Hogg, "A Small House in Order," *Economist,* 15 March 1981, Survey, p. 17; *Basler Zeitung,* 4 April 1979; and *St. Galler Tagblatt,* 15 August 1975.
77. *Vorarlberger Nachrichten,* 2 March 1979 and 12 December 1980.
78. This episode can be traced in the following newspapers: *Die Wirtschaft,* 14 July 1981; *Profil,* 20 July 1981; *Kurier,* 8 August 1981; *Tiroler Tageszeitung,* 13 August 1981; *Kurier,* 12 October 1981; *Wochenpresse,* 21 October 1981; *Salzburger Nachrichten,* 24 November 1981; *Kurier,* 25 November 1981; *Vorarlberger Nachrichten,* 17 and 22 April 1982; *Tiroler Tageszeitung,* 23 July 1982; *Börsen-Kurier,* 29 July 1982; and *Die Presse,* 21 January and 9 March 1983.
79. *Jahrbuch der österreichischen Wirtschaft, 1978/2,* p. 104; *Die Presse,* 5 and 25 January 1979; *Vorarlberger Nachrichten,* 27 February 1979; *Wirtschaft für Alle* 5 (May 1979); *Wiener Zeitung,* 15 May 1979; *Vorarlbergs Wirtschaft Aktuell,* 29 June 1979, pp. 4–6; and *Wiener Zeitung,* 30 March 1982.
80. *Österreichische Textil-Mitteilungen,* 25 April 1975.
81. Beirat für Wirtschafts- und Sozialfragen, *Vorschläge zur Industriepolitik II* (Vienna: Ueberreuter, 1978), pp. 45–46.
82. *Kurier,* 14 February 1979.
83. *Vorarlberg's Wirtschaft Aktuell,* 29 June 1979, p. 6.
84. *Die Presse,* 19 July 1977; *Oberösterreichische Nachrichten,* 10 August 1977; *Wiener Zeitung,* 3 August 1977; *Die Presse,* 26 July 1978; and *Die Wirtschaft,* 22 August 1978.
85. Alexander Vodopivec, *Die Dritte Republik: Machtstrukturen in Österreich* (Vienna: Molden, 1976), p. 55.
86. *Österreichische Textilmitteilungen,* 3 October 1975.
87. Ibid.; *Die Presse,* 27 September 1974; and *Frankfurter Allgemeine Zeitung* (Blicke durch die Wirtschaft), 2 October 1974.
88. *Arbeiterzeitung,* 10 March 1978; *Kurier,* 14 February 1979; and *Tiroler Tageszeitung,* 11 May 1979.

89. This episode can be traced in the following newspapers: *Die Presse,* 13 and 20 September 1975; *Die Presse,* 6 October 1975; *Volksstimme,* 10 October 1975; *Bank und Börse,* 8 November 1975; *Die Presse,* 15, 16, and 24 January 1976; *Wiener Zeitung,* 11 February 1976; *Arbeiter-Zeitung,* 15 February 1976; *Die Presse,* 3 March and 24 May 1976, 5 April and 12 May 1978; *Volksstimme,* 27 May 1978; *Neue Zeit,* 30 May 1978; *Wiener Zeitung,* 28 June 1978; *Die Presse,* 22 July 1978; *Frankfurter Allgemeine Zeitung,* 4 August 1978; *Arbeiterzeitung,* 29 November 1978; *Die Presse,* 7 and 9 December 1978; *Vorarlberger Nachrichten,* 12 December 1978; *Wochenpresse,* 13 December 1978. *Vorarlberger Nachrichten,* 27 February and 15 March 1979; and *Börsen-Kurier,* 7 August 1980.

CHAPTER 6. *The Politics of Change in the Steel and Watch Industries*

1. Organization for Economic Co-operation and Development (OECD), *Industrial and Structural Adaptation of the Iron and Steel Industry* (Paris: 1976).
2. See Erich Andrlik, "The Organized Society: A Study of 'Neo-Corporatist' Relations in Austria's Steel and Metal Processing Industry" (Ph.D. diss., M.I.T., 1983), especially pp. 243–88. See also Stephan Koren, "Sozialisierungsideologie und Verstaatlichungsrealität in Österreich," in Wilhelm Weber, ed., *Die Verstaatlichung in Österreich* (Berlin: Duncker & Humblot, 1964), pp. 165–265; Oskar Grünwald and Herbert Krämer, *Die verstaatlichte österreichische Metallindustrie* (Frankfurt: Europäische Verlagsanstalt, 1966); Margit Scherb, "Ökonomische Auswirkungen des Internationalisierungsprozesses auf kleine Industriestaaten: Dargestellt am Beispiel der verstaatlichten österreichischen Eisen- und Stahlindustrie," *Österreichische Zeitschrift für Politikwissenschaft* 1978, no. 3: 275–90; Dennison I. Rusinow, "Notes toward a Political Definition of Austria," Parts IV and V, *AUFS Reports* (June and July 1966); Otmar Kleiner, *Österreichs Eisen- und Stahlindustrie und ihre Aussenhandelsverflechtung* (Vienna: Hirt, 1969); Helmut Kramer, *Industrielle Strukturprobleme Österreichs* (Vienna: Signum, 1980); and Oskar Grünwald, "Steel and the State in Austria," *Annals of Public and Co-operative Economy* 51 (December 1980): 309–43.
3. Österreichisches Institut für Wirtschaftsforschung, "Die Ausbreitung neuer Technologien: Eine Studie über zehn Verfahren in neun Industrien," *Monatsberichte,* supplement 87 (September 1969): 5; Kurt Wicht, "Die Entwicklung des LD-Verfahrens und dessen Auswirkungen auf die VÖEST-AG von 1959 bis 1972" (Ph.D. diss., Hochschule für Welthandel, Vienna, 1975), p. 7; *Volksstimme,* 15 February 1980; Grünwald and Krämer, *Österreichische Metallindustrie,* p. 38; and Rusinow, "Notes," Part IV, p. 10, note 5. See also Robert A. Blecker, "The Diffusion of the Basic Oxygen Process and the Decline of the American Steel Industry" (paper prepared for the Social Science History workshop, Stanford University, 30 November 1982); G. S. Maddala and Peter T. Knight, "International Diffusion of Technical Change: A Case Study of the Oxygen Steel Making Process," *Economic Journal* 77 (September 1967): 531–58; and Guy Herregat, "Managerial Profiles and Investment Patterns: An Analysis of the International Diffusion of the Basic Oxygen Steel Process" (Ph.D. diss., University of Louvain, 1972).
4. One study estimates the cost reduction at 45 percent for a mill producing 1 to 2 million tons of steel annually. See Institut für Wirtschaftsforschung,

"Ausbreitung neuer Technologien," p. 6; Ferdinand Lacina, *The Development of the Austrian Public Sector since World War II* (University of Texas at Austin, Institute of Latin American Studies, Office for Public Sector Studies, Technical Papers Series no. 7, 1977), p. 21; and Kleiner, *Österreichs Eisen- und Stahlindustrie*, pp. 43–44, footnote 98.

5. A recent count of worldwide L-D capacity appears in the *L-D Process Newsletter* no. 71 (Linz: Voest-Alpine Engineering and Contracting Division, March 1981). On the international diffusion of Austria's technological innovation in steel and on the future of Austria's industry see also Franz Geist, "Die Zukunft der österreichischen Stahlindustrie," *West-Ost Journal* no. 6 (December 1976): 31–33.

6. Letters to the author by Nippon Kokan, 6 March and 8 April 1980.

7. Georg Vajta, "Die Zusammenhänge zwischen Stahlintensität und Sozialprodukt-Struktur in Österreich," *Wirtschaftspolitische Blätter* 21, 2 (1974): 195–98.

8. Scherb, "Ökonomische Auswirkungen," p. 283; Grünwald and Krämer, *Österreichische Metallindustrie*, p. 127. Furthermore, the iron and steel industries received more than half of the total aid given to the nationalized industries.

9. Koren, "Sozialisierungsideologie," pp. 112–14; Grünwald and Krämer, *Österreichische Metallindustrie*, p. 125.

10. Koren, "Sozialisierungsideologie," p. 123; *ÖIAG Journal* 1979, no. 2: 14; Rupert Zimmermann, *Verstaatlichung in Österreich: Ihre Aufgaben und Ziele* (Vienna: Wiener Volksbuchhandlung, 1964), p. 126; Herbert Koller, "Die wirtschaftlichen Aspekte der Stahlfusion," *Neue Technik und Wirtschaft* no. 8 (August 1973): 162–64; and *Die Presse*, 30 October 1975. It should be noted that in the 1970s the Voest's output of 4.5 million tons was only 10 percent of Japan's largest firm, Nippon Steel.

11. Herbert Koller, "Die österreichische Eisen- und Stahlindustrie in den vergangenen 50 Jahren," *Stahl und Eisen*, 20 December 1976, p. 1288. Erich Andrlik, "Labor-Management Relations in Austria's Steel Industry" (San Francisco, mimeo, 1982), p. 7, quotes from a study of the steel industry undertaken in 1968; see also Andrlik, "The Organized Society," pp. 253–54.

12. Scherb, "Ökonomische Auswirkungen," p. 286.

13. *Wiener Zeitung*, 22 July 1982.

14. Koller, "Die österreichische Eisen- und Stahlindustrie." For the interwar years, see the history by Grünwald and Krämer, *Österreichische Metallindustrie*. This acquiescence in public ownership in the iron and steel industry may be explained in part by the strong position that foreign firms occupy in Austria's metal industry. See *Die Presse*, 2 October 1971; *Frankfurter Zeitung* (Blick durch die Wirtschaft), 3 April 1976.

15. Grünwald and Krämer, *Österreichische Metallindustrie*, pp. 35–36; Scherb, "Ökonomische Auswirkungen," p. 282.

16. Franz Geist, "Zur Entwicklung der verstaatlichten Eisen- und Stahlindustrie," *Neue Technik und Wirtschaft* 25 (December 1971): 276–78; *Die Presse*, 14 January 1972; *Ecco*, 20 April 1974, pp. 16–20; and *Die Presse*, 12 June 1975.

17. *Die Welt*, 23 March 1972.

18. Koller, "Wirtschaftliche Aspekte," p. 162.

19. Ibid., pp. 162–63; *Die Presse*, 12 June 1975; *Frankfurter Zeitung* (Blick

durch die Wirtschaft), 11 April 1975; *Jahrbuch der österreichischen Wirtschaft, 1976/1: Tätigkeitsbericht der Bundeswirtschaftskammer* (Vienna: Budeskammer der Gewerblichen Wirtschaft, 1977), pp. 30–31; and *Die Presse*, 1 December 1977.

20. Erwin Plöckinger, "Die industrielle Forschung in der österreichischen Stahlindustrie," *Berg und Hüttenmannische Monatshefte*," no. 5 (May 1974): 191.

21. Quoted in Grünwald and Krämer, *Österreichische Metallindustrie*, p. 117.

22. Scherb, "Ökonomische Auswirkungen," pp. 283–84; Kleiner, *Österreichs Eisen- und Stahlindustrie*, pp. 30–31, 60–61.

23. Rusinow, "Notes," Part IV, p. 17; Zimmermann, *Verstaatlichung in Österreich*, pp. 27, 94.

24. OECD, *The Industrial Policy of Austria* (Paris: 1971), p. 69.

25. Different estimates are cited in Christian Smekal, *Die verstaatlichte Industrie in der Marktwirtschaft: Das österreichische Beispiel* (Cologne: Heymanns, 1963), p. 102; Grünwald and Krämer, *Österreichische Metallindistrie*, pp. 38–39; Kleiner, *Österreichs Eisen- und Stahlindustrie*, p. 32; and Scherb, "Ökonomische Auswirkungen," p. 283.

26. Scherb, "Ökonomische Auswirkungen," p. 285; Lacina, *Development of the Austrian Public Sector*, p. 19. More generally on the system of price supports see Smekal, *Die verstaatlichte Industrie*, pp. 100–107, 111–14; Eduard März, *Österreichs Wirtschaft zwischen Ost und West: Eine sozialistische Analyse* (Vienna: Europa Verlag, 1965), pp. 71–76; Koren, "Sozialisierungsideologie," pp. 135–50; and Zimmermann, *Verstaatlichung in Österreich*, pp. 125–26.

27. Smekal, *Die verstaatlichte Industrie*, p. 103; Zimmermann, *Verstaatlichung in Österreich*, p. 143.

28. *Eco*, 20 April 1974, pp. 16–20; *Die Presse*, 5 November 1974; and März, *Österreichs Wirtschaft zwischen Ost und West*, pp. 79–80.

29. Chris Cviic, "Their Own Kind of Miracle," *Economist*, 28 July 1973, Survey, p. 8; Andrlik, "Labor-Management Relations," p. 7.

30. Koller, "Österreichische Stahlindustrie"; *Stenographisches Protokoll*, 6. Sitzung des Nationalrates der Republik Österreich, XIV. Gesetzgebungsperiode, 3 December 1975, pp. 366–67; *Die Presse*, 30 October 1975; and *New York Times*, 12 October 1975.

31. Cviic, "Their Own Kind of Miracle," Survey, p. 8.

32. Ewald Nowotny, "Verstaatlichte und private Industrie in der Rezession: Gemeinsamkeiten und Unterschiede," *WISO* 2 (May 1979): 82; Sarah Hogg, "A Small House in Order," *Economist*, 15 March 1980, Survey, p. 9; and Andrlik, "Labor-Management Relations," pp. 9–10.

33. Nowotny, "Verstaatlichte und private Industrie," pp. 77–81 and p. 85, note 20.

34. Hogg, "A Small House in Order," Survey, p. 9.

35. *Die Presse*, 9 March 1978; *Arbeiterzeitung*, 12 and 27 September 1978; *Wiener Zeitung*, 21 November 1980; and *World Business Weekly*, 9 March 1981, p. 24.

36. Oskar Grünwald, "Austrian Industrial Structure and Industrial Policy," in Sven W. Arndt, ed., *The Political Economy of Austria* (Washington, D.C.: American Enterprise Institute, 1982), p. 144; *News from Austria*, 21 April 1981.

37. *News from Austria*, 25 November 1980, pp. 3–4; Grünwald, "Austrian

Industrial Structure," p. 145; *Arbeiterzeitung,* 3 March 1982 cites a 65 percent figure.

38. *Der Österreich-Bericht,* 8 July 1983, p. 1.

39. Helmut Krämer, "Österreich und die Dritte Welt: Am Beispiel der österreichischen Entwicklungshilfe," *Österreichische Zeitschrift für Politikwissenschaft* 1978, no. 3: 328–32, especially p. 330.

40. *Jahrbuch der österreichischen Wirtschaft* 1978/1, p. 102; *Die Presse,* 17 November 1977; *Arbeiterzeitung,* 22 November 1977; *Oberösterreichische Nachrichten,* 1 March 1978; *Die Presse,* 11 March 1978; *Oberösterreichische Nachrichten,* 1 September 1978; and *Die Presse,* 27 October 1978.

41. Grünwald, "Steel and State in Austria," p. 491.

42. Quoted in Charles Gaines, *Pumping Iron: The Art and Sport of Bodybuilding* (New York: Simon & Schuster, 1974), p. 54.

43. This episode can be traced in the following accounts. Andrlik, "The Organized Society," pp. 289–336; *Kleine Zeitung,* 12 July 1975; *Neue Zeit,* 7 February 1976; *Die Presse,* 26 August 1976; *Frankfurter Allgemeine Zeitung,* 27 September 1976; *Neue Zeit,* 26 March 1977; *Wiener Börsen-Kurier,* 15 September 1977; *Die Presse,* 23 November 1977; *Handelsblatt,* 27 January 1978; *Die Presse,* 9 March 1978; *Frankfurter Allgemeine Zeitung,* 15 April 1978; *Weg und Ziel* 5 (May 1980); *Die Presse,* 18 May 1978; *Die Presse,* 9 June 1978; *Kleine Zeitung,* 15 July 1978; *Finanznachrichten,* 21 July 1978; *Die Presse,* 20 October 1978; *Kleine Zeitung,* 24 November 1978; *Kurier,* 1 December 1978; *Volksstimme,* 1 December 1978; *Kleine Zeitung,* 25 January 1979; *Arbeiterzeitung,* 8 February 1979; *Österreichische Monatshefte* 4 (April 1979): 12–15; *Wiener Zeitung,* 7 July 1979; *Finanznachrichten,* 20 July 1979; *Kleine Zeitung,* 24 October 1979; *Wiener Börsen-Kurier,* 24 October 1979; *Gemeinwirtschaft* 11 (November 1979): 3–5; *Die Presse,* 24 November 1979; *Die Presse,* 28 November 1979; *Oberösterreichische Nachrichten,* 12 July 1980; *Neue Zeit,* 25 October 1980; *News from Austria,* 27 October 1980, p. 4, and 4 November 1980, p. 2; *Wiener Zeitung,* 10 January 1981; *Die Presse,* 4 March 1981; *Arbeiterzeitung,* 7 March 1981; *Wiener Zeitung,* 11 March 1981; *Kleine Zeitung,* 14 March 1981; *Wiener Zeitung* 15, 17, and 19 March 1981; *Neues Volksblatt,* 21 March 1981; *Frankfurter Allgemeine Zeitung,* 24 March 1981; *Die Presse,* 26 March 1981; *Wiener Zeitung,* 1 April 1981; *Kleine Zeitung,* 10 April 1981; *Neue Zeit,* 28 April 1981; *Wiener Zeitung,* 13 May 1981; *Kleine Zeitung,* 14 October 1981; *Die Presse,* 19 April and 10 October 1982; *Profil,* 8 November 1982; *Die Presse,* 28 and 29 January 1983; *Volksstimme,* 4 February 1983; and *Der Österreich-Bericht,* 14 June, 30 June, and 8 July 1983.

44. *Kurier,* 29 October 1982.

45. *Neue Zürcher Zeitung,* 11 July 1980; *Neue Zürcher Zeitung,* 12 June 1969. In 1981 Hong Kong became the world's largest watch producer; see *World Business Weekly,* 20 July 1981, p. 23; *Der Bund,* 14 July 1980. Fédération horlogère, "Projektionsstudie" (Biel: 1977), p. 19, speaks of a drop well below 40,000 by the middle of the 1980s. See also Bernard Kunz, *L'emploi dans la région horlogère* (Neuchatel: Groupe d'études économiques, University of Neuchâtel, 1978); Wirtschaftsförderung, *Artikeldienst* 22 (1 June 1981). More generally see David S. Landes, *Revolution in Time: Clocks and the Making of the Modern World* (Cambridge, Mass: The Belknap Press of Harvard University Press, 1983).

46. Ernst Güggi, *Die Schutzmassnahmen des Staates in der schweizerischen Uhrenindustrie und ihre Anwendung* (Solothurn: Buchdruckerei Vogt-Schild AG, 1951); *Allgemeine Schweizerische Uhrenindustrie AG, ASUAG: Darstellung ihrer Gründung und ihrer Entwicklung während 25 Jahre, 1931–1956* (Biel: Schüler, 1956); Harvard Business School, "Note on the Watch Industries in Switzerland, Japan and the United States" (Boston: 1972); OECD, Joint Working Party of the Committee for Scientific and Technological Policy and the Industry Committee on Technology and the Structural Adaptation of Industry, "Structural Change in the Swiss Watch-making Industry and the Development of Electronic Watch Technology" (Paris: DSTI, SPR, 77.46, and DSTI, IND, 77.79, November 1977); Walter Steinmann, *Die Entstehung öffentlicher und gemischtwirtschaftlicher Unternehmungen in der Schweiz,* (Zurich: Institut für Orts-, Regional-, und Landesplanung, Forschungsprojekt" Parastaatliche Verwaltung," May 1980), pp. 33–39; and Charbel Ackermann and Walter Steinmann, "Private versus State Policy: The Role of Public Policy, Industry and Banks in the Watch-Making Sector in Switzerland" (Paper prepared for the ECPR workshop "Instruments of Public Administration in the Mixed Economy," Aarhus, 29 March–3 April 1982).

47. The content of the industry's "collective convention" of 1936 is summarized in Douglas F. Greer, "United States," in United Nations, *Restrictive Business Practices: Studies on the United Kingdom of Great Britain and Northern Ireland, the United States of America and Japan* (New York, TD/B/390, 1973), pp. 68–69.

48. Henri Rieben, Madeleine Urech, and Charles Ifflaud, *L'horlogerie et l'Europe* (Lausanne: Centre de recherches européennes, 1959); Peter Stringelin, *Die schweizer Uhr und die europäische Integration* (Zurich: Schulthess, 1971).

49. *Neue Zürcher Zeitung,* 13 January 1967 and 21 April 1965; Percy W. Bidwell, *What the Tariff Means to American Industries* (New York: Harper, 1956), pp. 88–129.

50. *Neue Zürcher Zeitung,* 8 February 1961; *Neue Zürcher Zeitung,* 22 November 1961; and *Economist,* 30 December 1961.

51. Stingelin, *Die schweizer Uhr,* pp. 27–32.

52. *Vaterland,* 25 January 1971; *Der Bund,* 30 March 1973; *National-Zeitung,* 10 March 1975; and *Neue Zürcher Zeitung,* 23 November 1978.

53. "Die Handelsabteilung im Dienste unserer Volkswirtschaft," *Sysdata und Bürotechnik* (1976), p. 12.

54. *Neue Zürcher Zeitung,* 14 and 16 February 1971.

55. *Neue Zürcher Zeitung,* 23 February 1973; *Die Zeit,* 28 April 1978.

56. *Neue Zürcher Zeitung,* 12 January 1969, 14 and 16 February 1971; *Luzerner Neuste Nachrichten,* 29 May 1978. In the mid-1960s research and development was, despite the tenfold increase during the previous decade, still very small by Swiss standards. The watch industry employed only 86 full-time researchers as compared to more than 3,000 in chemicals and metals, and it accounted for less than 3 percent of Switzerland's total research and development expenditures. See *Schweizer Finanz Zeitung,* 15 March 1972.

57. *Neue Zürcher Zeitung,* 14, 16 February 1971; *Schweizer Finanz Zeitung,* 15 March 1972.

58. *Neue Zürcher Zeitung,* 12 January 1969; *Die Zeit,* 28 April 1978; and *Die Weltwoche,* 4 July 1979.

59. *Neue Zürcher Zeitung,* 3 May 1977; *World Business Weekly,* 25 May 1981, p. 43.

60. *Der Bund,* 20 March 1980; *Basler Zeitung,* 3 May 1980; *Neue Zürcher Zeitung,* 7–8 June 1980; and Peter Renggli, "Uhrenindustrie hat die Herausforderung der Elektronik bewältigt," *Schweizerische Kreditanstalt Bulletin* 86 (December 1980): 15.

61. Peter Renggli, quoted in *Die Zeit,* 28 April 1978.

62. Rudolf Eckert, "Schweizer Uhrenelektronik: Spät kommt sie doch sie kommt," *Wirtschaftsrevue* 16, 12 (1975): 18; *Die Weltwoche,* 4 July 1979; and *Neue Zürcher Zeitung,* 7 March 1971 and 21 January 1973.

63. *Neue Zürcher Zeitung,* 24–25 May 1975, reports a meeting attended by representatives of both the watch and the textile industry arguing their case unsuccessfully in Bern.

64. Quoted in *Der Bund,* 9 December 1978.

65. *Neue Zürcher Zeitung,* 1 and 16 December 1970. The definition stipulates that 50 percent of the value of all components must be Swiss products. See also Eidgenössisches Volkswirtschaftsdepartment, Der Beauftragte für die Uhrenindustrie und internationale Industriefragen, *Bericht und Kommentar zum Entwurf eines Bundesgesetzes über die offizielle Qualitätskontrolle in der schweizerischen Uhrenindustrie* (Bern: 19 February 1970); *Botschaft des Bundesrates an die Bundesversammlung über die offizielle Qualitätskontrolle in der schweizerischen Uhrenindustrie und die Ergänzung des Markenschutzgesetzes* (Bern: 2 September 1970).

66. *Der Bund,* 19 February 1971; *Thurgauer Zeitung,* 5 March 1971; *Neue Zürcher Zeitung,* 5 and 7 March 1971; and *National-Zeitung,* 25 April 1971. Analogous debates existed in the textile industry, which also moved, against the determined opposition of producers of lower-quality products, to a mandatory identification of Switzerland's textile products. See *Neue Zürcher Zeitung,* 12 November 1963 and 18 February 1970; C. M. Wittwer, "Die Zukunft der Qualitätskontrolle in der Schweizer Uhrenindustrie" (Informationsaustausch der Gruppe Industrie und Handel der Bundesversammlung, Bern, 30 September 1980, mimeo), p. 3; and *Aargauer Tagblatt,* 14 March 1981.

67. *Neue Zürcher Zeitung,* 10 March 1977. The role of groups under the "Watch Statute" is discussed generally in Juerg Lanz, "Die Heranziehung der Verbände bei der staatlichen Intervention auf Grund des Uhrenstatuts" (Ph.D. diss., University of Bern, 1964); and in Charles A. Junod, "Le statut légal de l'industrie horlogère suisse" (Ph.D. diss., University of Geneva, 1962).

68. *Neue Zürcher Zeitung,* 21 December 1967 and 25 March 1968; René Retornaz, "Stand und Probleme der schweizerischen Wirtschaft," *Wirtschaftspolitische Mitteilungen* 26 (March 1970): 6–7; and G. F. Bauer, "Ce que l'organisation professionelle peut apporter à une activité atomisée," *Entreprise,* 22 May 1965, pp. 45–50.

69. *New York Times,* 29 November 1982, p. 31. These Swiss figures exclude about 1,800 firms so small that they are not covered by the factory legislation that provides the legal basis for the collection of statistical information. See *Der Bund,* 25 April and 4–5 June 1966; "Die japanische Herausforderung," *Uhren Rundschau,* 7 and 15 September 1977; and *Neue Zürcher Zeitung,* 21 January 1973.

70. "Die schweizerische Uhrenindustrie und ihre Struktur," *Schweizerische Arbeitgeber-Zeitung,* 12 December 1974, pp. 893–95.

71. *Vaterland,* 25 January 1971; *Neue Zürcher Zeitung,* 19 February 1971.

72. *Der Bund,* 7 July 1979.

73. *Neue Zürcher Zeitung,* 23 November 1978; *Der Bund,* 23 March 1978.

74. *Neue Zürcher Zeitung,* 10–11 November 1979.

75. *Basler Zeitung,* 19 June 1980; *Der Bund,* 22 June 1979; and *Neue Zürcher Zeitung,* 10–11 November 1979 and 8–9 November 1980.

76. *Tages-Anzeiger,* 4 December 1979; André Beyner, "Influence de l'évolution technologique sur les structures des entreprises et de l'industrie horlogère," *Revue économique et sociale* 35, 1 (1977): 30–36.

77. Hilmar Stetter, *Schweizer Fabriken: Ab in die 3. Welt? Produktionsver-lagerung der Schweizer Grossindustrie* (Basle: Z-Verlag, 1980), pp. 26–43; René Retornaz, "The Swiss Watch Industry and the International Division of Labour" (Geneva: Centre for Applied Technology and the International Division of Labour, November 1980).

78. *Neue Zürcher Zeitung,* 26 January 1968.

79. *National-Zeitung,* 1 January 1972; *Finanz und Wirtschaft,* 4 November 1978; and Cyril Chessex, "L'industrie horlogère suisse au seuil de la mul-tinationalisation," *Revue économique et sociale* 33 (February 1975): 21–35.

80. Felix Müller, *Krise, Zufall oder Folge des Kapitalismus? Die Schweiz und die aktuelle Wirtschaftskrise. Eine Einführung aus marxistischer Sicht* (Zurich: Limmat, 1976), p. 53.

81. Quoted in *Neue Zürcher Zeitung,* 3 May 1977.

82. *Der Bund,* 7 July 1979.

83. Ibid.

84. Wirtschaftsförderung, *Kurzinformation,* 29 September 1980; *Tages-Anzeiger,* 6 May 1980; and Georges-Adrien Matthey, "Vor einer stabileren Zukunft für die Uhrenindustrie?" (Schweizerische Uhrenkammer, Bern, 30 September 1980). However, only 10 percent (8.2 of 96 million watches) were assembled or produced fully abroad. See *World Business Weekly,* 25 May 1981, p. 43.

85. *Neue Zürcher Zeitung,* 12 December 1980. The trend continued in 1981. See *Wall Street Journal,* 27 January 1982, p. 26; Ackermann and Steinmann, "Private versus State Policy," p. 12.

86. *Basler Zeitung,* 3 May 1980; Gil Baillod, "Die Zukunft der Schweizeri-schen Uhrenindustrie," *Bulletin-SKA* 87 (July 1981): 9.

87. A summary of the main study that the federal government commis-sioned is presented in *Schweizerische Finanz Zeitung,* 31 August 1977.

88. *Tages-Anzeiger,* 14 May 1979.

89. *Der Bund,* 31 August 1977.

90. *Tages-Anzeiger,* 14 May 1979.

91. *National-Zeitung,* 26 August 1976; *Neue Zürcher Zeitung,* 23–24 October 1976; and *Finanz und Wirtschaft,* 20 November 1976.

92. Interview, Bern, July 1981.

93. "Arbeitsbeschaffungsreserven der privaten Wirtschaft: Die Arbeitsbe-schaffungsaktion 1975/76 im Rückblick," *Mitteilungsblatt für Konjunkturfragen* 37, 1 (1981): 2.

94. *Finanz und Wirtschaft,* 18 November 1978; *Neue Zürcher Zeitung,* 1 Sep-tember 1976; and *Der Bund,* 9 December 1977.

95. Interview, Biel, July 1981.

96. Interview, Biel, July 1981.

97. *Neue Zürcher Zeitung,* 16 December 1977; Fédération horlogère, "Pro-jektionsstudie," p. 3.

98. Interview, Biel, July 1981.

99. Interview, Biel, July 1981. See also Fédération hologère, "Projektions-studie," p. 14.

100. *Schweizer Finanz Zeitung*, 4 May 1972.

101. *National-Zeitung*, 10 March 1973.

102. Güggi, *Schutzmassnahmen*, p. 44; *Neue Zürcher Zeitung*, 3 May 1977; and *Der Bund*, 4 July 1977.

103. Charbel Ackermann and Walter Steinmann, "The Representation of Private Actors in the Policy Implementation Structure" (Paper prepared for the ECPR planning session on "Implementation Seen from the Bottom Up," Lancaster, 30 March–4 April 1981), pp. 11–12.

104. Josef Hasler, *Der schweizerische Metall- und Uhrenarbeitnehmer-Verband SMUV* (Bern: SMUV, 1976), pp. 26–27.

105. *Neue Zürcher Zeitung*, 28 April 1975; *Handelsblatt*, 2 January 1976.

106. Schweizerischer Metall- und Uhrenarbeitnehmerverband, *Geschäftsbericht 1973, 1974, 1975* (n.p.: SMUV, n.d.), p. 133.

107. *Die Weltwoche*, 1 October 1980. The catalogue of demands that the union prepared in 1982 apparently has done little to change this situation. See *Neue Zürcher Zeitung*, 27 May 1982.

108. *World Business Weekly*, 25 May 1981, p. 43. Exports increased by 10 percent in 1981. See *Wall Street Journal*, 27 January 1982, p. 26; *Neue Zürcher Zeitung*, 25 April 1982; and *Der Spiegel*, 23 May 1983, p. 139.

109. *Die Weltwoche*, 4 July 1979; *Neue Zürcher Zeitung*, 18 June 1980.

110. David Landes, "Watchmaking: A Case Study in Enterprise and Change," *Business History Review* 53 (Spring 1979): 37.

111. This episode can be traced in the following accounts: *Die Weltwoche*, 1 October 1980; *Der Bund*, 11 October 1980; *Tages-Anzeiger*, 17 October 1980; *Neue Zürcher Zeitung*, 15 December 1980; *Finanz und Wirtschaft*, 20 December 1980; *Neue Zürcher Zeitung*, 20 February 1981; *Finanz und Wirtschaft*, 21 February 1981; *Neue Zürcher Zeitung*, 21 May, 5, 6–7, 13–14, and 17 June 1981; *Frankfurter Allgemeine Zeitung*, 21 May 1981; *Der Spiegel*, 25 May 1981; and *Die Weltwoche* 27 May 1981.

112. Peter A. Gourevitch, "The Second Image Reversed: The International Sources of Domestic Politics," *International Organization* 32 (Autumn 1978): 881–912; James R. Kurth, "The Political Consequences of the Product Cycle: Industrial History and Political Outcomes," *International Organization* 33 (Winter 1979): 1–34.

113. Laura Tyson and John Zysman, "American Industry in International Competition," in Zysman and Tyson, eds., *American Industry in International Competition: Government Policies and Corporate Strategies* (Ithaca: Cornell University Press, 1983), pp. 15–59.

CHAPTER 7. *Conclusion*

1. Sarah Hogg, "A Small House in Order," *Economist*, 15 March 1980, Survey, p. 8.

2. Chris Cviic, "Their Own Kind of Miracle," *Economist* 28 July 1973, Survey, p. 20.

3. Anton Pelinka, "Defense Policy and Permanent Neutrality: The Cases of

Switzerland and Austria" (Paper prepared for the annual conference of the Committee on Atlantic Studies, Wingspread, Racine, Wisconsin, September 1979), pp. 2–3, 8–9, 14. This aspect of Swiss and Austrian politics has received repeated and extensive scholarly attention.

4. Ibid., p. 3.

5. Ibid., p. 8.

6. Ibid., p. 14.

7. Peter C. Bettschart, "Exportförderung in der Schweiz," in *Exportförderung in der Bundesrepublik Deutschland, in der Schweiz und in Österreich: Ergebnisse eines Symposiums vom 9. Oktober 1979* (Vienna: Zentralsparkasse und Kommerzialbank, 1979), p. 30.

8. Cviic, "Their Own Kind of Miracle," Survey, p. 10.

9. This is a major theme of Wilhelm Hankel's *Prosperity amidst Crisis: Austria's Economic Policy and the Energy Crunch* (Boulder, Colo.: Westview, 1981).

10. Bernd Marin, ed., *Wachstumskrisen in Österreich*, 2 vols. (Vienna: Braumüller, 1979). See also "Modell Österreich—Abgewirtschaftet," *Der Spiegel*, 18 January 1982, pp. 92–94; "The Strains on Consensus," *World Business Weekly*, 9 March 1981, p. 27; and Anton Pelinka, *Modellfall Österreich? Möglichkeiten und Grenzen der Sozialpartnerschaft* (Vienna: Braumüller, 1981), pp. 60–61, 114.

11. Egon Matzner, "Sozialpartnerschaft," in Heinz Fischer, ed., *Das politische System Österreichs* (Vienna: Europa Verlag, 1974), pp. 429–51; Raimund Loew, "The Politics of the Austrian 'Miracle,'" *New Left Review* no. 123 (September–October 1980): 69–79.

12. Anton Pelinka, *Gewerkschaften im Parteienstaat: Ein Vergleich zwischen dem Deutschen und dem Österreichischen Gewerkschaftsbund* (Berlin: Duncker & Humbolt, 1980), pp. 86, 172, 198; Michael Pollak, "Vom Konflikt- zum Kompromissverhalten. Die Sozialpartnerschaft als Sozialisationsmittel politischen Handelns," *Austriaca: Cahiers universitaires d'information sur l'Autriche* (November 1979): 369–88.

13. Sidney Verba, Norman H. Nie, and Jae-on Kim, *Participation and Political Equality: A Seven-Nation Comparison* (Cambridge: Cambridge University Press, 1978), p. 107. See also pp. 75, 79, 110–11, 115, 118, 164–68, 172–82, 297–98. Similar findings are reported in Samuel H. Barnes, Max Kaase, et al., *Political Action: Mass Participation in Five Western Democracies* (Beverly Hills, Calif.: Sage, 1979).

14. Instructive articles include Frank J. Prial, "Unruly Youths Shatter Swiss Image," *New York Times*, 7 October 1980, pp. A1, A10; Paul Hofmann, "The Swiss Malaise," *New York Times Sunday Magazine*, 8 February 1981, sec. 6, pp. 35–39, 57–62; and Peter Bichsel, "Das Ende der schweizer Unschuld," *Der Spiegel*, 5 January 1981, pp. 108–9. See also *New York Times*, 10 May 1981, p. 13; *World Business Weekly*, 29 December 1980, pp. 23–24.

15. Quoted in Prial, "Unruly Youths," p. A10.

16. Francesco Kneschaurek, "Neue Probleme der Stabilitätspolitik im Zeichen der kommenden Entwicklung," *Schweizerische Zeitschrift für Volkswirtschaft und Statistik* 1979, no. 3: 253–71. As is true of Austria, only a few Swiss studies address problems of the future. They include *Entwicklungsperspektiven und -probleme der schweizerischen Volkswirtschaft: Zusammenfassung der Perspektivstudien über die Entwicklung der schweizerischen Volkswirtschaft bis zum Jahre 2000* (St. Gallen and Bern: Eidgenössische Drucksachen- und

Materialzentrale, 1974); Walter Wittman, *Wohin geht die Schweiz? Strategien des Überlebens* (Munich: Ehrenwirth-Athena, 1973); and Richard Schwertfeger, "Zukunftsperspektiven der schweizer Wirtschaft," *Civitas* 24, 5 (1969): 363–78.

17. *World Business Weekly*, 18 February 1980, p. 16. Hogg, "A Small House in Order," Survey, p. 21; *Austrian Information* 34, 2–3 (1981): 10. Since 1975 the marginal propensity to import has increased to 0.6 while the multiplier has decreased to 1.1. In other words, an additional schilling spent through larger budget deficits will generate only 1.1 domestic schillings of income. See Helmut Frisch, "Macroeconomic Adjustment in Small Open Economies," in Sven W. Arndt, ed., *The Political Economy of Austria* (Washington, D.C.: American Enterprise Institute for Public Policy Research, 1982), p. 51.

18. H. Androsch, "Die Rolle der österreichischen Wirtschaft," *Oberösterreichische Nachrichten*, 26 March 1977. The conflict pitted then Deputy Chancellor and Finance Minister Androsch against one of the directors of Austria's Nationalbank, Heinz Kienzl, with Chancellor Kreisky remaining silent on the issue.

19. Quoted in Paul Lewis, "The Austrian Economy Is a Strauss Waltz," *New York Times*, 22 March 1981, p. 9.

20. See in particular the articles by Marin, Klose, and Pelinka in Marin, *Wachstumskrisen in Österreich*, vol. 2.

21. Different interpretations are advanced by Robert Flanagan and his associates, specifically for Austria, and by Leo Panitch, more generally for modern capitalist states. See Robert J. Flanagan, David W. Soskice, and Lloyd Ulman, *Unionism, Economic Stabilization, and Incomes Policies: European Experience* (Washington, D.C.: Brookings, 1983), chap. 2; and Panitch, "The Development of Corporatism in Liberal Democracies," in Philippe C. Schmitter and Gerhard Lehmbruch, eds., *Trends toward Corporatist Intermediation* (Beverly Hills, Calif.: Sage, 1979), pp. 119–46.

22. Andrew Shonfield, *Modern Capitalism: The Changing Balance of Public and Private Power* (London: Oxford University Press, 1965), p. 193.

23. Hogg, "A Small House in Order," Survey, p. 4.

24. "Austrian Industrial Development," *Financial Times*, 29 August 1975, pp. 9–11.

25. OECD, *Economic Surveys: Austria* (Paris: 1981), p. 53.

26. Hogg, "A Small House in Order," Survey, p. 9.

27. *Austrian Information* 32, 6 (1979): 2.

28. This is the title of a recent book by Urs Schwarz, *The Eye of the Hurricane: Switzerland in World War Two* (Boulder, Colo.: Westview, 1980); the data are taken from Pelinka, "Defense Policy and Permanent Neutrality," pp. 2, 11–12, 14. In general see Karl Haltiner and Ruth Meyer, "Aspects of the Relationship between Military and Society in Switzerland," *Armed Forces and Society* 6 (1979): 49–81; Dietrich Fischer, "Invulnerability without Threat: The Swiss Concept of General Defense," *Journal of Peace Research* 19, 3 (1982–1983): 205–26. John McPhee, "A Reporter at Large: La Place de la Concorde Suisse I and II," *New Yorker*, 31 October 1983, pp. 50–117, and 7 November 1983, pp. 55–112.

29. Jane Kramer, "A Reporter in Europe: Zurich," *New Yorker*, 15 December 1980, p. 119.

30. See Richard Senti, ed., *Die Schweiz und internationale Wirtschaftsor-*

ganisationen (Zurich: Schulthess, 1975); Jacques Freymond and Nadine Galvani, eds., *La Suisse et la diplomatie multilatérale,* 2d ed. (Geneva: Institut universitaire de hautes études internationales, 1978).

31. *Der Spiegel,* 26 September 1977, p. 163. See also Michael M. Gunter, "Switzerland and the United Nations," *International Organization* 30 (Winter 1976): 129–52.

32. Bichsel, "Das Ende der schweizer Unschuld," p. 109. See also *New York Times,* 21 December 1980, p. 15.

33. *World Business Weekly,* 20 April 1981, pp. 24–25.

34. Albert Weitenauer, "Aussenpolitik und Aussenwirtschaft: Ausblick auf ein gemeinsames Ziel," *Schweizer Monatshefte* 57 (1977): 713–26; Heide Dechmann and Daniel Frei, "Der Platz der Schweiz im internationalen System: Eine deskriptive Studie," *Kleine Studien zur Politischen Wissenschaft* nos. 27–28 (Zurich: Forschungsstelle für Politische Wissenschaft, 1974), pp. 13–14, 40; Alois Riklin, *Gundlegungen der schweizerischen Aussenpolitik* (Bern: Haupt, 1975), p. 24; and Gottfried Berweger, *Investition und Legitimation: Privatinvestitionen in Entwicklungsländern als Teil der schweizerischen Legitimationsproblematik* (Diessenhofen: Rüegger, 1977), p. 66.

35. Hogg, "A Small House in Order," Survey, p. 3.

36. Herbert Lüthy, "Has Switzerland a Future? The Dilemma of the Small Nation," *Encounter* 19 (December 1962): 30.

37. Max Pfister, *Die Sonderstellung der Schweiz in der internationalen Wirtschaftspolitik: Aussenwirtschaftspolitik 1945–1959* (Winterthur: Keller, 1971), p. 88.

38. Jean-Christian Lambelet, "Switzerland's Economy: World Dependence vs. Domestic Stability," (n.p.: n.d., mimeo), p. 12.

39. Erich Andrlik, "Labor-Management Relations in Austria's Steel Industry" (San Francisco, 1982, mimeo), p. 37.

Index

Alpine-Montan, 203, 207; and steel merger, 204
Andrlik, Erich, 141
Androsch, Hannes, 71, 79
ASUAG (General Swiss Watch Corporation), 221; financial support for, 226–27, 234; government involvement, 217; restructuring, 218, 222–24, 231, 232
Austria
  compared to Switzerland, 133–34, 162–65, 239–41, 255–57
  description, 19–20, 22–26, 133
  economic sucess, 19–22, 26–27, 34–35, 239
  economy: foreign capital, 15, 43, 52, 56–57, 156, 182–83; foreign companies, 56–58; foreign trade and tariffs, 23, 52–56, 59, 79, 186; inflation, low, 19, 34; market outcomes, 41, 164–65; and nationalization, 205–6, 209–10; world markets, 46, 51, 54, 81–83, 206, 209
  federalism, 76
  institutions, 235–38; political, 59–66
  and international scene, 252–53
  political success, 20, 26–27, 34
  see also banks, nationalized; business community; democratic corporatism; democratic socialism; government; governmental policies; industry; interest groups; nationalization; policy process; political groups and organizations; public sector; Second Republic; social welfare; unions
Austrian Airlines, 159
Austrian Corporation for Industrial Administration (ÖIAG), 51, 57–58, 60, 66; political control of, 141; and

steel industry, 204, 205, 208, 210, 211
Austrian Industrial Corporation (ÖIG), 66
Austrian Trade Union Federation (ÖGB): and economic policy, 71; importance, 35, 48, 60–61; membership, 35, 61; organization, 37, 47, 61; and politics, 38, 39, 40, 48, 69, 70, 74; and public good, 39
automobile industry, 58, 272n151

banks, nationalized, Austria, 40; dominant role, 51, 142; and politics, 142; reorganization, 139. See also Nationalbank, Austria
banking, Swiss, 90–92, 124; and government, 116–18; growth, 89; importance, 98; as industry, 88–89; international orientation, 90, 156; ownership, 156–57; policies, 155; and textile industry, 170–71, 197, 310–11n35; and watch industry, 218, 224, 225, 226, 231, 232, 234, 238
banking organizations, Swiss: Banking Commission, 117; Banking Council, 125; Crédit Suisse, 117. See also Nationalbank, Switzerland
  Swiss Bank Corporation, 94, 174, 231
  Swiss Banking Association, 226
Bauer, Otto, 35, 73, 153
Beerbohm, Max, 20, 22
Benya, Anton, 26, 38, 48, 71, 275n209
Bettschart, Peter, 241–42
Biermann, Wolfgang, 22
Blecha, Karl, 42
Bloomfield Irirangi, 149
Booz-Allen and Hamilton, 207, 213
Bryce, James, 25
Bührle conglomerate, 169

Library of Congress Cataloging in Publication Data

Katzenstein, Peter J.
  Corporatism and change.

  (Cornell studies in political economy)
  Includes index.
  1. Industry and state—Austria. 2. Industry and state—Switzerland. 3. Corporate state—Austria. 4. Corporate state—Switzerland. 5. Austria—Politics and government—1945–   6. Switzerland—Politics and government—20th century. I. Title. II. Series.
  HD3616.A93K37 1984   338.9436   84-7676
  ISBN 0-8014-1716-3 (alk. paper)